Our Country Called

A Tribute To Washington County Servicemen and Servicewomen

Vol. II

Published by
The Herald-Mail Company
Hagerstown, Maryland
John League, Editor and Publisher

First Edition

ISBN: 0-9794278-0-0
Printed by:
HBP, Inc.
Hagerstown, MD.

Acknowledgments

The Project Staff

Michele Wills, Project Director/Veteran Interviews
Marie Lanser Beck, Book Editor/Writer/Veteran Interviews
Dennis Shaw, Gloria Dahlhamer, Writers/Veteran Interviews
Deb Lanzendorfer, Graphic Design Editor and Layout/Veteran Interviews
Susan Snyder, Veteran Interviews/Administrative Assistance
Kevin Gilbert, Yvette May, Joe Crocetta,
Ric Dugan, Deb Lanzendorfer, Photography
Andrew Schotz, Proofreading
Dave Thompson, Proofreading
Linda Boward, Sales
Brian Taylor, Technical Assistance
Brian Sease, Production Coordinator
Tom Crowell and **Skip Hutzell**, Scanning
John Frye, Proofreading/Historian,
Western Maryland Room —
Washington County Free Library
U.S. Army Military History Institute, Carlisle, Pennsylvania
Leon Brumback, Dieter Protsch, Massey Hirai, Oki Kang
and Eugene Nakada, Special Assistance

The names listed above are those who put the book together, but we must remember there would be no book except for the generosity of Washington County veterans and their families who provided information, photos and memorabilia.

These are their stories.
This is their book.

Editor's Note: "The Honor Was Ours"

The Herald-Mail Company is pleased to present Volume II of ***Our County Called: A Tribute to Washington County Servicemen and Servicewomen****. The veterans featured in this book and family members who supplied photographs and information for loved ones — some of whom are no longer here — have expressed appreciation for this effort to render an accounting of the service of local men and women in uniform from World War II through the current Global War on Terrorism.*

We have attempted, within the confines of space and time, to present experiences of those who have served under fire, in duty stations far away or close to home, in times of war and times of peace. We have sought to portray some sense of the experiences these men and women shared with their "band of brothers" (and, sisters) in service to our country.

It has been a profound privilege to hear the stories of soldiers, sailors, mariners, nurses, members of the Marine Corps and Cold Warriors who have rendered service, to pore over fading photographs or digitized images, to feel the remembered heat of a shipboard fire and to shiver at accounts of the bitter cold in Korea that bleak winter of 1951. Whether they served as Seabees on some South Pacific atoll or with the Strategic Air Command, or whether they were MPs in Southeast Asia or felt the recent sting of ancient sand in places with Biblical, or otherwise unpronounceable names, we salute them.

The late historian Stephen Ambrose, who helped the nation take stock of the sacrifice and suffering of a generation who saw the worst of war and fought for peace, said it best in the acknowledgment in James Brady's ***Flags of Our Fathers****, the powerful chronicle of the battle for Iwo Jima in World War II:*

> ***I was ten years old when the war ended. I thought the returning veterans were giants who had saved the world from barbarism. I still think so. I remain a hero worshiper. Over the decades I've interviewed thousands of the veterans. It is a privilege to hear their stories, then write them up.***

Those of us who had the opportunity to sit and talk and sometimes shed a tear with veterans who are represented in these two volumes have been touched by their sacrifice, service, pain and loss, and awed and humbled by the good humor and grace with which they put Uncle Sam's objectives above their own.

These are their stories. This is their book.

In the interest of disclosure, however, it must be acknowledged that the veterans themselves were often the most reluctant of interview subjects. Many of them would not have submitted themselves to our probing questions and insistent requests for additional information if not for the wives, sons, brothers, sisters, mothers, fathers, and, in one remarkable instance, the husband, who urged their loved ones to come talk to us. To those who shared their treasured keepsakes for veterans long gone, likewise, we are profoundly grateful.

The assembled accounts would not be here before you if not for the encouragement and support of those who value their loved ones' commitment to country and who, in a spirit of generosity and patriotism, sought to share them for the benefit of generations to come.

"Thank you so much for doing this," was an oft-repeated refrain from veterans or family members who shared their accounts. To this we can only say ...

The honor, to be sure, was ours.

Marie Lanser Beck

The items and photographs on both the front and back cover of ***Our Country Called Vol. II*** were selected from among the hundreds of images and items veterans and their families shared with us in the course of this project. Designer Deb Lanzendorfer created the cover, which incorporates the following items:

Front Cover (Clockwise from top left):

Front and back of Prisoner of War Medal presented to Army Air Forces gunner George F. Shinham, a POW in Romania during WWII, courtesy of George F. Shinham.
Vietnamese currency from the Vietnam War-era collection of Thurman W. Divelbliss, courtesy of Kitty Divelbliss and Kelly Cline.
Seabees insignia and photo of Daniel Watson reading in Iraq, courtesy of Daniel Watson.
"Tropic Lightning" shoulder patch of the 25th Infantry worn by Barry Melvin "Rick" Cunningham, shown upper right, along with the Purple Heart he was awarded for wounds received during the Vietnam War, courtesy of Karon Cunningham.
Fifth Air Force Patch from the Korean War, courtesy of Alvey Moser.
American Defense Service Medal presented to Lt. Howard H. Small during WWII, courtesy of Rose Sweeney.
Front and back of War Department identification card carried by Elmer O. "Whitey" Lewis in Europe in WWII, courtesy of Elaine Lewis.
NATO pin and photograph, courtesy of Curtis E. Shives.
Donald Spence in Inchon, Korea, during the Korean War, courtesy of Betty Spence and Debrah Siakowski.
War Bonds poster from the collection of Elmer O. "Whitey" Lewis, courtesy of Elaine Lewis.
Photograph of Orville Lee Knight, who was killed in action in Vietnam April 8, 1969, courtesy of Whylmenia Knight.
Camouflaged helmet worn by Larry F. Michael in Vietnam, courtesy of Larry F. Michael.
Operation Iraqi Freedom post card from the collection of Daniel Watson.
WWII USAAF Gunner's wings, courtesy of George F. Shinham.
Larry F. Michael reading a letter from home in Vietnam.
Photograph of Gary McDonald, courtesy of Lorraine McDonald.
Dog tags, ID card and diary from the collection of Charles L. Downey, courtesy of Patricia Martin.
Iraq Culture Smart Card issued to Marines, courtesy of Daniel Watson.
Army paratroopers preparing to make the first jump into Iraq, courtesy of Pat Bolland.
Army honor guard patch courtesy of John Beair.
Identity card and photo of Freda Nunamaker from WWII, courtesy of Cindy and Bill Wolfinger.
WWII "cricket" noisemaker, courtesy of Allen W. Myers.
Dog tags, courtesy of Michael Mardres.

Back Cover (Clockwise from top left):

Photo of Army Private Christina Carpenter Lawler, courtesy of her grandfather, Ramon Joy.
Okinawa Patch and dog tags belonging to James C. Mongold, courtesy of Dennis Mongold.
Navy dog tags belonging to Richard Pierce Lynch, courtesy of Betty Lynch.
Sewing kit carried by Charles L. Downey during WWII, courtesy of Patricia Martin.
Navy Lt. Michael Kamas on board a P-3 Orion military patrol aircraft, returning from a deployment in Europe on Feb. 5, 2003, courtesy of Michael Kamas.
Bronze Star awarded to George R. "Dick" Ambrose, shown on crutches in 1945 photograph, from his collection of WWII memorabilia.
WWII-era photo, courtesy of Calvin W. "Cal" Sheeler.
Patch for Iraqi Special Forces Support Battalion, courtesy of Ricky A. Pike.
"Ruptured duck" emblem pin from the collection of George R. "Dick" Ambrose.
Commemorative postage stamps from the 1950s recognizing the contribution of the National Guard, U.S. Coast Guard and U.S. Merchant Marine, courtesy of Dennis Shaw.
Lighter carried by William H. Ruck Jr. in WWII, courtesy of Helen Ruck and John Bryan.
Solomon Islands commemorative book, photo, ID bracelet and ID card, courtesy of WWII Navy Seabee D. Tolly West Jr.
White gloves and canvas bag belonging to Army Sgt. Elwood C. "Woodie" Pearman, a WWII-era military policeman, serving in Panama, courtesy of Bonnie K. Woodard.
Marine Corps commemorative knife, courtesy of Dennis Reeder.
Brother and sister Kevin Hurlbrink and Kelly Hurlbrink-Zamora in Kuwait in September 2003, courtesy of their mother, Lynn Jones.
Photograph and a Marine Corps medallion from his time in Vietnam, courtesy of Dennis Reeder.
Map case and cloth maps carried by Charles L. Downey during WWII, courtesy of Patricia Martin.
WWII Victory Medal presented to Howard H. Small, courtesy of Rose Sweeney.
Army "Eisenhower" jacket and campaign cap worn by Wilbur Hershberger in WWII, contributed by Beverley Hershberger.
WWII Army Air Forces Aviation Cadet wings belonging to Frederick G. Hill, courtesy of Carolyn E. Hill.
Photo of Lewis Watson, courtesy of Dr. Mary Watson.

JOHN McCAIN
UNITED STATES SENATOR
WASHINGTON, DC 20510

November 7, 2006

The Herald-Mail Company
c/o Michele A. Wills, Marketing Director
100 Summit Avenue
Hagerstown, MD 21741-0439

Dear Friends:

I write to recognize the veterans and their families who are gathered at the Valley Mall in Hagerstown, Maryland. I am honored to offer my personal thanks for the sacrifices you have made in defense of our nation, and regret being unable to be with you in person.

The sacrifices of veterans from the Tri-State area shall be remembered by generations to come. The documentation of Volume I of *Our Country Called: A Tribute to Washington County Servicemen and Servicewomen of Washington County* will help to chronicle the bravery of the area's veterans from wars past until this day.

Veteran's Day is a time to remember those who have put service before self and answered their nation's call to arms. Thank you for your distinguished and selfless service, your sacrifice, and the honor you have brought to our nation.

Sincerely,

John McCain

John McCain
United States Senator

NOT PRINTED AT GOVERNMENT EXPENSE

Letter sent by U.S. Sen. John McCain in recognition of a Veterans Day event sponsored by The Herald-Mail Co., HBP and the Valley Mall on Nov. 11, 2006.

Bang The Drum Slowly

by Emmylou Harris and Guy Clark

I meant to ask you how to fix that car
I always meant to ask you about the war
And what you saw across a bridge too far
Did it leave a scar

Or how you navigated wings of fire and steel
Up where heaven had no more secrets to conceal
And still you found the ground beneath your wheels
How did it feel

Bang the drum slowly play the pipe lowly
To dust be returning from dust we begin
Bang the drum slowly I'll speak of things holy
Above and below me world without end.

— Poodlebone Music/EMI April Music, Inc.

(Excerpt of a song written in honor of Emmylou Harris's father, a veteran of WWII)

(Photograph courtesy of Mrs. William K. Kendall, widow of William K. Kendall, Army Air Corps, WWII)

World War II

1941-1945

Okinawa (Contributed by Dennis Mongold)

Honolulu Star-Bulletin 1st EXTRA

Evening Bulletin, Est. 1882, No. 11387
Hawaiian Star, Vol. XLVIII, No. 15359

HONOLULU, TERRITORY OF HAWAII, U. S. A., SUNDAY, DECEMBER 7, 1941

★ PRICE FIVE CENTS

WAR!

(Associated Press by Transpacific Telephone)

SAN FRANCISCO, Dec. 7.—President Roosevelt announced this morning that Japanese planes had attacked Manila and Pearl Harbor.

OAHU BOMBED BY JAPANESE PLANES

SIX KNOWN DEAD, 21 INJURED, AT EMERGENCY HOSPITAL

Attack Made On Island's Defense Areas

By UNITED PRESS

WASHINGTON, Dec. 7. —Text of a White House announcement detailing the attack on the Hawaiian islands is:

"The Japanese attacked Pearl Harbor from the air and all naval and military activities on the island of Oahu, principal American base in the Hawaiian islands."

Oahu was attacked at 7:55 this morning by Japanese planes.

The Rising Sun, emblem of Japan, was seen on plane wing tips.

Wave after wave of bombers streamed through the clouded morning sky from the southwest and flung their missiles on a city resting in peaceful Sabbath calm.

According to an unconfirmed report received at the governor's office, the Japanese force that attacked Oahu reached island waters aboard two small airplane carriers.

It was also reported that at the governor's office either an attempt had been made to bomb the USS Lexington, or that it had been bombed.

CITY IN UPROAR

Within 10 minutes the city was in an uproar. As bombs fell in many parts of the city, and in defense areas the defenders of the islands went into quick action.

Army intelligence officers at Ft. Shafter announced officially shortly after 9 a. m. the fact of the bombardment by an enemy but long previous army and navy had taken immediate measures in defense.

"Oahu is under a sporadic air raid," the announcement said.

"Civilians are ordered to stay off the streets until further notice."

CIVILIANS ORDERED OFF STREETS

The army has ordered that all civilians stay off the streets and highways and not use telephones.

Evidence that the Japanese attack has registered some hits was shown by three billowing pillars of smoke in the Pearl Harbor and Hickam field area.

All navy personnel and civilian defense workers, with the exception of women, have been ordered to duty at Pearl Harbor.

The Pearl Harbor highway was immediately a mass of racing cars.

A trickling stream of injured people began pouring into the city emergency hospital a few minutes after the bombardment started.

Thousands of telephone calls almost swamped the Mutual Telephone Co., which put extra operators on duty.

At The Star-Bulletin office the phone calls deluged the single operator and it was impossible for this newspaper, for sometime, to handle the flood of calls. Here also an emergency operator was called.

HOUR OF ATTACK—7:55 A. M.

An official army report from department headquarters, made public shortly before 11, is that the first attack was at 7:55 a. m.

Witnesses said they saw at least 50 airplanes over Pearl Harbor.

The attack centered in the Pearl Harbor, Army authorities said:

"The rising sun was seen on the wing tips of the airplanes."

Although martial law has not been declared officially, the city of Honolulu was operating under M-Day conditions.

It is reliably reported that enemy objectives under attack were Wheeler field, Hickam field, Kaneohe bay and naval air station and Pearl Harbor.

Some enemy planes were reported shot down.

The body of the pilot was seen in a plane burning at Wahiawa.

Oahu appeared to be taking calmly after the first uproar of queries.

ANTIAIRCRAFT GUNS IN ACTION

First indication of the raid came shortly before 8 this morning when antiaircraft guns around Pearl Harbor began sending up a thunderous barrage.

At the same time a vast cloud of black smoke arose from the naval base and also from Hickam field where flames could be seen.

BOMB NEAR GOVERNOR'S MANSION

Shortly before 9:30 a bomb fell near Washington Place, the residence of the governor. Governor Poindexter and Secretary Charles M. Hite were there.

It was reported that the bomb killed an unidentified Chinese man across the street in front of the Schuman Carriage Co. where windows were broken.

C. E. Daniels, a welder, found a fragment of shell or bomb at South and Queen Sts. which he brought into the City Hall. This fragment weighed about a pound.

At 10:05 a. m. today Governor Poindexter telephoned to The Star-Bulletin announcing he has declared a state of emergency for the entire territory.

He announced that Edouard L. Doty, executive secretary of the major disaster council, has been appointed director under the M-Day law's provisions.

Governor Poindexter urged all residents of Honolulu to remain off the street, and the people of the territory to remain calm.

Mr. Doty reported that all major disaster council wardens and medical units were on duty within a half hour of the time the alarm was given.

Workers employed at Pearl Harbor were ordered at 10:10 a. m. not to report at Pearl Harbor.

The mayor's major disaster council was to meet at the city hall at about 10:30 this morning.

At least two Japanese planes were reported at Hawaiian department headquarters to have been shot down.

One of the planes was shot down at Ft. Kamehameha and the other back of the Wa-

Turn to Page [illegible], Column 1

Hundreds See City Bombed

Hundreds of Honolulans who hurried to the top of Punchbowl soon after bombs began to fall, saw spread out before them the whole panorama of surprise attack and defense.

Far off over Pearl Harbor the white sky was polka-dotted with anti-aircraft smoke.

Rolling away from the navy base were billowing clouds of ugly black smoke. Sometimes a burst of flame reddened the black sources of the smoke.

Out from the silver-surfaced mouth of the harbor a flotilla of destroyers streamed to battle, smoke pouring from their stacks.

Turn to Page [illegible], Column [illegible]

Names of Dead and Injured

The city emergency hospital reported at 10:30 a list of 6 killed and 21 injured.

The complete list will be carried later. Here is a partial list:

Peter Lopez, [illegible], of [illegible] Kamanaiki St., was reported at [illegible] a. m. to be in serious condition from wounds in the upper abdomen.

Bernice Gouveia, [illegible], [illegible] Kalihi St., is suffering from a mangled thigh, lacerations on the right leg and left arm.

A Portuguese girl, unidentified, 16 years old, died on arrival from puncture wounds.

Another victim who died on arrival was Frank Ohashi, [illegible], [illegible] Kamanaiki St., from puncture wounds in the chest.

Cecelia Brandt, [illegible], Honolulu gardens, was released from the hospital after treatment for lacerations.

Three were reported injured and one reported killed from the bomb that fell at Fort and School Sts.

Schools Closed

All schools on Oahu, both public and private, will remain closed until further notice, Edouard L. Doty, territorial director of civilian defense, announced at 11 a. m. today. This does not apply elsewhere in the territory.

Editorial

HAWAII MEETS THE CRISIS

Honolulu and Hawaii will meet the emergency of war today as Honolulu and Hawaii have met emergencies in the past—coolly, calmly and with immediate and complete support of the officials, officers and troops who are in charge.

Governor Poindexter and the army and navy leaders have called upon the public to remain calm; for civilians who have no essential business on the streets to stay off; and for every man and woman to do his duty.

That request, coupled with the measures promptly taken to meet the situation that has suddenly and terribly developed, will be needed.

Hawaii will do its part—as a loyal American territory.

In this crisis, every difference of race, creed and color will be submerged in the one desire and determination to play the part that Americans always play in crisis.

BULLETIN

Additional Star-Bulletin extras today will cover the latest developments in this war move.

(Contributed by Connie Daley)

Richard William Smith — Army — WWII

In the autumn of 1941, Richard William Smith of Hagerstown was an MP at Pearl Harbor with Company M, 21st Infantry. His Army career had been relatively low-key. He lied about his age to join up in 1939, when he was only 16, and he served stateside at Camp Pickett, Virginia, before being assigned to Hawaii. He was due to be discharged in December, and had already packed his bags for the trip home.

But then came the Japanese attack, and his service was extended. The photos on this page show him at Schofield Barracks, Hawaii, before he wrote the fateful entry in his diary on Dec. 7. Smith later saw action at Guadalcanal, seen on pages 132-133.

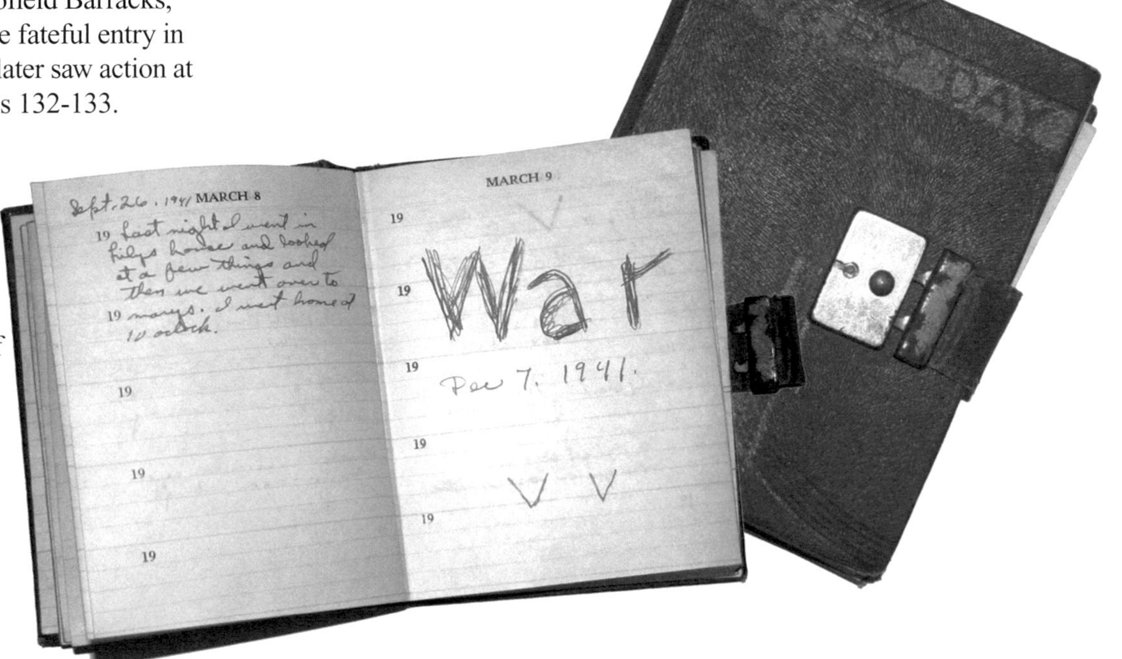

(Photographs and memorabilia courtesy of Gregory Smith, son of Richard William Smith)

PEARL HARBOR

It was on a Sunday morning when we saw them overhead,
Painted a dirty green, with emblems brilliant red.
Each man had a mission, which was to spell disaster,
For Pearl Harbor's personnel to remember ever after.

Their maps, well marked, showing completely our defense,
With the object of surprise to mislead our common sense.
Made the pilots duty easier from the land of Rising Sun,
And the first attack was over, the damage had been done.

Two thousand men they murdered that fateful Sabbath day,
And three ships were sinking, out there across the bay.
The estimated damage they had wrought, mounted even more,
As the final statements of loss from every source did pour.

Those men fought bravely, died valiantly to save our fleet,
And several of our future admirals executed brilliant feats.
The damage had been minimized by the courage of the personnel;
Who performed their duty through the terror of bomb and shell.

So the destiny of the Japanese, clearly to Americans appeared;
The much discussed war of hemispheres, now at last was here.
Only the future can decide the outcome of this tragical attack,
But we know; right will overcome this stabbing in the back.

We look into the future and the armistice seems far ahead,
But we will be victorious, in honor of those honored dead.
When the final peace is signed, and living is again worthwhile,
We'll know their death was not in vain; the Gods above will smile.

Private First Class, R. C. Urich, Jr.

Private Urich, who is stationed at Camp Malakole in the Territory of Hawaii, is a son of Mr. and Mrs. R. C. Urich, this city.

(Poem contributed by Darus Urich and Pearl Harbor pin contributed by Dennis Mongold)

Richard E. Messersmith — Marine Corps — WWII

Messersmith at his desk in Shanghai in 1940. His sister, Arlene Messersmith, said, "From his conversations throughout the years, his China experience made the most impression. He went alone, and young men at that time just stayed in Hagerstown and got a job and married."

Thoughts of American involvement in war were few and far between in September 1936, when 21-year-old Richard E. Messersmith of Hagerstown joined the Marines. But he saw some foretellings of war in August 1938, when he was sent to China with the Fourth Marines.

*Stationed in the International Settlement in Shanghai, where this photo was taken, he recalled his feelings in an interview with **The Daily Mail** after returning to Hagerstown.*

"The main job of the Marines seems to be letting the would-be aggressors realize that the Americans aren't going to be simple pushovers if contention ever does arise. The war has brought overwhelming influxes of refugees to Shanghai and the city is hard-pressed to feed them. Many die of starvation and the city government's biggest problem is providing enough coffins to go around. They had started burning the bodies when I left in May."

Messersmith returned to the States and was discharged from the Marines as a corporal in September 1940. His final pay voucher was $139.89.

But the war was coming home, and 16 months later, after the attack on Pearl Harbor, he would be inducted into the Navy to serve another three years.

Richard E. Messersmith's three brothers served in the Army in WWII while he was in the Navy. The top photo shows Pvt. Glenn Messersmith (left) with Richard in Hagerstown. Glenn served in Germany, where his duties included making sketches of the wounds of soldiers for medical purposes. The center photo shows Richard (left) with Harold A. Messersmith, a private 1st class in the Army. The bottom photo is of Cpl. Maurice L. Messersmith, who was in Alaska with the Army during the war.

The men's father, Joshua L. Messersmith, was awarded a Four-Star Emblem Pin by the Emblem of Honor Association of New York in 1942 in recognition of the services of his four sons. The proclamation read, "We believe that any parent who contributes so handsomely to the defense of his country is deserving of an award of this kind and recognition."

A local newspaper article at the time reported, "Messersmith was the first in Hagerstown to win the high honor. A similar honor was recently awarded to a Clearspring mother who has four sons in the service."

(Photographs courtesy of Arlene Messersmith, sister of Richard E. Messersmith)

*Messersmith was inducted into the Navy in February 1942 and retired as Yeoman 1st Class in September 1945, a month after the War in the Pacific was over. This photo shows him (right) with two shipmates in the captain's office of the USS **Monterey**.*

On the back of the photo, he wrote: "This is the Captain's office and crew. It isn't large, is it? It contains two typewriters, three desks (the long one I am sitting at is mine), two bunks (one mine), two lockers, three chairs, one locker for forms and paper and two book shelves. Except for about four hours, I am in this office 24 hours. There is also a blower and a fan which helps keep it cool.

"It looks as though my hair was geting thin (well, it is) ... The ship's photographer took this picture after a month of hinting. I wear the uniform at all times, about the same as on the railroad" (where he had been a brakeman).

*Messersmith served on the USS **Monterey** in 1943 and 1944, when he participated in the Marshall Islands Operation, in Asiatic-Pacific Raids, and in the Marianas Operation.*

*In 1945, he served on the USS **Enterprise** during the following engagements: occupation and defense of Luzon, attacks on Nasei Shoto, Formosa, Hong Kong area and French Indochina (Jan. 5-23, 1945). Also, Tokyo area raid (Feb. 16-17, 1945), occupation and defense of Iwo Jima, attacks on Bonins (Feb. 19-Mar. 9, 1945), and attack on Kyushu and Japanese Empire (Mar. 18-19, 1945).*

*He was "commended by the captain for a splendid and brave performance of duty under prolonged air attack on 20 March 1945 in Japanese waters while attached to the USS **Enterprise.**"*

Charles Leon Kendall

Army — WWII

Capt. Charles L. Kendall, Gen. J.M. Wainwright, Gen. B.C. Clark and an unidentified second lieutenant (left to right) review troops in Italy in 1943.

Kendall, Company Commander, 10th Armored Division, had come a long way since his birth in Hagerstown in 1913. Leaving Hagerstown High School after one year of study, he joined the Army in 1932 and spent the next 10 years as an enlisted man. He entered Officers Candidate School in 1941, graduated in September, and began active service as a lieutenant on Oct. 1.

During WWII, he served as a training center unit officer, an armored assault gun unit commander, an automotive maintenance and repair officer and a service company commander.

He was promoted to captain and retired in 1946 with the rank of major. He participated in four major campaigns — Algeria, Tunisia, Naples-Foggia and Rome-Arno, all with the 10th Armored Division under Gen. George S. Patton. He was wounded in fighting in Tunisia and Italy and received a Purple Heart.

(Photo courtesy of Edward Kendall, nephew of C.L. Kendall)

Aubrey Grumbine — Army — WWII

Aubrey Grumbine of Hagerstown was almost 25 when he joined the Army in July 1941. He took medical basic training at Camp Lee, Virginia, and Camp Wheeler, Georgia, and also was trained as a carpenter and clerk.

*His wife missed his departure by one hour as he sailed to Scotland on the **Queen Elizabeth**, unescorted through U-boat-infested waters of the North Atlantic. He was based in Swindon, England, for the duration of WWII, and returned home on the **Queen Mary**.*

Aubrey Grumbine, standing at left, with other medics on the grounds of the hospital in Swindon, England, where they treated soldiers wounded in battle in North Africa and Europe.

Among their patients were German prisoners of war. "Once a German general demanded treatment by someone his equal," Grumbine said. "A captain informed him that we could have the Russians treat him, and his attitude changed."

Though far from the battlefields, the medics experienced nightly bombings and attacks by German V-2 rockets, and Grumbine remembers "the incessant bombings, day and night." One member of their unit was killed in a bombing. "He didn't listen to orders and crawled under a truck that night," Grumbine said. "That's the worst place he could have been."

As an administrative NCO [non-commissioned officer], Grumbine also supervised the work of eight clerks and was responsible for all money and valuables of patients in the hospital.

He said he learned "a greater appreciation of human sacrifice and concern for world affairs. I see some of these boys coming home now," he said. "It brings back memories."

(Photos courtesy of Aubrey Grumbine)

Robert L. Bragunier — Army — WWII

Robert L. Bragunier of Williamsport switched gears, big-time, during his Army career from November 1942 to February 1946. He spent most of the first three years stateside with assignments at Camp Keesler Field, Mississippi; Camp Gore Field, Montana; Camp Howze, Texas; and Fort Ord and Camp Anza in California. His last six months, though, were spent engaged in heavy fighting in the Philippines.

According to his military separation papers, Cpl. Bragunier, who was assigned to the 21st Infantry in the Asiatic-Pacific Theater of Operations, "used a variety of hand weapons in the destruction of enemy personnel and to assist in the capturing of enemy positions. Weapons included rifle, automatic rifle, rifle grenade launcher, bayonet, trench knife, and hand grenades."

These uniformed "brothers in arms" assembled for a family photograph during WWII. Robert L. Bragunier in his Army uniform (center) is flanked by his brother-in-law, Wilbur Weishaar (left), and his brother, Allen (right), both of whom were serving in the Navy.

(Photographs courtesy of Gloria Bragunier, widow of Robert L. Bragunier)

Allen W. Myers — Army — WWII

Allen W. Myers was "just a little old country boy from Sharpsburg" when he was drafted in 1943. He was a man with memories of life-changing events when he came home from World War II in 1945.

Pfc. Myers was a messenger in the Army. After completing basic training at Camp McCall, North Carolina, and maneuvers at Camp Forrest in the Smoky Mountains of Tennessee, he shipped out from Boston's Miles Standish Port, bound for Liverpool, England. He underwent additional training in England, and then on Christmas Day 1944 was flown to Rheims, France, in preparation for front-line duty in the infamous Battle of the Bulge.

"We went into Rheims and took control of the American college there," he said. "After a couple of days, we were trucked by night to the woods outside Bastogne, Belgium, in preparation for marching into Bastogne and the battle."

As the messenger for E Company, 17th Airborne Division, Myers carried the radio for his lieutenant. Usually, he said, he stayed at headquarters, but radio transmission often was so poor he hand-carried messages to the troops in the field.

On the night his company was transferred to the area outside Bastogne, he was on duty at company headquarters. "The sergeant of the guard came running in and said he'd found four or five of the guards with their throats slit. He was so distraught I had to stay with him until an ambulance could pick him up."

Myers' outfit stayed in the Ardennes forest, caught up in the German offensive. They marched back to Bastogne on Jan. 6, 1945, trudging through snow and freezing weather. Their feet got so cold, he said, that his commanding officer, Lt. Leslie Telesca, unbuttoned the blanket lining of his overcoat so he and Myers could wrap their feet to keep them from freezing.

"He and I exchanged boots by accident," Myers laughed, "but he wore a size 8 and I wore a size 7. I was comfortable. He wasn't."

When they reached Bastogne, they met the enemy face-to-face.

"We were a green outfit, and this was the first battle we were in." he said. "The next morning we went up a hill and we faced German SS troops and a Panzer division — three crack German outfits. Their machine guns opened up, and our men were dropping right and left. They slaughtered us, but we held our own.

"There was an old sergeant there, and I asked him, 'How in the hell do you know where the front is up here?' He said, 'When you see lightning and hear thunder and the shells start flying.'

"The sergeant carried a bazooka. When I saw a puff of blue smoke, I asked him what that was. He said it was a smoke shell and get out of there ASAP. I ran up the hill and looked back to see the other men getting slaughtered."

Telesca was killed in that battle. The lieutenant's wife gave birth to a daughter within the following week. After the war was over, the daughter learned about Myers, looked him up and has kept in touch with him ever since.

"We started to circle back to where we'd come from," Myers continued his battle story, "when we were caught in German crossfire. I took two bullets through my left arm, one through bone. At that time, it was every man for himself. I got out my canteen, but the water was frozen. I laid on the ground quite a while. The blood in the sleeve of my coat froze, which is probably why I didn't bleed to death. After dark, I threw away everything I couldn't carry — my rifle, my canteen, my bandolier of ammunition. I started walking with only a hand grenade in my shirt pocket.

"I made it back to an aid station in the woods, where they gave me morphine. A jeep with four litters picked me up and took me to a triage unit in a big red barn outside Bastogne, where they put my arm in a traveling cast. Then I was transferred by train to Paris. I had to spend the night in Paris because the Germans had blown up the track, and I had to wait while they laid track around the blown-up section. The next day, I went by train to the English Channel and then by boat back to England."

In the British hospital, his doctor told Myers he wasn't sure he could save his arm. However, he was able to bridge the shattered bones and thus repair the arm.

"When I woke up after the surgery," Myers said, "the first thing I did was look to see if my arm was still there."

Myers remained in the hospital for seven or eight weeks before shipping home to New York aboard the *Queen Mary*. During that time, his records hadn't caught up with him and his mother, Ida Myers of Antietam Furnace, was notified that he was missing in action. It was 30 days before she learned that her son was "found."

Myers was transferred to a hospital in North Carolina, and then to Camp Pickett, Virginia, where he had physical therapy to regain the use of his arm and "eight weeks of training to be a civilian."

Myers had worked at Fairchild Aircraft before being drafted, and returned to his job when he was discharged in 1945. When Fairchild workers went out on strike, he took a job at the Veterans Administration Hospital in Martinsburg, West Virginia. In one of those truth is stranger than fiction incidents, one of the doctors who had treated him in the hospital in Great Britain was in charge of the orthopedic unit at the VA hospital. Myers remained at the VA for 26 years before retiring.

Allen W. Myers has some mementos of his Army service in the WWII Battle of the Bulge. At center is the cover of a booklet about the 17th Airborne Division. At upper right is a photo of two men — a Belgian doctor with whom Myers corresponds and who has visited him here, and an unidentified policeman who later participated in a 17th Airborne re-enactment. (Myers himself was a member of the Sharpsburg Rifles re-enactors at one time.) The photo at lower right shows one of the battlefields where he fought. Also pictured is the cricket, or "clicker," Myers carried as a messenger during the Ardennes Offensive.

(Photographs and memorabilia courtesy of Allen W. Myers)

Richard W. Huntzberry — Army — WWII

ASSOCIATION NATIONALE DES CROIX DE GUERRE, DES T.O.E.
ET DE LA VALEUR MILITAIRE
HOTEL DES INVALIDES . PARIS

DIPLÔME DE CROIX DE GUERRE 1939-1945

NOM Sergeant RICHARD W. HUNTZBERRY

CITATION À L'ORDRE DE L'ARMÉE

"MEMBER OF THE COMPANY "F" OF THE 168th INFANTRY REGIMENT OF THE 34th INFANTRY DIVISION, AN ELITE DIVISION, WHOSE LOYAL AND EFFICIENT COOPERATION WITH THE FRENCH DIVISIONS, WHICH BEGAN IN TUNISIA, WAS GLORIOUSLY CONTINUED THROUGHOUT THE ITALIAN CAMPAIGN. DURING THE OPERATIONS OF BELVEDERE, THE 34TH INFANTRY DIVISION, DESPITE THE DIFFICULTIES OF THE MOMENT, DISPLAYED THE MOST COURAGEOUS ACTIONS IN SUPPORT OF THE OPERATIONS OF THE 3rd ALGERIAN DIVISION."

CETTE CITATION COMPORTE L'ATTRIBUTION DE LA CROIX DE GUERRE AVEC PALME.

Décision N°843
PARIS, le 21 juin 1945
Signé: de Gaulle

1914 1918 — TOE — 1939 1945

Richard W. Huntzberry was posthumously awarded the Diplome de Croix de Guerre by the Republic of France in 1945. The citation, signed by Charles de Gaulle, commemorates the "loyal and efficient cooperation" of the elite "Red Bull" American combat unit with French divisions in fighting that began in Tunisia and continued throughout the Italian Campaign.

Huntzberry's body was returned to the United States and buried in Greenlawn Cemetery, Williamsport, in November 1948.

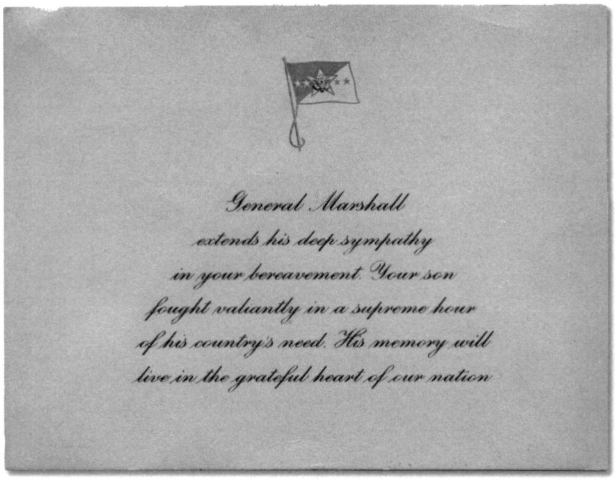

General Marshall
extends his deep sympathy
in your bereavement. Your son
fought valiantly in a supreme hour
of his country's need. His memory will
live in the grateful heart of our nation

Card sent by General George C. Marshall to the Huntzberry family expressing sympathy for the loss of their son.

Charles De Gaulle – Paris 1944

Snapshot of Gen. Charles de Gaulle in front of the Arc de Triomphe taken in 1944 by Maj. Charles L. Downey of Williamsport. (Contributed by Patricia Martin)

Family members preserved artifacts from Sgt. Richard W. Huntzberry's service with Company F, 168th Infantry Regiment of the 34th Infantry Division in WWII. Huntzberry, who had been working on his aunt and uncle's Downsville Pike farm before he was inducted into the Army in January 1943, was killed in action in Italy on Sept. 22, 1944.

He had been wounded in the early part of the Italian Campaign and had been awarded the Bronze Star for meritorious service in January 1944. Huntzberry was "cited for the daring rescue of a wounded man during which he crawled to within whispering range of the enemy," according to a newspaper account at the time.

Huntzberry was killed nine months later.

The case displays the following medals: the Bronze Star; Purple Heart; Good Conduct Medal; the European-African-Middle Eastern Campaign Medal; World War II Victory Medal; the French medal commemorating the Italian Campaign; and the Croix du Combatant Voluntaire.

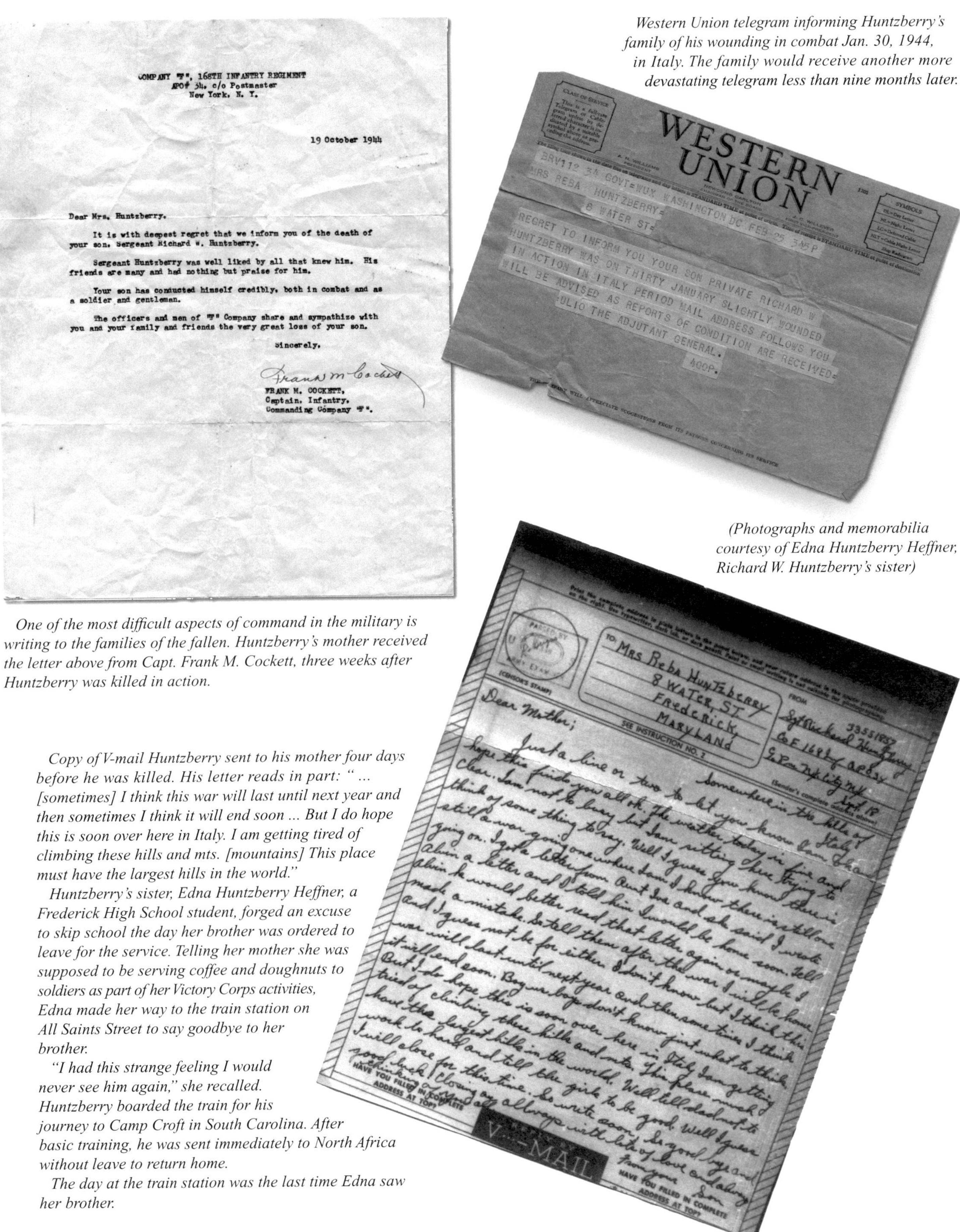

COMPANY "F", 168TH INFANTRY REGIMENT
APO# 34, c/o Postmaster
New York, N. Y.

19 October 1944

Dear Mrs. Huntzberry.

It is with deepest regret that we inform you of the death of your son, Sergeant Richard W. Huntzberry.

Sergeant Huntzberry was well liked by all that knew him. His friends are many and had nothing but praise for him.

Your son has conducted himself credibly, both in combat and as a soldier and gentleman.

The officers and men of "F" Company share and sympathize with you and your family and friends the very great loss of your son.

Sincerely,

Frank M Cockett

FRANK M. COCKETT,
Captain, Infantry,
Commanding Company "F".

WESTERN UNION

BRV112 34 GOVT=WUX WASHINGTON DC FEB 25 345P
MRS REBA HUNTZBERRY=
8 WATER ST=
REGRET TO INFORM YOU YOUR SON PRIVATE RICHARD W HUNTZBERRY WAS ON THIRTY JANUARY SLIGHTLY WOUNDED IN ACTION IN ITALY PERIOD MAIL ADDRESS FOLLOWS YOU WILL BE ADVISED AS REPORTS OF CONDITION ARE RECEIVED=
ULIO THE ADJUTANT GENERAL.
400P.

Western Union telegram informing Huntzberry's family of his wounding in combat Jan. 30, 1944, in Italy. The family would receive another more devastating telegram less than nine months later.

(Photographs and memorabilia courtesy of Edna Huntzberry Heffner, Richard W. Huntzberry's sister)

One of the most difficult aspects of command in the military is writing to the families of the fallen. Huntzberry's mother received the letter above from Capt. Frank M. Cockett, three weeks after Huntzberry was killed in action.

Copy of V-mail Huntzberry sent to his mother four days before he was killed. His letter reads in part: " ... [sometimes] I think this war will last until next year and then sometimes I think it will end soon ... But I do hope this is soon over here in Italy. I am getting tired of climbing these hills and mts. [mountains] This place must have the largest hills in the world."

Huntzberry's sister, Edna Huntzberry Heffner, a Frederick High School student, forged an excuse to skip school the day her brother was ordered to leave for the service. Telling her mother she was supposed to be serving coffee and doughnuts to soldiers as part of her Victory Corps activities, Edna made her way to the train station on All Saints Street to say goodbye to her brother.

"I had this strange feeling I would never see him again," she recalled. Huntzberry boarded the train for his journey to Camp Croft in South Carolina. After basic training, he was sent immediately to North Africa without leave to return home.

The day at the train station was the last time Edna saw her brother.

Ralph Allen Sheeler — Army — WWII
Calvin W. Sheeler Jr. — Navy — WWII

Private 1st Class Ralph Allen Sheeler

Brothers Ralph Allen Sheeler and Calvin W. "Cal" Sheeler Jr. both served in the military during World War II, despite a 16-year difference in their ages.

Ralph Sheeler was 34 years old when the Army beckoned on Oct. 2, 1943. Younger brother Cal was just 17 when he enlisted in the Navy seven months later on April 26, 1944. Both served with distinction in major campaigns, Ralph in the Battle of the Bulge in Europe and Cal in the battle for Okinawa in the South Pacific.

Ralph Sheeler served as a private 1st class in an antitank company, 10th Infantry, part of Gen. George S. Patton's 3rd Army. He saw action in four major campaigns, including the Ardennes Offensive and the Battle of the Bulge, as he moved with the Army across the Rhineland and Central Europe. Brother Cal said of him, "He found wherever he went that kids are the same the world over, and he saved his candy and gum for children he met between battles."

Ralph often regaled his family with a story about carrying a dead chicken across Europe. It seems his outfit killed and cleaned a chicken, and three days later finally got to cook it. The weather was so cold the chicken stayed frozen for the three days. When he finally got to taste the bird, Sheeler declared it "a great delicacy."

Ralph came home with a fistful of ribbons and medals including four battle stars. He was discharged on Oct. 6, 1945, and died in 1989 at the age of 79.

After Cal Sheeler enlisted in the Navy he saw service aboard the USS *Yokes* APD 69 [Auxiliary Personnel Destroyer], one of 192 crewmen and 13 officers on board. The *Yokes* provided convoy and transport duty in both the Atlantic and Pacific theaters and also did anti-submarine duty and beach bombardment in the battle for Okinawa. Sheeler's ship arrived at Okinawa about one week into the campaign and remained until the Japanese-held island was secured. During that last major offensive in the South Pacific, Sheeler said, 34 ships were sunk and 350 were damaged, resulting in some 10,000 casualties.

The *Yokes* served on the "ping line" off Okinawa, its underwater gear listening for Japanese submarines in the area. Sheeler said the ship also sailed in an assigned area, running figure eights to pick up planes coming off the southern tip of Japan.

Seaman 1st Class Calvin W. Sheeler Jr.

He said he and his crewmates were on watch 24 hours a day. They usually had a one-hour notice of kamikazes taking off from Japan, and he recalled one incident when he was standing guard on the bow and watched a kamikaze fly past him and crash into a storage unit on land. "I saw him explode," he said.

He saw Japanese pilots bomb a hospital ship, even though its big red crosses were well lighted. "It was horrible," he said.

Another time, he and his shipmates were equally dismayed to watch the Japanese bomb a freighter loaded with beer. "The freighter was coming out of the Philippines with beer for the ships' crews," he said, "and the Japanese sunk it. You should have heard the griping!"

He said when ships were in port, the Japanese often would swim up next to ships and throw grenades on board. "We had to stand watch," he said, "one on the bow, one on the stern, one on the port side and one on starboard side."

Cal was a member of a 5-inch gun crew, and it was his responsibility to pass ammunition from his post under the gun mount to the gunner.

During his service aboard the *Yokes*, he "steamed" some 70,000 miles. Like many of his shipmates, he was "initiated" when the ship crossed the Equator. He said he sailed as long as six weeks without seeing land.

Not unlike many young men of that era, he enlisted while still a student in high school. After his discharge on May 25, 1946, he came home to Hagerstown to complete his senior year at Hagerstown High School. He graduated with the Class of 1947.

Cal enlisted with high school classmate Jim Strine. Strine went into the naval air force, Cal went into the general pool. He served with fellow Washington Countian Guy Haines of Clear Spring aboard the *Yokes*, and found another hometown friend, Howell Hammond, on Okinawa. "We planned to get together," Cal said of Hammond, "but the war interfered. I saw him through my binoculars, and we waved."

(Photographs courtesy of Calvin W. Sheeler Jr.)

C. V. Eldridge — Army — WWII

In advance of D-Day, Pfc. C. V. Eldridge of Hagerstown was part of a camouflage unit in England that installed cue lights and apparatus on an open plain designed to look like an entire city from the air as part of efforts to deceive enemy reconnaissance planes. He is kneeling in front in the 1944 group photo below.

Eldridge received an Award of Merit for camouflaging Gen. Dwight D. Eisenhower's headquarters in London's Hyde Park.

This photo of a smiling band of brothers preparing to go to the front lines in Germany includes C. V. Eldridge (third from left in the back row), who was assigned to a camouflage unit — Company E, 263rd Infantry, 66th Division. Members of the "Black Panther" Division, as it was known, participated in five major European campaigns: Normandy, Northern France, Ardennes, the Rhineland and Central Europe.

*Eldridge recalls the general high spirits with which the young men headed to the battlefront. "We'd be riding in the back of the truck to the front lines singing **God Bless America** and other songs at the top of our voices. I think about that sometimes today and think we weren't too clever. We didn't realize what we were getting into."*

All throughout the fighting, Eldridge carried a photograph of his wife, Joy, inside his helmet.

*Eldridge, circled, and his fellow soldiers celebrated Hitler's defeat at a Paris restaurant in 1945. The acting career of his master sergeant, Sam Gilman (second from left), was interrupted by the war. Eldridge later saw his former sergeant, who went on to have a career in television, on an episode of **Gunsmoke**.*

View of "Rainbow Corner," an American Red Cross canteen in Paris, where American soldiers were given "donuts and Coca-Cola." Eldridge said the doughnuts didn't have any sugar on them, "but they sure were good."

Red Cross canteens were a welcome sight for most servicemembers, providing food, beverages and a place to relax. Eldridge spent a lot of time at the canteen during off-duty hours in France during WWII.

Red Cross volunteers were also on hand to greet soldiers when they returned from the war. Eldridge remembers seeing the Statue of Liberty on his return voyage and watching people waving sheets from their windows in welcome. He remembers Red Cross workers coming aboard to give the soldiers cookies and milk. "It was so great."

(Photographs courtesy of C. V. Eldridge)

George R. "Dick" Ambrose — Army — WWII

George R. "Dick" Ambrose, barely 21 years old, found himself in the middle of one of the greatest battles ever fought by the United States Army. Far from his Huyetts area home, just west of Hagerstown, Ambrose was one of hundreds of thousands of troops embroiled in what has become one of the most memorable of American military campaigns — the Battle of the Bulge.

Ambrose's unit had been tasked with guarding bridges and roads and keeping supply lines moving as American and Allied forces fought in the epic struggle to gain control of continental Europe, but as they moved closer to the front lines, "we saw many homes destroyed and could smell the stench of dead bodies. I then realized this was what war was all about," Ambrose wrote in a postwar reminiscence.

On Dec. 10, 1944, Ambrose's 817th Tank Destroyer Battalion got orders to move up and secure the area near the heavily forested Ardennes region in Luxembourg. In those days of heavy combat, Ambrose's tank destroyer unit had perfected the tricky art of blowing up tanks only a few paces away. Soldiers in the unit would get as close to an enemy tank as they could to damage the track and immobilize the deadly vehicle. "The tank can actually roll over you and that's when you throw a Molotov cocktail at the tank. It's nasty warfare," Ambrose recalled. "That guy [in the tank] didn't do nothing to me."

On that day, replacements were needed for another Third Army Group that had been depleted during the fighting, but Ambrose and his buddy didn't want to be transferred. His captain pulled two sticks from his pocket to determine who would go, and Ambrose drew the "short stick." He was wounded 45 minutes later.

"It had snowed the night before and the Germans had put mines in the snow," he wrote. While German soldiers had come prepared for the season with white uniforms as camouflage against the snow-covered terrain, Ambrose didn't even have combat boots. "Some of us went to the front lines with no combat shoes as they were stolen and sold to the black market. My feet were wrapped with toilet tissue (with stockings and

Private 1st Class George R. "Dick" Ambrose of Hagerstown was a welder at Fairchild Aircraft when he was drafted into the Army in February 1943. By the fall of that year, he was in England, bringing little more from home than memories and a small Bible that fit in his shirt pocket. A member of a tank destroyer battalion, he soon found himself in France in the Battle of the Bulge. While going to the rescue of two buddies in a minefield on Dec. 11, 1944, he stepped on a mine himself. The tourniquet he put on his left leg saved his life, but he eventually lost the leg. This photograph shows him a year after his return home.

"This is undoubtedly the greatest American battle of the war and will, I believe, be regarded as an ever famous American victory."

— Sir Winston Churchill, addressing the House of Commons following the Battle of the Bulge

Insignia of Ambrose's 817th Tank Destroyer Battalion, part of the Third Army in the Battle of the Bulge.

Shown in the photo at left are some of Ambrose's WWII medals (left to right): Good Conduct Medal; World War II Victory Medal; European-African-Middle Eastern Campaign Medal; and the American Campaign Medal.

Ambrose received two Purple Heart medals (below) for his service in WWII — one for when he lost his foot after stepping on a land mine and the second when another eight inches of his leg had to be removed at a stateside hospital some time later. The other medals include Ambrose's Expert Marksman Badge with rifle bar and the Bronze Star.

(Photographs and memorabilia courtesy of George R. "Dick" Ambrose)

galoshes pulled over top) which was not much protection against land mines," Ambrose recalled.

But when two of Ambrose's buddies, who were riding in a jeep, hit a land mine near the unit to which he had been reassigned, Ambrose rushed out to help them. He, too, hit a land mine. "I went up in the air and I saw blue flames at my feet, but I didn't know what happened." He didn't realize that the explosion had taken off part of his left foot.

"No one was there to aid us, so I took my belt off and tied it around my leg for ten seconds and then released it — on and off — to form a clot." The Army had trained its soldiers in the use of tourniquets. "When you see blood in the snow, you know you've got to do something." Applying his Army training and keeping his injured foot in the snow saved his life. "I'm just lucky I didn't bleed to death," Ambrose said.

Eventually, a military truck took him to a makeshift (tent) hospital, where his left foot was amputated at the ankle. As a result of nearly a dozen subsequent surgeries, he eventually lost much of his left leg.

Since that fateful day in 1944, Ambrose has "worn out" 25 prostheses and had to have his right knee replaced because of the strain on his remaining leg. Sixty-three years later, he still feels the "phantom pain" that many amputees experience. Ambrose went on to marry and father three children. In many ways, the period of child-raising was the most challenging time because "I realized I couldn't be the father I wanted to be to them — sports was out of the question — but I also realized maybe it gave them spunk and courage to be like their daddy," Ambrose said.

Spunk and courage may run in the family. His father, George Dewey Ambrose, was gassed in World War I. Ambrose, himself, received two Purple Hearts for his injuries and the Bronze Star for service in WWII. During the Vietnam War era, his son, Kenneth Ambrose, served as a Seabee "with a hammer, nails and a gun," and his son-in-law, Darryl Yost, also served in the Navy.

"Definitely want to thank the Man upstairs," said Ambrose pointing skyward. "I hear it takes only two to three minutes to bleed to death. There's somebody looking out for you. I know that now because I was able to live long enough to tell the tale."

Brothers in Arms — Robert Martin — Army Air Forces — WWII

Robert Martin is flanked by his parents, Percy and Bessie Martin (left), in a snapshot taken on Wilson Boulevard in Hagerstown when Martin was home on leave during the early days of WWII.

Robert Martin (right) stands under the shade of a palm tree in Florida during basic training in 1943.

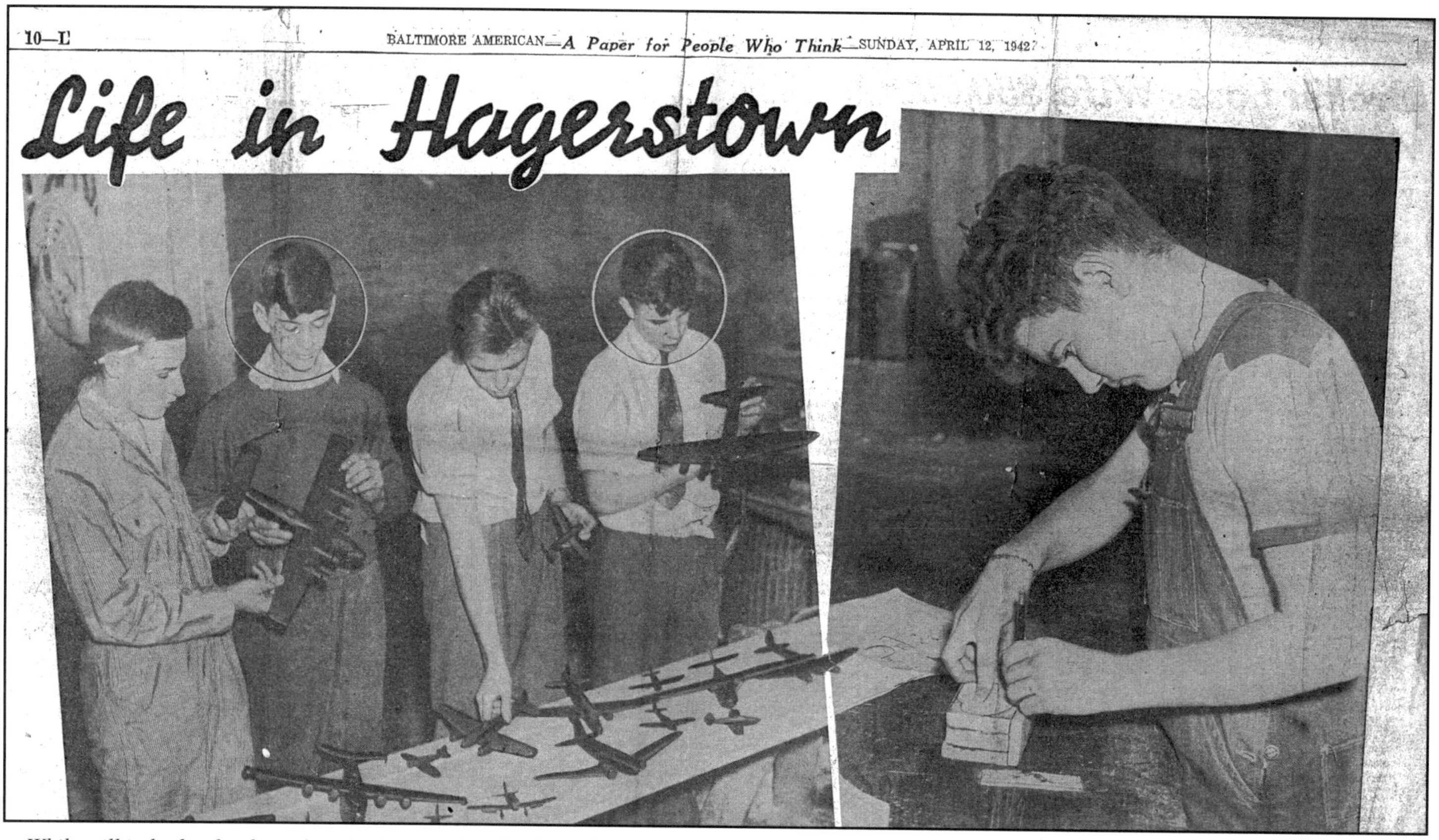

10—E BALTIMORE AMERICAN—A Paper for People Who Think—SUNDAY, APRIL 12, 1942

Life in Hagerstown

While still in high school, not long before entering the Army, Lawrence Martin and classmates in the woodworking shop at Hagerstown High School crafted solid wood models of aircraft to be used in Navy training. The meticulously rendered models were painted black so that Navy personnel could learn to distinguish the aircraft by silhouette alone.

The ***Baltimore American*** *printed this photo of Lawrence (third from left) in a full-page photo feature on April 12, 1942. The young men were identified in the photo (from left to right) as David, Ralph, Lawrence and Ken Martin. Although they all had the same last name, none of them were related. Two of the students' heads are circled as part of a promotion the Baltimore newspaper was running at the time. The student in the photo on the right, concentrating on tracing a template, is Lloyd Rockwell.*

Lawrence R. Martin — Army — WWII

A relaxed Lawrence Martin sits on the stoop of his brother Robert's 135 N. Locust St. home while on furlough from basic training in 1943. Visible in the glass door above his head is the "Sons in Service" flag families of servicemembers placed in full view to honor those serving in uniform during WWII. Robert's wife, Rebecca, placed the flag with a blue star in the center of the red-bordered white rectangle in the front window. The blue stars were replaced or covered with gold stars if the family member died in action. Happily both Robert and Lawrence Martin returned home safely from the war.

(Photographs and memorabilia courtesy of Lawrence R. Martin and his daughter, Vickie Layton)

Before shipping out to France, Lawrence Martin's unit camped out at Stonehenge Aug. 3 - Aug. 12, 1944. The troops spent many hours wandering around the mysterious arrangement of monoliths sitting out in an open field long before the ancient site became the fenced-in tourist attraction it is today.

During his time in France and Germany, Lawrence Martin enjoyed several furloughs in the little town of Madeley Heath in Staffordshire, England. "This was a very pretty section of the English Midlands," Martin recalled, and he and his fellow soldiers found the village to be "the closest thing to home with friendly people, quaint homes and little pubs." Lawrence Martin served with the Third Army under Gen. George S. Patton. As with many veterans of WWII, he knows exactly how many days he was overseas: 1 year, 6 months and 14 days. He participated in five major campaigns of the European offensive: Normandy, Northern France, Ardennes, Rhineland and Central Europe.

Lewis Ruth — Army — WWII

Lawrence Martin (right) and Lew Ruth (left) were both Hagerstown boys and the same age, but they didn't know each other until they were inducted into the Army in 1943. Martin and Ruth went into the Army the same day and their serial numbers (the identification numbers every servicemember was assigned) were just one number apart.

*Martin and Ruth were together all through basic training. They came home to Hagerstown on furlough together after they completed training, and then went back to the same company — the 305th Ordnance Maintenance Company. They were in the same artillery section and traveled overseas together on the ship **Louis Pasteur**.*

*When their company camped, the two Hagerstown boys shared a tent. They were together all through their travels in Europe during the war, and they came home together on the Liberty ship **James Hoban**. They arrived at Hampton Roads, Virginia, and both were discharged on the same day.*

Francis Bernard Rang — Army Air Forces — WWII

Bernard Rang (in photo at right) was awarded the Silver Star in 1942 during ceremonies at an air base near Tel Aviv. The Silver Star is the fourth-highest military decoration that can be awarded to any member of any branch of the service.

Rang had previously been awarded the Distinguished Flying Cross, the second-highest military decoration, for his service with the crew that routinely transported mail and dignitaries back and forth across the Atlantic during the early days of the United States' entry into WWII.

President Franklin Delano Roosevelt and British Prime Minister Winston Churchill were among the passengers on flights in which he served as a navigator with the Air Corps Ferry Command. The award was given in recognition of Rang's service after a particularly harrowing flight when one of the key figures of WWII was on board. Caught in a storm, Rang safely navigated the plane (with its distinguished cargo) to a landing strip in Newfoundland.

In one of the last photos taken of Major Bernard Rang of Hagerstown, the officer raises a toast to an unknown photographer in Tel Aviv on June 7, 1943. Rang, an Army Air Forces navigator/bombardier, was reported missing and presumed dead following a bombing raid over Messina, Sicily, on July 14, 1943.

Rang looking out over the sea wall in Tel Aviv. Rang was a navigator trained on both the B-17 "Flying Fortress" and B-24 "Liberator" bombers. From bases in the Mediterranean, the heavy bombers "softened up" enemy positions in Sicily in preparation for the landing of Allied troops on the Italian peninsula.

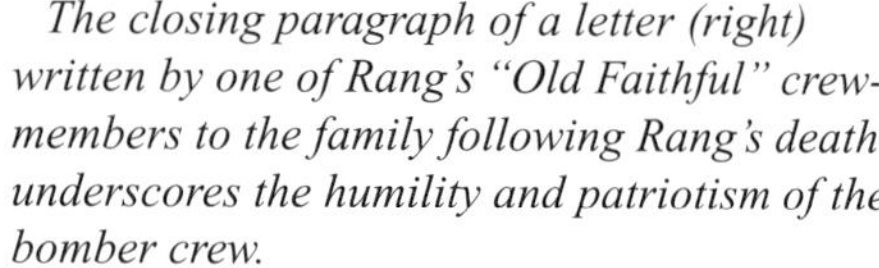

The closing paragraph of a letter (right) written by one of Rang's "Old Faithful" crewmembers to the family following Rang's death underscores the humility and patriotism of the bomber crew.

3.

stuck his head up in the astro-dome and yelled: "Come on you buggers, let's fight!"

But Lt. Rhoades had other ideas. He noticed that our formation had been broken up and there were only three of our ships in the element. When he pointed this out to the Major, he again stuck his head up into the astro-dome and started to sing, "Please go away and let me sleep!"

Everyone laughed and stood by their stations as Colonel Kalberer t turned back with his two other ships to help the rest of the formation out.

After we had landed and the pictures of the mission had been printed, they showed that Major Rang's bombs had splattered the entire deck of the transport frombow to stern.

The boys in the elements back of us said the boat reared up on the stern and sank in three minutes/

We are just eight of thousands of airmen who do the same thing every day. And our adventures and successes and failures are the same as all the others. We are proud to be part of this vombat crew, and we are proud to be Americans, and part of the Army Air Forces.

You get 'em Flying and we'll keep Jerry dying.

"Old Faithful's Enlisted Crew"

Aerial photographs of "four of 70 B-24s" dropping their payloads in a "most successful mission," according to an inscription by "Bernie" on the back of small snapshots mailed home to his mother and two sisters in Hagerstown.

Rang was the navigator/bombardier of "Old Faithful," a bomber that flew missions targeting enemy shipping in the Mediterranean. In a letter to Rang's family, an unnamed surviving crewmember describes bombing runs the aircraft made in 1942. Rang, who often sang to fellow crewmembers over the intercom system, called his vulnerable glass-enclosed gunner position in the plane's nose "the Green House." Rang was known to belt out, "Oh, she jumped in bed and covered her head ..." when the aircraft was in sight of a target as a cue to the crew in advance of the "Bombs Away!" command.

Rang [standing far left] with fellow crewmembers in 1941 in front of a B-24 bomber.

Rang graduated from Hagerstown High School in 1935 and attended the College of William & Mary on a fencing and boxing scholarship. He was working for Douglas Aircraft in California when the United States entered the war. Following his enlistment, he trained as a navigator in Florida. In 1942, Rang [with foil on right] used his fencing skills as recreation and as entertainment for the crew at his Mediterranean air base in between bombing raids.

News clippings, a V-mail envelope indicating Maj. Rang was "Missing in action . . . Return to sender," and a memorial service program testify to Rang's ultimate sacrifice on behalf of his country.

Rang had volunteered to be an observer in a raid over Sicily on July 14, 1943. He and another crewmember were lost when the aircraft was hit by flak and severely damaged. An order was given for the crew to bail out, but the pilot was able to coax the hobbled bomber back to base. Rang and another occupant were reported missing in action.

"They never found a trace of either one of them," said Rang's sister, Mary Halligan Berkenbaugh of Hagerstown. A plaque commemorating Rang's service in WWII was placed at his family's burial plot in Hanover, Pennsylvania, on June 25, 1988.

Photographs of Bernard Rang and his son appear side-by-side in a framed memento cherished by Rang's sister. Before the war, Rang had married Mary Theresa Dodson, a young woman from San Pedro, California. She was working as a nurse at Douglas Aircraft, and they met when Rang came to the infirmary with a tiny sliver of metal in his eye. Their son, Francis Bernard Rang II, was not yet one year old at the time of his father's disappearance over Sicily. The photograph of the major's son was taken at the age of 5. The younger Rang is one of an estimated 183,000 American children who lost fathers in combat during WWII.

(All photographs and memorabilia courtesy of Bernard Rang's sister, Mary Halligan Berkenbaugh)

Julia Donovan — WAAC — WWII

Less than four months after the bombing of Pearl Harbor, Congress created the Women's Army Auxiliary Corps [WAAC] on March 15, 1942, and life changed dramatically for Julia Hogan of Hagerstown. Leaving her job in the payroll department at Hagerstown Shoe & Legging Co. in October, she was inducted into the WAAC and sent to administrative specialist school in Des Moines, Iowa. Upon graduation, she was assigned to Fort Custer, Michigan, to work in the finance department.

She remembers the day in 1943 when the WAAC became the WAC [Women's Army Corps], and her post commander "welcomed us WACs into the Army ranks." But the best was yet to come. On Feb. 1, 1944, while working at post headquarters as administrative "acting sergeant major" for the post's three WAC companies, she received the telegram she'd been hoping for: she was being given an overseas assignment.

"Our unknown destination," she said, took her by ship to Cairo, Egypt, to work in the finance office at headquarters for USAFIME [United States Army Forces in the Middle East]. This was a unified Army command established in August 1942 to oversee the Egypt-Libya Campaign. Working with its British counterpart, it had command over Army forces in North Africa and the Middle East.

Though the war in Europe ended on May 8, 1945, "ships home were very limited," Julia said, and it was November before she was able to leave Egypt. Back in the States, she went to George Washington University and art school in Washington, D.C. There she met her future husband and moved to New York City, where the Donovans have lived for the last 54 years. She continued to work for the Army as a statistician, and after retirement, she began to volunteer, and continues to do so, for the aged. "I should be there myself," she said.

The idea of women in uniform was still a novel concept at the beginning of WWII, even though small numbers of American women had served their country during WWI, most visibly, as nurses. A distinctive feature of the WAAC uniform was the khaki hat that accompanied the tailored jacket and skirt.

WAAC recruits were issued five shirts, three skirts, four pairs of rayon hose, four pairs of cotton hose, six panties, three brassieres, one raincoat, two girdles, two anklets, one khaki jacket, one pair of slippers, one pair of athletic shoes, one bathrobe, one exercise suit, two pairs of pajamas, one khaki cap, one hat, one pair of gloves, three slips and two barracks bags.

(WAAC cap courtesy of Lloyd Sigler)

Recruiting posters such as the one above were displayed widely during WWII in the hope that women would enlist in the Women's Army Auxiliary Corps, predecessor to the Women's Army Corps.

Russell "Clarke" Urich Jr. — Army, Army Air Forces — WWII

Russell "Clarke" Urich Jr. wore two hats during WWII — in the Army in the Pacific and in the Army Air Forces in Europe. A graduate of Hagerstown High School, Urich was working as an accountant for the Western Maryland Railway when he joined the Army in April 1941. He was in the coast artillery at Pearl Harbor when the Japanese attacked on Dec. 7, which was his most memorable experience of the war. A poem he wrote about that day appears at the beginning of the WWII section of this book. This photo shows him in Hawaii or Fiji.

Urich served in the Fiji Islands before returning stateside in 1943 to realize his ambition to fly.

After training for an officer's job in the Army Air Forces, he was sent to Europe as a bombardier — the member of a bomber crew who operates the bombsight and bombing release mechanism. He flew a B-17 Flying Fortress heavy bomber with the 18th Army Air Force's 368th Bomber Squadron, 306th Bomber Group. He served in Europe for nine months, completing 35 combat missions (283 combat hours) over Northern France, Germany and the Ardennes. When he returned home after the war, he brought a piece of a parachute from a forced landing.

(Photos courtesy of Darus Urich, widow of Russell "Clarke" Urich Jr.)

Galen R. Warden — Merchant Marine — WWII

Galen R. Warden was permitted to graduate early from high school in April of 1945 so he could go into the service. He really wanted to join the Navy, but there was only one problem — the Antietam Street resident was color-blind, and unable to distinguish the hues of signal flags used by the Navy. He decided to join the Merchant Marine instead.

Warden (second from the left in the first row) completed his training at Sheepshead Bay, near Coney Island in New York. He did one tour of duty with the Merchant Marine and then was permitted to enlist in the Army in December 1945. He trained at Fort McClellan in Alabama and Camp Carson in Colorado. He was never sent into combat because WWII had ended and he was discharged as a corporal in 1947.

(Photograph contributed by Marlene Shank, sister of Galen R. Warden)

James M. Hamby — Navy — WWII

Ladders, Hatches Worst Hazards On County Boy's Battlewagon

"Just the fact that you have this letter," writes James M. Hamby, S 1/c, to his parents, Mr. and Mrs. Harry Hamby, Sr., Clearspring Route 1, "tells you that I'm well, that the ship is still steaming along with a full crew and, so far, no serious difficulties have marred our activities."

Considering that Jim writes from the midst of a Pacific battle zone, that's a pretty optimistic statement, but Jim and his fellow crew members make a habit of being optimistic. One of his shipmates is William Middlecamp, who used to live on Mulberry street in Hagerstown.

"There are always some minor problems," the Clearspring youth confesses, "like men falling down ladders, dropping hatches on their heads, bumping into 'doorknobs,' etc. All of these are run-of-the-mill casualties and we expect them. We also expect an emergency appendix before every campaign. We have had one before each of the last three and it has reached the point where the doctor feels that an emergency appendectomy is an augur of success if it comes a day or two before we tangle with 'Tojo's Tots.'

"Four jobs have been checked off our list since last I wrote to you. Each one has been duly recorded through the press at home. You, of course, had no way of knowing

(Continued on Page 2)

carriers need us as much as we need them. Our plane craftsmanship is superb but some day when the whole story is told, it will be one of unity and splendid organization. All parts work in perfect harmony.

"Dropping back from the battle line," he continues, "we picked up our tankers and fueled for the next operation that followed right along. Yet better still we picked up mail from home. What a cheer as a destroyer came alongside with 12 wonderful bags of reports from home. There are few things more satisfying than letters from home when we are far from land and in the midst of battle operations."

Bringing things up to date: "This morning we fueled destroyers. The little ships that are doing such a big job can't go as far as we can on their fuel supply, so after a week or so they must call on the 'gas station of the deep,' the battlewagon. Again it is cooperation that counts, and the skill with which our boys perform their work shows the hours of careful training which have made each man letter perfect.

"Well, this is about all for now, Unfortunately we must wait for the Japs as we can chase them only so far without consolidating our own supply lines. But we are on the way—it may be a long way, but we have what it takes and will take what the Japs have. Don't forget me in your prayers. That is your part of the job. Will write soon again. Your loving son, Jim."

Excerpts of James M. Hamby's letter to his parents in Clear Spring during WWII provide a glimpse of life aboard ship in the midst of fighting in the Pacific. Hamby details the incidental hazards of life aboard ship "like men falling down ladders, dropping hatches on their heads, bumping into 'doorknobs,' etc. All of these are run-of-the-mill casualties and we expect them," Hamby wrote. He goes on to acknowledge the importance of fuel supplies in keeping fighting ships in action and the joy of a rendezvous with a destroyer and picking up "12 wonderful bags of mail" from home.

Hamby and his buddies pose for the camera near laundry drying in the sun. Hamby served with the Navy in the Pacific in WWII.

Post cards Hamby mailed home from Japan.

(Photographs and memorabilia courtesy of Brian D. Ruth, nephew of James M. Hamby)

Harold B. Nunamaker — Army Air Forces — WWII
Freda Davis Nunamaker — WAC — WWII

Harold and Freda Nunamaker worked for their country as civilians in the early years of WWII at Fairchild Aircraft in Washington County. Harold started in 1940, working in the plant at the Fairgrounds, cutting and forming sheet metal used in the assembly of aircraft parts. Later, he also was foreman of 30 men.

Mutual friends introduced Harold and Freda at a skating party at Braddock Heights Park. They married on July 12, 1941. Freda started work at Fairchild in 1942, inspecting sheet metal and motor parts for airplanes at the Pennsylvania Avenue plant.

Harold left Fairchild in 1943 to join the Army Air Forces. Freda left in 1944 to join the Women's Army Corps. They are shown above in 1943 in California, where Freda had gone to see Harold off as he shipped off to India.

Nunamaker (right) and a buddy in India display the flag of the 377th Service Squadron of the 10th Air Force, where they worked repairing damaged aircraft.

WWII was still raging on two fronts when Freda Davis Nunamaker joined the Women's Army Corps in December 1944. When she was discharged from the Army less than a year later, peace reigned in both Europe and the Pacific.

Upon enlisting, Freda Nunamaker left behind her expertise with sheet metal and learned typing and administration. She took a clerk's course in May while completing basic training at the First Women's Army Corps Training Center at Fort Des Moines, Iowa. She was assigned to Post Headquarters at Camp Shanks, New York, where this photo was taken. Her work there consisted of distributing special orders for men returning from overseas to various headquarters. She retired from the military as a private on Dec. 9, 1945.

Identity card and photo of Freda Nunamaker when she served in the WAC at Camp Shanks, New York, in 1945. She is now 85 and in good health.

(Photos and memorabilia courtesy of Bill and Cindy Wolfinger. Cindy is the daughter of Harold and Freda Nunamaker)

Harold and Freda Nunamaker both appear in this photo taken in Los Angeles, in 1943. It shows the graduating class of a Sheet Metal Repair Technical School, from which Harold had just graduated, first in his class. Harold can be seen in the photograph, sitting at the table, just below the portrait of Franklin D. Roosevelt. Freda is the taller of two women in dark suits with white blouses, seated together in the upper lefthand corner. She had gone to California for the graduation.

After basic training in the Army Air Forces in Salt Lake City, Utah, Nunamaker was sent to India, where he served in the China-Burma-India Theater. This was commonly known as "Confusion Beyond Imagination," Nunamaker remembered.

Thanks to his experience at Fairchild, he knew the work: repairing sheet metal parts of aircraft damaged by enemy fire or caused by crash-landings for the 377th Service Squadron of the 10th Air Force. The planes were hauling supplies to the 14th Air Force in Kunming, China, because it was the only way to supply them.

He had vivid memories of flying over "The Hump" of the Himalayas, also known as "The Aluminum Highway" because of the aircraft that went down there. One time, Nunamaker served as co-pilot on a mission over the mountains even though he didn't know how to fly. The pilot needed a second man in the cockpit to be allowed to take off.

Nunamaker returned from Asia in late 1945 and retired as sergeant in March 1946. He died in March 2002.

Army Air Forces collectors' pillow that Nunamaker sent home to his parents from Utah, where he was in basic training. On it is written: MOTHER & DAD: The voice of parents, the voice of gods, for to their children they are heaven's lieutenants. SALT LAKE CITY, UTAH." From India, Nunamaker brought home a "bail-out" map printed on silk and an ivory bracelet carved with the insignia of U.S. pilot's wings.

Percy Albert Jr. — Army — WWII

"No story about the Normandy Campaign would be complete without mention of the hedgerows of France." Thus begins a narrative written by the late Private 1st Class Percy Albert Jr. of Boonsboro, who served and was wounded during that WWII campaign.

Writing about the almost impenetrable rows of hedge which defined the French farmers' plots of land, Albert said, "Often German was on one side, American on the other, each trying to be the first to destroy the other."

Albert served in the Army for three years, from March 12, 1943, until his discharge on Feb. 14, 1946. Assigned to the 4th Infantry Division as a sharpshooter, he served with Company B and A, 1st Battalion, 22nd Infantry Regiment. He landed on Utah Beach on D-Day and saw action in Normandy, Northern France and the Rhineland campaigns.

According to his widow, Mary Jane Albert, "Percy always said his military service made a man out of him and made him want to stand up for what he believed in and gave him love for those who served with him."

In his hand-written account of his overseas experiences, Albert tells how his platoon was loaded on a huge English ship at the port of Southampton and was "finally told this was the invasion of D-Day. The weather was cold, rainy and bone-chilling. Then the storm swept in and no one thought there could be any serious attempt to set sail across the Channel. How wrong we were! As we left the harbor the waves were angry, whipping and roaring, tossing that English tub like a cork. So many were seasick that I personally wondered how many could be effective fighting men if ever we reached shore. But those British sailors seemed unconcerned as they would ring their bell, 'Tinky, Tinky, Tink' and announce 'Tay Time.' Despite Hell or stormy sea they had to take time for the serving of tea!"

Albert posed for this photo with his brother, Eugene S. Albert Sr., who served with the Navy at the submarine base in New London, Connecticut.

According to his journal, Albert's ship bobbed around for three days "in water so rough and skies so murky it seemed we were alone with no other ships in sight and certainly no signs of shore."

Finally, he wrote, "the sailors threw rope nets overboard and we were ordered to climb down the nets and jump into the LSTs [Landing Ship Tanks]. There was a young lieutenant directly ahead of me on the ropes when a huge swell brought the LST directly against the side of the ship, crushing his body in between. Without giving a moan, his body slid into the water. It was the first casualty I saw before reaching the beach."

Albert landed on Utah Beach on D-Day + four, June 10, 1944, and he noted in his journal that "from all the discarded wreckage I knew the guys from the Fourth Infantry Division who had landed ahead of me ... had not had an easy time of it."

His platoon was assigned to capture a small town near the beach and "we had our first taste of small arms fire ... and I finally realized that only the most dedicated soldier who had absorbed his training in the USA had much chance to survive in this holocaust."

Albert noted that airborne glider troops had landed in trees in an apple orchard. "When our platoon came upon this area, we saw the Germans had captured these men, hung them on the trees with their own tent ropes, and then mutilated their bodies so horribly that I cannot be more specific ... As I looked upon these young bodies and the mutilation done to them, I knew my training sergeant had not really prepared us for the full blow of man's inhumanity to his fellow man. Then I knew the dedicated German soldiers would give us no quarter and expect none. In an encounter it would be death to the finish. I had at last become a fully dedicated fighting man."

Albert and his fellow soldiers encountered heavy fighting in many villages near the beaches as they followed the road to Cherbourg. "Nothing prepared me for the sight of ten-wheeler Army trucks loaded with bodies stacked like cord wood," he wrote.

Since darkness didn't fall until approximately 11 p.m. and dawn broke at 5 a.m., he wrote, there were many hours when fighting didn't abate even after darkness fell. Under cover of that darkness, "patrols were sent out to harass the enemy, penetrate their lines to destroy ammunition dumps and seek information about enemy maneuvering and enemy strength. When sent on patrol, a soldier carried only a trench knife, dog tags covered with a section of gas mask hose so they wouldn't rattle, no helmet liner or helmet, just a fatigue hat or, later when winter set in, a knitted mask.

"The life expectancy of those picked for patrol was not very high. Once on a nine-man patrol to blow up an ammunition dump ... only three of us survived. We came back through the 29th Division lines and because a piece of shrapnel had penetrated my left thumb so deeply it couldn't be picked out and red streaks had begun to run up my arm, I was sent back to Birmingham Hospital in England for medical treatment. Since the 29th Division medic sent me back, the 4th Division had no record of my whereabouts and reported me missing in action." His mother, Mrs. Daisie Albert, received a telegram stating her son was missing. It was an anxious 25 days until she received a second telegram saying the MIA report was "erroneous" and that he was back on active duty.

Albert received the Purple Heart, and later, in the Hurtgen Forest campaign, would receive the oak leaf cluster to go with it, signifying a second time being wounded in action.

Continuing the written saga of his WWII experiences, he wrote, "Since we were run out of St. Lo three times by the German army who were determined to hold it at all costs, there remained only rubble and partial skeletons of buildings. But a sight I will not forget was a chimney standing proudly against the skyline with a clock still on the mantel. How incongruous it seemed amidst all that rubble!"

Albert's division was part of the American forces that captured five German armies near Avranches in Normandy on July 30. "German soldiers everywhere surrendered to tired, dirty G.I.'s who were so bone-weary we were not really elated," he wrote. The next day he was sent to England for treatment of his wounded thumb.

After the fall of Paris, he was sent back to his unit, still wearing bandages on his thumb. He got back just in time for the Belgium campaign. He was among the first American troops to penetrate the Siegfried Line on October 4, 1944.

Writing in his journal, Albert recalled the event. "Our general, General Raymond Barton, drove up in a jeep and asked how we were doing and told us to carry on. It is a matter of historical record that he was the first American general to enter German soil, but I had reached there before him." His journal entry continues: "As part of the Belgium Campaign there is something every American should not forget since it has been finally admitted by our Government in the Freedom of Information Act.

"The Fourth Infantry Division consisted of 3 Infantry Regiments. There is a village in Belgium called Malmedy. Here there was furious fighting of such intensity that all units, German and American alike, were fighting tooth, claw and nail to be the victors. When pockets of the 8th Regiment were reduced to no ammunition, no rations, and many wounded, they surrendered. The Germans took their empty weapons and herded them into a clearing where they were ordered to sit until trucks could be brought to take them behind German lines. Eventually trucks arrived and backed up to the Americans.

Photograph of "Dragon's Teeth" in the Siegfried Line, near Ubach, Germany, was taken in December 1944 by Maj. Charles L. Downey. The Siegfried Line was the name Allied troops gave to a 392-mile expanse of bunkers, tunnels and tank traps that stretched along Germany's western frontier from the border of the Netherlands to Switzerland. The dragon's teeth were blocks of reinforced concrete placed in rows on a single foundation, designed to serve as tank traps. U.S troops broke through the Siegfried Line near Aachen on Sept. 13, 1944.
(Contributed by Patricia Martin)

Suddenly, the Germans jerked open the rear tarpaulins to reveal machine guns and began firing into the Americans. Realizing what was happening, some Americans began running for the woods behind them. Some made it safely, even though hunted with determination. They later returned to see what happened to their buddies who were slaughtered by the Germans. The Germans brought in bulldozers and dug ditches, shoved the dead Americans in, buried them, and when they thought all traces of their deed had been eradicated, passed on.

"When those few Americans who had escaped were able to return to American lines, this story was disbelieved and discredited. When the Germans finally surrendered, these few soldiers from the 8th Regiment persisted in efforts to find the site, while the German government said it had never happened. All the reports remained secret. After several decades passed and with persistence from members of the 4th wanting the truth exposed, our government finally exhumed the bodies of our American soldiers and brought them home, finally admitting the truth of the Malmedy Massacre. I can't remember the exact number of the slaughtered men, but it is nearer 300 than 200 victims. This is really what war is all about. Not the glamour seen on TV or tales of wonderful generals, but ordinary infantrymen."

Albert noted in his written account of the massacre that Sam Crone of Jefferson, Maryland, was among the Malmedy survivors.

"Then, his story continues, "in to the hell of Hurtgen Forest. Ask any man who participated in the Normandy Campaign and it was the Hurtgen Forest which he dreaded worst. To any fighting man who was really there, the Hurtgen Forest was Hell inferno itself. Over 125 percent of the men who fought there as a division were lost. You might ask how can a Division lose 125 percent of its strength. When you start with the original number in a Division, replace all dead and wounded with replacements who are killed or wounded in turn, the figures mount heavily. So it was with the 4th Infantry Division in this horrible battle. I made it through the forest and was dug in waiting with a few others to be replaced by the 83rd Division when I was hit on December 3, 1944.

"What was the forest really like? It was ridges of mountain ranges so heavily forested as to be almost impenetrable, with cliffs so sheer that the cliffs of Harpers Ferry look miniature in comparison. It is still a dank, dark, haunted place even today with an atmosphere that makes shivers run over the body. There was a prize of $100 offered to anyone who could find a tree which had escaped destruction from military action. Needless to say the money had never been claimed."

Albert compared battle notes while touring Antietam National Battlefield when home on medical leave after being wounded in Germany. He suffered severe leg wounds in the battle at Hurtgen Forest and was left with a permanent disability.

Albert's platoon of eight men was on the front line in the battle for Hurtgen Forest, due to be relieved the next day. He was given orders for him and his men to hold their position at all costs. He ran from foxhole to foxhole delivering the order, which put him in the open under heavy fire. He was struck by an 88 mm shell and severely wounded — 13 wounds in this one encounter.

His widow says, "As far as he knew, Percy was the only man out of the eight to survive."

In his written account of the battle, Albert said he did not remember being wounded "until I awoke with the sun shining in my face." He was evacuated to Aachen and later put on a train to Paris. There, he wrote, he was put on a plane for a hospital in England, where he waited for space on a hospital ship bound for home.

Mary Jane Albert says her husband remembered coming home in a full body cast. "He commented that every time he regained consciousness, there was always medical personnel right with him. When the ship landed, he was carried off by handles attached to his body cast. He asked the Navy corpsmen carrying him to let him look around. They positioned his casted body upright for a few minutes, and he was amazed at the number of men he watched being carried from the ship."

Albert was moved to Camp Kilmer, New Jersey. On his 21st birthday, March 7, 1945, he woke up to two nurses singing "Happy Birthday" and holding a cupcake. He couldn't believe it had taken from Dec. 3, 1944, to March 7, 1945, to make it to a hospital in the U.S. "I could not believe three months had passed with no recollection of my past," he wrote.

Albert recovered from his wounds at McGuire Army Hospital in Richmond, Virginia. But the wound to his leg was so severe that the leg was several inches shorter once it healed. "He spent the rest of his life with his disability," Mary Jane said.

CLASS OF SERVICE
This is a full-rate Telegram or Cablegram unless its deferred character is indicated by a suitable symbol above or preceding the address.

WESTERN UNION
A. N. WILLIAMS
PRESIDENT

1201

SYMBOLS
DL=Day Letter
NL=Night Letter
LC=Deferred Cable
NLT=Cable Night Letter
Ship Radiogram

The filing time shown in the date line on telegrams and day letters is STANDARD TIME at point of origin. Time of receipt is STANDARD TIME at point of destination

BRD5 43 GOVT=WASHINGTON DC 15 238A

1944 AUG 15 AM 7 37

MRS DAISIE ALBERT=

BOONSBORO MD=

THE SECRETARY OF WAR DESIRES ME TO EXPRESS HIS DEEP REGRET THAT YOUR SON PRIVATE PERCY ALBERT JR HAS BEEN REPORTED MISSING IN ACTION SINCE THIRTY ONE JULY IN FRANCE IF FURTHER DETAILS OR OTHER INFORMATION ARE RECEIVED YOU WILL BE PROMPTLY NOTIFIED=

ULIO THE ADJUTANT GENER

THE COMPANY WILL APPRECIATE SUGGESTIONS

Pfc. Percy Albert Jr.'s mother, Mrs. Daisie Albert, was notified her son was missing in action after he sustained a shrapnel wound to his thumb during a raid on an ammunition dump in Normandy. Because he was separated from his division and sent to a hopital in England by medics from another division, he was erroneously reported MIA. Later, she received the good news that her son was alive and well and back on active duty.

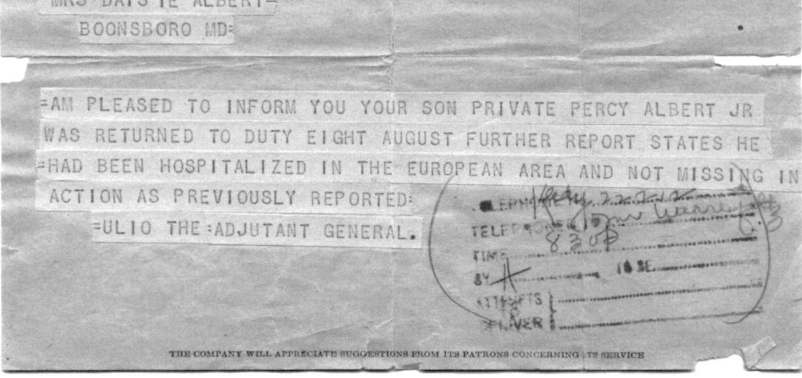

CLASS OF SERVICE
This is a full-rate Telegram or Cablegram unless its deferred character is indicated by a suitable symbol above or preceding the address.

WESTERN UNION
A. N. WILLIAMS
PRESIDENT

1201

SYMBOLS
DL=Day Letter
NL=Night Letter
LC=Deferred Cable
NLT=Cable Night Letter
Ship Radiogram

The filing time shown in the date line on telegrams and day letters is STANDARD TIME at point of origin. Time of receipt is STANDARD TIME at point of destination

BRD190 36 GOVT=WUX WASHINGTON DC 22 757P

1944 AUG 22 PM 3 26

MRS DAISIE ALBERT=

BOONSBORO MD=

=AM PLEASED TO INFORM YOU YOUR SON PRIVATE PERCY ALBERT JR WAS RETURNED TO DUTY EIGHT AUGUST FURTHER REPORT STATES HE =HAD BEEN HOSPITALIZED IN THE EUROPEAN AREA AND NOT MISSING IN ACTION AS PREVIOUSLY REPORTED=

=ULIO THE=ADJUTANT GENERAL.

THE COMPANY WILL APPRECIATE SUGGESTIONS FROM ITS PATRONS CONCERNING ITS SERVICE

A shadowbox frame contains memorabilia from Percy Albert Jr.'s service in the Army during WWII. His medals at the bottom of the case are (left to right): the Bronze Star; Purple Heart w/oak leaf cluster; Good Conduct Medal; European-African-Middle Eastern Campaign Medal; American Campaign Medal; WWII Victory Medal; and (at top) Liberation of France Medal, presented by the French government. At lower right is a medallion presented to Albert, who was a delegate to the 1960 Maryland State American Legion Convention in Baltimore. The case also includes his Fourth Infantry Division patch (upper left and center), his dog tags, Combat Infantryman Badge (top row center), his ribbon rack, his marksmanship badge and discharge pin.

Robert Carl Hixson — Army Air Forces — WWII

Sgt. Robert Carl Hixson served with the Army Air Forces in the snow-clad Aleutian Islands during WWII.

Washington County resident Robert Carl Hixson served as a draftsman and an interrogation officer with the 404th Bombardment Squadron in the Aleutian Islands during World War II, in what has been described as a brutal environment which proved to be the worst enemy of U.S. and Japanese troops alike.

Serving as a sergeant in the Army Air Forces for three years, Hixson spent most of his military time in the Aleutian chain. For 41 days at the end of WWII, he surveyed on the Seward Peninsula while on detached service with the Army's 331st Engineer Construction Battalion. It was quite an adventure for a young man from Paramount to be flown by a bush pilot 90 miles above Nome, and then dropped off on a waterway in the middle of nowhere.

According to memories shared by his widow Jane E. Hixson, "he was left there all alone with a sleeping bag and some food, but no gun. He did have a knife, and he slept on the ground with his knife by his side." She said he didn't know if there were bears or other wild animals roaming the island.

His crew and surveying equipment followed him via an overland route.

The crew worked from August 6 to September 15, 1945, to accomplish their special mission. They constructed the building which served as their base of operations, and depended on trade with the native Inuit people for fresh food.

Jane Hixson recalled her husband telling her how friendship with the Inuits began: "One morning they took a skiff up a waterway to find the local inhabitants. Their commander had told them to make friends with the Inuits. Bob walked up to a group of them ... when he got close he asked if anyone spoke English. Silence. He asked again. Eventually, they got to know this group of people and began to trade candy and cigarettes for berries and fish."

Sgt. Hixson spent the majority of his service in the Aleutians, traveling from island to island behind combat forces. As each island was wrested from Japanese invaders, he followed all the way to Attu, a little fog-shrouded island at the western end of the chain. The Battle for Attu had been a fiercely fought campaign in the summer of 1943. The entire Aleutian campaign was the only battle of WWII fought on North American soil — and on a national wildlife refuge.

U.S. bombers were hitting Japanese strongholds in the Kurile Islands during this wartime period, and Hixson helped debrief those pilots when they returned to base with aerial reconnaisance photographs. As an interrogator working with the pilots, he was able to gain essential information and to map critical sites.

Alaska's Aleutian chain is a place of forbidding weather and desolate terrain. The islands are swept by cold winds and often engulfed in dense fog. Hixson told his wife he could never forget the "willowaws," violent squalls characterized by piercing wind which hampered U.S. forces throughout the Aleutian campaign. Hixson and his crew lived in Quonset huts heated by stoves, but Jane Hixson said he never complained about his living arrangements.

A surveyor by occupation, Hixson enlisted in the military on Sept. 30, 1942, and was discharged on Nov. 9, 1945, not long after the Japanese surrender in August of that year. He spent two years in Alaska and its Aleutian chain after completing basic training in Florida and attending Air Force Clerical School at Fort Logan, Colorado.

Jane Hixson said he made a lot of friends in the service and kept in touch with them for years following his discharge. "He really valued the friendships he made," she said.

Although Robert and Jane went to school together, Jane Hixson said they didn't really know each other until he came home from the service and she came home from Washington, D.C., where she had worked for the Canadian Department of Munitions and Supplies during the war years. Friends introduced them, and they were married in 1946.

Hixson worked as a surveyor and draftsman with J.B. Ferguson Company after his return from military service. He died in 1992.

Because he knew the altitudes of the mountains, Sgt. Hixson hated to fly over the fog-shrouded Aleutian Islands, where the planes' wings would ice over and pilots would have to dip down to de-ice. His widow said he never liked to fly once he returned to civilian life.

One of Sgt. Hixson's prized mementos of his service in the cold and snowy Aleutian Islands was a hand-carved bracelet given to him by the native Inuit people.

Hixson lived and worked in Quonset huts during his service in the Aleutians, where he was a surveyor and draftsman. Dogsleds were a familiar mode of transportation.

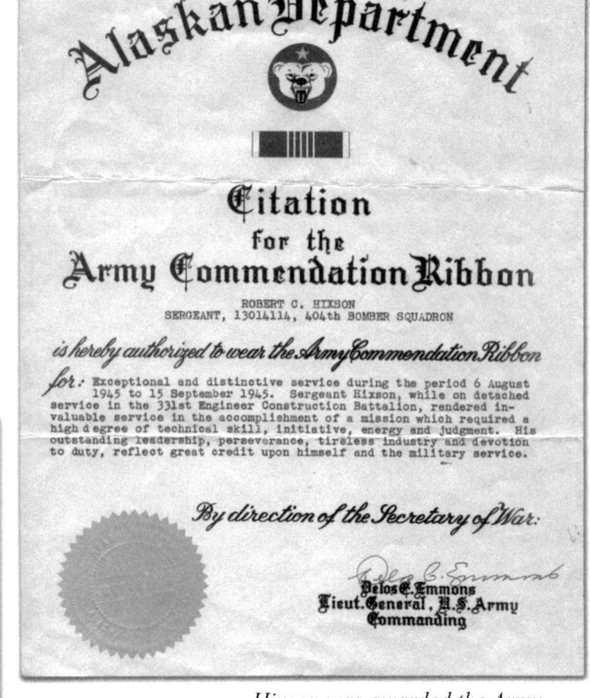

Alaskan Department

Citation
for the
Army Commendation Ribbon

ROBERT C. HIXSON
SERGEANT, 13014114, 404th BOMBER SQUADRON

is hereby authorized to wear the Army Commendation Ribbon

for: Exceptional and distinctive service during the period 6 August 1945 to 15 September 1945. Sergeant Hixson, while on detached service in the 331st Engineer Construction Battalion, rendered invaluable service in the accomplishment of a mission which required a high degree of technical skill, initiative, energy and judgment. His outstanding leadership, perseverance, tireless industry and devotion to duty, reflect great credit upon himself and the military service.

By direction of the Secretary of War:

Delos C. Emmons
Lieut. General, U.S. Army
Commanding

Hixson was awarded the Army Commendation Medal for his work building an airline runway in the Aleutians at the end of WWII.

(Photographs and memorabilia courtesy of Jane Hixson, widow of Robert Hixson)

Jonas William "Buck" Zeigler — Navy — WWII

Jonas William "Buck" Zeigler was living in the Washington County community of Security, just east of Hagerstown, when he joined the Navy and became a Seabee in WWII. The Seabees were the Naval Construction Battalions (CB), hence the nickname "Seabee." During his time in the Navy, he mastered many trades in the electrical, plumbing and construction fields. He participated in the landing on Guam on July 21, 1944, and helped rebuild damaged airstrips and infrastructure after the island was secured on Aug. 9, 1944. American forces used the island as a base for B-29 bombing raids on Japan.

Zeigler brought home this photograph of Chamorro children riding on a water buffalo along an airstrip in Guam in 1945.

Marie Zeigler didn't meet her husband until after WWII, when she went to work in the fall of 1948 at the trucking company where Zeigler worked as a driver. "It was love at first sight. We were married a year later and shared 44 good years together," she wrote in a letter accompanying this 1955 photograph. "I lost my Seabee to a massive heart attack on Dec. 28, 1993. He was a one-of-a-kind husband and the love of my life."

Zeigler strikes a jaunty pose in front of an intricately decorated B-29 bomber on a Guam airstrip. The likely name of the aircraft: "20th Century Fox." Bomber crews and those flying in other types of fighters often customized their planes by painting popular images on the nose or sides of the aircraft in an effort to personalize the machinery upon which their lives often depended.

In addition to his work in construction, Zeigler was trained to drive jeeps, trucks and operate heavy equipment. Following the war, these skills proved valuable. Zeigler returned to Hagerstown and got a job as a tractor-trailer driver. He worked for Charlton Brothers Transportation Co. for more than 40 years.

(Photographs courtesy of Marie V. Zeigler, widow of Jonas William "Buck" Zeigler)

UNITED STATES NAVY

RATING DESCRIPTION

MACHINIST'S MATE
(CB) (Equipment Operator), Third Class

Jorde M. ZEIGLER
Name and Service Number

927-96-31
Rating

MM3c
Signature of Certifying Officer

FEB. 18 1946
Date of Issuance

NAVY DEPARTMENT
BUREAU OF NAVAL PERSONNEL

NAVPERS 15586

Rating description booklet published by the Navy setting out the many requirements, duties and responsibilities ascribed to a Machinist Mate 3rd Class in the Seabees — the construction arm of the U.S. Navy.

Harvey L. "Teter" Brown

Navy — WWII

Navy Seabees may best be known for their depiction in the popular musical ***South Pacific****, but they were the true workhorses of the Navy — bulldozing, paving roads and landing strips and building the structures that provided shelter for military forces. More than 325,000 men served across the world as Seabees in WWII.*

The official Seabee motto was "Construimus, Batuimus" — "We Build, We Fight," but the unofficial motto is "Can Do." The other, less official, description, as indicated on a post card Seabee Harvey L. "Teter" Brown mailed home from his WWII duty station in Milne Bay, New Guinea, in 1944, is probably closer to the truth:

"A Seabee Is A Soldier In A Sailor's Uniform, With Marine Training And Doing Civilian Work At WPA Wages."

WPA refers to the Works Progress Administration, part of President Franklin Roosevelt's New Deal economic program designed to help pull the country out of the Great Depression.

Brown, a Williamsport native, was part of the 104th U.S. Naval Construction Battalion building airfields on New Guinea in the South Pacific.

(Photograph and post card courtesy of Harvey L. "Teter" Brown's widow, Barbara Brown)

Seabees are the construction battalions of the Navy.
(Contributed by Marie V. Zeigler)

CAMP ENDICOTT
DAVISVILLE R.I.
SEABEES
UNITED STATES NAVAL CONSTRUCTION BATTALIONS

PLACE ONE CENT STAMP HERE

POST CARD

' A SEABEE IS A SOLDIER IN A SAILOR'S UNIFORM, WITH MARINE TRAINING AND DOING CIVILIAN WORK AT W P A WAGES.'

D. Tolly West Jr. — Navy — WWII

The United States Navy has its share of admirals and captains, but it is said that chief petty officers are the ones who *really* run the Navy.

During World War II, at the ripe old age of 25, D. Tolly West Jr., a Naval storekeeper on the island of Tulagi in the South Pacific, was promoted to chief petty officer. He had spent two years stateside, much of the time at a Navy blimp station near Elizabeth City, North Carolina, but was shipped overseas two weeks to the day after he married a young woman he met in North Carolina.

West was assigned to Tulagi, a bustling Naval supply depot in the Solomon Islands that was a critical link in the resupply chain for ships operating in the South Pacific and nearby shore bases. Located very near Guadalcanal, the small tropical island was mostly out of harm's way by the time West arrived. He was one of thousands of storekeepers assigned to supply stations scattered across the Pacific providing what the Navy needed to keep its ships afloat as the war moved closer to Japan's shores.

Because most of the fighting was over by the time he reached Tulagi, "the only grief I had during the war was leaving my wife and the baby that was on the way, and the fear that I would never get home," West said.

The island boasted everything needed to sustain personnel and equipment of a sprawling navy — all kept under lock and key in Quonset hut warehouses. Design of the prefabricated structures was commissioned in 1941 in response to the need for portable, easily assembled structures for men and materiel.

"A chief petty officer in the Navy who is in charge of beer has some real clout!" — Tolly West

As the senior petty officer in charge of beer, soft drinks, cigarettes, clothing and nonperishable items, West suddenly found himself "in a whole new ballgame." Being the chief in charge of beer brought him "considerable respect from my peers," West wrote in a memoir he published for his family several years ago. "Our unit was always busy and all issues [transactions] were for cash." Three combination safes were kept on the island to accommodate all of the accumulated currency.

While serving in the Pacific Theater during WWII, West's thoughts were at home with his bride, Connie, and their infant son, who was born Nov. 21, 1944. Letters from home were a treasured diversion while stationed at a Navy staging center on Tulagi. Mail deliveries were made every two weeks and West would often receive a dozen letters at a time. "My happiest time is to sit down, arrange the letters by postmark date and read those sweet words," West wrote.

West (center) stands in front of the wooden structure he and two others built and lived in on Tulagi Island. They named their shack "Flvaca" in honor of ***FL****orida,* ***V****irgini**A** and South* ***C****arolin**A**, the states they called home. The roof was designed with a long overhang as protection against torrential rains.*

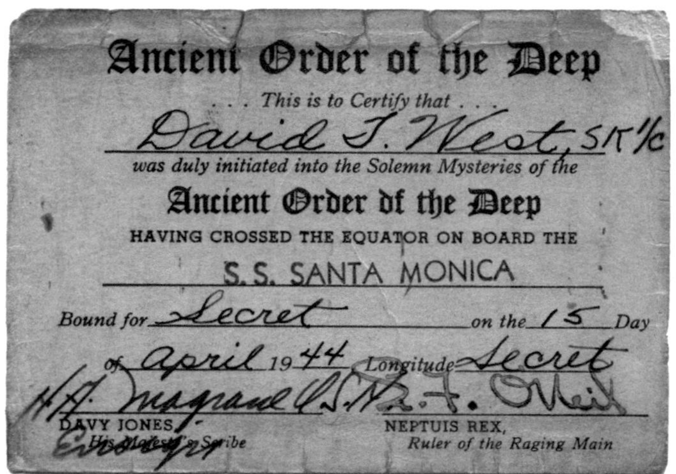

Ancient Order of the Deep

. . . This is to Certify that . . .

David T. West, SK1/c

was duly initiated into the Solemn Mysteries of the

Ancient Order of the Deep

HAVING CROSSED THE EQUATOR ON BOARD THE

S.S. SANTA MONICA

Bound for Secret on the 15 Day

of April 1944 Longitude Secret

DAVY JONES, His Majesty's Scribe

NEPTUIS REX, Ruler of the Raging Main

A card identifying Tolly West as having been initiated into the solemn mysteries of the Ancient Order of the Deep — an honor bestowed on seafarers following the traditional hijinks that accompany a sailor's first crossing of the Equator. West crossed the Equator on April 15, 1944, while on board the troopship SS ***Santa Monica***.

In a diary entry written at the time of the crossing, West wrote: "On a troopship the initiation is a little awkward, but they managed to run us through several gauntlets of belt swingers and a few other things just so we don't get the honor scot-free. Once initiated you are a shell-back." Note the destination is marked "Secret."

After 30 days at sea, West disembarked at the island of Neumea, New Caledonia, and later made the 1,000-mile trip north by sea to Tulagi for duty.

West returned home from his tour of duty in the Pacific, trading cigarettes for a variety of war clubs and beads made of shells by the native people

West had 25 copies printed of an 80-page memoir he wrote not long after his 80th birthday at the urging of his granddaughter.

This excerpt details one particularly nerve-racking delivery that took place in 1945 under his supervision.

I am at the dock watching a huge ship being tied up preparing for unloading. It contains a resupply of beer for our warehouses. I don't know it at the time but there is nothing on this ship but beer. Every hold is packed full. We were notified of its arrival and all precautions are in place to prevent theft on the quarter mile between the ship and our warehouses . . . I will be on duty during the whole process with no sleep . . . In spite of security precautions truck personnel make several attempts to throw off cases of beer on the way to the warehouse, hoping their buddies can pick them up without getting caught. Some make it, some don't. One of the truck drivers hijacked a loaded truck to the Seabees compound only to be captured by a jeep load of armed shore patrol. It is a rowdy 72 hours. I go onboard the ship to watch the unloading process. Slings are lowered into the holds and loaded with cases of beer by sailors. It is a sight to see. Some of them are obviously drunk and staggering all around. One or two have had too much and are sick. I don't know who is in charge but it sure is a mess.

When the ship is finally unloaded, we have two 40' x 100' Quonset huts loaded solid with beer, front to back and bottom to top. I find myself thinking, how can they commit a huge ship to bring nothing but beer when there must be a need for more important things to win the war?

Following a four-week trip to New Zealand, West returned to Tulagi only to discover that one of his warehouses had been torn down and hauled away, a sign of the shrinking importance of Tulagi as a resupply depot near the end of the war. In a never-ceasing quest to find diversions on the tropical island, West got permission to convert the concrete base of the demolished Quonset hut into a tennis court. Requisitioning lumber and wire for the backstops from the general stores, he arranged work crews and secured a net, rackets and balls from the recreation officer: "And bingo! We have our own private tennis court. I keep the supply of rackets and balls in my shack. I let other people use it, but mainly it's used by the people in our area. We now spend a lot of time playing tennis and it's enjoyed by a lot of people."

Recreation helped West and others cope with the boredom and tedium on the island far from home. "It's another routine day on Tulagi, just like yesterday was a routine day and tomorrow will be a routine day; when suddenly, the island is jolted with the news that the United States has dropped an atomic bomb on one of Japan's largest cities. The devastation is unbelievable. There is great excitement and hope that this will bring Japan to its knees," West wrote.

"Several days later we learn that another atomic bomb was dropped and news that Japan has surrendered. The word atomic is new to me. I have never heard of an atom but explanations and descriptions are traveling fast around the island. The important thing to me and everyone else is that the war is over. It's hard to believe with all the planning for an invasion of Japan. Discharges from the armed forces will be based on points accumulated for the time in the service and time served overseas. I have more than enough points to be discharged."

When West finally received orders home, it took six weeks to cross the Pacific. A severe storm just seven days out of San Francisco caused an agonizing week's delay and forced a rerouting to Seattle. After a long train ride to the East Coast, West arrived at the Norfolk Naval Base Nov. 13, 1945, for discharge.

Following the war, at the urging of his friend and Maryland native, Jordan Bean, West moved to Hagerstown with his wife and son, David. He went to work for Jamison Door Company in 1946, and the couple had three more children. West eventually became president of the company, the first president who was not a member of the Jamison family. He retired in 1982.

West remembers that movies were shown every night under the stars at the island's outdoor Halsey Theatre. On April 15, 1945, the theater was the backdrop for a memorial service in honor of President Franklin Delano Roosevelt, whose death stunned the nation and members of American fighting forces around the world.

(Photographs and memorabilia courtesy of D. Tolly West Jr.)

Robert Lee Heiberger — Navy — WWII

Robert "Bob" Heiberger (below left) and three Navy buddies ride in a donkey cart in Tijuana, Mexico, on Sept. 22, 1943, on R&R when they were based in San Diego during WWII. Heiberger was a machine operator at Hagerstown Shoe & Legging Co. when the Japanese bombed Pearl Harbor in December 1941, and three weeks later, he was in the Navy. During the war he worked as a shipfitter striker on the USS *Porter* and the USS *Castor*, which took him to New Zealand, the Philippines, Fiji, the Aleutians and Pearl Harbor.

(Photos courtesy of Mildred Heiberger, widow of Robert Lee "Bob" Heiberger)

Quonset huts

In 1941, the Navy sought to design an all-purpose lightweight structure that could be shipped anywhere in the world and assembled quickly.

A commission was given to George A. Fuller Construction Company of New York and the units were manufactured at Quonset Point, Rhode Island — hence the name of the nearly 170,000 prefabricated structures that were produced rapidly and scattered across the globe for military use.

The Quonset hut skeleton was a row of semicircular steel ribs covered with corrugated sheet metal. The ribs sat on a low steel-frame foundation with a plywood floor. The basic model was 20 feet wide and 48 feet long with 720 square feet of usable floor space. The larger models, designed to serve as temporary warehouses, such as the ones used on Tulagi, where D. Tolly West Jr. was stationed, were 40 feet by 100 feet.

Following the war, the U.S. military sold the surplus Quonset huts to the public for $1,000 each. A number of the structures are still in use, more than 60 years after they were made.

Versatile Quonset huts (above) provided shelter from the extreme elements in the Aleutian Islands, where Robert Hixson was assigned on detached service as a draftsman with the Army Air Forces during WWII. The huts, covered in corrugated sheet metal, were used for barracks, offices and storage at Hixson's Alaskan outpost, and were quite cozy as seen in the interior view (right) of Hixson's humble Alaskan shelter. (Photos contributed by Jane Hixson)

While assigned to the island of Guam in WWII, Jonas William "Buck" Zeigler was part of a Seabee team tasked with constructing prefabricated Quonset huts for Marines, similar to the one being assembled in the photo on this post card included in an album of photographs and memorabilia he brought home with him after the war. (Contributed by Marie V. Zeigler)

Robert Henry Kelsh — Army — WWII

Robert Henry Kelsh was a short-order cook at the Savoy Cafe at 100 W. Washington St. in Hagerstown before he joined the Army in 1939. However, his cooking style had to change when he found himself feeding more than 200 soldiers in a company mess, and he sometimes wondered what he'd gotten himself in for. But upon leaving the Army he became a chef and was still cooking the day he died.

The Pennsylvania native, who came to Hagerstown in 1936, cooked on a grill as a civilian. But as a soldier, according to his Army separation record, he "prepared meats, gravies, soups, and salads ... he made desserts, salads and baked bread, pies, cakes and other pastries ... he cooked on coal, gas and steam in garrison and on gasoline field ranges."

Enlisting in the Army, Kelsh honed his cooking skills at the cooks and bakers school at Fort Benning, Georgia. There, the course of his military career was set and he found himself preparing meals in places including England, Tunisia, Corsica and Italy during the Rome-Arno Campaign, January-September 1944.

Kelsh's cooking expertise might have kept him in the Army a bit longer than he liked, however. He wrote to his wife in 1945 from Camp Patrick Henry, Virginia:

CERTIFICATE No. 3029
DATE ISSUED May 18, 1946

158329

UNITED STATES OF AMERICA
VETERANS ADMINISTRATION
CERTIFICATE OF ELIGIBILITY
THIS IS TO CERTIFY THAT

NAME OF VETERAN: Robert H. Kelsh
SERIAL NO. [illegible] ☒ ARMY ☐ NAVY ☐ MARINE CORPS ☐ COAST GUARD DATE OF BIRTH 11-22-19

IS ELIGIBLE FOR THE BENEFITS OF TITLE III OF THE SERVICEMEN'S READJUSTMENT ACT OF 1944, AS AMENDED, PUBLIC LAW 268, 79TH CONGRESS.

THE AMOUNT OF AVAILABLE GUARANTY BENEFIT FOR THE GUARANTY OR INSURANCE OF A LOAN, IF ANY, SHOWN ON THE REVERSE HEREOF, IS EITHER THE AMOUNT RESERVED FOR A PARTICULAR LOAN OR LOANS IDENTIFIED BY THE NUMBER SHOWN OR IS THE AMOUNT NOT USED WHICH WILL BE AVAILABLE FOR FUTURE LOANS WHEN RESERVED.

THIS CERTIFICATE MUST BE COUNTERSIGNED BY THE VETERAN IDENTIFIED HEREIN BEFORE THE CERTIFICATE MAY BE USED IN APPLYING FOR THE ABOVE CITED BENEFITS. SIGNATURE OF THE VETERAN MUST BE THE SAME AS THAT TO BE SIGNED ON A NOTE OR OTHER EVIDENCE OF AN OBLIGATION TO BE GUARANTEED OR INSURED BY THE VETERANS ADMINISTRATION.

ADMINISTRATOR OF VETERANS AFFAIRS

Robert H. Kelsh
SIGNATURE OF VETERAN

June 7, 1946
DATE OF VETERAN'S SIGNATURE

William H. Ensor
SIGNATURE OF AUTHORIZED AGENT

Baltimore Regional Office
1315 St. Paul Street, Baltimore 2, Md.
ISSUING OFFICE

Veterans Administration Certificate of Eligibility dated May 18, 1946, authorizing Kelsh to receive Title III veterans benefits.

"I am wondering how come I had to be a cook in this man's army. I sure wish now that I didn't know anything about the trade."

"I am wondering how come I had to be a cook in this man's army. I sure wish now that I didn't know anything about the trade."

But by September of that year he was a civilian again, and a chef at the eatery he owned at 631 Pennsylvania Ave. in Hagerstown — the Pennsylvania Avenue Confectionery, popularly known as "Mr. Bob's."

Kelsh quit his second job with the Western Maryland Railway to devote himself full-time to being a chef and father of three young children, after the death of his wife, Mary Slaughter Kelsh, who had worked at Fairchild Aircraft during the war.

His daughter Janice Kelsh remembers how the family house was right next door to the restaurant. "There was a bell set up in the house," she said. "He'd get up and go to work at 5 a.m.

He'd ring it to wake us, and then he'd fix us breakfast. When it was ready, he'd ring the bell again to alert us he was bringing it over to the house." Such preferential treatment was easy to explain: "We were Daddy's little girls," Janice said.

"He was a good father," she said. And he was cooking until the day he died. He worked that day. Robert Henry Kelsh died on Nov. 6, 1976, at age 56.

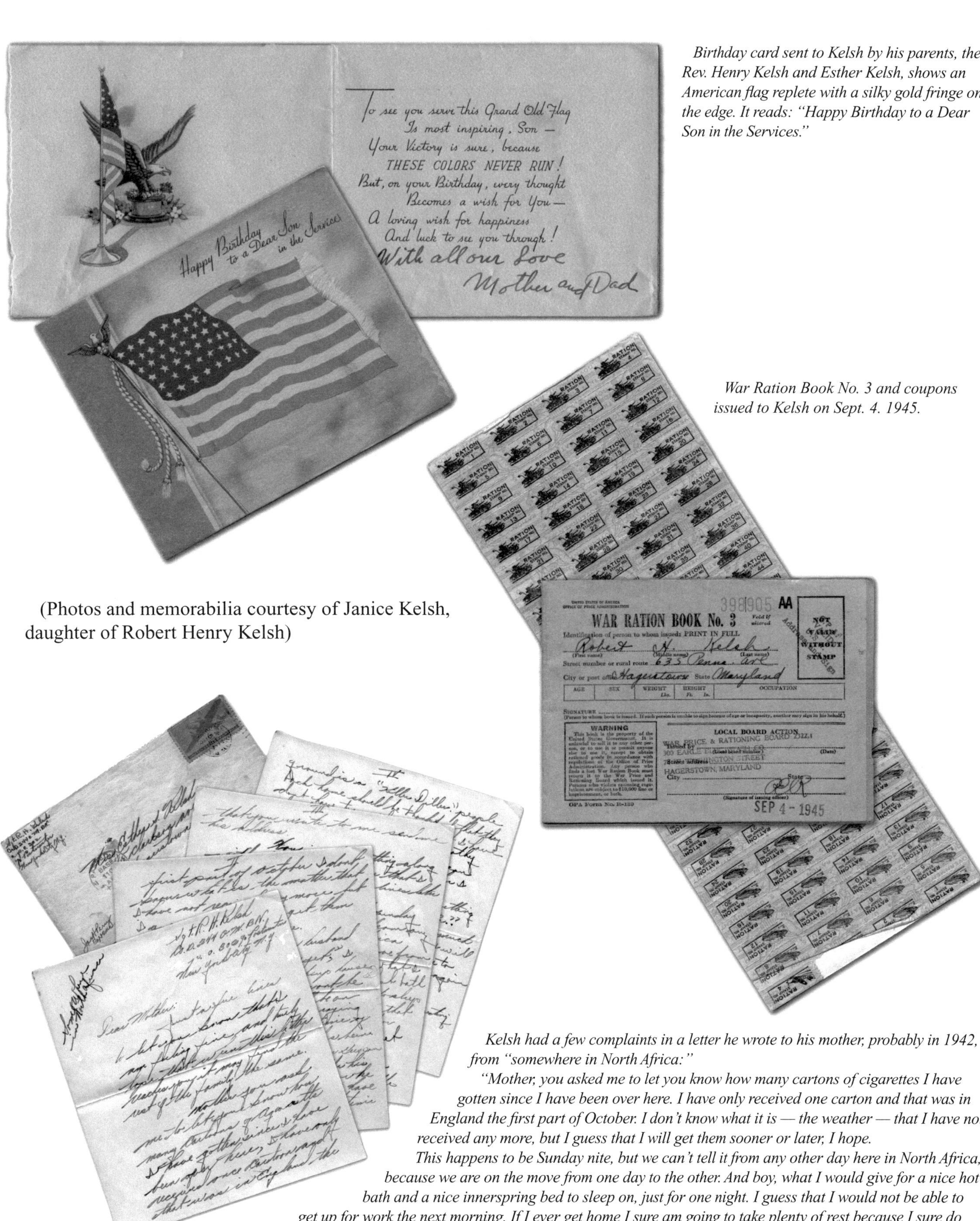

Birthday card sent to Kelsh by his parents, the Rev. Henry Kelsh and Esther Kelsh, shows an American flag replete with a silky gold fringe on the edge. It reads: "Happy Birthday to a Dear Son in the Services."

War Ration Book No. 3 and coupons issued to Kelsh on Sept. 4. 1945.

(Photos and memorabilia courtesy of Janice Kelsh, daughter of Robert Henry Kelsh)

Kelsh had a few complaints in a letter he wrote to his mother, probably in 1942, from "somewhere in North Africa:"

"Mother, you asked me to let you know how many cartons of cigarettes I have gotten since I have been over here. I have only received one carton and that was in England the first part of October. I don't know what it is — the weather — that I have not received any more, but I guess that I will get them sooner or later, I hope.

This happens to be Sunday nite, but we can't tell it from any other day here in North Africa, because we are on the move from one day to the other. And boy, what I would give for a nice hot bath and a nice innerspring bed to sleep on, just for one night. I guess that I would not be able to get up for work the next morning. If I ever get home I sure am going to take plenty of rest because I sure do need it because this sleeping on the ground is a "Killer Diller." People back home should be thankful that they don't have to go through what I have already gone through. Tell Dorothy that I am going to be a mean man when I do get home tell her I said hello."

Poster bearing the autographs of many surviving members of the 101st Airborne Division, including members of Easy Company of ***Band of Brothers*** *fame. The paratroopers of Co. E, 506th Parachute Infantry Regiment, of the 101st Airborne Division, were portrayed in historian Stephen Ambrose's best-sellng book* ***Band of Brothers****, and immortalized in Steven Spielberg and Tom Hanks' Emmy-award-winning HBO miniseries of the same name.*

The autograph of Major Richard "Dick" Winters, who commanded Easy Company from Normandy to Berchtesgarden, appears in the lower left margin of the poster, near the edge of the shield bearing the division's distinctive "Screaming Eagle." The autographs were collected during 101st Airborne Division reunions over several years by Donna G. Allen's husband, Richard Allen. Donna Allen is the daughter of Roy U. Talhelm, a member of the 506th Parachute Infantry Regiment, who landed at Normandy on D-Day, was wounded two days later, and died June 12, 1944, less than three months before his 18th birthday. (Poster courtesy of Donna G. and Richard G. Allen)

Roy U. Talhelm — Army — WWII

Roy U. Talhelm, who was born in Hagerstown, used an altered birth certificate to join the Army when he was only 16 years old. Soon, he was on his way to Camp Toccoa, Georgia, to join the 506th Parachute Infantry Regiment that was to become part of the 101st Airborne, a division nicknamed the "Screaming Eagles." At the time he left for boot camp, he did not know he had a daughter on the way.

Talhelm did not meet his daughter, Donna, until after he completed paratrooper training and knew he would be headed to Europe. On a return visit to the area, before shipping out to England as part of the largest invasion force ever assembled, Talhelm got to hold his tiny daughter for the first and only time.

Talhelm was wounded on June 8th during the D-Day Invasion and died of his wounds on June 12, 1944. Talhelm is buried in the American Cemetery at St. Laurent-sur-Mer (Colleville-sur-Mer), block C, row 9, grave 32.

Talhelm's daughter, Donna, has no memory of her father and little trace of him was preserved by her teenage mother's parents, who destroyed his letters, photographs and other reminders of him. She was told only that as an infant when her father visited her 242 S. Locust Street home, she had cried in his arms. Donna was 48 before she ever saw a photograph of her father. She spent more than 15 years piecing together fragmentary information about her father, who was among the youngest to die at Normandy. She joined the American WWII Orphans Network (www.awon.org), which was founded in 1991 and is based in Indianapolis, Indiana. The Network provides a forum and assistance to the estimated 183,000 American children whose fathers were killed in WWII.

"Since then I have visited his grave at the American Cemetery in Normandy three times," Donna said. A photograph of Donna as a baby was delivered to her father's grave site by 101st paratrooper Guy Whidden, from Frederick, Maryland, on the 50th anniversary jump in Normandy as President Bill Clinton spoke to those assembled.

"My father was only a few weeks shy of his 18th birthday when he gave his life for all of us. The baby who cried in his arms as he held her for the first and last time, spent many years aching to find out about him, missing him always," Donna wrote in a tribute to her father, expressing the sentiment of many who lost their fathers in WWII.

Every year since 1994, Donna and her husband, Richard Allen, have placed a wreath at the 101st Airborne Monument in Washington, D.C., in honor of her father. Richard Allen, who served with the 101st Airborne Division in the 1960s, is sergeant at arms for the National Capitol Area Chapter of the 101st Association in Washington, D.C.

American WWII Orphans Network

In Their Memory

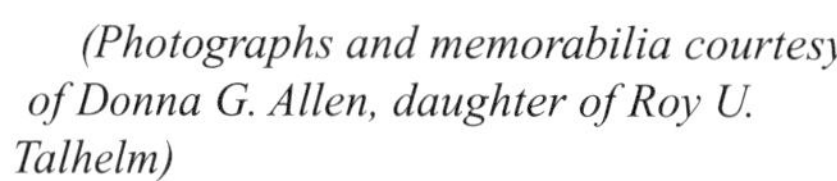

(Photographs and memorabilia courtesy of Donna G. Allen, daughter of Roy U. Talhelm)

George W. Lushbaugh Jr. — Army — WWII

George W. Lushbaugh Jr. was an Army combat engineer in Europe in WWII, landing in Normandy on D-Day + 5 and fighting his way to Germany until its surrender. He took part in the liberation of the Nordhausen concentration camp in April 1945 with the 49th Engineers Combat Battalion.

In this letter written on June 29, 1944, to his parents, Viola Mowen Lushbaugh and George W. Lushbaugh Sr., he tells what it was like as his unit pushed eastward.

"I just came back from taking a nice hot shower ... the first since we left England and we were pretty dirty ... The other night it rained all night long, and I was trying to sleep in about four inches of mud and water ... One thing good is that we get to go to church ... Don't worry about me as I am in the best of health and happy."

"We move almost every day, and we have to dig us a fox hole to sleep in every time we move. It just looks like a grave after you dig it. It's about three feet deep and six feet long."

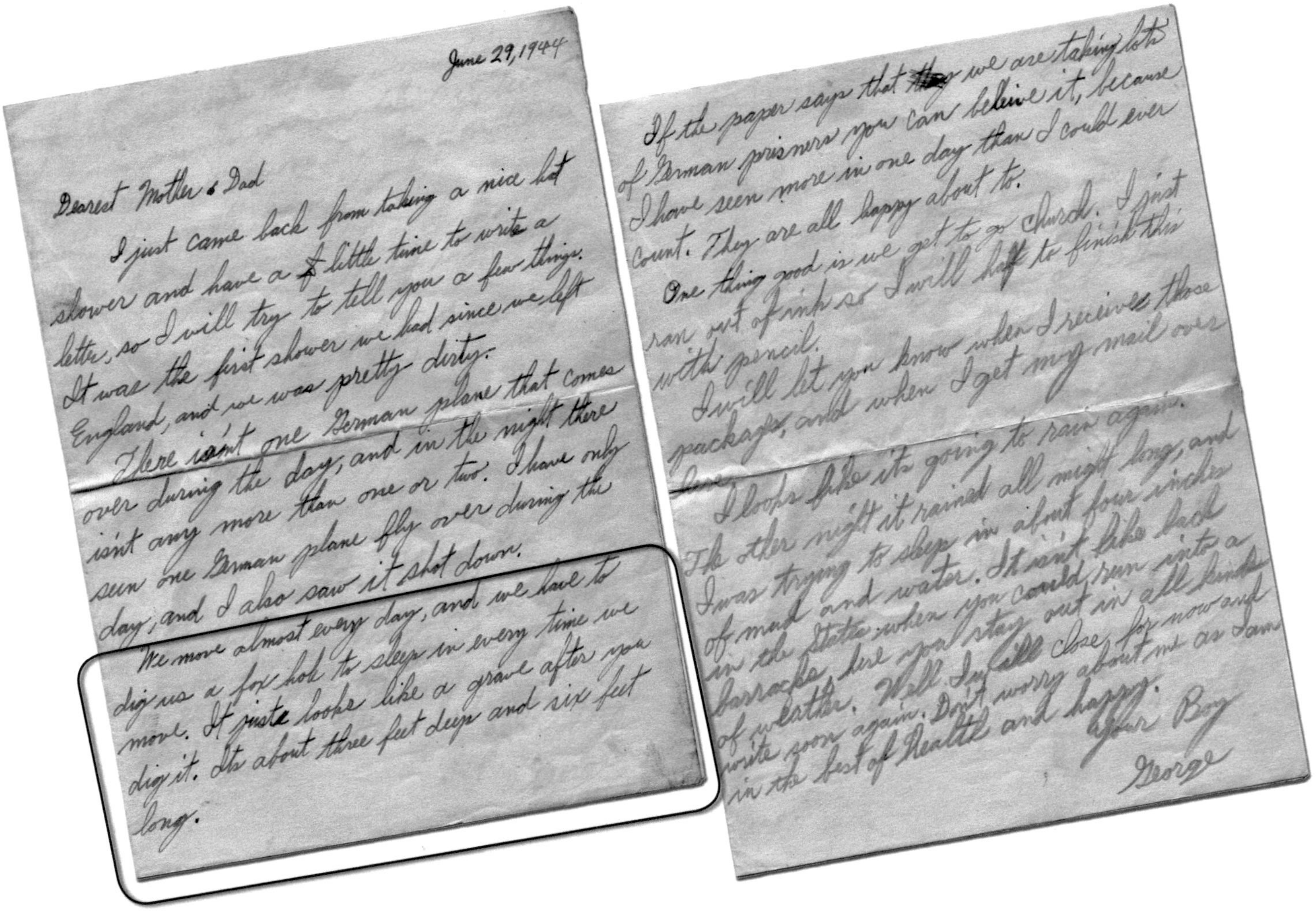

June 29, 1944

Dearest Mother & Dad

I just came back from taking a nice hot shower and have a little time to write a letter, so I will try to tell you a few things. It was the first shower we had since we left England, and we was pretty dirty.

There isn't one German plane that comes over during the day, and in the night there isn't any more than one or two. I have only seen one German plane fly over during the day, and I also saw it shot down.

We move almost every day, and we have to dig us a fox hole to sleep in every time we move. It juste looks like a grave after you dig it. Its about three feet deep and six feet long.

If the paper says that ~~they~~ we are taking lots of German prisners you can believe it, because I have seen more in one day than I could ever count. They are all happy about to.

One thing good is we get to go church. I just ran out of ink so I will haff to finish this with pencil.

I will let you know when I receives those packages, and when I get my mail over ~~here~~.

It looks like its going to rain again.

The other night it rained all night long, and I was trying to sleep in about four inches of mud and water. It isn't like back in the States when you could run into a barracks and stay out in all kinds of weather. Well I will close for now and write soon again. Don't worry about me as I am in the best of health and happy.

Your Boy
George

George W. Lushbaugh Jr.'s collection of WWII memorabilia includes, clockwise from upper right: soldiers' eating utensils; a pack of playing cards marked "Gift of the American Red Cross"; a brush used for cleaning rifles; a cigarette lighter; a flag hung in the window of the homes of families with a star to show they had a family member in the military; a brass Army insignia. At the center is a medal of Saint George — the patron saint of Boy Scouts, soldiers, farmers and England.

(Photo and memorabilia courtesy of Margaret Richards, sister of George W. Lushbaugh Jr.)

Marian Freed Cain — Cadet Nurse — WWII

Marian Freed Cain has fond memories of her Cadet Nurse Corps uniform.

"I'll never forget walking down Antietam Street in my official Cadet Nurse uniform and having an enlisted GI salute me," she said. "That uniform has put me where I am today."

Now retired from the Veterans Administration in Martinsburg, West Virginia, after more than 30 years of service, Cain earned a wealth of practical experience in the nursing corps established by the federal government to alleviate a shortage of nurses in World War II. She is one of more than 124,000 nurses who graduated from the Corps between 1943 and 1948.

As a Cadet Nurse, she worked at Washington County Hospital from July 1, 1943, to June, 1946, under specifications and guidelines set up by the U.S. Public Health Service.

That uniform Cain was so proud of was designed by leading fashion designers of their day. The summer uniform was a suit of gray and white striped cotton featuring a jacket with red epaulets and large pockets and a gored skirt. It was worn with a simple round-neck white blouse. The winter uniform was a guard's coat of gray velour, belted in the back, with pockets and red epaulets, plus a single-breasted gray suit with buttoned pockets, and a white blouse.

The Cadet Nurse Corps at Washington County Hospital School of Nursing stands in front of the hospital in this 1946 photograph. Marian Freed Cain is standing in the fourth row, fifth from the left.

Cain said the Cadet Nurse Corps uniform was only worn on special occasions like public programs and parades. Mostly, she says, "we wore our school uniforms while working."

Cain enrolled in Washington County Hospital School of Nursing in June 1943, immediately following her graduation from Hagerstown High School. Like most of her nursing class, she opted to join the Cadet Nurse Corps when it was established one month later.

"When we were inducted," she said, "we committed to nursing until the war was over. I stayed in the Corps until it was disbanded and continued on at Washington County Hospital until October 1949, when I went to the VA Hospital." If the war had not ended when it did in 1945, she said, she would have gone on to military service.

According to a published essay recording the history of the Corps, written by Heather Willever-Farr and John Parascandola, Congress in 1942 passed the Labor-Security Agency Appropriation Act, which appropriated funds for nursing schools and assigned the responsibility for allocating those funds to the Public Health Service. However, the funding was insufficient and there were no centralized recruiting efforts. As the war progressed, the demand for nurses increased, but young women were opting for higher-paying factory jobs instead of nursing.

Working with nursing groups, Representative Frances Payne Bolton of Ohio introduced a bill that would establish the Cadet Nurse Corps (originally designated the Victory Nurse Corps) to persuade more young women to join the ranks of the nursing profession. Under the Bolton Act, the Corps would grant scholarships and stipends to qualified applicants for providing "military or other Federal governmental or essential civilian (nursing) services for the duration of the present war." The Act became public law on July 1, 1943.

Women regardless of color qualified for the Cadet Nurse Corps if they were between the ages of 17 and 35, had graduated from an accredited high school, had earned good grades, and were in good health. Washington County Hospital School of Nursing was accepted as a participating school, and Cain qualified for a scholarship that covered tuition, fees, and a small monthly stipend. The Corps also paid \$35 to \$45 for her room and board. She graduated in 1946.

When Cain entered the local nursing school, students were housed in the old Keymar College building on the hospital campus. Later, she recalled, they lived in houses purchased by Washington County Hospital, one on King Street and another on Frederick Street.

"Things were pretty strict in those days," she said. "We worked eight hours in the hospital and had classes in the old gymnasium on the hospital lawn. Margaret Mullen was the director of nurses, and local doctors were our instructors." She rattled off a long list of doctors who had a hand in her nursing education, including Drs. B.B. Kneisley, Frank Lusby, Vic Miller, Earl Young and Peregrine Wroth.

"We worked from 7 to 7," she said. "It was a long day, but generally we had a two-hour break according to how our hours were scheduled. We spent most of our time on campus."

The nursing school had some tough rules. Students had study hall from 7 to 8 every night, and were required to be in their rooms by 10 p.m. "We were allowed one overnight to go home, or one 'late' night until 11 o'clock per week," Cain said.

The retired nurse recalls a rare vacation break in 1944. She and her roommate, Betty Lillard McCauley, took a bus to Ocean City for a few days. "We wore our Cadet Nurse Corps uniforms, and people took notice of us. This sounds disrespectful now," she said, "but back then the uniforms gave us priority for seats on the bus."

Cadets were expected to graduate in 30 months and to provide essential nursing services for the duration of the war, either in the military or in civilian life. Like Cain, most senior cadets provided nursing services on the home front, where many positions were vacated by nurses who went overseas to care for the wounded.

In their Cadet Nurse Corps history, Willever-Farr and Parascandola write: "Many organizations and institutions were involved in the active recruitment campaign of the Corps. Corporate, cinema, radio and magazine promotions of the Corps were the most influential and visible elements of the recruitment campaign. More than 300 national radio programs broadcast information about the Corps. Film stars posed with 'pretty Cadets in Hollywood' and 'Cadets in Washington were photographed with notables.' Companies such as Eastman Kodak, Pond's Cold Cream, Kotex, Pepsi-Cola, Old Spice, Sanka Coffee and National Biscuit Company ran ads featuring Cadet Nurses.

"Vanguard Films produced a 10-minute film starring Dorothy McGuire as Cadet Nurse Peggy Adams and co-starring popular screen artists Aline MacMahon, Spring Byington and James Brown. Actresses donning Cadet Nurse uniforms were also featured in other films such as Shirley Temple's *Kiss and Tell, Lady on a Train*, and *The Blonde from Brooklyn*.

The end of the war brought an end to the Cadet Nurse Corps. The last class was admitted to the Corps on Oct. 15, 1945, and the last Cadets were graduated in 1948.

Cain recalled a parade in Hagerstown at war's end. "The local Cadet Nurse Corps marched in the parade, right down Potomac Street, but I was working and couldn't participate."

After the Corps disbanded, Cain remained at Washington County Hospital until October 1949, when she went to work for the Veterans Administration in Martinsburg. Ironically, she said, there she worked with veterans from all wars "from WWI until 1980."

Cain is registered at the Women In Military Service For America Memorial, Arlington, Virginia.

(Photographs courtesy of Marian Freed Cain)

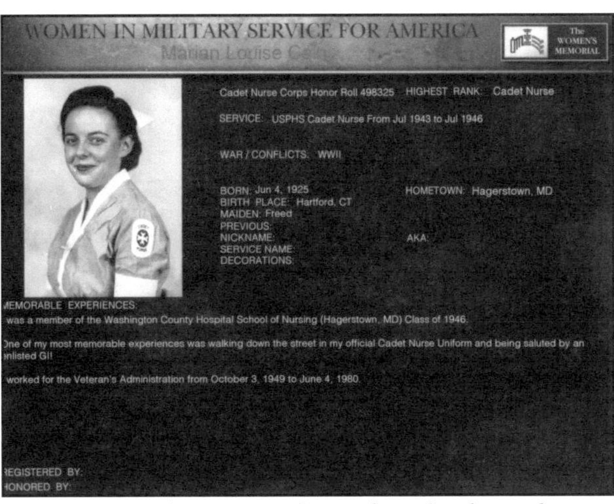

WOMEN IN MILITARY SERVICE FOR AMERICA

The WOMEN'S MEMORIAL

Cadet Nurse Corps Honor Roll 498325 HIGHEST RANK: Cadet Nurse

SERVICE: USPHS Cadet Nurse From Jul 1943 to Jul 1946

WAR / CONFLICTS: WWII

BORN: Jun 4, 1925 HOMETOWN: Hagerstown, MD
BIRTH PLACE: Hartford, CT
MAIDEN: Freed
PREVIOUS:
NICKNAME: AKA:
SERVICE NAME:
DECORATIONS:

MEMORABLE EXPERIENCES:
I was a member of the Washington County Hospital School of Nursing (Hagerstown, MD) Class of 1946.

One of my most memorable experiences was walking down the street in my official Cadet Nurse Uniform and being saluted by an enlisted GI!

I worked for the Veteran's Administration from October 3, 1949 to June 4, 1980.

REGISTERED BY:
HONORED BY:

Marian Freed Cain's certificate of membership in the Women In Military Service For America Memorial recognizing her as a "woman in military service in America."

"I didn't think twice when the Navy Nurse Corps came courting. Nurses were needed to win the war."
— Laura-Nel (Bowen) Carlisle
LTJG, NC USN, WWII

APRIL 2006

NURSING GIs

World War II was one of those rare events in history that galvanized the public's resolve and millions put country before self. Most remarkable was the service of women. Thousands left the comforts of home to work in factories and businesses or to volunteer with organizations like the USO, Salvation Army and American Red Cross, both on the home front and abroad. Of critical need were registered nurses – some 75,000 worked in Army and Navy hospitals across the country. Over 57,000 women joined the Army Nurse Corps and more than 14,000 were Navy nurses. But no men need apply. Serving as commissioned officers in every theater of war, on the world's oceans and in the skies, the nurses accompanied invasion forces and some became POWs. Many women supported the effort by joining the Public Health Service, working hand-in-hand with the military. Nursing care was so vital that the government formed the Cadet Nurse Corps and trained some 124,000 women as nurses, a few who were black. By 1945, the fear of a nurse shortage spurred President Roosevelt to request a nurse draft. The bill passed the House, but the war ended in Europe before it reached the Senate.

Marian Cain was recognized for her service in the Cadet Nurse Corps in the April 2006 calendar produced by the Women's Memorial.

The Women In Military Service For America Memorial, Arlington National Cemetery, honors women who served in all branches of the military.

Robert W. "Bob" Johnson — Army Air Forces — WWII

"It's different now, but it wasn't then."

Aviation had never been a particular interest of Robert W. "Bob" Johnson as a young African American male growing up in Sheridan, Pennsylvania — "a town about this big," said Johnson, pinching two fingers together.

Not really a surprise, since opportunities for black pilots were few and far between and African Americans had been banned from military aviation until President Franklin D. Roosevelt signed an executive order creating the aviation training school at Tuskegee, Alabama, in 1940.

The summer after graduating from high school, Johnson was at his sister's home in Baltimore, waiting to be drafted into the Navy — "something I wasn't sure I wanted to do" — when a friend asked Johnson to accompany him to an aviation cadet qualifying exam. "He was going to take a test for pilot training and he wanted me to go along to keep him company." When they got to the post office, his persuasive friend encouraged Johnson to take the test, too. They both passed and "I was sworn in that very day," Johnson said.

His trip to basic training at Keesler Field in Biloxi, Mississippi, was his first exposure to the American South. "Segregation was rampant, but I stayed on the base. I didn't want to be bothered with that kind of hatred," Johnson said. But even at the military installation, African American soldiers were not allowed to go to the PX [post exchange] or the clubs for noncommissioned officers.

But Johnson and the other cadets paid little attention to the double standard. They were simply too preoccupied with mastering the demanding curriculum and the harassments peculiar to their aviation cadet training. "At the time, all new cadets were called either knucklehead or dummy. We didn't answer to anything else," Johnson said.

Johnson had attended integrated schools in his hometown in Lebanon County, Pennsylvania, and had few expectations beyond "graduating from high school and getting a job at the blast furnace like everyone else." But just short of 18 years of age, he was among the youngest of the pool of African American aviation cadets from across the country who had been selected to train as pilots. This was his first association with African American college graduates and professionals who sat next to him in class — all of them under the watchful eye and firm tutelage of veteran Tuskegee Airmen, who themselves had battled discrimination and racial prejudice to earn what would eventually be recognized as an unparalleled role in aviation history. Tuskegee Airmen flew 1,500 missions over Europe in WWII without losing a single bomber they were assigned to protect.

His aviation cadet training "was a turning point in my life," Johnson said. "It changed my outlook. I wanted to do things better." He and fellow cadets put up with the harassment by senior cadets. "All upperclassmen were considered to be officers," Johnson explained. When responding to a question by a superior, Johnson recalled there were only three acceptable responses: "'Yes, sir,' 'No, sir,' and 'No excuses, sir.' They didn't want any quibbling." Sixty-two years later, he can still recite with rapid recall the incoherent string of nonsense phrases, called "dodo verses," junior members were required to memorize and repeat perfectly

Robert W. "Bob" Johnson, with goggles on his head, takes a breather during training at Tuskegee Institute in 1945.

at any time of day at the whim of an upperclassman. The strict regimentation, rigorous classroom instruction, physical training and drill had a purpose: to instill discipline. "A lot of cadets washed out ... They couldn't handle it. But if you can take that harassment and still keep a smile on your face," you would do fine.

Johnson successfully completed ground school, and preflight, basic and advanced training. He also attended radio school at Scott Field in Illinois. In the beginning, ground school proved to be the biggest challenge, along with the physical training the cadets endured. "We would run and run and run and do thousands of push-ups," Johnson said. In comparison, actual flight training was a breeze.

By flying single-engine AT-6's that "looked a lot like Japanese zeros" in advanced flight training, Johnson learned to love being in the air. Night-flying on cross-country trips put the young cadet's skills to the test. On one particular flight, Johnson was flying solo on a cross-country flight. An approaching storm precipitated a decision to ground the planes, but Johnson's radio wasn't working and he didn't get word the mission had been scrapped. His only clue came when another pilot eased his plane close to Johnson and caused his plane's tail to "wag" — a universal sign among pilots indicating "follow me." His ground reception included being "chewed out by instructors."

Johnson and his fellow cadets were accustomed to the routine dressing down that kept the trainees on their toes. Johnson remembers a particularly harsh "chewing out" when he was flying in the traffic pattern preparing to land. He slowed up a little in response to a decrease in speed by the plane ahead of him, not knowing an officer was piloting the plane immediately behind him. No sooner had the rubber of his wheels touched ground than the officer pulled up right beside him screaming: 'What were you trying to do, pull up and park up there? Knucklehead!'"

As an aviation cadet, Johnson learned to fly on the AT-6 trainers, but the camera caught him posing for this photograph in the cockpit of a B-25 in a snapshot taken during his days of flight training at Tuskegee Institute. The photo was turned into a greeting card by his brother decades later.

Johnson was a young aviation cadet at Tuskegee when he sent this holiday photo greeting home to his family.

Young Johnson would be called a lot worse in Mississippi and other parts of the United States during the days of segregation. When he first enlisted, he and seven other would-be aviation cadets were given first class train tickets from New Cumberland, Pennsylvania, to Biloxi, Mississippi, by way of Cincinnati. From Pennsylvania to Ohio, they rode in immaculate air-conditioned Pullman cars. But from the time they switched trains in Cincinnati for the long journey south, even though they held the higher-priced tickets, they were relegated to a car without air-conditioning, located immediately behind the locomotive, that was filled with soot and cinders. Racial slurs would accompany their walk through the passenger cars to the dining car.

But racial discrimination "really smacked you in the face" in New Orleans, where Johnson and a few buddies went for a Christmas break in 1944. Fueled by the spirit of the season and a bottle of rum, the fellows had the misfortune to miss their train back to Keesler Field in Biloxi and were forced to take the bus instead. They walked into the well-kept lobby of the bus terminal, but were told to go around back to buy their tickets. At the rear of the building, they entered a filthy room and purchased their tickets through a hole in the wall. When the bus arrived, the driver told them only three of them could board because there weren't enough seats on the bus. "But the bus is half full," Johnson remembered pointing out. Only two other blacks had taken their seats at the rear of the bus, but the driver insisted there was only room for three more.

The pre-aviation cadets waited for the next bus. But "the real humiliation" came later. After they took their seats, the driver came to the back and pulled down "a leather curtain with tiny pin holes in it" to hide them from the view of other passengers. All during the journey, they could hear the white passengers comment on the beauty of the water as they traveled along the coast, "but we couldn't see a thing," Johnson said. "It's different now, but it wasn't then."

WWII came to an end before Johnson was able to fly with the 99th Pursuit Squadron, so he never fulfilled his dream of flying overseas in service of his country. All of the cadets were given the option of finishing the program, but that meant a three-year commitment in the Army Air Forces. Johnson knew there was no future for black pilots in either military or commercial aviation, so he opted to go to Morgan State University on the GI Bill.

Johnson came to Hagerstown in 1950 to do his student teaching at the segregated North Street School and taught there until 1956, when he went to North High as a physical education teacher. He was also the North High assistant football coach for 18 years and varsity baseball coach for eight years. He later served as assistant principal of E. Russell Hicks Middle School. His cadet training served him well. He often admonished his own children, his students and the players he coached: "No quibbling."

It wasn't until the airing of the 1996 HBO movie about the Tuskegee Airmen that family and friends began to ask Johnson about his days at the legendary training institute in Alabama. Speaking invitations and media attention followed.

As with many of his generation, war service was not a common topic of discussion and he never regarded his time as an aviation cadet as anything unusual. "None of us did. Everyone was going into the service. It was nothing to talk about. You just did what you had to do."

ARMY AIR FORCES EASTERN FLYING TRAINING COMMAND

Upon the recommendation of his Tactical Officer I do hereby appoint Aviation Cadet Johnson, Robert W., a Sergeant in the 2164th AAF Base Unit, CPSP to rank as such from the thirtieth day of June, 19 45 He is therefore carefully and diligently to discharge his duties as Cadet Flight Sergeant, and all cadets coming under his command are strictly charged and required to be obedient to his orders as such. And he is to observe and follow such orders and directions as he shall receive from his military superiors, according to the rules and discipline of War.

Given under my hand at 2164th AAF BU CPSP Tuskegee Institute, Alabama this thirtieth day of June in the year of Our Lord one thousand nine hundred and forty-five.

DANIEL J. SORRELLS,
1st Lt., Air Corps
Commandant of Aviation Cadets

Aviation Cadet Form No. 31 EFTC 1824-44

Johnson served as a cadet flight sergeant for the 2164th Army Air Forces Base Unit at the Army Air Forces Eastern Flying Training Command's Tuskegee Institute where African Americans trained as pilots, navigators, bombardiers and aircraft mechanics during WWII.

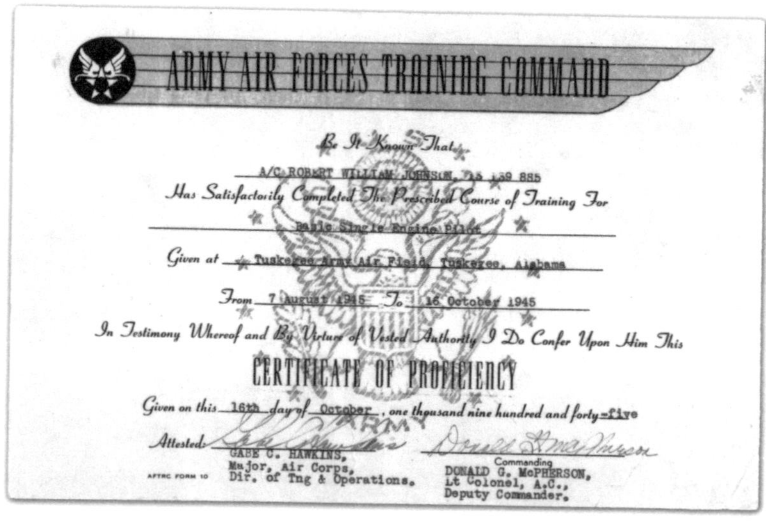

ARMY AIR FORCES TRAINING COMMAND

Be It Known That

A/C ROBERT WILLIAM JOHNSON, 15 139 885

Has Satisfactorily Completed The Prescribed Course of Training For

Basic Single Engine Pilot

Given at Tuskegee Army Air Field, Tuskegee, Alabama

From 7 August 1945 To 16 October 1945

In Testimony Whereof and By Virtue of Vested Authority I Do Confer Upon Him This

CERTIFICATE OF PROFICIENCY

Given on this 16th day of October, one thousand nine hundred and forty-five

Attested: GABE C. HAWKINS, Major, Air Corps, Dir. of Tng & Operations.

Commanding DONALD G. McPHERSON, Lt Colonel, A.C., Deputy Commander.

AFTRC FORM 10

Army Air Forces Training Command certificate reflecting Johnson's completion of training as a single-engine pilot in October 1945.

(Photographs and memorabilia courtesy of Robert W. Johnson)

In March 2007, Congress awarded Tuskegee Airmen who served in combat in WWII with the Congressional Gold Medal, the highest civilian honor Congress can bestow — 62 years after their unparalleled record of service.

Carroll S. Hose — Army — WWII

Carroll S. Hose (left) of Boonsboro took only the clothes he was wearing and some writing material with him when he went off to war in March 1942. He participated in the brutal Guadalcanal campaign and takes satisfaction in the fact that his Army unit participated in the massive effort that helped prevent Japan from occupying Australia.

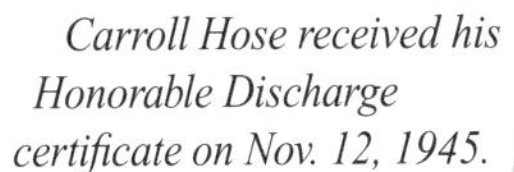

Carroll Hose received his Honorable Discharge certificate on Nov. 12, 1945.

(Photographs and memorabilia courtesy of William R. Suffecool on behalf of Carroll S. Hose)

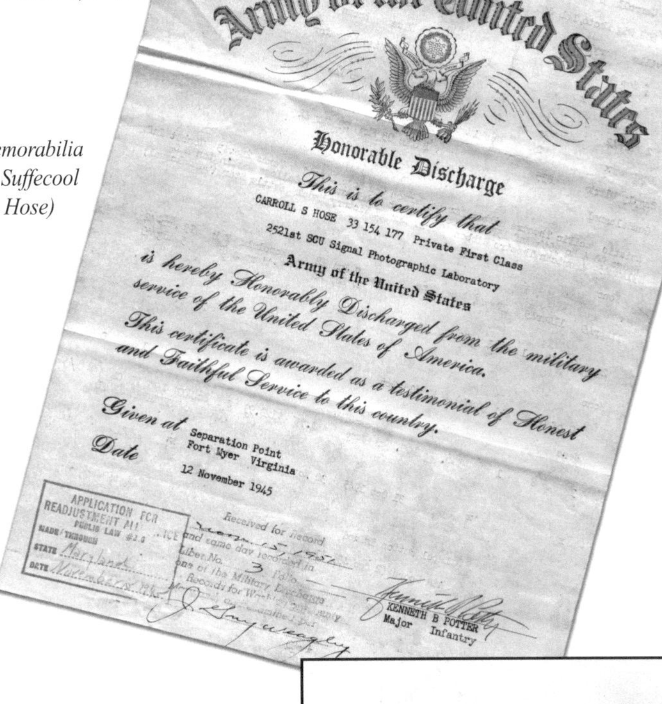

7

Army of the United States

Honorable Discharge

This is to certify that

CARROLL S HOSE 33 154 177 Private First Class

2521st SCU Signal Photographic Laboratory

Army of the United States

is hereby Honorably Discharged from the military service of the United States of America.

This certificate is awarded as a testimonial of Honest and Faithful Service to this country.

Given at Separation Point Fort Myer Virginia

Date 12 November 1945

APPLICATION FOR READJUSTMENT ALLOWANCE

Received for Record

KENNETH B POTTER
Major Infantry

Carroll Hose (left) shares some laughs with friends Donald Betts, Paul Green and Carroll's brother, Fred Hose, in front of the bowling alley in Boonsboro, while home on leave during WWII.

Carroll Hose and friends made the most of their time on leave. In this group photo, Hose stands at left in front of his future wife, Nellie Carson. Next to them are Donald Betts and an unidentified young woman. Good friend Paul Green and Nancy Clopper are the couple on the right.

Carroll Hose said his military experience "helped me appreciate our liberty to a greater degree." Another benefit was the fact that "during leave, being in uniform helped attract the local ladies, one of which later became my wife."

In this photo, Hose and his future wife, Nellie Carson, and their friends Paul Green and Nancy Clopper, practice mouth-to-mouth resuscitation in Boonsboro's Shaffer Park during the soldiers' time home on leave in WWII.

Stanley R. Brown Sr. — Navy — WWII

Stanley R. Brown entered the Naval Reserve in July 1943. Following nine weeks of basic training in Great Lakes, Illinois, Brown was given one week's leave to return to his Smithsburg home before shipping out of San Francisco to Australia. He was later shipped to New Guinea for placement with the amphibious service and served during four island invasions with the Army in the Pacific. Brown happened to be home on leave when the war ended.

After the war, Brown served in the regular Navy on the newly built aircraft carrier USS **Coral Sea**, which was launched in April 1946. He visited France, Spain, Portugal, Italy and many other countries before his discharge in October 1949. Television fans will appreciate the fact that the USS **Coral Sea** has appeared as a location for the television show **JAG**.

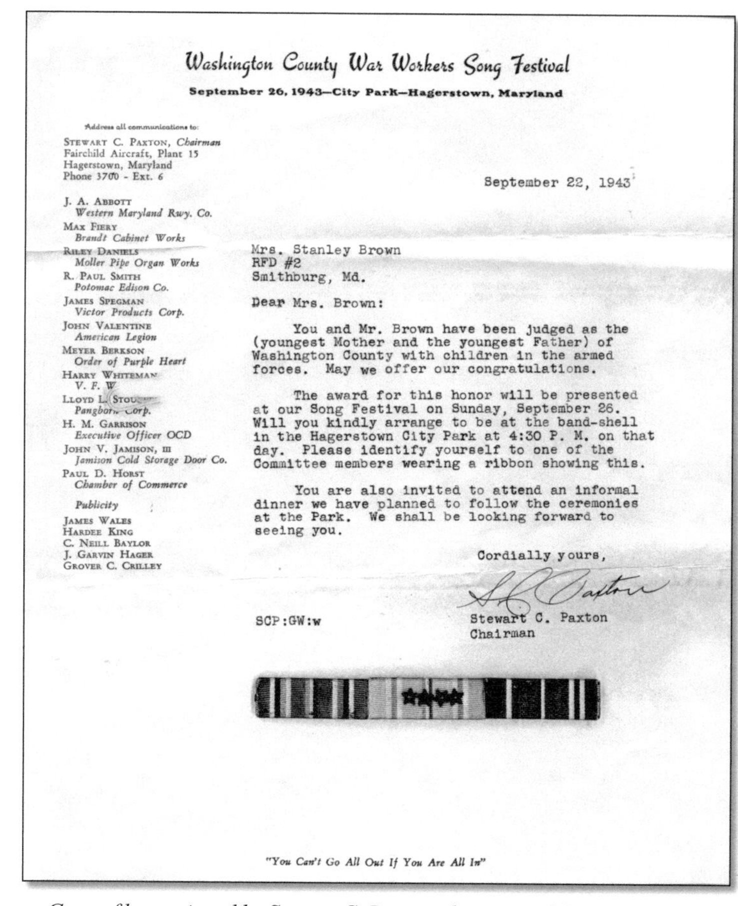

Washington County War Workers Song Festival

September 26, 1943—City Park—Hagerstown, Maryland

Address all communications to:
Stewart C. Paxton, *Chairman*
Fairchild Aircraft, Plant 15
Hagerstown, Maryland
Phone 3700 - Ext. 6

J. A. Abbott
Western Maryland Rwy. Co.
Max Fiery
Brandt Cabinet Works
Riley Daniels
Moller Pipe Organ Works
R. Paul Smith
Potomac Edison Co.
James Spegman
Victor Products Corp.
John Valentine
American Legion
Meyer Berkson
Order of Purple Heart
Harry Whiteman
V. F. W
Lloyd L. Stou[illegible]
Pangbor[illegible] Corp.
H. M. Garrison
Executive Officer OCD
John V. Jamison, III
Jamison Cold Storage Door Co.
Paul D. Horst
Chamber of Commerce

Publicity
James Wales
Hardee King
C. Neill Baylor
J. Garvin Hager
Grover C. Crilley

September 22, 1943

Mrs. Stanley Brown
RFD #2
Smithburg, Md.

Dear Mrs. Brown:

You and Mr. Brown have been judged as the (youngest Mother and the youngest Father) of Washington County with children in the armed forces. May we offer our congratulations.

The award for this honor will be presented at our Song Festival on Sunday, September 26. Will you kindly arrange to be at the band-shell in the Hagerstown City Park at 4:30 P. M. on that day. Please identify yourself to one of the Committee members wearing a ribbon showing this.

You are also invited to attend an informal dinner we have planned to follow the ceremonies at the Park. We shall be looking forward to seeing you.

Cordially yours,

Stewart C. Paxton
Chairman

SCP:GW:w

"You Can't Go All Out If You Are All In"

Copy of letter, signed by Stewart C. Paxton, chairman of the Washington County War Workers Song Festival, sent to Stanley R. Brown's parents in 1943. (Photographs and memorabilia courtesy of Stanley R. Brown Sr.)

Brown's parents, Stanley and Gladys Brown of Smithsburg, were recognized as the youngest Washington County parents to have a child in the armed forces, at a ceremony in Hagerstown City Park on September 26, 1943. Gladys, seated at right, and her husband, Stanley, were honored during ceremonies held in conjunction with the Washington County War Workers Song Festival. The older woman receiving an award in the foreground is not identified.

The Long Brothers — Army — Navy — Army Air Corps — WWII

William Russell Long was one of three Keedysville brothers who served in the military in WWII. He served as a member of the 407th Infantry, part of the Ninth Army in Germany. He had just gone overseas in September 1944 and was wounded in action in Germany that November. Shrapnel from an 88 mm gun hit him in the left side, breaking his shoulder and wounding his chest wall. He convalesced in a military hospital in Cambridge, England, and then returned to the United States. He was honorably discharged from the 38th Station Hospital, at Fort George Meade, Maryland, Dec. 22, 1945.

Howard F. Long, a seaman 2nd class, eventually went to the Pacific where he served on a minesweeper in Nagoya and Kobe, Japan; Shanghai, China; and then in the Philippines. After the war, he returned to the States by way of the Panama Canal.

Pfc. John W. Long Jr. went into the military in March 1944, serving with the Army Air Corps at Stinson Field in San Antonio, Texas. The former Fairchild employee carried cards identifying him as a munitions worker and as one certified in the repair of self-sealing fuel cells, following his training in Detroit, Michigan.

(Photographs courtesy of Rosalie V. Long, wife of John W. Long Jr., and Howard and William Long's sister-in-law)

Three Keedysville Brothers Are In Service

Pfc. William R. Long, whose wife is the former Betty Jane Mose of Sharpsburg, is pictured at the Guild Hall in Cambridge, England, where he and other convalescents from two nearby U. S. military hospitals were entertained. The lady at the left is the Mayoress of Cambridge. Going overseas in September 1944, the county man has been hospitalized since last November, when schrapnel from an 88 hit him in the left side, breaking his shoulder and wounding the chest wall. He was serving with the Ninth Army in Germany when wounded.

Now in a replacement center, Pfc. Long has recovered from his wounds. He is 23 years old and the son of Mr. and Mrs. John W. Long, Keedysville. His two brothers are shown below.

Howard F. Long, S 2-c, who graduated from the Boonsboro high school in 1943, has been in the Navy since November 29, 1944, and is now attending a signal school at Bainbridge Naval Training Station.

Cpl. John W. Long, Jr., who entered the Army a year ago, is now at Stinson Field, San Antonio, Tex. He recently spent an 18-day delay en-route at his home in Keedysville, while being transferred to his present post. A former Fairchild employee, he graduated from the Boonsboro high school in 1938.

William Russell Long's convalescence in England and an account of his two brothers' military service was reported in the local newspaper.

AIR TECHNICAL SERVICE COMMAND

THIS CERTIFIES THAT

Pvt. John W. Long Jr. 33843921

GRADE NAME ASN

IS A QUALIFIED

MUNITIONS WORKER

CLASSIFICATION OFFICER SIGNATURE OF SOLDIER

DATE 11 April 1945

Proper entry has been made in the service record (WD AGO Form 24) and on the qualification card (WD AGO Form 20)

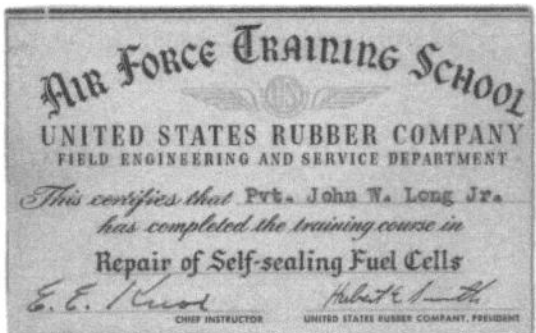

Air Force Training School

UNITED STATES RUBBER COMPANY

FIELD ENGINEERING AND SERVICE DEPARTMENT

This certifies that Pvt. John W. Long Jr. has completed the training course in Repair of Self-sealing Fuel Cells

CHIEF INSTRUCTOR UNITED STATES RUBBER COMPANY, PRESIDENT

Patches, dog tags and cards from John W. Long Jr.'s service in the military in WWII.

Elwood C. "Woodie" Pearman — Army — WWII

Elwood C. "Woodie" Pearman of Williamsport was 26 when he was drafted into the Army in October 1941. After basic training at Camp Wheeler, Georgia, he was selected to be an MP [military policeman] with Company B of the 14th Infantry Military Police, 7th Army. His duties took him to many countries in Central and South America, including Fort Davis in the Panama Canal Zone. He left Panama on a POW [prisoner of war] ship and then served as an MP at a POW camp in Ahoskie, North Carolina. During his four years in the Army, Pearman also worked as a postal clerk at a military post office. On this page are photos and memorabilia of his time as an MP, including white gloves, Army-issued canvas bag, Panama map, armband, baton, sergeant's stripes, collar insignia, bullet and 7th Army patch.

An arrow pointing to his feet, Pearman stands facing a superior officer while training to be a military policeman in the Army. MPs are responsible for law enforcement on military property. Their duties can include installation security, traffic control, personal protection of senior officers, criminal investigation and management of prisoners of war and military prisons. They are generally not front-line combatants, but especially when directing military convoys, can be near or at the front lines. Traditionally, the Army has selected tall soldiers to serve as MPs. Pearman stood 6'2".

Pearman left some unfinished business behind him when he was drafted on Oct. 1, 1941, and sent to basic training at Camp Wheeler, Georgia. Eight weeks later, he went AWOL [absent without leave] and returned to Williamsport to marry his girlfriend, Annabelle "Belle" Ditto. They were married at the Williamsport Methodist Church on Christmas Day 1941, and photographed here on Dec. 27 at Union Station in Washington, D.C., before he boarded a train that would take him back to Camp Wheeler. He didn't get into trouble for being AWOL; his lieutenant covered for him.

Little is known about the military careers of Wilbur and Melvin Pearman, brothers of Elwood C. "Woodie" Pearman, who were drafted at the same time he was in 1941. It is known that Wilbur, pictured here, was stationed in Africa, where he lost some of his fingers when a gun he was working on blew up. All three brothers returned alive from WWII.

(Photos and memorabilia courtesy of Bonnie Pearman Woodard, daughter of Elwood C. "Woodie" Pearman and Annabelle "Belle" Ditto Pearman)

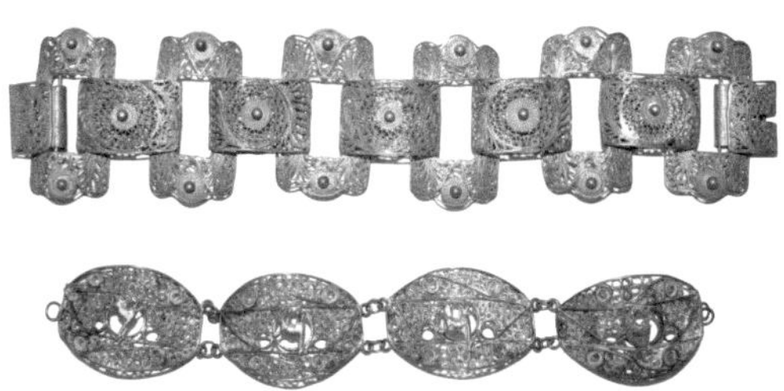

Sterling silver bracelets that Elwood C. "Woodie" Pearman brought back from Peru while he was stationed in Central and South America during WWII. He also acquired a knowledge of Spanish that was unknown to his daughter, Bonnie Pearman Woodard, until she was learning the language in school and he surprised her by speaking to her fluently.

Vernon Jenkins — Army — WWII **Weston Jenkins** — Army — WWII

The Jenkins brothers, Weston (left) and Vernon (right), examine the underside of a C-82 Packet — known locally as a "Flying Boxcar" — produced by Fairchild Aircraft in the closing days of WWII. Weston went into the Army but received a medical discharge during basic training. He worked at Fairchild and become the company's official photographer. Vernon was trained as an Army ranger specializing in sabotage — disrupting enemy communications and transportation lines. He was captured in Italy and spent two-and-a-half years as a prisoner of war. After he was liberated, Vernon returned to Hagerstown. His ill-fitting uniform testifies to the dramatic weight loss he suffered as a prisoner of war.

Vernon Jenkins

Weston Jenkins

Weston Jenkins made this plaque listing the names of 22 individuals from 17 homes on South Street in Hagerstown who served during WWII, including the name of his brother, Vernon, who was a prisoner of war, and another neighbor, who was killed in action. The block-long expanse of South Street had an average of nearly two soldiers per household serving in uniform during WWII. This wooden plaque was erected on a vacant lot on South Street in 1943. The lot is still vacant, but the sign is no longer there.

(Photographs courtesy of Ray L. Nalley, Vernon and Weston Jenkins' brother-in-law)

Carl J. Reed — Army — WWII

Carl J. Reed of Big Spring carried his Bible from Orchard Ridge Church and photos of his family and his girlfriend when he joined the Army in November 1942. After training at Fort Campbell, Kentucky, and Fort Meade, Maryland, he was sent to England before seeing action in France, Belgium and Germany with Company M of the 335th Infantry.

(Photos and memorabilia courtesy of Mrs. Carl J. Reed, widow of Carl J. Reed)

Rosen, Daily, Reed, Harden, Ebersole

Carl J. Reed (center) is surrounded by his buddies as they pose on their half-track M3 personnel carrier, an armored vehicle used extensively in WWII. An armorer, or "the spare parts man" in his division, Reed was also an experienced machine gun technician and operator, and was called "the champion foxhole digger of the division." He said his most memorable experiences during WWII included crawling across a battlefield to help a fellow soldier while carrying a machine gun, crossing the Rhine River, and getting home alive and safe.

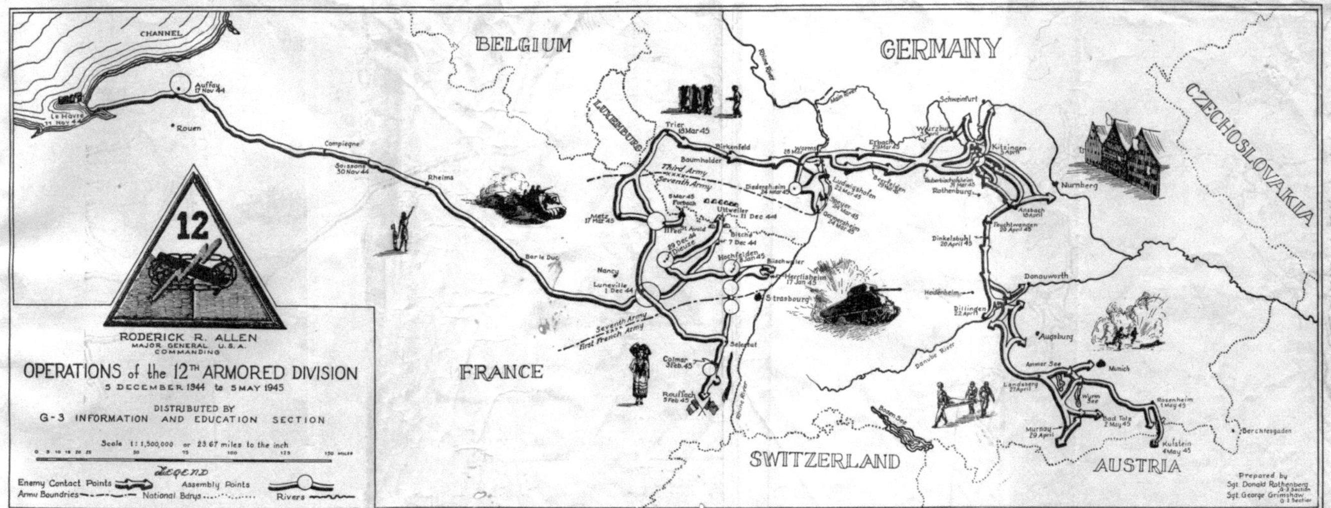

Map showing operations of the 12th Armored Division in Belgium, Germany and Austria between Dec. 5, 1944, and May 5, 1945, including the Rhineland Campaign. Carl J. Reed had expected to fight in the Battle of the Bulge, but orders were changed at the last minute, and his division joined Patton's Third Army to spearhead the march to the Rhine River.

John Aubrey Hill — Army — WWII

In a playful photograph taken in front of a shoe store in Anniston, Alabama, near Fort McClellan, Carolyn Ridenour Hill dons her husband, John Aubrey Hill's Army hat. The snapshot was taken in 1943, just before Hill shipped out to Australia on his way to New Guinea, the Philippines and, eventually, Japan. It was their last time together until the end of the war. Carolyn did not see John again for another three-and-a-half years. Although she wrote to him every day, and he wrote as often as he could, when he returned, "it was like meeting a stranger," Carolyn said.

This family photograph was taken in Hagerstown after Hill completed his military service. Hill had been gone for more than three years. His son, Jack, was only six months old when he left. Carolyn taught Jack to call her husband "Daddy John," but young Jack, not unlike countless other children born during WWII who failed to recognize their returning fathers, "didn't know him when he got home."

John Aubrey Hill's dog tags and a ***Pocket Guide to Australia****, prepared by the War and Navy Departments, designed to acquaint American soldiers dispatched to Australia in WWII with the customs of their fellow English speakers "down under." Carolyn Hill recalled her husband telling her that upon their arrival, the soldiers were invited to the home of an Australian family and he told her how he danced to the song* ***Waltzing Matilda****.*

Hill sent home a bracelet he made from Australian coins, a tiny boomerang he purchased as a souvenir, and a shell bracelet he made in New Guinea. He also sent home a decorated coconut, a grass skirt and this photograph taken of him with natives of New Guinea, where Allies waged a furious battle to push back the Japanese.

Hill also kept a small book entitled ***My Life in the Service*** *which included an account of his time in Australia, New Guinea, the Philippines and Japan during WWII. The book also provided room for autographs from Army buddies.*

Shown below is the cover of a booklet with the emblem of Hill's Ship & Gun Crew Command in Australia in 1944.

Frederick Hill

Frederick Hill, John Hill's older brother, went into the Army Air Forces in July 1941. Because of a shortage of pilots at the outbreak of WWII, the Army Air Forces initiated the Army Air Forces Cadet Program. Aviation cadets received $75 a month. They had to swear that they were single and take an oath that they would not marry while in training.

Hill was sent to Luke Field, Glendale, Arizona, where the Army Air Forces had its advance fighter flying school, and was later posted to Baton Rouge, Louisiana, in 1943.

To the right of the photo are the Army Air Forces Aviation Cadet wings belonging to Frederick Hill of Hagerstown, who was drowned in Baton Rouge, in August 1943. The family was never able to find out the circumstances of his death. Hill was only 23 at the time of his death.

The aviation cadet wings (above) feature a winged propeller instead of a winged eagle as its insignia.

(Photographs and memorabilia courtesy of Carolyn Ridenour Hill, widow of John Aubrey Hill, and sister-in-law to Frederick Hill)

Max Krumpe — Merchant Marine — WWII

For Max Krumpe of Hagerstown, going to sea was a bit of a family tradition. "My grandfather had come from Germany before 1913 as a merchant seaman," said Max Krumpe's son, Rudolph. "When the war broke out, he stayed here and joined the U.S. Coast Guard." Krumpe had always dreamed of joining the Navy, but tests revealed that he was color-blind, and "the Navy wouldn't take him." The Merchant Marine, however, whose valiant efforts to keep Europe supplied went unheralded for decades, wasn't nearly so picky. "By 1943, they needed sailors."

Members of the crew of the American Liberty ship, Button Gwinnett, who arrived at Leith yesterday after having had to run for port when their vessel sprang a leak during gales in the North Sea.

Krumpe, circled at right, appeared in this undated photograph from a Scottish newspaper showing members of the crew of the ***Button Gwinnett****, an American Liberty ship that arrived at Leith after having "had to run for port" after their vessel "sprang a leak during gales in the North Sea."*

Son Rudolph Krumpe believes this may have been his father's closest call during WWII. "They were taking on water. But they made it back to port."

United States Merchant Marine

Certificate of Service

This is to certify that

MAX KRUMPE

is a

U.S. Merchant Marine Veteran

having served aboard oceangoing merchant ships in service to the United States during World War II.

MARITIME ADMINISTRATOR

Although the U.S. Merchant Marine was a civilian operation, it suffered the second highest casualty rate of any of the branches of the service — second only to the Marine Corps. Forty-five years after the end of WWII, President Ronald Reagan awarded members of the Merchant Marine veteran status if they had served during 1941-1943 on the North Atlantic supply lanes.

More than 200 merchant ships were lost as a result of submarines, mines, enemy destroyers, and kamikaze pilots. Approximately 8,300 merchant mariners were killed during WWII. Because 1 in 26 mariners serving aboard merchant ships in WWII died in the line of duty, the service suffered a greater percentage of war-related deaths than all other U.S. services. The heavy casualty rate was kept secret during the war to prevent the enemy from determining the success of its efforts and to attract and keep mariners at sea.

(Photographs and memorabilia courtesy of Rudolph and Clara Krumpe)

NEW YORK

MAX KRUMPE

SEAMAN

USMS TRAINING STATION
Sheepshead Bay, New York

WAR SHIPPING ADMINISTRATION
TRAINING ORGANIZATION
UNITED STATES MARITIME SERVICE
(IDENTIFICATION CARD)

KRUMPE, Max

Date of birth 2-9-26

Height 5' 9½"

Weight 150

AS

Service No. 4314-30970

Issued NOV 24 1943

Void after NOV 24 1945

Comdr., USNR

Executive Officer

Identity cards bearing Krumpe's photograph from his days at the U.S. Merchant Marine Training Center at Sheepshead Bay, New York. He graduated in November 1943.

The center was dedicated in December 1942. At the time, it was the largest training station in the world with the capability of training 30,000 apprentice seamen a year.

In coverage of the dedication ceremony, ***The New York Times*** *quoted New York Gov. Charles Poletti as saying:*

> *When the history of this great conflict is written the story of the transportation and supply of our armed forces across the seven seas will be one of its most glorious chapters. Valiant and resolute — braving enemy torpedoes and enemy bombs — they are fighting a winning fight against ruthless, cunning enemies.*

Krumpe served aboard the **Walter Forward**, one of the 2,751 Liberty ships that navigated the treacherous oceans during WWII. Liberty ships were cheap and hastily built cargo vessels produced by the United States in response to the decimation of British cargo ships by German U-boats at the beginning of WWII. Using prefabricated parts produced throughout the United States, huge 270-ton sections of the Liberty ships could be welded together in less than 70 days. President Franklin D. Roosevelt, nicknamed the merchant ships "ugly ducklings," but they were the means by which men and supplies could be shipped to Europe and Asia to defeat the Axis powers.

*Krumpe looks right at home of the helm of the **Walter Forward**, under the watchful gaze of the first mate in this 1946 photo. Krumpe, who had signed on originally as a deck hand, served as the night cook and baker. He stayed in the Merchant Marine until 1947 and traveled around the globe, before returning to Hagerstown to make the famed doughnuts that bear his family name at Krumpe's Do-Nut Shop.*

(Stamp courtesy of Dennis Shaw)

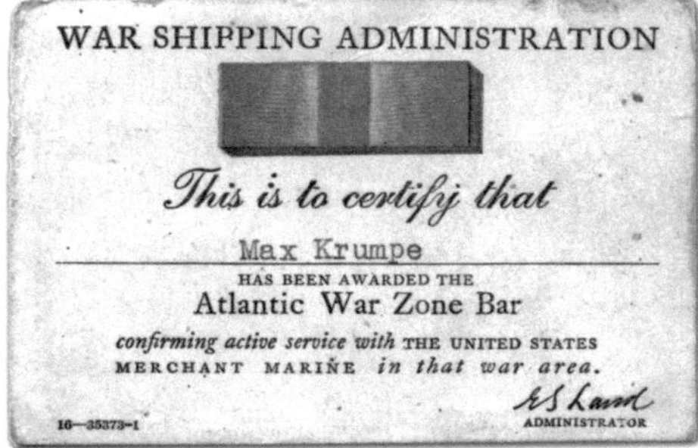

WAR SHIPPING ADMINISTRATION

This is to certify that

Max Krumpe

HAS BEEN AWARDED THE

Atlantic War Zone Bar

confirming active service with THE UNITED STATES MERCHANT MARINE in that war area.

ADMINISTRATOR

16—35373-1

Krumpe was awarded the Atlantic War Zone Bar for his service in the Merchant Marine during WWII. It wasn't until President Ronald Reagan's administration, four decades after WWII, that merchant mariners received the recognition they were due. The bar was retroactively designated the Atlantic War Zone Medal and members of the Merchant Marine who served between Dec. 7, 1941, and Nov. 8, 1945 are eligible for the commendation.

The back of this wallet-sized card bears the names and addresses of two Scottish lasses the American seaman apparently met when his ship was held over in Edinburgh, Scotland, for repairs.

SERIAL NUMBER E511510

BOOK NUMBER 3 44077

UNITED STATES COAST GUARD

CERTIFICATE OF SERVICE

(OTHER THAN ABLE SEAMAN OR QD MEMBER OF THE ENGINE DEPARTMENT)

This certifies that M Krumpe having taken oath required by law is hereby qualified to serve aboard american vessels of 100 tons gross and upward in Steward's Department in a rating 2nd Cook & Baker (7.4)

Issued under signed officer in charge Marine Inspection this 24th day of March 1944

Commander,

Officer in charge Marine Inspection

Port of NEW YORK, N.Y.

Signature of Seaman

In this March 1944 certificate of service from the United States Coast Guard, Krumpe is deemed qualified to serve aboard vessels of 100 tons gross as "a cook and baker."

Five-Star Family — The Kellers — WWII

Mr. and Mrs. Hubert Keller, shown here at their home on South Cannon Avenue in Hagerstown, watched and waited nervously during WWII as their five sons left home to serve in the Army. From left, they are: Pvt. Cecil Keller, in Italy; Pvt. Robert Keller, in England; Pfc. Chester Keller, in the Pacific; Pvt. Earl Keller, in England; and Pvt. Richard Keller, in France. All five brothers came home alive, although Richard, who suffered severe frostbite in France, lost his foot, his leg, and soon afterwards, his life.

(Photos courtesy of Robert Stotelmyer, nephew of Earl Keller)

Milton M. Gillan — Army Air Forces — WWII

Milton M. Gillan spent most of WWII on the bleak, cold Aleutian Islands at the top of the Pacific Ocean, as shown in the photos here. The 27-year-old Hagerstown man became a member of the Army Air Forces in 1941 and served as a ground manager on the islands of Adak and Attu in the island chain located strategically between Alaska and the Soviet Union.

Parts of the Aleutians were occupied by Japanese forces in June 1942 when Attu and Kiska were invaded to divert American forces away from the Japanese attack at Midway. Thc Navy, having broken Japanese codes, suspected this was a diversion and did not expend much effort defending the islands. A few Americans were taken to Japan as prisoners of war. Adak Army installations allowed the U.S. forces to mount a successful offensive against Attu and Kiska and regain control of the islands. The Aleutians were also a stopping point for aircraft sent from California to Russia as part of the war effort.

Milton M. Gillan shares a meal with USO volunteers in Alaska in this 1943 photo.

(Photographs courtesy of Lorraine McDonald, daughter of Milton M. Gillan)

Doris Stevenson Sager — WAVES — WWII

Doris Stevenson Sager was scheduled to graduate with the Penn State University Class of 1944, but the advent of World War II changed her plans and the plans of millions of others. In an effort to graduate as many students as quickly as possible, the university switched to a trimester system, accelerating the academic program, so that students could graduate a full year earlier. The journalism major then took a job with her hometown newspaper, *The Record Herald*, in Waynesboro, Pennsylvania, while she waited for her application to the WAVES [Women Accepted for Volunteer Emergency Service] to be processed.

The WAVES were a WWII-era division of the Navy made up entirely of women performing support functions designed to free uniformed men for combat duty overseas.

"My mother thought this was just great," said Sager, referring to her decision to apply for service in the WAVES. Her father was encouraging as well. "But on the day he was to take me to the train station, he must have had some misgivings. We tarried a little too long over breakfast and when we drove up to the train station in Greencastle, the train was pulling out of the station. We jumped in the car and raced the train to Chambersburg," where 21-year-old Doris boarded for the remainder of her trip to Philadelphia to complete the necessary tests and interviews prior to her induction.

Once accepted, she was off to Midshipmen's School at Smith College in Massachusetts for basic training, where she spent a lot of time in physical training in the gym, "swinging down ropes" and marching in formation. From there, Seaman Stevenson was assigned to Mt. Holyoke, another women's college in Massachusetts, used as a training site for the new phalanx of women in uniform.

After completing special training in communications, she was assigned to the Communications Annex near Ward Circle, close to the American University campus in Washington, D.C. She worked nights in the code room, encrypting and decoding the flurry of messages that flowed in and out of Washington as the war proceeded. She was eventually promoted to a job in the mail room, where a large number of enlisted women and one civilian routed "bags and bags" of mail to offices in the highly secure building. The most difficult aspect of working in wartime Washington, according to Sager, was the critical housing shortage caused by the flood of military and civilian personnel from all over the country into the nation's capital as the war intensified.

At first, she and two other WAVES shared a tiny bedroom at the local YWCA before she and nine other WAVES were able to rent the spacious house of a Navy commander assigned overseas. "We moved in and hung our banner with its 10 stars in the window. No other neighbor could top that.

Doris Stevenson Sager hurried off to Chicago to see her younger brother, Harlan Quinn Stevenson, a Navy recruit, on the last weekend before he shipped out to the Philippines in November 1945. The Lt. (jg) and her brother, five years her junior, took time out to have a studio photo taken during their short time together.

We were now within walking distance of our work," Sager said. Because they all worked shift work, the young women, including two married WAVES whose husbands were overseas in combat, were seldom all there at the same time. "In our house, someone was always coming or going, sleeping or eating. We all survived and remain good friends to this day, keeping in touch via 'round robin' letters and infrequent reunions." A few of her former colleagues have since died and their daughters were asked to be included in the continuation of the letters that are mailed in sequence to each of the original group — everyone adding a little news and forwarding the letters on.

Even before the outbreak of the war, the young Pennsylvania girl had an affinity for the Navy. From childhood, she had cheered for the Navy's team in the yearly contests with rival Notre Dame, her father's and brother's favorite team. And then there were the handsome Navy ensigns, detailed to special engineering classes at Penn State, who briskly walked around the State College campus in their smart-looking uniforms.

In the end though, she fell for a 4-F Duke University graduate, whose military deferment was a result of a childhood accident in which he lost some vision in one eye. Tom Sager worked for Noland Company in Washington, but often traveled to his hometown of Hagerstown. She was frequently headed to her Waynesboro home and their paths crossed. "I met him on the bus from Washington, and a year later, he gave me an engagement ring on the bus."

When the war ended, Sager stayed on as a civilian employee, performing the same job "for less pay." In 1950, she and her husband and the first of their three children moved to Hagerstown when her husband went to work for his family's business, the Sager-Redford Wholesale Lumber Company.

The Navy sought to recruit women into the WAVES to fulfill critical support functions. WAVES worked as clerks, members of the Judge Advocate General's Corps, in the medical professions, as well as the communications, intelligence and technology fields. Membership in the WAVES peaked at 86,000 in August of 1942. Doris Stevenson Sager was one of 8,000 officers who served in the WAVES in WWII.

On a chance visit to her home in Waynesboro, Pennsylvania, in the spring of 1944, first cousins William Stevenson, an Army Air Forces lieutenant, and Doris Stevenson Sager snap to attention in a smart salute for the camera.

Ribbons representing medals Sager was awarded for her service in WWII. They include the American Campaign Ribbon, the WWII Victory Ribbon and a Navy Unit Commendation Ribbon. The bars below are the insignia for a lieutenant senior grade, Sager's rank upon discharge.

With the SPARS

Priscilla Ruth Wishard, S 1-c (Y), (above) is now located at the Coast Guard Recruiting Office in Charlestown, South Carolina.

Miss Wishard, 22-year-old daughter of Mr. and Mrs. Fred R. Wishard, 218 Park Street, was inducted into the Spars on July 21, 1944, in Baltimore. She took her basic training at the Spars Training Center at West Palm Beach, Fla. Having graduated from the Washington Township High School in the class of 1940, she was employed at the Landis Tool Company before entering the service.

Serving your country in uniform was just something young men and women did during WWII, as evidenced by a scattering of snapshots of some of Doris Stevenson Sager's contemporaries.

Sager's friend William H. Gelbach Jr., of Leitersburg Pike, is shown (on the right in the first photo above) holding a fish caught in the South Pacific, and, at center, riding a motorcycle in New Guinea in 1943. Donald Sensenbaugh (photo at right), another friend of Sager's, who was a Smithsburg High School graduate, served in the Marine Corps.

Men were accustomed to donning uniforms in times of war. But the advent of WWII created new opportunities for women to wear the uniform of their country as well. In addition to service in the WAVES and WACS [Women's Army Corps], women could serve with the Coast Guard, as did Sager's classmate, Priscilla Ruth Wishard of Waynesboro, Pennsylvania (shown in the newspaper clipping above), who was a member of the SPARS — the women's auxiliary of the U.S. Coast Guard. The SPARS took their name from a contraction of the Coast Guard motto ***Semper Paratus*** (Always Ready).

Also shown (above) are an embroidered version the WAVES emblem and Navy dog tags bearing the name Frances Doris Stevenson.

Sager has been an enthusiastic supporter of the Women In Military Service For America Memorial at Arlington National Cemetery. The memorial is designed to recognize the contributions of women who have served in the military. Women served in every theater of WWII including North Africa, Europe and the Pacific Islands, China, India and Burma.

(Photographs and memorabilia courtesy of Doris Stevenson Sager)

Edmund Ray "Slats" Easterday — Army Air Corps — WWII

Boonsboro native Edmund Ray "Slats" Easterday saw the world through the sights of a .50-caliber machine gun on the left side of a B-17 while flying missions in Germany and the Mediterranean during WWII. Easterday entered military service in 1942 and served as a corporal in the Army Air Corps until his discharge on Jan. 1, 1946. He served both as a military policeman and as a gunner.

His nickname "Slats" came from a minister who was working with him building a roof in Boonsboro. In the process of constructing the roof, Easterday was climbing a ladder with two long slats of wood. The wind was blowing that day and caught hold of the slats, making them uncontrollable. Easterday had a choice: drop the wood or fall off the ladder. He dropped the wood. As the boards hit the sidewalk they shattered. The minister looked down, saw what had happened, and called him a "dumb slats." Thereafter he was "Slats."

BOMB GROUP MESS
Kirtland Field, Albuquerque, New Mexico
NAME EDMUND R. EASTERDAY
RANK Private
ORG. 871st A.S.N.
Is authorized to ... in this organization.

KIRTLAND FIELD
Albuquerque, New Mexico
This certifies that
NAME EDMUND R. EASTERDAY
RANK Pvt A.S.N.
ORG. 871st Guard Squadron
is permitted to be absent from the reservation when not on any prescribed duty.
ROBERT A. FULLER, Major, AC
COMMANDING:
OFFICIAL
Date Issued 1-1-44
Expires 12-31-44
By PAUL E. BAIR, 1st Lt., AC
Adjutant

*Cpl. Easterday was a military policeman during production of the movie **The Bombardier** at Kirtland Field in Albuquerque, New Mexico, in 1943. Characterized as a WWII propaganda film, the movie concentrated on the technical job of the bombardier. Easterday took these photos of the film stars including actresses Anne Shirley and Marjorie Stewart, and their male counterparts Randolph Scott, Walter Reed and Pat O'Brien.*

Easterday's military police unit was "cannibalized" due to significant losses sustained by the 8th Army Air Force in the daylight bombing campaign over Germany. "Cannibalization" was done during WWII in order to fill the needs of the Army at any specific time due to losses. Stationed in England with the 8th Air Force, Easterday flew ten missions into Germany on a B-17. His flight gear served as a record of the Corps' accomplishments. He was transferred to a base on the Mediterranean in Africa to fly B-24s, and flew another 28 missions including a mission to bomb the oil fields in Ploesti, Romania.

According to stories shared with his family, the planes came in low and had to fly into heavy smoke from burning oil that blanketed the sky while German anti-aircraft guns were waiting for them. The bombs that were dropped had delayed fuses, and some of the planes were hit by shrapnel from the exploding oil storage units. Easterday was in Africa when victory in Europe was declared in 1945, but didn't have enough points to come home immediately. He was transferred instead to the Pacific in anticipation of the invasion of Japan and was stationed on an atoll close to Tinian Island.

A skilled mechanic, he served on a ground crew while on duty in the Pacific. He was wounded during a Japanese air attack while trying to move a plane out of the line of fire with a tow rig. A bomb exploded close by, and a piece of metal was lodged in his knee. The metal remained with him the rest of his life.

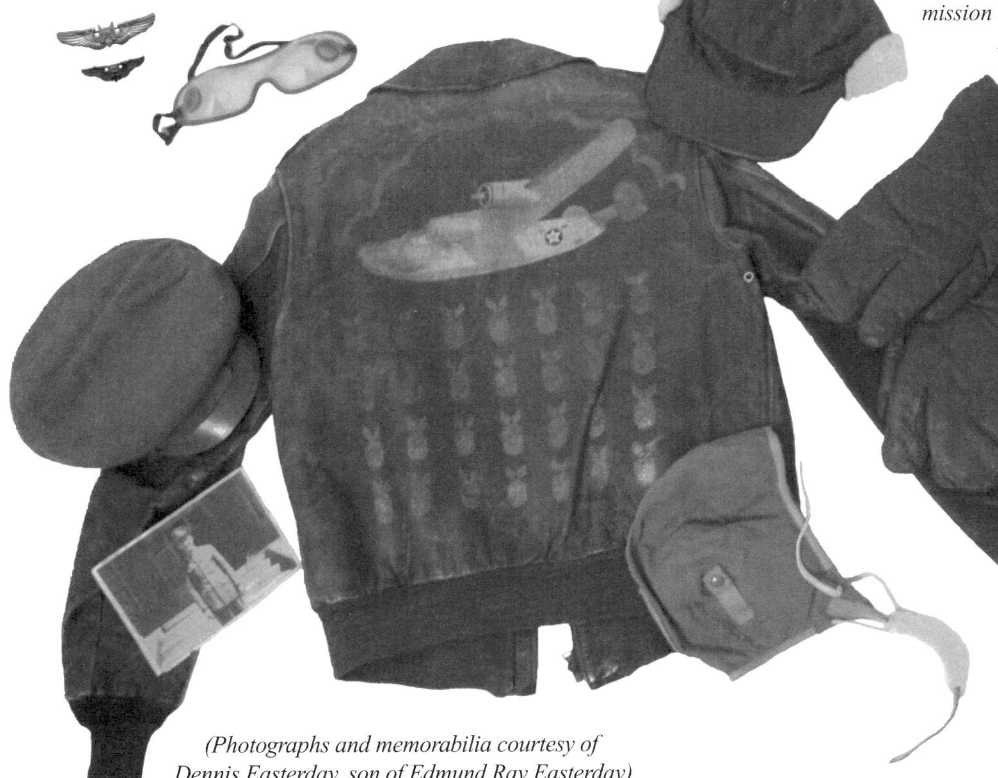

(Photographs and memorabilia courtesy of Dennis Easterday, son of Edmund Ray Easterday)

Eisenhower Army jacket and cap worn by Wilbur Hershberger, photographed against the 48-star American flag that existed during WWII. The Eisenhower, or "Ike," jacket is a shortened coat that terminates in a waistband. Modeled after a British battle dress coat, it was introduced in 1943 by Gen. Eisenhower, supreme commander of the Allied Expeditionary Force, as a modified version of the Army's regulation service uniform coat. Made in the shortened form later on, it became popular among officers and enlisted men as standard additions to their uniforms. Convenient to wear while operating a vehicle or carrying a sidearm, jackets of this style were widely used by civilian police agencies after the war.

(Photos courtesy of Beverley Hershberger, widow of Wilbur R. Hershberger)

Wilbur R. Hershberger — Army — WWII

Wilbur Hershberger was only 19 years old when the photo above was taken while at basic training at Camp Swift, Texas, in 1943.

Born in Boonsboro, Wilbur R. Hershberger joined the Army in February 1943 and took basic training at Camp Swift, Texas, where this photo was taken. After completing radio school at Fort Leonard Wood, Missouri, he was made squad leader and sent overseas with the 137th Infantry, Company A. Attached to Patton's Third Army, he was in the third wave of the Normandy landings and fought in campaigns in Northern France, Ardennes [The Battle of the Bulge] and the Rhineland.

His widow, Beverley Hershberger, remembers him talking about his service. In France, she said, they were ordered to take the town of St. Lo, but had to fall back and secure the perimeter. "One American plane flew over with leaflets telling French residents to evacuate and Germans to surrender," she said. "The next morning, so many planes flew over that the ground shook from the sound of the engines. They leveled the town ... the only thing left standing was one church steeple."

Hershberger was shot through the knee on Sept. 9, 1944, and sent to a hospital in England. But no bones were broken, and upon his release he returned to active duty. But he had not been issued liners for his boots, and while marching into the Battle of the Bulge, his feet froze. He was told to sit down and wait for a medic, then sent back to England. "The rest of the group went on," Beverley said. "Many did not return."

Hershberger also spoke of a time near the end of the war when his unit was ordered to secure the perimeter of a particular area. "They didn't understand why," his widow recalled. He said, "there was a horrible odor, and ashes in the air like powder." Later they learned they were securing the perimeter of the Dachau concentration camp.

Returning home a sergeant with a Purple Heart, Hershberger worked for Potomac Edison from 1945 to 1986 and lived in Maugansville, where he raised two sons and a daughter and enjoyed feeding squirrels and birds in his yard and going fishing. He died of cancer in 1993.

"The war had a lifelong effect on him," Beverley said. "He suffered nightmares and the aftereffects of his frost-bitten feet."

Ralph I. Gibney Jr. — Army — WWII

Ralph I. Gibney Jr. was a 26-year-old illustrator working for Potomac Edison in Hagerstown with a wife and two children when he was drafted into the Army in 1944. Gibney, a self-taught artist who demonstrated artistic talent from an early age, exchanged his pen and ink for a rifle and bayonet and fought with the 1st Infantry Division in the Battle of the Bulge.

Gibney came to love the quaintness of the German villages with the half-timbered homes, according to his stepdaughter Barbara Bachtell. But he also remembered in the last days of the war when "walking down the street in a small German town, an elderly German soldier came up out of a hole behind him with his rifle and his hands in the air surrendering. Ralph didn't know he was there and the guy could have shot him in the back," recalled Bachtell, remembering the story Gibney had shared with family members.

Cover of pamphlet commemorating the 1st Infantry Division's role in WWII and the inside front cover with a letter by Commanding General Clarence R. Huebner commending members of the "Fighting First" for "your courage, your caginess, your teamwork and your spirit."

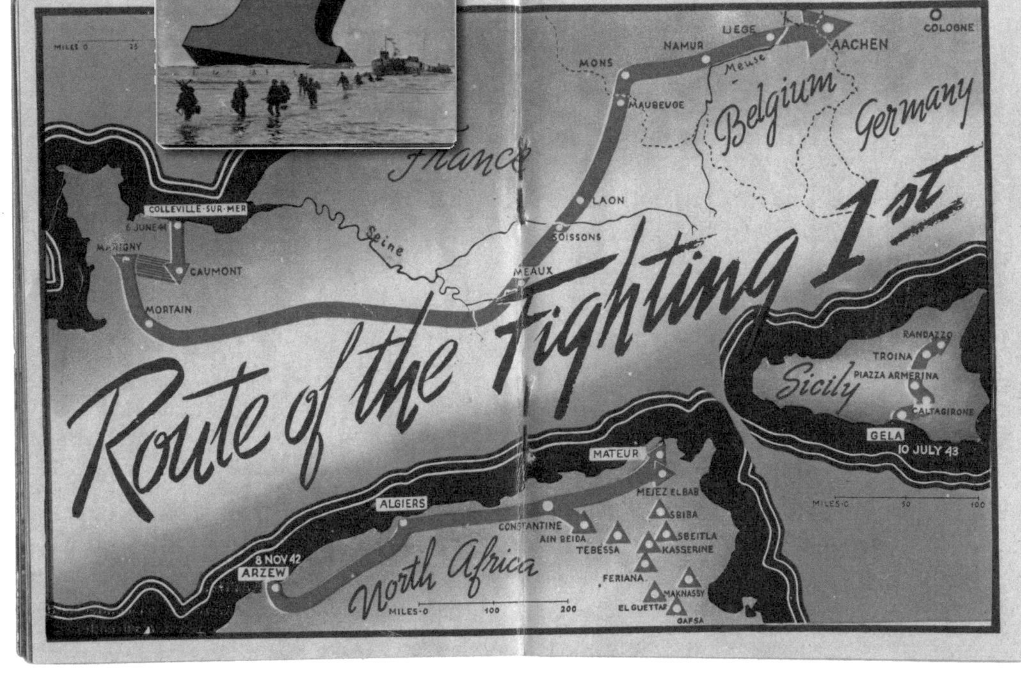

(Photographs and memorabilia courtesy of Barbara Bachtell, Ralph I. Gibney Jr.'s stepdaughter)

With an artist's eye, Gibney created this poster for the 1st Infantry Division entitled "Echoes from the ETO." He also sketched a humorous depiction of life in occupied Germany entitled "Mädchen on Wheels."

Traces of Gibney's exposure to postwar Europe appear in the commercial art he produced for his own Gibney Studio on Virginia Avenue in Hagerstown.

THE AMERICAN TRAVELER

1st United States Infantry Division

Vol. XV. No. 7 | Ansbach, Germany | Thursday, September 6, 1945

Division Will Share Station For Broadcast

ERLANGEN, Sept. 5—Special Service scored another entertainment and service triumph today with the announcement that the division would sponsor programs on a 200-mile-radius radio network here in about two weeks in cooperation with the Ninth Tactical Air Command which is using the station part-time now.

According to Maj. Lloyd M. Barnett, Division Special Service officer, the new radio feature will include broadcasts of USO shows, GI talent programs, unit orchestras and bands, sports and world news, and items about division units.

Studio in Nurnberg

The main division studio will be located in the Nurnberg Opera house so that a greater variety of programs can be sent over the air. Radio technicians will have their control room in an inclosed room built in one of the theatre's boxes.

Signal Corps personnel from the 1st Division and 9th TAC have conferred on running lines from Nurnberg to Erlangen, where the radio station is located.

Radius Now 200-Miles

The station operates on the centimeter band at 950 kilocycles. Because it is now used only part-time, the station's radius of broadcasting is

Nurnberg Opera House Where Division Will Broadcast

Pictured above is the famous Opera House in Nurnberg where Division Special Service plans to install a broadcast studio for 1st Division programs in conjunction with the radio station in Erlangen. Despite the damaged appearance of the building's exterior, the inside was hardly marked by countless air raids during the war.

Rubble Moving Is 26th's Job; Trials Delayed

NURNBERG, Sept. 5—Three additional companies moved into Nurnberg this week to aid preparations for the trials of Europe's major war criminals, postponed until sometime in October because of the collapse of a section of the floor of the courtroom.

Clearing of Nurnberg's rubble has been turned over to the 26th Infantry, while the 1st Engr. Bn. is providing necessary help. Co. C. of the Engineers and one platoon of Co. B are busy operating earth augers and building prefabricated houses.

Attached Units Help

The three companies which joined the list of 1st Division units in Nurnberg are: Co. C of the 70th Tank Bn., attached to the 774th TD Bn.; Co. A of the same battalion, attached to the 610th TD Bn., and Co. A, 18th Infantry.

Meanwhile a four-power agreement signed in London by representatives of the United States, Great Britain, France and the Soviet Union defined the crimes to be tried by the court to include:

Violation of the peace by undertaking or participating in a war of aggression; criminal violation of the international laws of warfare, such as mistreating of civilian populations

After the cease-fire in Europe, Gibney worked as an artist for the American Traveler, a 1st Infantry Division newspaper, published in Anspach, Germany.

William L. Harbaugh — Army — WWII

William L. Harbaugh was one of the boys from George Street in Hagerstown who went off to war in 1943. Harbaugh, his two brothers — Martin "Jack" Harbaugh and Allen Harbaugh — and his uncle, Charles Russell, were among the estimated 44 servicemembers from that three-block expanse to serve in uniform during World War II.

Just as so many of his generation answered their country's call, Harbaugh entered the Army on March 3, 1943, crossing the ocean for training in England and landing with the 29th Infantry Division on Omaha Beach on D-Day. Debrah Siarkowski's father talked a lot about the good times he had in England as troops prepared for the invasion of continental Europe, but for decades he refused to say much about his time in combat in WWII.

"When people started telling war stories, he would get up and leave the room. I couldn't get him to talk about his experiences," Debrah said. "It wasn't until a French historian working on a book contacted him for an interview that he began to talk openly of the carnage he witnessed. Laurent LeFebvre got him to talk about what happened in those fateful days after the D-Day invasion. LeFebvre collected oral histories and published *They Were On Omaha Beach: The Story of D-Day Told by Veterans* (2004).

Only then did Debrah learn more details of her father's service with the famed 29th Infantry Division, which landed on the Normandy beachheads. The 29th Infantry Division, made up primarily of National Guardsmen from Maryland, Virginia, Delaware, New Jersey, Pennsylvania and the District of Columbia, faced devastating fire after a tortured beach landing. Remarkably, its soldiers seized the steep bluffs despite intense firepower raining down upon them. Once the bluffs were taken, they pressed on to the French city of St. Lo.

Harbaugh recalled the hours leading up to the invasion as excruciating. Because of the one-day delay in the planned invasion due to bad weather, he and his fellow soldiers hadn't been fed. "All they had had to eat was cream of celery soup," Debrah remembered her father saying. "They were all scared," and "nothing would stay down" in the violent pitch of the landing craft as they motored to their targeted point on the beach. Debrah remembered her father saying they kept playing Xavier Cugat's song *Brazil* over and over again on the loudspeakers all night long. To make matters worse, "they all had diarrhea."

Harbaugh, an ammo-bearer, was designated a machine gunner to replace one of the gunners who was killed immediately. A young solider "who idolized Dad" offered to be his ammo-bearer. As Harbaugh got out of the LCD, burdened by his heavy pack and weaponry, his .30-caliber machine gun sank into the mud in the waist-high water. By the time he pulled it free and called for his ammo-bearer to hurry off the craft, the boy had already been shot between the eyes. "He was killed even before he could get off the boat," Debrah said. "Out of the 100 men in his group, only seven were left alive."

What followed next was a blur of bullets and blood. In 1998, Harbaugh saw the acclaimed Steven Spielberg movie *Saving Private Ryan* — a depiction that "didn't come close" to approximating the confusion and horror of that day. "The actual beach scene was even worse than what they showed," Debrah remembered him saying.

Harbaugh survived the mine fields and withering fusillade in the capture of the Normandy beachhead, and fought on for two more days until he was wounded by "friendly" artillery fire in "Purple Heart Valley" near St. Lo. He was evacuated to a hospital in England, and following his recuperation, he rejoined the division in February 1945.

"Don't Forget Us, Love, Margret"

Many of the details are now lost to history, but sometime during the war Harbaugh met a German woman by the name of Margret Walters. Margret, a nurse, was sitting in a cafe with a group of other nurses the first time he saw her. According to Harbaugh's daughter, the young American soldier and the young German nurse very quickly fell in love.

Time and circumstance would intervene. Harbaugh was part of the push to liberate Europe from the yoke of the Third Reich. Finally, the interminable war in Europe came to an end with a surprising suddenness. Harbaugh, who had lost contact with Margret, was shipped back to the States with the daunting realization for him and his fellow soldiers that although the war in Europe was over, they would soon be fighting the Japanese.

Only after the fighting was over did he learn that Margret, who had corresponded with his sister, Betty, had had a child — a son she named Frank. But by this time — October 1946 — Harbaugh was already back home and the global war was over.

Thus began an intermittent correspondence, plagued by time and distance in the chaos of devastating war. Margret would write, telling him of the progress of their young son and gently reproving him for not writing. Harbaugh kept sending letters, and his mother and sister shipped care packages to Margret in Bremen. It was clear from the letters with German postmarks that the powdered milk, baby clothes, money and other items of particular value in war-ravaged Europe never reached her. Bureaucratic obstacles, a shattered economy, a flourishing black market, and American military policies discouraging relationships between German women and American soldiers, all conspired to keep them apart.

Still, she tried to maintain contact, sending Harbaugh a carefully compiled photo album with snapshots of their brief time together, and later, images of herself holding their infant son. On the back of one of the photos she wrote: “Don’t Forget Us, Love, Margret.”

In the plaintive, almost heart-breaking final letter Harbaugh received in late 1946, Margret muses that Harbaugh must surely have forgotten her or she would have heard from him. She concluded the letter sadly, conceding that it was probably best that she no longer try to contact him.

He never heard from her again.

Harbaugh shared this story with his future wife, Evelyn Sledge, before they married in 1946. Harbaugh had worked at Fairchild before the war and resumed his job when he was discharged. Evelyn was a real-life “Rosie the Riveter,” who had come from North Carolina to work in the aircraft industry as a welder during the war. They met, fell in love, and were married for 54 years.

Debrah did not learn the story of her father’s first child until she was 18 years old.

In deference to Debrah’s mother, no real effort was made to try to locate Margret during the years that William and Evelyn were raising their family in Hagerstown. But when Debrah’s mother died in 2000, her father asked his daughter to help him renew efforts to find his long-lost love and their now-grown son. Letters were written to German officials and Debrah engaged a German citizen to help locate Margret, but to no avail. She and her father and her aunt traveled to Europe in April 2005 and tried to find Margret when they were in Germany. The whereabouts of Harbaugh’s former love and son remained a lingering question to him until the day he died of cancer, one month after his return.

Whatever happened to Margaret and her son remains a mystery.

Inside cover of the photo album Margret Walters compiled in 1945 and sent to William L. Harbaugh, that included photos of their time together in Bremen, Germany. A later photograph is of Margret with their infant son, Frank — the son Harbaugh never knew.

Margret's brother, Peter Walters, shown in German uniform in the center of the collage, was a Luftwaffe pilot who managed to survive the war. Peter Walters gave some of these artifacts from Nazi Germany to Harbaugh, who was in love with Walters' sister. (Photographs and memorabilia courtesy of Debrah Siarkowski)

Local Heroes of George Street — WWII

A decade ago, William L. Harbaugh was given a photocopy of an undated article from a copy of a WWII-era local newspaper in which an unknown writer waxed eloquent about a little street in Hagerstown, which the article suggested, produced block-for-block more uniformed servicemembers than any other small town in the United States — a total of 44 fellows in uniform from the 17 households on the tiny street.

Harbaugh, his two brothers, Martin "Jack" Harbaugh and Allen Harbaugh, and uncle, Charles Russell, were among the George Street residents who served in the military in WWII.

FORTY-AND-FOUR AND MAYBE MORE

(Contributed)

There is a street in Hagerstown, one of our older streets, but one which has never had any particular mention, and which boasts no great industries and contains no pretentious mansions. Time was when there was a furniture factory and a laundry, but the furniture factory burned down and the laundry died abornin'.

It is a street where live a class of folk who are just about the average of the 139,000,000 people who go to making America what it is, the type that contributes quietly and without fanfare to the needs of the community and the nation, asking few questions but giving freely of their substance and themselves when the occasion requires or the call comes.

The street I have in mind — George Street — is three blocks long, bounded on the east by Foundry street and the Western Maryland Railroad, and on the west by Alexander street.

While George street may not be famous for its great industrialists, civic wizards or noted educators, there is one thing it can point to with pride — its Patriotism. And in singling out George street we have no thought of belittling or minimizing the patriotism of any other street or community. There may be some which have an even greater percentage of boys in the service. But today we think more particularly of the street in question, which has surely come into its own in this hour of national crisis.

In reading the lists published from time to time by the Draft Board I was attracted by the repetition of the name George street, George street, George street, and knowing it was but a short span I was curious to find where all the young men came from and how many there really were, so I took time out to walk the length of the street and count stars. I found that, counting the corner houses on the four streets that intersect, there are forty-four, and probably a few who have not displayed a star as yet for the one in the service. Various branches of the armed service are represented, and the banners carry anywhere from one to four stars.

As stated in the opening paragraph George Street is one of our older thoroughfares. The block from Foundry to High street was built first and its residents numbered some of the best known of our older West End families, such as Seigman, McKane, Loudenslager, Ranels, Baughman, Coffman, Cummings, Lewis, Miller and others.

At that time there was just one house beyond High street, the little log house, still standing, just west of Winter street. Later on "Petey" Zittle, George Warner and others built in the second block and at one time there was a three-room frame school house about midway of the block, now occupied as a residence. Houses then began to appear on the third block and now there are few vacant lots on the street with the exception of the one side from High to Wise street frequently occupied by carnivals and tent meetings. There used to be a rockbreak adjoining this stretch, and opposite it a baseball diamond on the commons where the kiddies learned their A, B, C's of the national pastime.

George street may well be proud of their boys in the service. And if the time ever comes when a roll-call of streets is made to determine where our fighting lads come from, the representative from George street can hold his head high when he responds to the roll.

I think this is an exceptional record. Forty-And-Four, and Maybe More of the nation's finest from such a limited area. May these boys cover themselves with glory, as they have brought credit to the city and the community which they call home.

(Newspaper contributed by William L. Harbaugh's daughter, Debrah Siarkowski, and his sister, Betty Spence, with George Street photograph contributed by Gregory Smith, son of Richard Smith)

In this photograph taken on George Street in 1945, Russell Sipes (the soldier third from the left, with his father standing in the background) was one of the George Street patriots.

The other men in uniform include (left to right) Herb Andrews, Jim Godlove and Richard Smith (next to Russell Sipes), who was serving as an MP in Hawaii at the time of Pearl Harbor and later participated in fighting in Guadalcanal.

Elmer O. "Whitey" Lewis — Army — WWII

This group of Hagerstown veterans gathered on Nov. 11, 1946, in front of the Pioneer Hook & Ladder Company on West Franklin Street. The two sailors kneeling in front as part of this Veterans Day photo are Gene Mowen and Elmer Hoover. Standing in back in Army uniform (left to right) are Woodrow "Woody" Decker, William "Bill" Baker and Elmer "Whitey" Lewis, whose parents lived at 45 1/2 W. Franklin St.

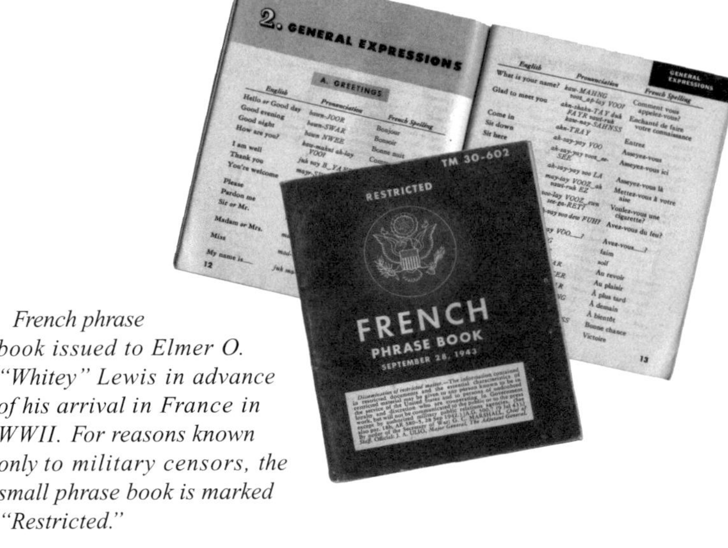

French phrase book issued to Elmer O. "Whitey" Lewis in advance of his arrival in France in WWII. For reasons known only to military censors, the small phrase book is marked "Restricted."

Lewis's dog tags and War Department Identification Card with a red cross on the reverse side signifying the bearer as "engaged exclusively in the removal, transportation and treatment of the wounded and sick ... and entitled to respect and protection from the enemies of the United States as required by Article 9 of the Geneva Convention of July 27, 1929."

In Europe, covenants protecting medics and other non-combatants were generally honored by the Nazis, but evidence suggests that Japanese forces specifically targeted medics, recognizing their effectiveness in saving the lives of wounded soldiers — soldiers who, once patched up, were likely to return to the battlefield.

Metal-shielded copy of the New Testament Lewis carried with him during his service in Europe in WWII. The small Bible with a plated steel cover, when carried in a soldier's chest pocket, was believed to protect the bearer from bullets to the heart.

Many servicemembers returned to the States with wartime mementos. While some battlefield souvenirs were not authorized, the Army set up a system whereby individual servicemembers were allowed to bring approved trophies home. This certificate permitted Lewis to mail home a .32-caliber Italian pistol. Lewis also brought back Nazi emblems recovered during his time in Europe.

(Photographs and memorabilia courtesy of Elaine Lewis, widow of Elmer D. "Whitey" Lewis)

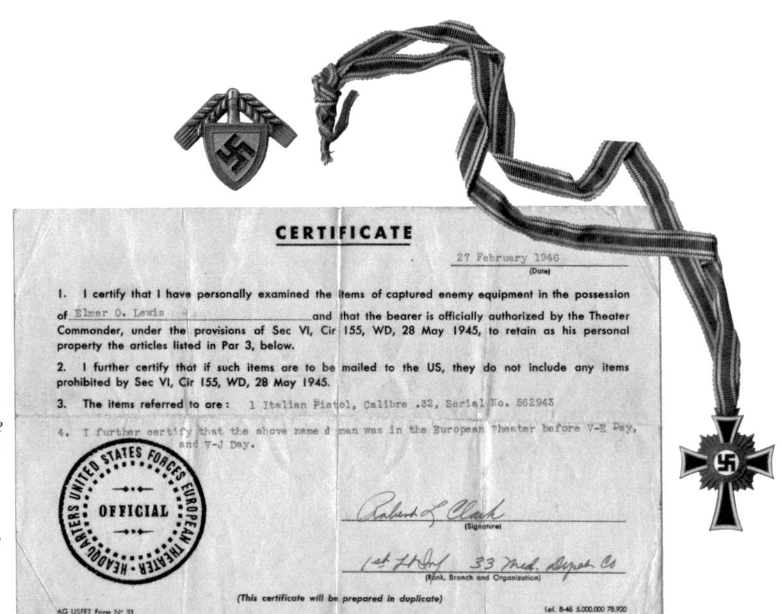

CERTIFICATE

27 February 1946
(Date)

1. I certify that I have personally examined the items of captured enemy equipment in the possession of Elmer O. Lewis and that the bearer is officially authorized by the Theater Commander, under the provisions of Sec VI, Cir 155, WD, 28 May 1945, to retain as his personal property the articles listed in Par 3, below.

2. I further certify that if such items are to be mailed to the US, they do not include any items prohibited by Sec VI, Cir 155, WD, 28 May 1945.

3. The items referred to are: 1 Italian Pistol, Calibre .32, Serial No. 862943

4. I further certify that the above named man was in the European Theater before V-E Day, and V-J Day.

HEADQUARTERS UNITED STATES FORCES EUROPEAN THEATER · OFFICIAL

Robert L. Clark
(Signature)

1st Lt Inf 33 Med. Depot Co
(Rank, Branch and Organization)

(This certificate will be prepared in duplicate)

AG USFET Form No 33

Oscar K. "Bud" Keller — Navy — WWII

*Oscar K. "Bud" Keller describes himself as "a young boy of 17" when he joined the Navy in 1943. He took only a gold cross and a Bible with him when he left his North Mulberry Street home for training in Sampson, New York, and then to Brooklyn, where he was assigned as an armed guard to the SS **William G. Fargo**. As a gunner, Keller made six trips across the Atlantic on the **Fargo** before being transferred to the SS **Samuel Adams**, where he participated in one of the largest convoys to cross the Atlantic during WWII. Of the 100 vessels that made the treacherous crossing, 35 were lost.*

Service on underarmed and undermanned merchant ships was often a dreaded assignment, given the constant danger of attack, and the fact that the ships were often the last to receive new equipment and weaponry.

*Keller made six trips between the United States and Europe on the **Samuel Adams** and served for a time at the Naval Training Center at Newport, Rhode Island, before being transferred to the aircraft carrier USS **Princeton**.*

The most memorable experiences of the war for Keller were the massive project of taking supplies to the troops in preparation for the D-Day landing, and the gift of a small gold band presented to him by a German prisoner of war as an expression of appreciation for the kindness Keller showed him.

Keller, who lived in Hagerstown until 2000, when he moved to North Carolina, said his wartime service taught him "to appreciate each day."

(Photograph courtesy of Oscar K. "Bud" Keller)

Eugene P. Snyder — Army Air Corps — WWII

Eugene P. Snyder graduated from Hancock College of Aeronautics, Santa Maria, California, and enlisted in the Army Air Corps in 1942. In short order, he was flying P-38s with the Eighth Air Force in Europe.

From an air base at Mount Farm, England, 1st Lt. Eugene P. Snyder was sent on air reconnaissance missions over enemy territory. The photographic images Snyder obtained were used to pinpoint targets and evaluate the effectiveness of bombing raids. Snyder is shown here in January 1944 following one of his missions over Germany.

Snyder, who had a picture of his wife, Marion, painted on the nose of his plane, sent letters home telling her as much as he was allowed to say about his missions.

On Nov. 29, 1943, he wrote: "I'm behind on my writing again. Was forced down on the coast on my way back from a mission. I spent three days there waiting for repairs on my plane. Finally made it back here this afternoon. I'm getting damn tired of being chased around France by someone who is trying to shoot hell out of me."

Five months later, Snyder was seriously injured in a plane crash. On April 19, 1944, his P-38 was hit by anti-aircraft fire over Belgium and he coaxed the plane to a crash-landing in England. Snyder's back was broken in two places and his jaw was broken in six places.

Snyder recovered from his injuries and went on to raise a family in Hagerstown. His wife, Marion, is shown with their children, Tommy, 5 (left), Donna, 8 (right), and Suzie, 3, (center) in this 1951 photo.

Snyder was safety director and personnel manager at Marquette Cement Co. when he retired in 1977.

"I'm getting damn tired of being chased around France by someone who is trying to shoot hell out of me."

Richard P. "Dick" Lynch — Navy — WWII

Richard P. "Dick" Lynch in seaman's cap and his Navy dog tags.

Photo of Lynch's ship — Landing Craft Support (L)(3)-37 — pulling out of Portland, Oregon. The ship, produced by Albina Engine & Machine Works and Commercial Iron Works in Portland, was launched on Sept. 23, 1944. The support craft was damaged beyond repair at Okinawa and was destroyed March 7, 1946, at the Naval Repair Base on Manicani Island in the Philippines.

Fresh-faced crew of the Landing Craft Support (L)(3)-37 in 1945 on Manicani Island in the Philippines. An account of the history of a sister ship, the (L)(3)-35, reported that the average age of its crew of 66 men and 6 officers was younger than 20. Lynch's crew appears to be just as young.

Betty Lynch, who attended several reunions of the landing ship crew before her husband's death on July 10, 2003, is amazed how 75 men could serve on such a small vessel. She recalled with awe the stories the former sailors would share when they gathered together. "Can't imagine what they went through ... the good times and the bad times."

Additional information about Landing Support Craft is available at www.navysource.org.

On a post card of famed Diamond Head, Lynch writes to his mother's sister, Mrs. Edna Davies of Corbett Street in Hagerstown, that he was having a "fine time" in Hawaii. "They do have some pretty scenery here, though the girls aren't much to look at though," he wrote.

R. P. Lynch F2c
U.S.S. LCS(L) 39
% Fleet Post Office
San Francisco, Calif.

12-5-44

Dear Edna & all,
Having a fine time. Wish you were in my place. They do have some pretty scenery over here, though the girls aren't much to look at though.
Write again soon. Richard

Mrs. Edna V. Davis
1000 Corbett Street
Hagerstown
Maryland

(Photographs and memorabilia courtesy of Betty Lynch, widow of Richard P. "Dick" Lynch)

Lynch in his Navy uniform stands next to his mother, in this photo taken during WWII. Lynch was an only child and his mother, Hilda Spielman Lynch and father, Hillary Lynch, were "very proud" of their son, according to Betty Lynch.

January 4, 1946
Manicani Island.
4:30 A.M.

Dear Thelma and Pres,

I received your letter of Dec 19 yesterday and really enjoyed hearing from you. The picture you sent me of the snowfall in Buffalo has gone all over the ship and the fellows really enjoyed it. Practically all of us had heard about it but that was the first picture we had of it. Mother and Dad sent me the same picture out of the Daily Mail but it was slightly smaller.

I'm sure glad that Ralph is out and I hope he was able to spend Christmas at home. That would make the season complete for him. Maybe sometime I will get home too.

I'm writing this while on watch 4-8 AM and about 8:30 we are going to move our gear up to the barracks. This is a helluva morning to be moving because it is raining but I hope by then it will be all rained out. Last night we had

Lynch wrote a letter to his aunt and uncle, Thelma and Pres Jacobs of Hagerstown, at 4:30 a.m. January 4, 1946, while he was on a miserable rainy night watch. In the letter he describes preparations for the crew's departure from the ship and a dreaded move to shore the next day. Lynch's ship had been so heavily damaged in the fighting for Okinawa that it was beyond repair. "It will seem funny to live in a barracks after being aboard ship for so long. On here we have everything real close at hand and on the base things are scattered from here to China ... One thing we will miss will be our hot water. Wash water and drinking water is all the same temperature, piss warm."

Roderick C. Reed — Army Air Forces — WWII

Roderick C. Reed, a 1933 graduate of Hagerstown High School, had enlisted in the Army Air Corps in Baltimore in 1940, so he was already in uniform and stationed at MacDill Field, Tampa, Florida, when the Japanese attacked Pearl Harbor on Dec. 7, 1941.

He had completed basic training at Langley Field, in Virginia, before he was assigned to the 21st Reconnaissance Squadron at MacDill. Reed, who was detailed to Gander, Newfoundland, was part of the "rehearsal" squadron "of big planes that went to Newfoundland in the summer of 1941," according to the April 1942 *New Yorker* magazine article which profiled the crew of the "Dixie Demo Jr." — one of the first of the American B-17 crews to arrive in England in the early days of U.S. involvement in the war.

In due course, Tech Sgt. Reed was stationed in Great Britain as a maintenance crew chief. He flew his first combat mission over France on Aug. 13, 1942. After 12 of these flights, all maintenance personnel were grounded because of their technical expertise. As the *New Yorker* reported in its profile: "Reed used to fly in B-17's, but was grounded, like most of the best noncommissioned engineers; such men were considered more valuable on maintenance work."

While stationed in Bishra, Tunisia, in North Africa, in 1943, Reed provided critical mission support to the Allied effort to push back Italian and German forces in his role as line chief for the 414th Bomb Squadron, 97th Group. During his time there, Reed shared a tent for approximately two weeks with famed WWII correspondent Ernie Pyle. Pyle traveled to various combat theaters. His folksy writing style and realistic portrayal of the Americans on the battle front, made him a beloved figure to men and women in the military. According to Reed's son, Jeffrey, Pyle "used Dad's typewriter" to produce his chronicle of the war in Tunisia — sections that were included in Pyle's acclaimed 1943 book ***Here is Your War***. Contained in the family's copy of the book are the loose-leaf pages with corresponding carbons of sections Pyle worked on while he stayed with Reed — original drafts that made their way into the published book.

In December 1943, Reed received a battlefield commission and became the 341st Bomb Squadron maintenance officer. Shortly thereafter, he joined the 15th Air Force in Italy, commanded by Gen. Nathan Twining, who, a decade later, was chief of staff of the armed forces. By the time the war was over, Reed had supervised operations of aircraft maintenance and repair units, serving overseas for two years with the 8th, 12th and 15th Air Forces. Upon his return to the United States, he was a production line maintenance officer for B-17 aircraft at Sebring Field in Florida.

Reed was released from service in September 1945, and worked as a liaison engineer at Fairchild Aircraft. A year and a half later, though, he was back on active duty at Reading, Pennsylvania, as the maintenance officer for the 12th Fighter Wing. In July 1949, he resigned from the service, and once again was employed by Fairchild, this time in the service division.

Reed, wearing a life jacket, stands proudly in front of the nose of a B-17 bomber in Tunisia in 1943 — the stenciled bombs alongside the nose reflecting the number of bombing missions the aircraft completed.

Reed's "Fire From the Clouds" shoulder insignia represents the devastation rained down by B-17 bombers.

(Photographs and memorabilia courtesy of Jeffrey and Douglass Reed, sons of Roderick C. Reed)

The immediacy and poignancy of a mother's letter to her son comes across in a letter written to Roderick C. Reed by his mother, Emma Craig Reed, on Dec. 8, 1941. Reed was a private 1st class, assigned to MacDill Field, in Tampa, Florida, when the Japanese attacked Pearl Harbor.

Dear Son, I don't know if I can write you a sensible letter to-night, or not. I intended to do a few notes yesterday afternoon, and our letter too; but I turned the radio on when I was looking at the paper a minute, first — and the news came on about the Jap's attack —well, I have been like in a daze, yet. It all comes back when Uncle Bill & Harold had to go in the other war — you were a little white-haired youngster playing around and I never thought that for a minute I'd see you in a return war ...

A number of boys from here were in Hagerstown and left at once yesterday when the radio call was made — the Fogle boy was home and left for Norfolk at once, his mother told Daddy at church last night. The trucks of soldiers from S. Carolina have been going thru all day & the paper says, to-morrow also.

She closes the letter with "My love & kisses," and shares these parting thoughts:

I'll be waiting for some word from you, if it only has your name & postmark on. Remember that this all will clear away, and we must keep faith in our living ... Good-night, dear, and I'm going with you every minute.

In a stronger hand, at the bottom of the last page, Reed's father, Donald C. Reed, penned:

"Give a good account of yourself when you get a crack at the Japs. Sorry I can not be with you. Dad."

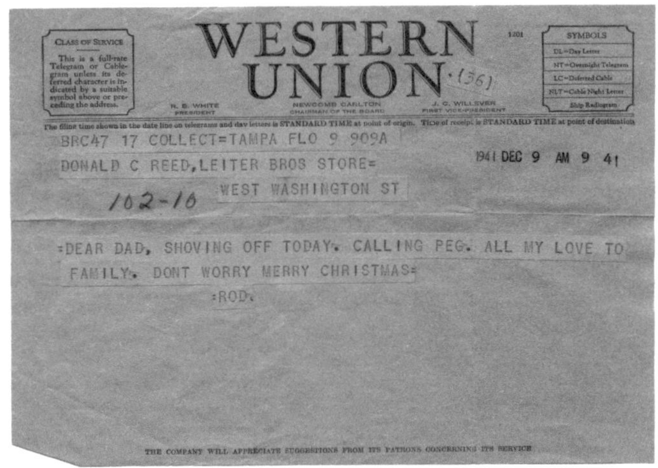

WESTERN UNION

BRC47 17 COLLECT=TAMPA FLO 9 909A

1941 DEC 9 AM 9 41

DONALD C REED,LEITER BROS STORE=

102-16 WEST WASHINGTON ST

=DEAR DAD, SHOVING OFF TODAY. CALLING PEG. ALL MY LOVE TO FAMILY. DONT WORRY MERRY CHRISTMAS=

=ROD.

Telegram Reed sent to his parents in the days after the Japanese attack on Pearl Harbor. He wishes his parents a Merry Christmas even though the telegram was sent Dec. 9, reflecting the real sense that Reed and others already in uniform would not be stateside for very long.

Reed's roommate in Tunisia in 1943 turned out to be none other than famed war correspondent Ernie Pyle. Some of the copy that would be included in Pyle's 1943 book, ***Here is Your War****, was typed on Reed's typewriter.*

Reed carried a small New Testament with him and kept a diary during his time in uniform during WWII. The photo of Reed in a heart-shaped frame on the back of a small mirror was something his wife, Frances, kept close while he was away at war.

Reed gave the small New Testament to his Marine Corps son, Douglass C. Reed, who would take this treasured token with him to another war more than two decades later — this one in Vietnam.

Paul D. Bailey — Army — WWII

Paul D. Bailey hadn't seen much of the world when he enlisted in the Army on May 29, 1944. As an 18-year-old country boy from Clarksville, Maryland, Bailey says traveling and seeing other countries made a big impression on him. In fact, he said, "I grew up during those two years between 18 and 20."

After completing basic training, he joined the 71st Division. An infantryman, he was trained in use of the Browning automatic rifle which he is holding in the photo at left taken in Austria after World War II. He transferred to the 9th Infantry occupation forces at war's end because he didn't have enough points to be sent home. Bailey guarded German POWs at Camp Sheridan, taking truckloads of prisoners out to cut wood for the camp.

His most memorable experience in Austria was liberating the Gurskirchen Lager, Mauthausen-Gusen concentration camp in May 1945. The camp was the last to be liberated.

Bailey went into combat in Biche, France, with the Seventh Army, and later was transferred to General Patton's Third Army. "We fought our way across Germany and were in Austria at war's end," he said. While overseas, he went on leave for 10 days in December 1945 to Nice, France. Bailey is pictured at right, among the palm trees along the French Riviera. He said enlisted men went to Nice, officers went to Cannes. He was discharged on June 6, 1946.

SOLDIER'S INDIVIDUAL PAY RECORD

Bailey, Paul D Pfc T/5

W. D., A. G. O. Form No. 28
March 26, 1942

SOLDIER'S INDIVIDUAL PAY RECORD

IMPORTANT

No payments to you will be made without this pay record if you are separated from your organization. Retain on your person at all times.

No changes or alterations will be made in this record other than as provided in instructions on page 8.

If this pay record is lost, report at once to your organization commander.

If this pay record is found and owner cannot be located, drop in U. S. mail—without postage.

(1)

W. D., A. G. O. Form No. 28
March 26, 1942

16—28144-1

Bailey worked in the laundry on the ship going overseas, and worked in the ship's kitchen on the voyage home.

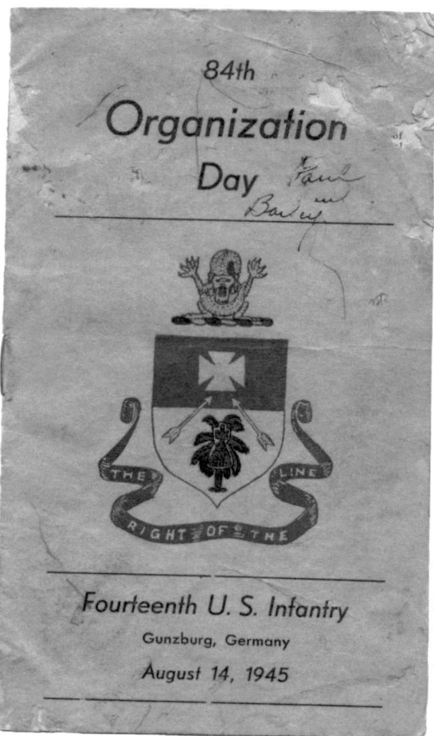

84th
Organization
Day

Fourteenth U. S. Infantry
Gunzburg, Germany
August 14, 1945

84th Organization Day, Fourteenth U.S. Infantry, Gunzburg, Germany, August 14, 1945. Bailey received the 14th Infantry Regiment Pin which dates back to the regiment's service during the Boxer Rebellion in China.

(Photographs and memorabilia courtesy of Paul D. Bailey)

Joseph Charles Finfrock — Marine Corps — WWII

NABISCO BRANDS RETIREES
PITTSBURGH DIVISION

Just as the September,1995 Nabisco Brands Pittsburgh Division Retirees Newsletter was being stuffed in the envelopes and sent off to you, the Editor got a very pleasant surprise from Barbara Reeder, former Office Clerk in Williamsport, MD Branch. She sent me a section of the August 27, 1995 edition of the Hagerstown, MD Herold Mail Newspaper. It honored the local World War II veterans on the 50th Anniversary of the ending of the WAR TO END ALL WARS.

The newspaper printed the names of more than 750 area men and women who served in World War II, and interviewed several people who represent all these veterans, and served in the Pacific Theater of War. One of these was our own Joe Finfrock, who also served Nabisco as a Sales Rep for 40 years. Here is his story:

World War II
Joseph Finfrock

Joseph Finfrock enlisted in the Marine Corps seven days after Pearl Harbor. He was 19, living in Funkstown and working at M.P. Moller Organ Inc. in Hagerstown.

He participated in the invasion of the Solomon Islands on Aug. 7, 1942. His outfit took Tulagi in three days then joined the fight for Guadalcanal. The battle lasted until February 1943 and added the name of the island to history books.

The Navy, outnumbered by a superior Japanese fleet, dropped the Marines on the island and pulled out.

Finfrock was wounded twice. The second time he was sent to recover in a New Zealand hospital.

He was reassigned to the Fifth Marine Division for landings on Cape Gloucester and New Guinea. Later he was at Peleliu, site of another bloody Marine fight.

"How I got out alive I'll never know," Finfrock said. "I put a lot of it out of my mind. I never liked remembering it," he said in true Marine fashion. "I have no regrets and I ask for nothing."

Finfrock was sent home for Christmas in 1944 after 31 months in combat. He was on leave in Fall River, Mass., when the Japanese surrendered.

Finfrock met his future wife at a party on the night of V-J Day.

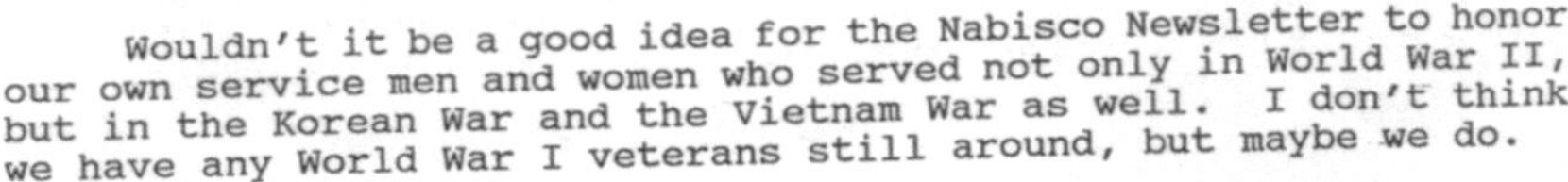

Wouldn't it be a good idea for the Nabisco Newsletter to honor our own service men and women who served not only in World War II, but in the Korean War and the Vietnam War as well. I don't think we have any World War I veterans still around, but maybe we do.

(Photograph and newsletter courtesy of Barbara Reeder, friend and former co-worker of Joseph Charles Finfrock)

Joseph Charles Finfrock, who was originally from Funkstown, served 31 months in combat in the Pacific in WWII. The first time was with the 1st Marine Raider Battalion from February 1942 until November 1942 at Guadalcanal where he was wounded twice. The second time was with the 2nd Battalion, 5th Marines from November 1942 until December 1944, participating in combat at Cape Gloucester, New Guinea and the Battle of Peleliu, in the Palau Islands. That battle had the highest casualty rate of any amphibious invasion in terms of men and materiel in the entire war in the Pacific.

Finfrock completed his Marine Corps service at the Naval War College in Newport, Rhode Island, assigned as an aide to Vice Admiral William S. Pye, president of the college.

Finfrock, who worked as a sales representative for 40 years for the Pittsburgh Division of Nabisco Brands, in Martinsburg, West Virginia, was featured in this copy of a 1995 regional newsletter for Nabisco retirees. The feature, reprinted from ***The Herald-Mail****, prompted a series of similar articles in subsequent newsletters highlighting the wartime service of former employees in the wake of the 50th anniversary of the end of WWII. Renewed interest in the experiences of WWII veterans has continued to this day, fueled in part by the 1998 publication of NBC news anchor Tom Brokaw's* ***The Greatest Generation****.*

William K. Kendall — Army Air Corps — WWII

William K. Kendall of Smithsburg told Army officials he wanted to be a cook, but after basic training at Fort Meade, Maryland, he was sent for armament training at Buckley Field and Lowery Field in Colorado. The Army then sent him to the Tyndall Field Aerial Gunnery School in Panama City, Florida, before shipping him overseas.

In April 1944, William K. Kendall got an all-expense-paid trip to Scotland on the luxury liner *Queen Mary*. But in April 1944, when Kendall and the 16,000 other recruits boarded the ship in New York City, their accommodations were anything but luxurious. "We were literally packed in the ship like sardines in hanging bunks," Kendall wrote in a short account of his wartime service. His assigned bunk was in the *Queen Mary's* drained swimming pool, located on a lower deck below sea level.

For five long days on the unaccompanied cruise, the uniformed passengers tried not to think about the danger of German U-boats trolling the Atlantic for unprotected targets or complain about the twice-daily meals consisting mostly of beans and rice.

After departing the ship in Scotland, Kendall boarded a train to Little Walden in Essex, England, to serve as a gunner's mate with the 409th Bombardment Group, 641st Squadron. His first mission was on May 19, 1944, in an A-20 Havoc searching the skies for unfriendly aircraft from his turret. The A-20 was a light bomber and night-flyer designed for high-altitude bombing. The squadron's mission, as part of the Ninth Air Force, was to bomb enemy installations, bridges, railroads and ammunition dumps to disrupt the German offensive as a prelude to the D-Day invasion of June 6, 1944.

During the invasion, Kendall and his crew provided aerial support high above the soldiers storming the beaches of Normandy. Kendall's squadron flew additional missions over Corbeil and Lyon, France, following the invasion. Of the 65 missions Kendall flew with the 409th, the most harrowing was a bomb run from England over a target in Thury Harcourt, France, when both engines on their A-20 Havoc quit. He described in detail the potentially fatal mission:

> *In a maneuver to restart the plane's engines, [Lt.] Deane switched from our bomb bay tanks to the main fuel tanks and hit the booster pumps. Our engines started and we dropped our bombs.*
>
> *Deane thought we would run out of fuel and not make it back to England, so he looked for a place to land. It was pitch dark, and we knew we were still over enemy territory from observing flashes of fire from the ground. We were flying pretty low.*
>
> *After checking his maps, Deane headed northwest and spotted an airfield with British Beauforts [bombers]. We thought we were in the clear, and Deane entered a pattern to land at the British airstrip.*
>
> *Then myself and our other gunner noticed we were being fired on by small arms fire. I quickly yelled over the intercom to Deane, and he pulled up, readjusted his pattern and we landed safely.*

There was no rest for the weary flyboys though:

> *The British put us up in a tent for the night. We didn't get any sleep as the British artillery gun located on the other side of the wall by our tent fired into the German lines, and the Germans strafed the airfield and blew up an ammunition dump that night. We were glad to fly out the next morning back to base in Little Walden.*

An emergency landing made the crew's 50th mission memorable. They knew they were in trouble when the landing gear on their A-26 Invader wouldn't pull up just after takeoff. They continued their bombing run anyway through heavy cloud cover and headed to their target — the Ahr River bridge, just north of Bonn, Germany. Surrounded by flak [anti-aircraft fire] they made three passes over the bridge before releasing their bombs. "Returning to base, Lt. Deane got lost in the 'soup' (clouds) and then discovered he had fuel line trouble. Gas was pouring in the gunner's section," Kendall wrote.

The pilot got a bearing over an emergency field, but the flares could not be lit because of the danger of setting the plane on fire. To make matters worse, the plane lost its hydraulic pressure and had no brakes. The pilot was able to "cut the switches" and set the plane down where it rolled on, jumped over a railroad track and crash-landed on a highway. Its landing gear buckled underneath the plane. According to Kendall, the rough landing occurred on the pilot's birthday. "Deane said it was the best birthday present he ever had getting his crew back safe."

Kendall's last mission was on March 23, 1945, and by his own account, he "returned home to Smithsburg and married his sweetheart Doris Wiles on Aug. 14, 1946." He was honored on Feb. 21, 2002, with a "Thank You America" diploma from the French government in a ceremony and reception at the French embassy in Washington, D.C. Kendall's name, along with those of millions of other veterans, is included in the National World War II Memorial's registry in the nation's capital.

Staff Sgt. Kendall was a turret gunner on the A-20 Havoc and A-26 Invader bombers in Europe during WWII. The high-altitude bombers targeted key military installations and transportation sites in an effort to disrupt the enemy before and after the D-Day invasion. A-20s were light bombers adept at high-altitude flying. The A-26 Invaders were introduced in Europe in November of 1944 and were the fastest bombers used in WWII.

Kendall (left) poses with combat crew members of the 409th Bomb Group (L) on March 28, 1944. Kendall was a turret gunner on both the A-20 Douglas Havoc and the A-26s and participated in 65 missions over continental Europe during WWII. Members of his crew included the pilot Lt. William W. Deane (center) and J. Calvin Jones, engineer gunner (right).

(Photographs courtesy of Mrs. William K. Kendall, widow of William Kendall)

Douglas P. Weaver Jr. — Navy — WWII

Douglas P. Weaver Jr. stood on Virginia Avenue in Hagerstown in front of a billboard promoting Fairchild Aircraft. He was home on leave from the Navy, which he joined in July 1943, one year shy of completing high school. After basic training and gunnery practice, where he "fired everything from small arms to large surface guns," he was assigned as a Naval Armed Guard on the merchant ship SS *Jose Bonifacio*.

In his "World War II Memoirs," Weaver wrote: "It was a liberty cargo ship and looked so very big to me. The longshoremen loaded all sorts of ammunition in the holds and six P-51 fighters and a tugboat on the deck. We set sail from New York and headed to the Florida Keys to pick up a convoy."

The convoy, consisting of 180 Merchant Marine ships and a large Naval escort, crossed the Atlantic without incident until rough weather caused it to be split up. The sailors "saw many floating mines and had to be careful, and one tanker was sunk by an enemy sub."

After spending Christmas 1943 in Port Said, Egypt, Weaver wrote, "On the return trip we hit a terrible storm in the North Atlantic where once again the convoy was split up. The empty ships pitched over as much as 30 degrees in the rough seas and I thought that they would never roll back upright. After two days, the weather broke and the convoy came back together."

Learning of the death of his brother Robert, Weaver was given two weeks' leave before being assigned to the tanker SS *Sachen*, where he was promoted to petty officer 3rd class and "assigned to a 5 inch .38 mm surface and anti-aircraft gun. I really liked that gun!" With a crew of 20, the ship made numerous trips across the Atlantic to England, Ireland and France, carrying "only aviation fuel and a lot of it."

Weaver's assignments took him to such diverse places as Cuba, the port of Marseilles, Iran, India, Australia, Panama and Aruba, and then through a hurricane to France, when "the storm took all but one lifeboat and two rafts off the ship." But it was after his return to New York that he experienced "the worst trip I ever made!" This trip was by train, to Oakland, California. "It was like cattle cars," he wrote.

After six weeks in Oakland, he was put on a troopship for Okinawa and "arrived just in time for the worst typhoon ever that flattened the island." Six months later he was shipped home on a carrier and discharged in February 1946.

"In conclusion," Weaver wrote, "I traveled 50,000 miles on one trip that took me around the world. I landed on six continents: North America, South America, Europe, Asia, Africa and Australia."

(Photographs and memorabilia courtesy of Douglas P. Weaver Jr.)

Douglas P. Weaver Jr. (front, second from right) and fellow sailors in Port Said, Egypt, at Christmas 1943. Weaver returned to Egypt at Easter 1944, "where I had the opportunity to see the pyramids. I turned down the chance and should have had my butt kicked!"

Typhoon Louise, which struck Okinawa just as Weaver was arriving on Oct. 9, 1945, was "the worst typhoon ever that flattened the island," he wrote. "I lost all my gear except for what I had on my back."

A Christmas card that Weaver sent home to his brother Bill and his cousin Stan in December 1945. The following Christmas, Weaver would be out of the Navy and home in Hagerstown.

Weaver saved this notice making clear that the U.S. Naval Armed Guard and the Merchant Marine are not the same thing. He served as an armed guard on mechant marine vessels.

US Naval Armed Guard and WWII Merchant Marine

We were NOT guards. We WERE US Navy Gun Crews consisting of Gunners, Coxswains and Boatswains, Radiomen, Signalmen, an occasional Pharmacist, and toward the end of the war a few radarmen serving at sea on Merchant Ships. The Merchant Marine ran the ships and we provided gunnery protection and communications services. Our crews were small, our hearts were large. The Merchant Crew took the same risks and many of them had been rejected by the military services or requested to stay in the Merchant Marine where they were badly needed.

Roscoe D. Corderman — Army — WWII

As a railway engineer with three dependents, Roscoe D. Corderman had the option of a military deferment. But in early 1945, he enlisted and was sent to the Philippine Islands.

"Being a married man with two children (a daughter 6 years old and a son only 4), the time away from them was a mental strain ... I missed my family," he said.

On leave before his overseas assignment, Corderman (right) chatted with Ann Knodle, the daughter of a neighbor.

Late in the war, Corderman enjoyed a brief furlough to visit his family. As soon as he reached his California posting, however, he had orders for an emergency leave back home. His son had fallen out of the back of a moving car and received serious head injuries. Corderman took the next train home. Fortunately, his son recovered and since the war was winding down, the Army assigned Corderman to a railroad battalion in Virginia until his discharge on June 30, 1946.

(Photographs courtesy of Roscoe D. Corderman)

Army cooks enlisted the help of Filipino personnel to perform KP [Kitchen Patrol] duties in the preparation of the hundreds of meals served each day. The most memorable, and possibly the most frightening times for Corderman, were the 31-day troopship ride on the SS ***Mexico*** *from Louisiana to Manila Bay and the train ride from Manila Bay to Clark Field. Troops were crowded onto gondola train cars with canvas roofs, traveling by night without lights because of the danger of raids by concealed Japanese fighters.*

In a light-hearted moment in the waning days of WWII, Corderman poses with a statue on Manila Boulevard a few blocks from his barracks that was miraculously undamaged in the barrage that liberated Manila.

Paul D. Koontz — Army — WWII

Army Tech Sgt. Roscoe Corderman was happily working as an engineer on the Western Maryland Railway when he volunteered for military service in January 1945 and became a cook. Corderman (standing second from left) was one of several company cooks assigned to the 35th Transportation Corps Service Group in Manila during WWII.

Corderman's "Home Sweet Home" away from home in 1945 was this "air-conditioned" tent in humid Manila.

Evidence of damage inflicted on buildings on Manila Boulevard near Corderman's barracks by U.S. artillery and aircraft fire that forced out occupying Japanese troops.

Capture of the Philippines was an essential part of Japan's plans for dominance in Asia. The island was bombed the day following Pearl Harbor and Japanese forces landed on the Bataan peninsula on Dec. 9, 1941.

Allied forces were compelled to surrender on May 8, 1942, and remaining personnel and citizens of Allied nations were imprisoned. The campaign to liberate the Philippines began on Oct. 20, 1944, with the largest armada of ships in the Pacific War. More than 200,000 soldiers of the 6th Army began the arduous job of liberating the Philippines from Japanese control.

Cpl. Paul D. Koontz of Hagerstown served three years in the Army during WWII, spending the bulk of his service time in Africa and Italy. Inducted on Nov. 11, 1942, he served as a military policeman, guarding military supplies going to the front lines and later guarding Italian prisoners of war en route from Africa to Italy. Only four months of his service time was stateside, all the rest was served overseas.

Pictured here in front of the tent that served as his home in Casablanca, Koontz said the most valuable item he took with him when he was inducted into the Army was his New Testament. His most memorable experience, he said, was "coming home." He was discharged on Nov. 30, 1945. Although he was not involved in any major battles in the European-African-Middle Eastern Campaign, he nonetheless said, "I learned a lot in the military." The patch pictured is the Allied Forces insignia.

(Photos courtesy of Paul D. Koontz)

Paul C. Green — Army — WWII

Three of the four sons of Mr. and Mrs. Perry Green of Boonsboro served in WWII — Paul (shown at left), Russell and Arvine. All survived the war. Paul and Russell continued on in the Army Reserve and Arvine became a career serviceman.

Paul, after basic training at Camp Blanding, Florida, was sent to France in 1944 as an infantryman with Company D, 310th Infantry, 78th Lightning Division, 1st MG [machine gun] Platoon. He fought in Belgium and Germany at Remagen Bridge and the Battle of the Bulge, and when Germany surrendered he was in Wuppertal, approximately 100 miles from Berlin. Spreading out into small "cow towns," he and his comrades manned checkpoints set up to catch fleeing German storm troopers.

"They'd steal clothes off clothes lines" to disguise themselves, Green said, "but we'd catch them. I took 50 prisoners with a Colt .45, and I couldn't hit the broad side of a barn with it."

He then served with the Occupation forces in the American sector of divided Berlin, where this photo of him was taken at the gate to the newly-established quarters. When his division was deactivated, he was transferred to the 3rd Infantry Division, returned home in July 1946, and served in the reserves for three years.

Paul Green served under Gen. George S. Patton, and remembers the experience well. "I saw him, and he saw me," Green said. "He gave me a good chewing-out because I didn't salute him. He got out of his jeep and he had a few choice words for me. I pointed out to him that his jeep jockey hadn't uncovered his plate, and then he went after the jeep jockey. A while later, when he was awarding Presidential Unit Citations and came down the line to me, he recognized me. He said, 'You were right.' That was his form of apology."

(Photos courtesy of Clara Green, wife of Paul Green)

Arvine A. Green — Army Air Corps — WWII

A graduate of Boonsboro High School, Arvine A. Green joined the Army in 1936 and became a member of the Army Air Corps, where he was a turret gunner on a B-17 bomber. He was a career serviceman, staying on when the Army Air Forces became the Air Force in 1947 and retiring from the service in 1960, after 22 years of active duty during two major wars.

Russell L. Green — Army — WWII

Russell L. Green joined the Army in 1937 and became a medical corpsman. During WWII, he served in England and France. One time in France he was working in a field hospital not far from where his brother Paul was fighting. Neither brother knew the other was close by, however. "If I'd been wounded I'd have probably ended up being cared for by him," Paul said. Russell stayed on in the reserves after WWII ended. He was called back into service when war broke out in Korea and served stateside rather than being sent to the front.

Francis "Skunk" Knight — Navy — WWII

Francis "Skunk" Knight of Dargan served in the Navy during WWII and saw action in the Pacific as a crewman aboard Landing Craft, Infantry (Large) 1021. He participated in landing operations on enemy territory at Nasugbu, Luzon; Iloilo, Panay; and the initial landing operation against the Japanese at Pulupandan, Negros, all in the Philippine Islands.

Seaman Knight got his nickname of "Skunk" when he picked one up and was given a smelly initiation by the animal. The smell left, but the nickname stuck. He was drafted in January 1944 after working four years at Victor Products in Hagerstown. He completed basic training at the Great Lakes Naval Training Station in Illinois, and took additional training at the Amphibious Training Station at Solomons, Maryland.

Seaman Knight often remarked that he found it amusing that he served on a ship when he couldn't swim a stroke. He crossed the Equator on Aug. 24, 1944, and like seamen before him, was initiated into the Royal Domain of Neptunus Rex and qualified as a "trusty shellback." He is pictured here aboard his landing craft in April 1944. He is the second from the left in the top row in the group photo.

After his discharge on Dec. 17, 1945, he returned to his job at Victor Products. When that plant shut down, he went to work at Pangborn Corporation until his retirement. He died on March 18, 1999.

(Photos courtesy of Whylmenia Knight, widow of Francis Knight)

Glenn W. Andrews — Army Air Forces — WWII

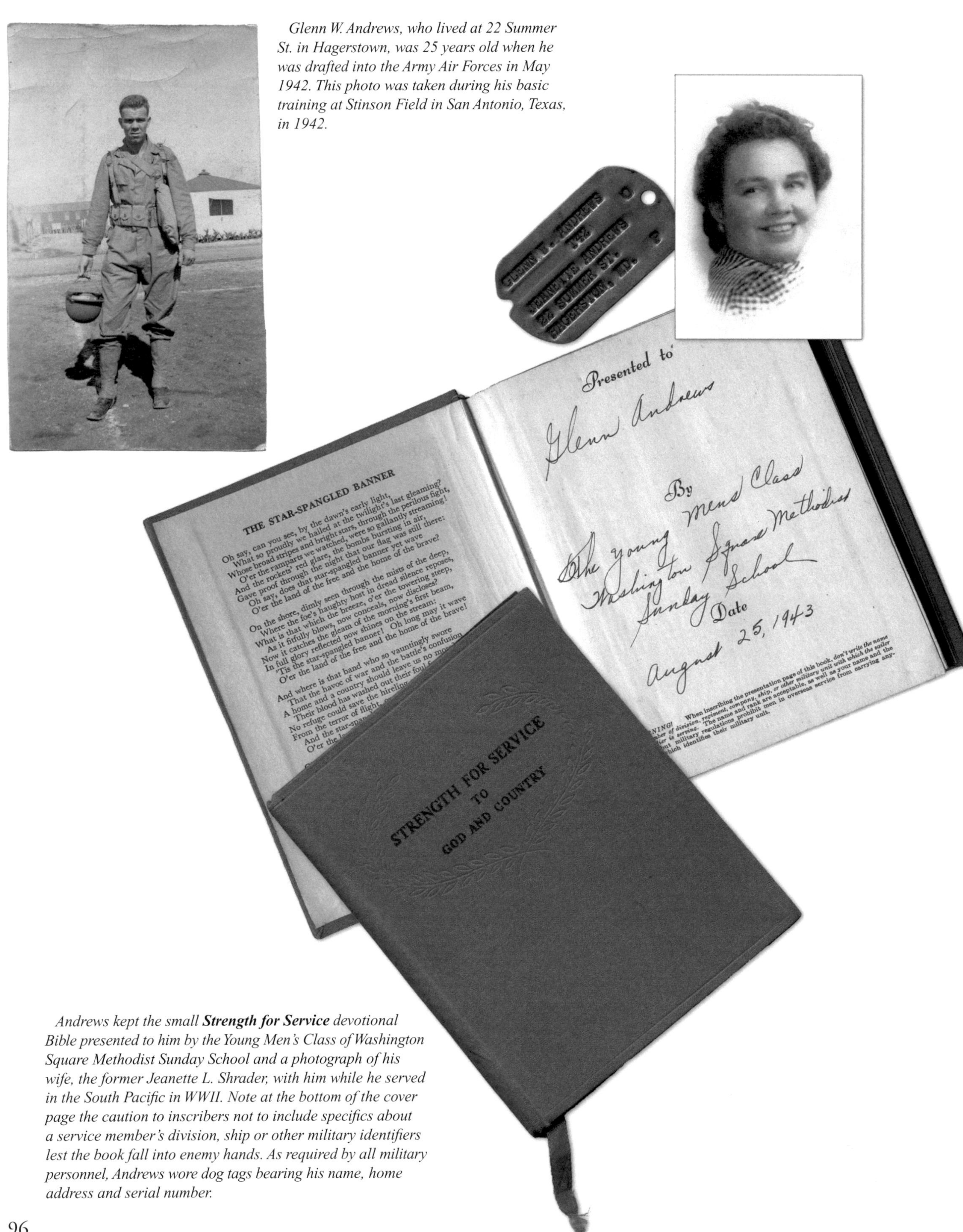

Glenn W. Andrews, who lived at 22 Summer St. in Hagerstown, was 25 years old when he was drafted into the Army Air Forces in May 1942. This photo was taken during his basic training at Stinson Field in San Antonio, Texas, in 1942.

Andrews kept the small ***Strength for Service*** *devotional Bible presented to him by the Young Men's Class of Washington Square Methodist Sunday School and a photograph of his wife, the former Jeanette L. Shrader, with him while he served in the South Pacific in WWII. Note at the bottom of the cover page the caution to inscribers not to include specifics about a service member's division, ship or other military identifiers lest the book fall into enemy hands. As required by all military personnel, Andrews wore dog tags bearing his name, home address and serial number.*

A-24s, the Army's version of the Navy's Douglas Dauntless Dive-bombers prepare their approach to one of three airfields on the South Pacific island of Biak. The Japanese had established the air bases on the 45-mile-long island in the center of Geelvink Bay, near the western end of New Guinea. American and Australian troops invaded the island on May 27, 1944, in a battle that resulted in 2,700 Allied casualties and an estimated loss of Japanese that ranges from 6,100 to 9,000. The capture of Biak was an important part of the Allies' island-hopping strategy. The airfields at Biak supported Allied heavy bombers that were instrumental in operations against Japanese forces occupying the Philippines and Borneo. This photo was taken from the top of a hill which was used as a marker to the aircrafts' approach prior to landing.

Andrews stands in front of barracks on the island of Biak, off the coast of New Guinea in 1945, his staff sergeant stripes clearly visible on both sleeves. He served as a construction foreman with the Army Air Forces in the South Pacific during WWII, moving from New Caledonia, to Guadalcanal to New Guinea and finally to Biak, in the brutal struggle against entrenched Japanese forces on the islands.

The war in the Pacific was waged with more than bullets and bombs. In an effort to persuade Japanese soldiers to give up their arms, the U.S. military employed psychological tactics to undermine enemy morale. In this leaflet brought back by Andrews from his time in the South Pacific, a Japanese soldier is depicted reading a newspaper whose headline blares: "War in Europe is Over." The upper righthand corner contains a form of haiku designed to make Japanese soldiers homesick. The poetic verse reads:

A leaf is falling to the ground.
How sad.
A sentimental song.

The leaf referred to is that of the paulownia, also known as a "Princess Tree," a species widely cultivated in Japan, whose heart-shaped leaves and delicate purple blooms are evocative of home. In Japan, it was customary to plant a paulownia tree when a baby girl was born, and then to make it into a dresser as a wedding present when she got married.

On the reverse side, in the black shaded area, is the phrase: "Peace comes to Europe." Washington County veteran Eugene Y. Nakada provided a paraphrase of the subsequent text, which roughly translates:

"The slaughter in Europe has finally come to an end. Peace has finally arrived. The bells are thundering over there. Those who starved on the front lines, suffered from disease and were lost in the gunsmoke ... how they wish they too could enjoy peace. Soldiers vanishing in the gruesome battle smoke are wishing they were back home with their families." The closing phrases pick up the theme conveyed in the haiku "... the trees are beginning to show young leaves back home and the happiness of a peaceful life is not that far away. The dream of the century is about to be realized."

The propaganda piece is subtle in that it appeals to the soldiers' basic emotional needs, according to Nakada. The paulownia tree was also a badge of the Japanese government, not unlike the chrysanthemum, which is the imperial seal of Japan, hence the significance of the paulownia leaf falling to the ground. "The psychology used is brilliant, planned by someone with a thorough knowledge of the Japanese psyche," Nakada said. The only problem is that the calligraphy is of such an archaic style that it is doubtful that the ordinary Japanese soldier would have been able to read it.

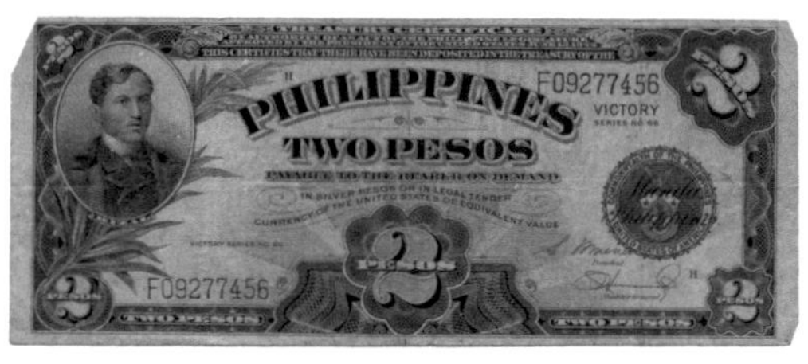

Paper currency from Japan, Indochina and the Philippines that Andrews collected during his time in the Army Air Forces in the Pacific during WWII.

Andrews kept this printed pamphlet marking his "Magic Carpet" homeward bound trip from Biak, identified as "the jungle," to Los Angeles, marked as "civilization." The 1945 journey across the Pacific, aboard the USS ***Olmsted****, took 19 days.*

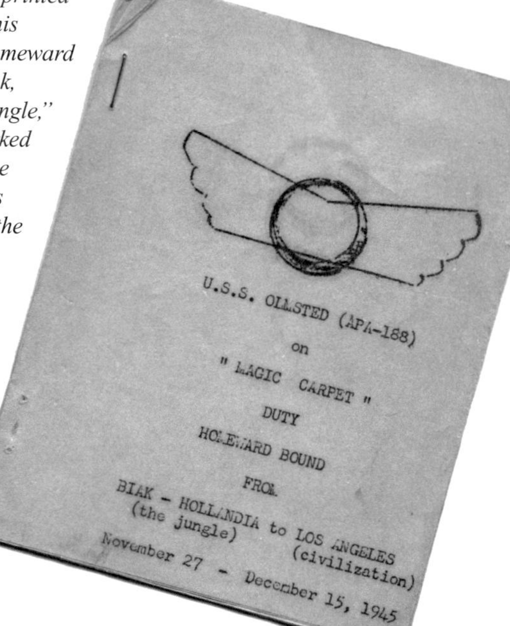

U.S.S. OLMSTED (APA-188)

on

" MAGIC CARPET "

DUTY

HOMEWARD BOUND

FROM

BIAK - HOLLANDIA to LOS ANGELES
(the jungle) (civilization)

November 27 - December 15, 1945

ARMY AIR FORCES

Certificate of Appreciation

FOR WAR SERVICE

TO

GLENN W. ANDREWS

I CANNOT meet you personally to thank you for a job well done; nor can I hope to put in written words the great hope I have for your success in future life.

Together we built the striking force that swept the Luftwaffe from the skies and broke the German power to resist. The total might of that striking force was then unleashed upon the Japanese. Although you no longer play an active military part, the contribution you made to the Air Forces was essential in making us the greatest team in the world.

The ties that bound us under stress of combat must not be broken in peacetime. Together we share the responsibility for guarding our country in the air. We who stay will never forget the part you have played while in uniform. We know you will continue to play a comparable role as a civilian. As our ways part, let me wish you God speed and the best of luck on your road in life. Our gratitude and respect go with you.

H H Arnold
COMMANDING GENERAL
ARMY AIR FORCES

(Photographs and memorabilia courtesy of Sandy and Matt Andrews, Glenn W. Andrews' son and grandson)

Certificate of appreciation for wartime service in the Army Air Forces, presented to Andrews and signed by Henry H. "Hap" Arnold, commanding general of the Army Air Forces.

Irvin Shipley — Army — WWII

Pfc. Irvin H. Shipley was two months shy of his 20th birthday when he was killed in Germany on April 10, 1945. The Downsville native was a member of the 7th Armored Division and saw action in Holland, France, Belgium and Germany. Before his induction in February 1944, Shipley had been employed at the Victor Hosiery plant in Hagerstown.

(Photograph and newspaper clippings courtesy of Marion C. Gaylor, Irvin H. Shipley's sister)

Pfc. Shipley Rites Sunday

Body Of Countian Killed In Germany In 1945 To Arrive Today.

The body of Pfc. Irvin H. Shipley, who was killed in Germany on April 10, 1945, will arrive today for reburial on Sunday afternoon. Funeral services will be held at 2 o'clock at the Christian Church at Downsville, with the Rev. C. W. McDonald officiating. Interment in Greenlawn cemetery, Williamsport.

Pfc. Shipley was a member of the Bethany Church of Christ at Downsville. He was inducted into the army in February, 1944,

PFC. IRVIN H. SHIPLEY

and received his training at Camp Blanding, Fla. He was a member of the armored division. Pfc. Shipley was born June 15, 1925, at Downsville.

He is survived by parents, Mr. and Mrs. Lewis G. Shipley, Downsville; sisters, Mrs. Gladys Roberts, Fairplay; Mrs. Mildred Lizer, Williamsport; Mrs. Margaret Hildebrand, of this city; Mrs. Nellie Reid, Halfway; Mrs. Thelma Kimmel, Frederick; Mrs. Marion Gaylor, Williamsport; Lois, Fern and Mary Ellen, all at home; brothers, Ralph, Funkstown; Melvin, at home.

Full military honors will be tendered by the Williamsport American Legion, Post 202.

TWENTY-EIGHT

Pvt. Shipley Rites Sunday Afternoon

Body Of Countian Killed In Germany In 1945 Arrives

The body of Pfc. Irvin H. Shipley, who was killed in Germany on April 10, 1945, arrived yesterday for reburial on Sunday afternoon. Funeral services will be held at 2 o'clock at the Christian Church at Downsville, with the Rev. C. W. McDonald officiating. Interment in Greenlawn cemetery, Williamsport.

Pfc. Shipley was a member of the Bethany Church of Christ at Downsville. He was inducted into the army in February, 1944,

PFC. IRVIN H. SHIPLEY

and received his training at Camp Blanding, Fla. He was a member of the armored division. Pfc. Shipley was born June 15, 1925, at Downsville.

He is survived by parents, Mr. and Mrs. Lewis G. Shipley, Downsville; sisters, Mrs. Gladys Roberts, Fairplay; Mrs. Mildred Lizer, Williamsport; Mrs. Margaret Hildebrand, of this city; Mrs. Nellie Reid, Halfway; Mrs. Thelma Kimmel, Frederick; Mrs. Marion Gaylor, Williamsport; Lois, Fern and Mary Ellen, all at home, and Mrs. Jane Hammond, Downsville; brothers, Ralph, Funkstown; Melvin, at home.

Full military honors will be tendered by the Williamsport American Legion, Post 202.

Killed In Action

Pfc. Irvin H. Shipley (above), son of Mr. and Mrs. Lewis G. Shipley, Downsville, who was killed in action in Germany on April 10. He was a former employe of the Victor Hosiery plant in Hagerstown.

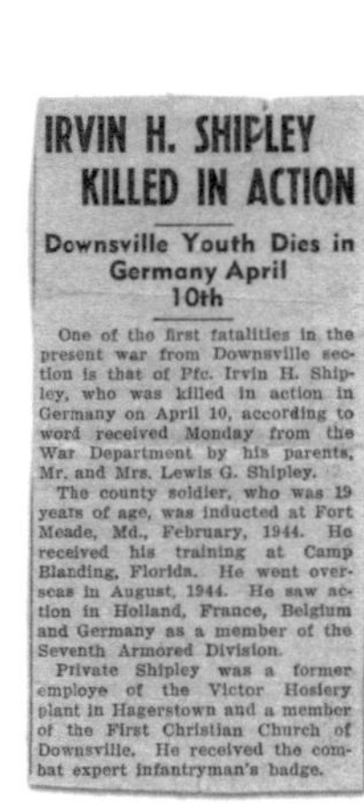

IRVIN H. SHIPLEY KILLED IN ACTION

Downsville Youth Dies in Germany April 10th

One of the first fatalities in the present war from Downsville section is that of Pfc. Irvin H. Shipley, who was killed in action in Germany on April 10, according to word received Monday from the War Department by his parents, Mr. and Mrs. Lewis G. Shipley.

The county soldier, who was 19 years of age, was inducted at Fort Meade, Md., February, 1944. He received his training at Camp Blanding, Florida. He went overseas in August, 1944. He saw action in Holland, France, Belgium and Germany as a member of the Seventh Armored Division.

Private Shipley was a former employe of the Victor Hosiery plant in Hagerstown and a member of the First Christian Church of Downsville. He received the combat expert infantryman's badge.

Samuel Baker — Army Air Forces — WWII

Samuel Baker of Hagerstown sent these handkerchiefs, embroidered with the symbol of the Army Air Forces, home to his wife, Marie, when he was serving at Chanute Air Force Base, Illinois, during WWII. Baker and his wife now live in Maugansville.

(Photographs and memorabilia courtesy of Samuel Baker)

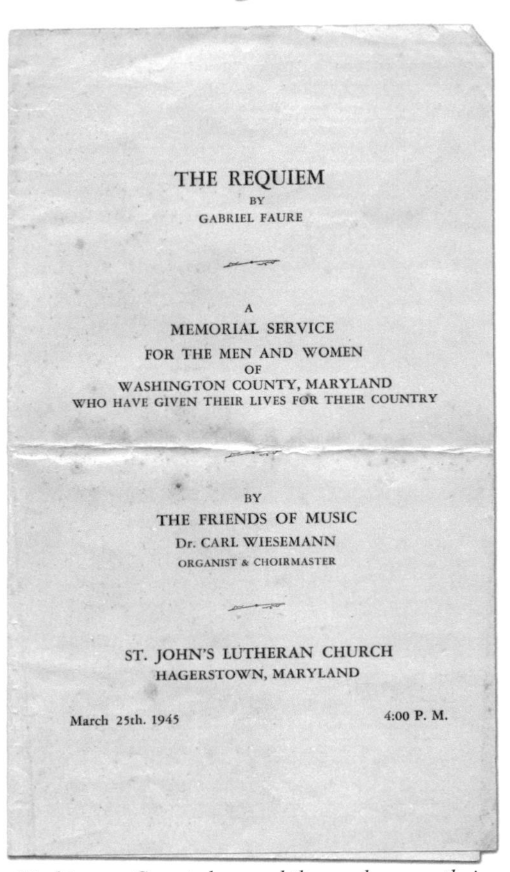

THE REQUIEM
BY
GABRIEL FAURE

A
MEMORIAL SERVICE
FOR THE MEN AND WOMEN
OF
WASHINGTON COUNTY, MARYLAND
WHO HAVE GIVEN THEIR LIVES FOR THEIR COUNTRY

BY
THE FRIENDS OF MUSIC
Dr. CARL WIESEMANN
ORGANIST & CHOIRMASTER

ST. JOHN'S LUTHERAN CHURCH
HAGERSTOWN, MARYLAND

March 25th. 1945 — 4:00 P. M.

Washington County honored those who gave their lives in WWII at a community-wide memorial service at St. John's Lutheran Church in Hagerstown on March 25, 1945.

(Contributed by Robert C. Geiser)

Four Friends

William M. "Bill" DeLauder, John Grosh, Charlie "Gordy" Myers, Earl Sam Myers

Hagerstown buddies John Grosh, Gordy Myers, William M. "Bill" DeLauder and Sam Myers, Gordy Myers' cousin, posed for this group photo in uniform in 1946 after their return from WWII. "We were all buddies," said DeLauder, "we all ran around together." Sailors Grosh, DeLauder and Gordy Myers spent much of their wartime service at sea, but Sam Myers, a member of the 82nd Airborne Division, fought in Europe and "had his feet frozen at the Battle of the Bulge," according to DeLauder.

DeLauder was part of the Navy flotilla participating in the bombardment of Corregidor and Okinawa. His ship was one of the first American vessels to arrive at the port of Nagasaki after the atom bomb was dropped on that major Japanese metropolis. "We went into Nagasaki, and at first you didn't see anything moving. It was spooky," DeLauder said. (Photograph courtesy of William M. DeLauder)

"This is the story of four friends, veterans of World War II," began Mrs. William DeLauder's account of her husband William M. "Bill" DeLauder's service in WWII and that of his three good friends. "Their friendship began in 1940. William DeLauder, John Grosh, Charlie "Gordy" Myers and Sam Myers."

William M. "Bill" DeLauder

*"'Bill' DeLauder begged his mother to allow him to enlist in the Navy, which she finally did, when he turned 17. He had basic training at Bainbridge, Maryland, and spent several weeks in Anacostia, near Washington, D.C. He traveled by train to California to board a transport ship **General George O. Squire** packed with servicemen and sailed to New Caledonia. Boarded a ship to Guadalcanal, onto Munda to board the USS **Montpelier** (Cleveland class cruiser, Div. 12). Proceeded to bombard Saipan prior to the Marine's landing, in the Marianna Islands and the Philippine Campaign. The ship returned to Mare Island Navy Yard, California for repairs, was overhauled and painted camouflage colors. Onto the Philippines, Corregidor, Bataan, bombarded Luzon prior to General MacArthur's arrival. They proceeded to Subic Bay where the crew had shore leave, 1st time in a year. Sailed to Borneo with Australians on board preparing for landing. The ship cruised East China Sea hunting for Japanese Supply ships; onto Okinawa awaiting orders for the invasion of Japan when the war ended. The **Montpelier** along with hospital ships were dispatched to Japan to evacuate Allied Prisoners of War at Honshu. Crewmembers were allowed ashore to sightsee, some of whom went to Hiroshima. They supported the Occupation of Japan. The ship took several torpedo hits, but luckily several were duds, survived a ferocious typhoon and a Japanese kamikaze plane which hit the ocean and then slammed into the ship and shattered into pieces, but no explosion.*

Bill received the rank of Petty Officer 2nd Class and awarded the American Campaign Medal (3 stars), The Asiatic-Pacific Campaign, World War II Victory Medal, The Honorable Service Lapel Button WWII, and Good Conduct Medal.

The ship proceeded to San Diego where some crew members had earned enough points to be discharged. They traveled through the Panama Canal, up the East Atlantic Coast to the Brooklyn Navy Yard and picked up new recruits and traveled to Massachusetts where Bill was discharged April 1946.

Bill and his wife, Helen, live in Hagerstown and have two sons and a granddaughter.'"

Earl Sam Myers

"Earl Sam Myers Sr. of Hagerstown enlisted in the Army May 1942 and was assigned to the West Coast. He transferred to the Paratrooper, Co. D, 508 Parachute Infantry, hoping to be assigned to the East Coast closer to home. He was sent to Ft. Benning, Ga., and Camp McCall, N.C. Upon completion of Basic Training he was shipped to Scotland. He participated in the African [campaign], parachuted into Holland, Belgium and the Battle of the Bulge. He was hospitalized with frozen feet and an injured knee. He attained the rank of Sergeant and received two purple hearts. He was assigned to guard General Eisenhower's headquarters in Germany and was discharged January 1946.

Sam and his wife, Betty, an L.P.N., resided at South Pointe; they have a daughter living in Halfway with 2 daughters, and a son living in Martinsburg, W. Va. with his daughter. They have 3 granddaughters and a great grandson. Sam passed away May 16, 2004 and was buried in Cedar Lawn with full military honors."

Charlie "Gordy" Myers

"Charlie 'Gordy' Myers of Hagerstown enlisted in the Navy in May 1943. He trained for Medium Bombers and Gunnery Crew in Memphis, Tenn. and Beaufort, S.C. He was assigned to Medium bomber and Training Patrol Squadron in Florida. He was assigned patrol duty via Seaplane from Guantanamo bay north along the Atlantic Coast; also dispersed patrol squadrons for duty. He was awarded Air Crew Wings upon completion of training and discharged in 1945. He met his wife in Beaufort, S.C.

They have two sons, Terry, who lives with his wife and two children in Hagerstown, and son, Randy, who served in the U.S. Marines 29 years. He and his wife and two daughters live in South Carolina. He retired as a full Colonel.

Charlie and wife, Betty, live in Ft. Myers, Florida."

John Grosh

"John Grosh of Hagerstown was drafted in early 1944 and requested the U.S. Navy. He received Basic Training at Bainbridge, Md. He applied for Amphibian School training for PT Boats. He spent six weeks training at Martha's Vineyard. He was a mechanical engineer in the Engine Room on PT Boats, based in Louisiana. He spent nine months on patrols in the Marshall Islands. His classification was Fireman 1st Class and discharged in 1946.

John resides in Wilmington, N.C. and has two sons and five grandchildren in Hagerstown."

John Alvey Smith — Army Air Forces — WWII

John Alvey Smith flew 35 missions between 1944 and 1945 as a tail gunner on B-17s and B-24s, with the 8th Air Force's 493rd Bomb Group in Europe during WWII. On one of the bombing runs, Smith's plane was riddled with 102 holes from enemy flak. One of the pieces of shrapnel lodged itself into his parachute pack, sparing his leg from injury. In addition to the parachute that helped save his life, Smith brought home the lingering effects of frostbitten fingers — a result of the time he spent in high altitudes in unpressurized, unheated B-17 bombers. Smith flew in support of the D-Day invasion and the subsequent European campaigns that liberated Europe from Nazi control.

(Photographs and memorabilia courtesy of Dorothy Smith, John Alvey Smith's widow)

Hagerstown brothers H. Miller Smith and John Alvey Smith had their photograph taken when they met up in England in 1944. Miller Smith served as an LCI [Landing Craft, Infantry] crewmember in the Navy while John Alvey Smith served his country in the skies over Europe.

A 1945 Wehrmacht joke:

When we see a silver plane, it's American.
A black plane, it's British.
When we see no plane, it's German.

The 8th Air Force patch was worn on the left shoulder of the uniform. Combat losses for the 8th Air Force in Europe were heavy. According to some accounts, individuals had a better chance of being killed, wounded or captured while flying in the 8th Air Force than if they served in the infantry in the front line.

Smith is shown in the middle of the front row, holding the crew's mascot, with members of his B-17 flight crew in a photo taken at McCook Army Airfield, Nebraska, before the crew headed to England in 1944.

Allan Powell — Navy — WWII

Allan Powell, a native of Washington County, joined the Navy at age 17 in 1942. After gunnery school, he was assigned to a PBY [Patrol Bomber Consolidated Aircraft Corp.] Squadron operating out of Guantanamo Bay, Cuba. These large seaplanes ranged the Atlantic and Caribbean doing anti-submarine patrol duty. After his tour of duty in the South Pacific, Powell was stationed at Corpus Christi, Texas, in a PBY squadron. These huge Martin "Mariner" flying boats also engaged in anti-sub reconnaissance.

He retired as a 2nd Class Aviation Ordnanceman in 1945, after the fighting in Europe was over but before the war in the Pacific ended. He got his GED in Corpus Christi and after his discharge, thanks to the GI Bill, he studied for the ministry, then switched to philosophy and majored in social sciences and history. He became a teacher, working at Washington Street School, Woodland Way School, North Hagerstown High School, and then on educational television. His last teaching stop was Hagerstown Junior College, where taught for 33 years, for a total of 41 years of teaching. "I loved every minute of it," he said.

Allan Powell and his mates had a lot of free time on their hands while in the Solomons. They went diving in coral reefs, where they found and collected shells. To help pass the time, they used the shells to make necklaces like this one. Some of them also made jewelry from aluminum that was used in conjunction with TNT to activate bombs. Powell brought this necklace back from the Solomons, along with a coffee mug that he now uses as a shaving mug.

(Photos and memorabilia courtesy of Allan Powell)

Navy uniform worn by Allan Powell during his service in WWII. Medals on the uniform, from left, are: Good Conduct Medal; Air Medal; WWII Victory Medal; Asiatic-Pacific Campaign Medal; Navy & Marine Corps Commendation Medal. Above them are gunner's wings, with the maximum three stars. On the shoulder is the patch for Aviation Ordnance 2nd Class Seaman, showing a bomb, and on the cuff is an apprentice patch.

Model of a PBY-5A aircraft like the one on which Allan Powell served in the Solomon Islands. An amphibious plane like those seen in the movie **Midway***, it was used to spot Japanese warplanes and detect enemy fleet movements. Another service was rescuing shot-down air crew. It flew missions every four days lasting from 12 to 18 hours. In addition to performing reconnaissance, it dropped bombs on vessels or land installatons. A "Catalina" type aircraft, the PBY-5A had a 104-foot wingspan and carried four 500-pound bombs. These bombs had fuses to arm for both land and water. Powell's unit, U.S. Navy Patrol Squadron VP-81, was part of the "Black Cat" operation in the Pacific. These planes were painted black and the missions were primarily at night. Pacific operations commenced at Guadalcanal, and from there they went island-hopping up the Solomons between Nov. 25, 1943, and July 15, 1944. They saw action in Bougainville, New Georgia, Green and New Britain islands.*

Powell's most memorable experience in the Pacific was on Green Island. "We were there for fueling, and a Betty [a Japanese bomber] came over and started dropping bombs on the runway. We had a full tank of gas, so we ran into the jungle and watched. You could see the plane. But they ran out of bombs before they got to us."

Helen P. Eslick — Army — WWII

Helen Powell Eslick of Washington County, now living in Cincinnati, Ohio, was the only woman among five siblings who joined the military during and after WWII. Eslick went to the Hospital for the Women of Maryland in Baltimore. She then took a three-month course in Operating Room Techniques at Johns Hopkins Hospital before enlisting in the Army Nurse Corps in 1943. She was sent to Europe, where she worked as an operating room nurse until her discharge in 1946.

(Photograph courtesy of Evelyn Stape, Helen Eslick's sister)

Clarence "C.K." Powell — Army — WWII

Clarence Kenneth "C.K." Powell joined the Navy shortly after Pearl Harbor was attacked on Dec. 7, 1941. An Aviation Radioman 1st Class (ARM1), he served in WWII as a radio and radar operator on an airplane in the South Pacific. He was stationed on a light cruiser, flying an amphibious reconaissance plane with pontoons. It was catapulted off the ship, performed its reconaissance and then landed on the water, where it was picked up by the cruiser and put back on board.

After leaving the Navy, C.K. attended Hagerstown Junior College, got a pilot's license at Hagerstown Airport, and went to work for Fairchild Aircraft. He re-enlisted in the Navy to make a career there, but died from Hodgkin's Disease in 1952, at age 28.

(Photograph courtesy of Evelyn Stape, Clarence Powell's sister)

Fred S. French — Navy — WWII

Gunner's Mate 3rd Class Fred S. French saw military service in the South Pacific during WWII and participated in the invasions of both Iwo Jima and Okinawa. A resident of Downsville when he enlisted in the Navy in September 1943, he served aboard the USS ***Berrien****, an attack transport, during the Pacific Campaign. Among his wartime memories are the rescue of the crew of a B-24 that had crashed into the ocean, and the retrieval of a teenage Japanese suicide bomber pilot from the Pacific. French's job aboard ship was maintaining the ship's guns.*

(Photograph courtesy of Fred S. French)

A Japanese kamikaze aircraft like those used in suicide missions against Allied forces. (Photograph courtesy of Dennis Mongold)

George F. Shinham — Army Air Forces — WWII

The Second World War and the draft pulled George F. Shinham away from the family farm in Cearfoss in March 1943 and took him to basic training in Miami Beach, Florida, where he is pictured here. A flight engineer and gunner with the Army Air Forces, he flew 13 missions on B-24 "Liberator" bombers in Air Offensive Europe over Italy (Rome-Arno), Southern France and Romania. Shot down over Romania, he was a prisoner of war for a short time, but was freed and returned home in October 1945.

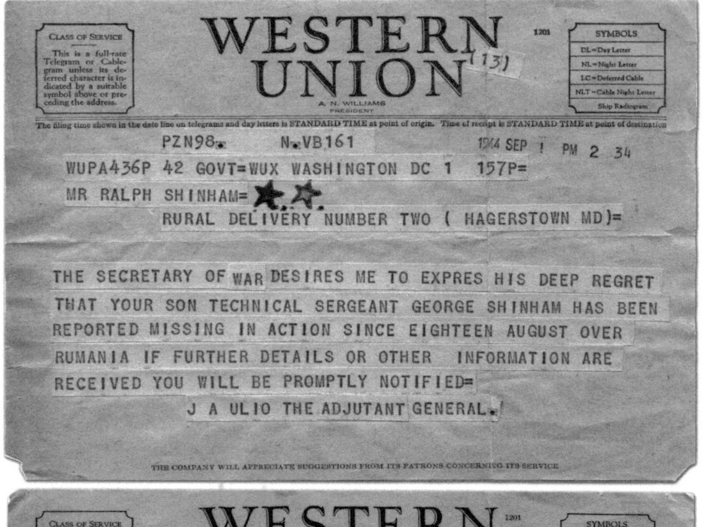

WESTERN UNION (13)

A. N. WILLIAMS PRESIDENT

PZN98 N.VB161 1944 SEP 1 PM 2 34

WUPA436P 42 GOVT=WUX WASHINGTON DC 1 157P=

MR RALPH SHINHAM=

RURAL DELIVERY NUMBER TWO (HAGERSTOWN MD)=

THE SECRETARY OF WAR DESIRES ME TO EXPRES HIS DEEP REGRET THAT YOUR SON TECHNICAL SERGEANT GEORGE SHINHAM HAS BEEN REPORTED MISSING IN ACTION SINCE EIGHTEEN AUGUST OVER RUMANIA IF FURTHER DETAILS OR OTHER INFORMATION ARE RECEIVED YOU WILL BE PROMPTLY NOTIFIED=

J A ULIO THE ADJUTANT GENERAL.

THE COMPANY WILL APPRECIATE SUGGESTIONS FROM ITS PATRONS CONCERNING ITS SERVICE

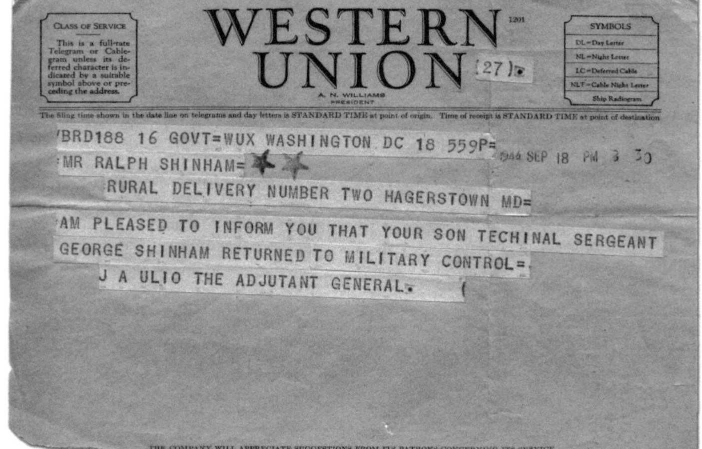

WESTERN UNION (27)

A. N. WILLIAMS PRESIDENT

BRD188 16 GOVT=WUX WASHINGTON DC 18 559P= 1944 SEP 18 PM 3 30

MR RALPH SHINHAM=

RURAL DELIVERY NUMBER TWO HAGERSTOWN MD=

AM PLEASED TO INFORM YOU THAT YOUR SON TECHINAL SERGEANT GEORGE SHINHAM RETURNED TO MILITARY CONTROL=.

J A ULIO THE ADJUTANT GENERAL.

THE COMPANY WILL APPRECIATE SUGGESTIONS FROM ITS PATRONS CONCERNING ITS SERVICE

Gunner's wings worn by Shinham for his service on a B-24 bomber. The Consolidated B-24 "Liberator" was an American heavy bomber produced in greater numbers than any other American combat aircraft during WWII. It was used by every branch of service, in the European, Pacific, African and Middle Eastern theaters. One of the most valuable contributions to Allied victory was its use against German U-boats in the North Atlantic. When the long-range planes started attacking the submarines, the so-called "Atlantic Gap" was soon closed, allowing shipping convoys to reach Britain in relative safety.

Telegrams sent to Ralph Shinham, George's father, reporting on Sept. 1, 1944, that his son was missing in action, and on Sept. 18 that he was back in Allied territory. Ironically, due to the time lag before the telegrams were delivered, George Shinham was actually safe in Italy on the day the telegram arrived reporting that he was MIA.

Prisoner of War Medal awarded to Shinham for events that began on Aug. 18, 1944. It was his fourth mission over Romania bombing the Ploesti oil refineries — which he calls "the best defended target in Europe." His plane was hit and "three engines quit running." He still remembers "the free fall out of the plane when we bailed out, before the chute opened." Of the 10-man crew, only the pilot was seriously injured, with shrapnel in his leg. The men were taken prisoner and sent to a Romanian POW camp in Bucharest infamous for its "39 percent survival rate."

But luck was with them. "We arrived at the camp at 7 p.m., and at 11 p.m. Romania joined the Allied side. I never had to endure being a prisoner," he said. But he had to get out of Romania fast, for the Germans retaliated swiftly and began bombing Bucharest. After only 13 days as MIA [missing in action], Shinham was safely back in Italy.

Mary Shinham Downing —
Army Nurse — WWII

A letter George Shinham wrote to his father on Sept. 2, 1944, says: Dear Dad and all, Here I am back in Italy again. Believe me it took more than just luck to get here too. The statement that there are no atheists in fox holes also applies to bomb shelters.

"Everything here is fine and there is nothing at all wrong with me. When we got here we had a physical checkup, shower, delousing, and an issue of new clothes from shoes to cap.

At present we don't know definitely what the score is, but I expect to soon be on my way home. Of course I'm still in the Army and by experience I know that they can't be held responsible for what they do on such matters. I'll write more as soon as I get more time. Your son, George."

When Mary Shinham Downing graduated from Hagerstown High School, she completed a three-year program at Washington County Hospital and became a nurse. But after seeing her brother, George, drafted into WWII, she enlisted as an Army nurse. She served in Europe, and nursed injured troops during the Battle of the Bulge.

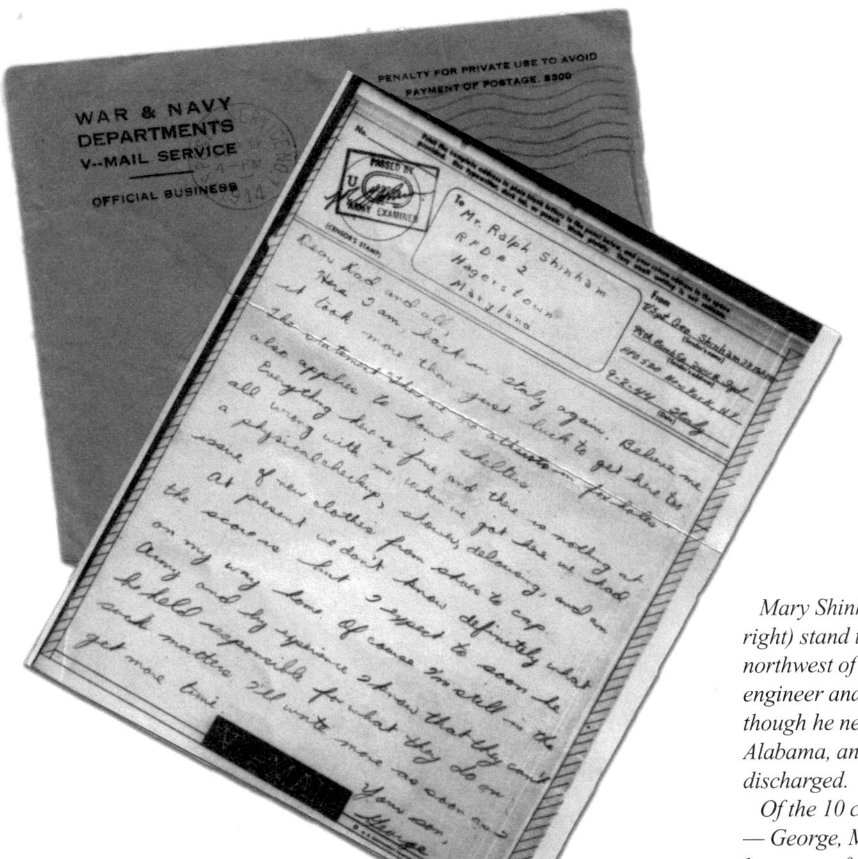

WAR & NAVY
DEPARTMENTS
V--MAIL SERVICE
OFFICIAL BUSINESS

PENALTY FOR PRIVATE USE TO AVOID
PAYMENT OF POSTAGE, $300

To Mr. Ralph Shinham
RFD # 2
Hagerstown
Maryland

9-2-44

Dear Dad and all,
Here I am back in Italy again. Believe me it took more than just luck to get here too. The statement that there are no atheists in fox holes also applies to bomb shelters.
Everything here is fine and there is nothing at all wrong with me. When we got here we had a physical checkup, shower, delousing, and an issue of new clothes from shoes to cap.
At present we don't know definitely what the score is but I expect to soon be on my way home. Of course I'm still in the Army and by experience I know that they can't be held responsible for what they do on such matters. I'll write more as soon as I get more time.
Your son,
George

Mary Shinham Downing, Ralph Shinham and George F. Shinham (left to right) stand together in uniform around 1943 at the family farm in Cearfoss, northwest of Hagerstown. Mary was an Army nurse and George was a flight engineer and gunner in WWII. Their father, Ralph, was in the Army in WWI, though he never saw action. He finished basic training in Montgomery, Alabama, and was about to be sent overseas when the war ended and he was discharged.

Of the 10 children in the Shinham family, six were involved in WWII — George, Mary, and four sisters who married servicemen. In addition, at least two of the sisters worked in defense industries, one at Fairchild and one at Pangborn.

(Photos and memorabilia courtesy of George F. Shinham)

Roger E. Stottlemyer — Army — WWII

Sergeant Roger E. Stottlemyer

Mt. Lena native Roger E. Stottlemyer believes war "is one of the most stupid of things," but it was in some of the bloodiest fighting of World War II that he witnessed what he can only characterize as "miracles."

A sergeant in the Army's S2 Section [Intelligence Section], 99th Infantry, he saw action on Elsenborn Ridge overlooking the Siegfried Line along the French border in Germany just prior to the Battle of the Bulge, and later in the battle for Ludendorff Bridge over the Rhine River in Remagen, Germany.

*It was while on line on Elsenborn Ridge that Stottlemyer vented his frustration with war in general and the artillery in particular in a poem which was subsequently published in the **Herald-Mail** newspapers.*

*In an interview with Frank Woodring for **Cracker Barrel** magazine in 2001, Stottlemyer told the story this way:*

"When I went on line, I was placed in an observation post. Around December 14, 1944, I saw hundreds and hundreds of German troops coming down this gully and going into these bunkers. I had a telephone in my foxhole, so I called for artillery. They sent a shell in and it was too far to the right, so I called in and gave them a corrected reading and called for more artillery. They dropped a second shell, and it was right on target. You could see the German troops fall to the side of the gully, so I called for more artillery. The response I got was 'Sorry, we have fired our quota for the day'."

He said he was so distressed because he had called for artillery with the enemy right there, and gotten that kind of response.

"I asked myself, What kind of war is this?"

His call for artillery went out on Dec. 14 or 15, 1944, he's not sure which day it was. The Battle of the Bulge started on the 16th.

Stottlemyer penned his poem on New Year's Day 1945, recalling what he termed "a terrible situation." By his recollection, the poem was printed in the local newspapers later that January.

Recalling those December days in 1944, Stottlemyer said, "We were soon surrounded. They [the Germans] had dropped paratroopers behind us. We were completely cut off, so we started to withdraw. The snow was waist deep, and the fog was so dense that visibility was down to several feet. It was so bitter cold the fog froze on our overcoats. The flaps on the overcoats would smack; it sounded like two boards hitting together."

He said he didn't know how long he and his comrades walked. "We walked and walked. I think we were going around in circles. It was our objective to break through the German line and get back and join the 99th Division at Elsenborn."

Eventually, he said, they did rejoin their outfit. "We had no air support whatsoever, and it stayed that way from Dec. 18 right through to Christmas Day.

"Christmas Day - it was just like a miracle! The fog lifted, the skies cleared, and the sun came out.

"The sky was just filled with bombers. You wouldn't believe the sky was almost dark with bombers. I said, 'Thank God they're on our side.'"

Stottlemyer said he was in a foxhole on Elsenborn Ridge on Christmas Day, 1944. On that day he got his first hot meal in more than a month. "The cook delivered us a hot Christmas dinner. We had turkey and all the trimmings." Another miracle.

The joy of a hot meal soon dimmed. By March 1945, the sergeant had gone from Elsenborn Ridge to the Ludendorff Bridge over the Rhine at the city of Remagen, Germany. The 9th Armored Division had captured the bridge intact, and Stottlemyer's 99th Division was trucked down to the bridge.

"The Germans had had instructions to blow up the bridge, but they didn't do it," he said. "They would drop shells in there about every 30 seconds. It was after dark. During breaks in the shell firing, [our commanding officer] would send twelve of us running across that bridge. Of course, once that shell fell, that's when we started off.

"While we were running across the bridge, there were soldiers underneath it building a pontoon bridge."

The bridge remained intact for two or three days until it collapsed, but by that time the engineers had put the pontoon bridge across the river. After that, Stottlemyer said, "we went into what was called the Ruhr Pocket."

Stottlemyer had eight men under him in his S2 [intelligence] section. Their job was to escort German prisoners behind the lines for interrogation. One of the boys in his section had been to the front lines, where the Americans had taken some German prisoners, and had reported back to Stottlemyer's section for reinforcements to secure the prisoners.

"Somehow he got confused," Stottlemyer said, "and we didn't go back the road we were supposed to [to pick up the prisoners]. We ran right into a German burp gun. There were six of us in the jeep. Two were sitting on the front fenders, two on the back fenders, and two were sitting in the seats.

"When they opened fire on us, they were in a creek washout. We rolled off the jeep into a ravine on the side of the road. One of the soldiers who was riding on the back fenders was wounded. The jeep ran down the road and crashed into a stone embankment. It was full of bullet holes.

"I asked the boys in my section, 'Would any of you volunteer to make a break and try to get back to battalion headquarters and get an ambulance down here for this boy?'

"I was always of the opinion that I wouldn't ask anybody to do anything I wouldn't do. I was their sergeant."

When he didn't get a response to his question, Stottlemyer said he

Sgt. Roger E. Stottlemyer brought home a few trophies of war including this dagger he took from a German prisoner of war. The name of the German soldier had been etched in the metal. According to a story told him by another soldier, the dagger may have been presented to the German officer by Adolf Hitler. When the officer fell out of favor with Hitler, his name was removed. The dagger also is etched with the words "Alles fur Deutschland" [All for Germany].

told his group to "keep constant fire going" while he made a break for it himself.

With laughter in his voice, he described how he made the break. "I came out of there, and if anybody had seen me going down that road, he'd have sworn I was crazy, 'cause I was zigzagging this way and that, and I was jumping up in the air, and I was bending way down low. But I made it back to headquarters and there they gave me a four-man patrol to help get the others back to safety."

Taking a mountain route, Stottlemyer led the patrol back to the wounded soldier. He later was awarded the Bronze Star for his efforts.

Referring to the incident, Stottlemyer voiced real compassion for the German soldiers.

"Those poor guys, I don't know why they were so stupid. They could have withdrawn down that creek bed, but instead they came out of there and tried to run up the side of that hill. I could hear those guys screaming whenever they got hit. That thing lived with me for months after I came home.

"I regret war, period. Had a person met those boys in civilian life, they probably could have been good buddies to one another. But instead of that, we were out there trying to kill one another. War is one of the most stupid things. It's only because of somebody's lust for power."

The Mt. Lena resident's military service was sprinkled with many "miracles" besides the one he witnessed on Christmas in 1944.

While manning his observation post near the Siegfried Line, he had climbed a pine tree to secure several boughs to cover his foxhole when he heard strange noises. Realizing that a German sniper had him in his sights, he scrambled out of that tree just in the nick of time.

On another day, he was standing beside his foxhole with four other soldiers when a German artillery shell hit the foxhole. The four other men were wounded, but he remained unscathed.

When he returned to the U.S. at war's end, Stottlemyer and his brothers Woodrow and Charles opened a service station on Route 40 near what is now Greenbrier State Park. Later, he took over the station by himself and when I-70 "doomed" Route 40 businesses, he moved his Amoco station west to the Dual Highway near the I-70 interchange.

*Stottlemyer's mother, Annie Stottlemyer, and his nephew, George Brandenburg, hold a copy of the Hagerstown **Daily Mail** announcing the surrender of Germany near the end of WWII.*

(Photos and memorabilia courtesy of Roger E. Stottlemyer}

This is the poem Sgt. Roger E. Stottlemyer wrote on New Year's Day 1945 after calling for artillery fire on German soldiers along the Siegfried Line and being told the artillery had fired its quota for the day and would fire no more.

With pen in hand, America dear,
I sit me down to write you here.
These amateur but pleading lines
I'll attempt to put for you in rhyme.

Old father time came out today
To start a new year on its way.
It's ours to do with what we will.
Let's win the war, then pay the bill.

If this whole world would look at time
The way I do they'd surely find
That life is much too short to waste
On wars that mar its charm and grace.

I start the new year with the hope
Around Hitler's neck we put a rope.
Then draw that rope so gosh-darned tight
That Nazism fades out of sight.

Then maybe man can have the peace
That I, for life, would like to lease.
And never again in future years
Go through an era of blood and tears.

But you, America, must do your part
As the year gets off to a hopeful start.
Please no more strikes that prolong the war.
This is our prayer and what we're pleading for.

We're short on tires and ammo, too.
The supply we get depends on you.
So if you'd have us "hurry back"
Some extra effort could take up the slack.

Compare what you have with what you give.
It's for the things you have that we care to live.
Yet many of us will pay the price of death,
So won't you sacrifice.

— Roger E. Stottlemyer

Paul F. May — Army Air Forces — WWII

It was a long way from Boonsboro to Amarillo in November 1942 when Florence E. May traveled to Texas to see her husband, Paul F. May, before he left for the Pacific in 1943. The Boonsboro native spent most of his time with the Army Air Forces repairing aircraft in New Guinea and the Philippines.

May sent this photo of himself leaning against a truck in New Guinea to his wife, Florence, and young daughter, Judy. The photograph is dated Nov. 17, 1943.

"The boys of the Electric Shop" is how this Sept. 22, 1945, photograph taken in New Guinea is labeled on the back.

Members of the 482nd Air Service Squadron are shown with tool kits at the ready, gathered around an aircraft engine. The aircraft mechanics are identified as (top row from left) Robert C. Barrett, Dale J. Bennett and G. Van Winkle. John C. Yanzanitis is crouching on the left side of the engine and Paul F. May is shown to the right.

Keeping planes in the air was an important component to Allied success in the war against Japan.

Earl E. May — Army — WWII

While Paul May was serving in the Pacific, his younger brother, Earl, was serving with the Army's tank corps as part of the 3rd Armored Division in Europe. Tank crewmembers often wore helmets similar to the one shown at right. Earl May was wounded and awarded a Purple Heart.

(Photographs courtesy of Florence E. May, widow of Paul May)

(Helmet courtesy of Lloyd Sigler)

Two Brothers — **Leroy “Roy” Elgin** — Army — WWII

Roy Elgin, in the photo at left, looked into an oven in a crematorium at a German concentration camp liberated by American troops in 1945. The camp is believed to have been somewhere in Belgium, but Roy's brother, Phil, said he can't be sure, because Roy, who died in 1988, "never talked about that, or the Bulge, or much of anything from his time in the service." The photo below, also from Roy's collection, shows newly-liberated camp inmates in their bunks at the camp.

Leroy "Roy" Elgin's first assignment after joining the Army in 1937 at age 18 was a three-year stint as an infantryman in Panama. There he also played the bugle in the Army band. When the U.S. entered WWII in 1941, he was transferred to Europe, where he operated anti-aircraft artillery during the invasion of Normandy, the Battle of the Bulge and the liberation of German-occupied territories. After the war he served in the Army Reserve in Baltimore until his retirement as Chief Warrant Officer in 1952. He is shown here on leave in Baltimore in 1942.

(Photos contributed by Phil Elgin, Roy Elgin's brother)

John “Jack” Elgin — Air Force — WWII, Panama, Pacific

John "Jack" Elgin stood next to a 1941 Willys he bought from Snowberger Oldsmobile on East Washington Street in Hagerstown. A private in the Army Air Forces, Jack was shipped overseas in January 1942 to serve as a mechanic in the East Indies, including Papua, New Guinea. He returned to the States in October 1945 and received an honorable discharge with the rank of staff sergeant.

Re-enlisting in the Air Force in 1948, he worked stateside and in Germany and Japan, before retiring as a sergeant major in 1965 after 26 years of service. He died in 1974.

(Photo and memorabilia contributed by Lorraine Elgin, Jack Elgin's widow, and Phil Elgin, Jack's brother)

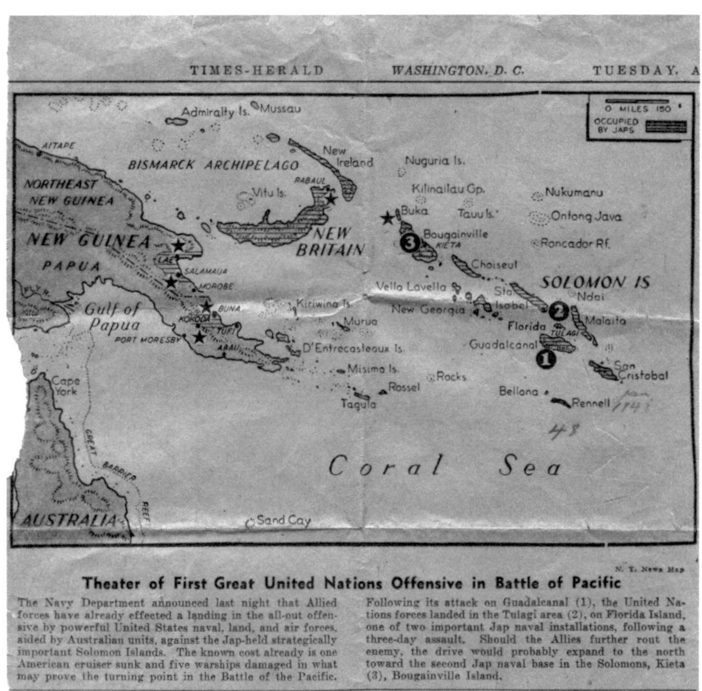

TIMES-HERALD WASHINGTON, D. C. TUESDAY, A

N. Y. News Map

Theater of First Great United Nations Offensive in Battle of Pacific

The Navy Department announced last night that Allied forces have already effected a landing in the all-out offensive by powerful United States naval, land, and air forces, aided by Australian units, against the Jap-held strategically important Solomon Islands. The known cost already is one American cruiser sunk and five warships damaged in what may prove the turning point in the Battle of the Pacific. Following its attack on Guadalcanal (1), the United Nations forces landed in the Tulagi area (2), on Florida Island, one of two important Jap naval installations, following a three-day assault. Should the Allies further rout the enemy, the drive would probably expand to the north toward the second Jap naval base in the Solomons, Kieta (3), Bougainville Island.

Map clipped from a newspaper in August 1942 by Jack Elgin's father, Leroy Elgin Sr., after U.S. forces landed on Guadalcanal.

Peter Badrich — Army Air Forces — WWII

In the photo above, Peter Badrich and his sidekick, Oscar, prepare to head overseas in November 1944 for active duty in the Army Air Forces. Born east of Hagerstown in Security, Md., in 1921, Pete was 13 when he saw a picture of a ventriloquist's dummy and was hooked. When his parents offered to give him a bicycle, he asked for a dummy instead, and soon Oscar — a "Charlie McCarthy style" dummy — arrived in the mail.

Pete and Oscar entered show biz when they performed in junior high school at Woodland Way School, and they played a big role in the "Jitterbug Lunatics" show at Hagerstown High School, where they were cheerleaders. After graduating in 1940, Pete went on to Western Maryland College and did a few public performances. But things changed dramatically after Dec. 7, 1941.

"I remember the day vividly. My dorm was crowded into a big room listening to the radio about Pearl Harbor. The first week of January, I enlisted with a Greek friend, Tom Pappas. A few months later, he was killed in a plane crash. On my first furlough, I ran into his mother and brother, which made me feel guilty that I was still alive. Ironically, he was the one who persuaded me to enlist. His name is on the plaque in front of the courthouse listing WWII veterans."

Oscar helps Pete (above) with office work at their Special Services desk at Scott Field in Missouri in 1942, where they took basic training. "I went to radio school," Pete said, "but I wasn't doing too well. A friend knew I was a ventriloquist and told the major, who asked for a demonstration." Soon he was emceeing shows that came to the base, or going out on War Bond tours with a band. He worked with the singer Hildegarde, among many others. When the Army was looking for men to appear in Irving Berlin's musical revue, ***This is the Army****, Pete was asked to audition, but his Special Services officer refused to let him go.*

Meanwhile, Oscar, whom Pete called his "sub-private officer," was insisting on having a uniform of his own. So Pete took him to "a kindly tailor" in nearby St. Louis for special measurements. "He made a ceremony dressing the figure," Pete said. "Once dressed, his small office staff applauded. It was the first time I was applauded for NOT performing. The tailor wouldn't accept any money, saying it was his contribution to the war effort. You can imagine the elation of a young GI returning to his base."

Pete and his future wife, Maisie (above), on their second date, July 10, 1944, at the Belleville Hotel in Belleville, Ill., near Scott Air Force Base. Maisie, who worked for the Army, married Pete just before he was sent to India in November 1944.

Oscar shows Pete his pistol (left) while the two are waiting to be sent to tour in China in 1945. The duo arrived in India in November 1944 as part of a replacement pool of 200 entertainers who spent 30 days at sea to reach Bombay. "Landing in India, I thought we were being attacked," Pete said, "but it was Indians looking for black-market cigarettes and chocolate. They saw my dummy and thought it was magic."

Pete and Oscar went by train to Calcutta and then to base camp in Kurmitola, in what is now Bangladesh, with a 1345th Army Air Forces Base Unit. Singer Tony Martin was in charge of entertainment for the China-Burma-India Theater, and also working there was actor and officer Melvyn Douglas. "Tony Martin went on tour with us a couple of times ... He was so nice, so smooth," Pete said.

The troupes made tours of Army bases for three weeks, then returned to home base to prepare to go out again with another GI entertainment group. "The tech sergeant took me to officers' clubs to perform, and we did shows for the troops in all the bases. One show was a seven to eight minute training skit on dental hygiene."

(Photos courtesy of Peter Badrich)

In the photo below, a troupe of entertainers in Kunming, China, includes a piano player, Pete and Oscar, "an impressionist who thought he was Eddie Cantor," a violinist, a singer and a dancer. Pete and Oscar found themselves in China two or three weeks after their arrrival in India, when they flew with the Air Transport Command "over the hump," a five-hour trip across the Himalayas.

"It was the first time I flew," Pete said. "I was nervous. The fellow next to me was wearing a parachute. On a flight to India, he had crash-landed, and this was the first time he was flying back to China. At every bit of turbulence he jumped, so I was a nervous wreck, too."

The troupe spent two to three days doing shows in Kunming, and also went to Chengdu and Chongqing. Pete, who was in charge of the group, said, "The men really enjoyed the shows. There was a lot of laughter."

The men were in Chengdu when the atomic bombs were dropped on Japan. "We didn't really know what it meant then," Pete said. "We were asked to do a special show. Madame Sun Yat-sen was in the audience."

After the war, Pete and Oscar returned to the U.S. by ship by way of Port Said, Egypt. "When we arrived in New York, we were all crying," he said.

Pete's performances in the military led to a career as a civilian, and he worked as a ventriloquist for more than 40 years, under the civilian stage name Peter Rich. He got a new dummy, named Rawhide, and together they worked with entertainers Minnie Pearl, Louise Mandrell and many others.

Among other things, Pete took four 10-week tours to the Orient as a civilian entertainer, which included shows in officers' clubs in Okinawa, Taipei, Manila, Bangkok and Japan. He also performed on cruise ships for 20 years, retiring in 1989. "I was fortunate, doing what I wanted to do," he said. "It amazes me that I made a living doing this."

Pete Callas — Navy — WWII

Callas (right) and a Navy buddy in New London, Connecticut, during WWII.

Pete Callas went skydiving in a dive bomber in Florida, saw naval duty on the high seas in the Pacific and Indian oceans, and served aboard a destroyer off the coast of Korea during military service in two wars.

Callas was following in the footsteps of his father and three brothers, all of whom volunteered for military service.

He and his high school buddy, Howard "Pete" Smead, wanted to enlist in the Navy in 1943. Smead was too young, so, Callas said, "I think he changed dates on his birth certificate."

Both enlisted.

But in order to graduate from high school before going off to see the world, they had to complete all class requirements by December 1943. Hagerstown High School Principal John D. Zentmyer gave the boys permission to take extra English classes, and they got their diplomas. They were the only HHS students to complete graduation credits in the middle of the year.

Callas went off to boot camp in Sampson, New York, in February 1944, and Smead went to the Great Lakes, Illinois, Naval Training Station. After completion of boot training, Pete was assigned to Fire Control School in Fort Lauderdale, Florida. He subsequently saw duty in the Pacific and Indian oceans.

While stationed in Fort Lauderdale, he and Tony Cavalero, a friend he made on base, hitchhiked to Opa-locka, Florida, for some flying. It cost them one dollar. The plane was a Dauntless dive bomber. "It was not a routine flight," Callas recalled with a chuckle. "To my surprise, it was dive bombing practice!"

Callas served as a fire controlman 3d class aboard the submarine tender USS **Clytie** *during WWII. He was discharged in May 1946.*

Five years later, he was recalled to active duty during the Korean War and served as a radar range-finder operator aboard the destroyer USS ***John R. Craig****. His ship was almost sunk by a mine off the coast of Korea. He said the mine exploded and damaged the ship's navigation systems. "We fired on the mine, but it was too close," he said, "and our ship was damaged to the point that we returned to the States."*

Callas' three brothers also served in the military, one in the Army, the other two in the Navy. They all followed the patriotic bent of their father, George J. Callas, who came to the United States as a Greek immigrant in 1910 and went back to Greece in 1911 to fight with his countrymen against the Turks in the First Balkan War. The senior Callas returned to Greece a second time to fight for Greece against the Bulgarians in the Second Balkan War.

Callas said he learned both discipline and patriotism during his military career.

"The military allowed me to bypass many of the problems of growing up and kept me focused," he said.

Best of all, he said, the GI Bill, which came out of WWII, "provided opportunities that I took advantage of." Callas earned his bachelor's and master's degrees at Western Maryland College. In 1949, he attended the University of Stockholm, Sweden, where he received a licentiate degree. He was employed in the foreign exchange department of the Scandinaviska Banken of Stockholm in 1950. Following completion of his master's degree at Western Maryland College, he attended Columbia University Teachers College and George Washington University, where he earned his doctorate in school administration, "all with the help of the GI Bill."

Callas was employed by the Washington County Board of Education, first as a teacher and principal, then as director of general administration in the central office. In 1965, he and his late wife, Margaret, spent 27 months in Nigeria, where he was a technician and evaluator of the Modern Aids to Education Project for Nigeria and Washington County Board of Education. He took an early retirement in 1975.

In 1987, he was elected to the Washington County Board of Education and served as its president. After four years he was elected to the Maryland House of Delegates, where he was delegation chairman for eight years. He served three terms.

(Photographs courtesy of Pete Callas)

Fire Controlman 3rd Class Pete Callas on an island off the coast of Australia in June 1945.

Support On The Home Front — WWII

Copy of War Bonds poster, one of many that appeared in Hagerstown and across the country designed to encourage people on the home front to buy government bonds supporting the war effort during WWII. (Contributed by Elaine Lewis)

Helen Warden of Hagerstown, whose son Galen would serve in the Merchant Marine, used her seamstress talents to make patriotic Halloween costumes for her daughter Norma Warden Winpigler (the young sailor); her son William J. Warden (Uncle Sam), and her daughter Marlene Warden Shank (the pouting infantryman). They were preparing to appear in the 1942 Hagerstown Mummers Parade.

(Photograph contributed by Marlene Shank, Helen Warden's daughter)

Hagerstown's Lester Jerl Warden wanted to do his bit for the country when the nation went to war in WWII, but as a 37-year-old father of four, he was not accepted in the military, as attested by his Notice of Classification card, identifying him as Class III-A-H. As a volunteer Minuteman though, Warden policed his Antietam Street neighborhood, enforcing wartime blackouts and air raid drills and assembling at City Park for training with fellow Minutemen.

(Photograph contributed by Marlene Shank, Lester J. Warden's daughter)

Washington County servicemen home on leave during WWII got more than parties and dancing at the USO in Hagerstown; they also got a second mother. Mary H. "Ma" Luipersbeck, a dedicated USO volunteer (shown here baking her world-renowned cookies for the USO), welcomed soldiers into her heart and her home.

Born in Austria in 1895 into a family of 10 children, Mary worked in canteens and hospitals during WWI. After marrying and having two children, she moved in 1922 to Washington County, where her husband, John's, brother lived. She joined St. Mary Catholic Church in Hagerstown and soon got involved in a multitude of volunteer activities. During WWII she became a fixture at the local USO, where she was called "Ma" or "Mom" and was considered a second mother to many a lonely soldier.

Senior hostess and girls' advisor for the Girls Service Organization of the USO, she opened her home on Security Road to more than 400 servicemen in need of lodging while on leave during the war. And they never forgot her.

In a local newspaper article about her in later years, she said hundreds of letters from servicemen would pour into her home, and she would answer every one personally.

> *Many have written wanting me to meet the girls they have chosen to marry. They want to bring them here, to my house, to get my approval. They have their own parents, but I don't know why they do this ... they just do.*
>
> *"But don't say so much about me," she said. "Please tell everyone how fine the girls of Hagerstown are. They deserve a lot of credit for the efforts and time they spent trying to make the fellows feel at home during the war. It wasn't always such a pleasant and easy job for them. I couldn't possibly have done as much as they. I am only one person.*

In 1959, Ma Luipersbeck was honored by the enlisted personnel of the Lake View Service Club at Fort Ritchie as their Mother's Day Queen. She is shown above during the ceremony at the Mother's Day dance, flanked by Pfc. Nina J. Goodman (left) and Pfc. Eileen M. Snyder of Fort Ritchie.

In 1976, Ma was recognized as one of the Outstanding Women of Washington County by the Hagerstown branch of the American Association of University Women. She passed away on Dec. 28, 1981.

(Photos courtesy of Gisele Klincewicz, daughter of Mary H. "Ma" Luipersbeck)

Gerald L. "Mannie" Ebersole

(Photo, badge and certificate courtesy of Lorraine and Gerald "Mannie" Ebersole)

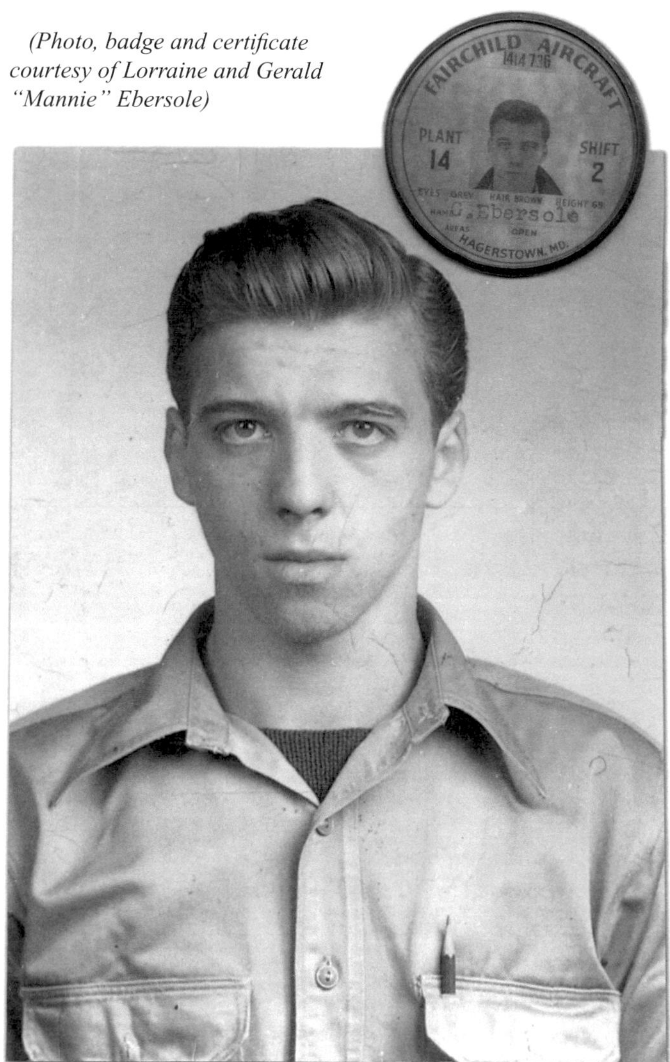

Gerald L. "Mannie" Ebersole's work at Fairchild Aircraft kept him out of active duty in the armed forces during WWII. Ebersole welded landing gear for bombers at Fairchild's plant #14 on Baltimore Street in Hagerstown from 1940 to 1943. The certificate presented to him represents the Army Navy E Award, which was given to workers who were deferred from active service due to their production of vital war materials in the defense industries. Workers in 4,283 of the nation's war production facilities earned the award "for their part in the defeat of the Axis Powers," according to the War and Navy Departments. This number includes Navy E Awards made prior to July 1942, when the Navy E, the Army A and the Army-Navy Munitions Board Star awards were merged and became known as the Army-Navy E Award.

ARMY E NAVY

CERTIFICATE OF AWARD

TO

G. L. Ebersole

WHOSE PERSONAL EFFORTS AND CONTRIBUTIONS TOWARDS THE PRODUCTION OF VITAL WAR MATERIALS IS RECOGNIZED IN THE PRESENTATION OF THE

Army-Navy E Award

TO FAIRCHILD AIRCRAFT

HAGERSTOWN, MARYLAND
February Seventh
Nineteen hundred and forty-three

VICE-PRESIDENT AND GENERAL MANAGER
FAIRCHILD AIRCRAFT division of
FAIRCHILD ENGINE & AIRPLANE CORPORATION

Guy Wingert — Army — WWII

Guy Wingert and his bride, Elizabeth, are shown here on their wedding day in 1945. Wingert enlisted in the Army in 1942 and spent virtually his entire time in uniform overseas. He was engaged in heavy fighting during the Battle of the Bulge and served for a time with Gen. George S. Patton's Third Army. He carried a picture of Elizabeth with him the entire time he was away to remind him of her and of home. Once he returned from the war, his wife said, he did not talk about his combat experiences, and she would often find him staring into space for long periods of time. Sometimes Wingert would start to shed tears and shake all over.

Wingert worked for Fairchild Aircraft when war was declared, but the 22-year-old Hagerstown man was deemed too valuable a worker in the critical war industry to be inducted and was granted a military deferment. Finally, because so many of his buddies were being drafted, Wingert asked to be released from Fairchild so he could enlist. He wanted to serve his country on the battlefield. Wingert returned to Fairchild after the war, but then went to work for Mack Truck, retiring in 1985. Wingert died in January 2001.

(Photograph contributed by Marlene Shank, Guy Wingert's niece)

Linwood E. Orange — Army Air Corps — WWII

Linwood E. Orange went from airplanes to airplanes when he entered military service in June 1942. A resident of Cavetown at the time, Orange was working as clerk of field and secretary to Dick Henson, chief of flight test at Fairchild Aircraft, prior to joining the Army Air Corps. He completed his primary flight training in a PT-19 produced by Fairchild like the one pictured above with Dick Henson at the controls.

Commissioned a second lieutenant, Orange served stateside, primarily in Texas, flying multi-engine planes. He said his most memorable experience was flying a B-29 similar to the one he is pictured with in this 1995 photograph, taken in Pueblo, Colorado, during the 50th anniversary of the graduation of Pilot Class 44F.

Orange's brother, George W. Orange, also served in the Army Air Forces during WWII, with overseas duty as a fighter pilot in France. In July 1945, while he was stationed at Hendricks Field, Sebring, Florida, Linwood said, his brother George "spent some of his precious leave time visiting me. We had always been very close, and we decided to take advantage of this occasion to have our pictures taken, for family history and all that. After all, it might be a spell until the two of us were together again and had another chance. So we hunted up the Post Photo Studio and got the job done. This is my picture. [George had his photograph taken separately that day.] As it turned out, this was our last chance." Linwood's brother was killed on Sept. 27, 1946, when his AT-6 crashed just a few miles north of Hagerstown.

Now a resident of Hattiesburg, Mississippi, Orange said his military experience paved the way to "a fine professorial career." It gave him "enough GI Bill time" to complete a Ph.D. at Duke University.

Charles L. Downey — Army — WWII

A weary-looking Charles L. Downey (left) in combat gear and helmet Jan. 4, 1945. "Yours truly" is written on the back of the photo. Downey was posted in Ubach, Germany, a town near the Netherlands border, from Nov. 27, 1944, until Feb. 28, 1945.

Major Downey of Williamsport served as assistant quartermaster of the 102nd Infantry Division during WWII, participating in the liberation of Holland and the fighting that ended the war with Germany.

In an account completed some time after the fighting, Downey described a 1944 German bombing raid in Holland in which he and other soldiers grabbed their helmets and lay on the floor "scared stiff."

Later, he wrote of an English-speaking Dutch family, named Horio, that was hired to do the soldiers' laundry, and a meal of baked rabbit and potatoes the family and soldiers shared. Thirty-two years later, Downey would be reunited with the family's young son, who had helped with translations.

When John Horio (at center of inset photo above) visited his Kemps Mill Road home in the summer of 1976, Downey (right) returned a handmade coverlet intended to be passed on as a family heirloom (inset above). Horio's mother had presented the coverlet to Downey in appreciation for his role in the American liberation of her country.

A map with a tiny compass, the metal shaving mirror and a leather sewing case with regulation color thread Downey carried with him throughout the fighting in Europe.

After the war, Downey worked in The Herald-Mail Co.'s advertising department. He eventually became personnel manager and was later promoted to general manager for Schurz Communications, the newspaper's parent company. He was also the third of four generations of Downeys to serve as Washington County commissioners. Both his grandfather, Lewis Downey, and father, Simon Downey, were county commissioners, as was his son, R. Lee Downey.

In a tape recording made several years ago, Downey recalled the last days of the war in April 1945. Having scouted out an advance location for his unit in a girls school in a small German village, Downey recalled two memorable events: learning of the death of President Franklin Roosevelt and escaping a German bombing raid.

. . . during the evening, a German observation plane was flying over and he was no doubt looking for some targets, and the next morning, we were having some pretty good hot cakes for breakfast. We had the kitchen set up in the big garage of the school.

We had all these trucks in the courtyard, and I feel sure the Germans were really looking for us. And they dropped the bomb, but it landed downtown, really about a quarter of a mile from us. But it was quite a percussion — killed quite a few people in the town — but missed us.

But the percussion did knock the plaster off the wall and the ceiling and it fell down in the hot cake batter, and that put us out of the hot cake business for breakfast. End of story."

Menu (below) served on Sept. 23, 1945, signed by some of the men with whom Downey served in the closing days of WWII.

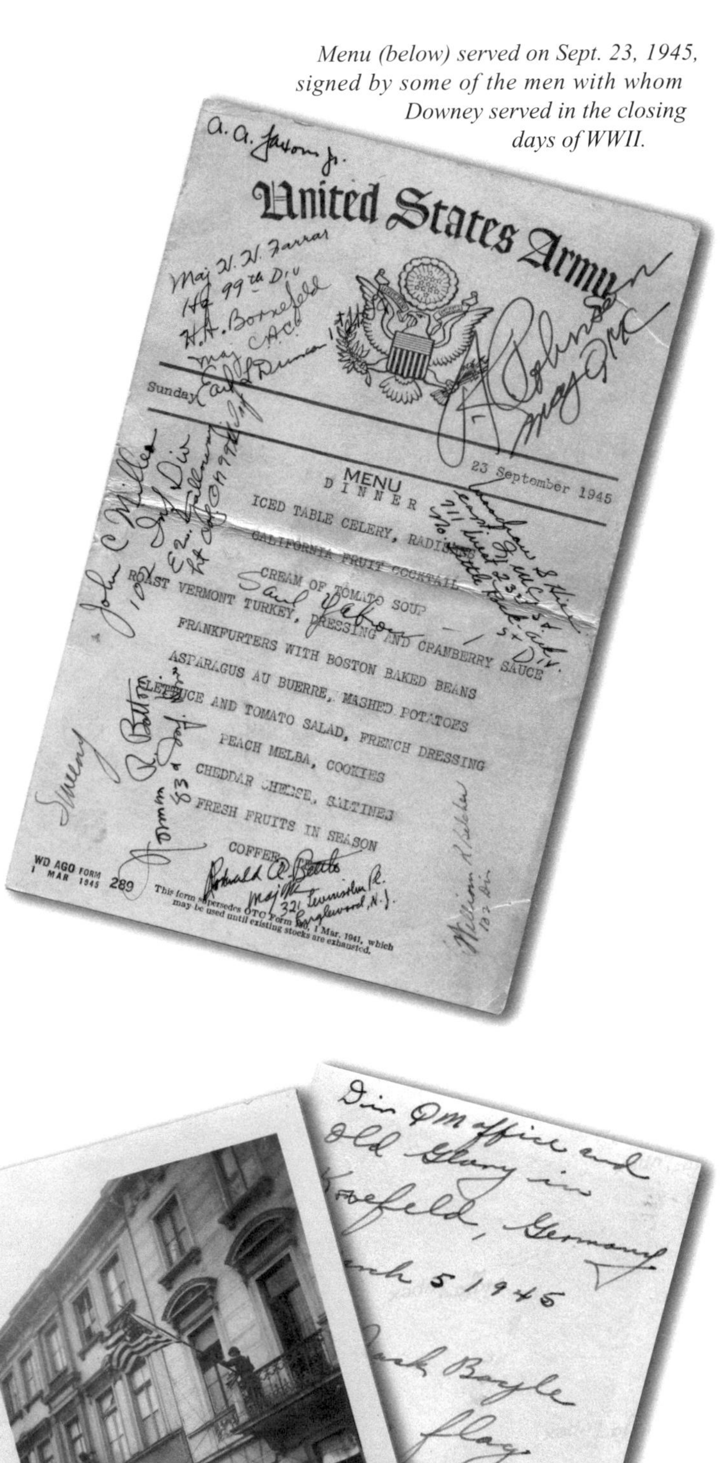

United States Army

Sunday

23 September 1945

MENU
DINNER

ICED TABLE CELERY, RADISHES
CALIFORNIA FRUIT COCKTAIL
CREAM OF TOMATO SOUP
ROAST VERMONT TURKEY, DRESSING AND CRANBERRY SAUCE
FRANKFURTERS WITH BOSTON BAKED BEANS
ASPARAGUS AU BUERRE, MASHED POTATOES
LETTUCE AND TOMATO SALAD, FRENCH DRESSING
PEACH MELBA, COOKIES
CHEDDAR CHEESE, SALTINES
FRESH FRUITS IN SEASON
COFFEE

WD AGO FORM 289, 1 MAR 1945

This form supersedes OTC Form ..., 1 Mar. 1941, which may be used until existing stocks are exhausted.

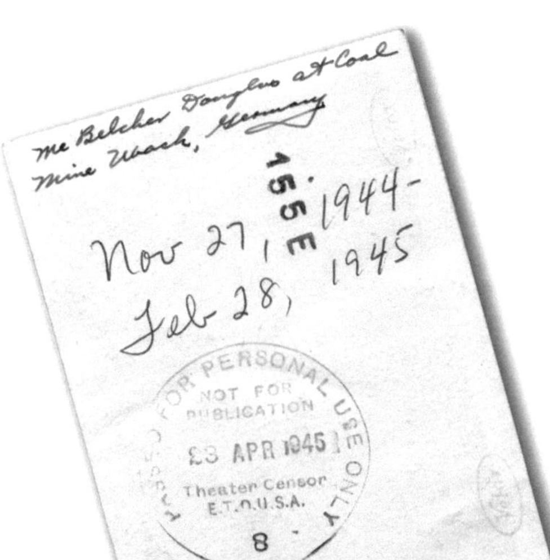

Maj. Downey, Capt. Belcher, and Col. William R. Douglas [Downey's supervising officer] at coal mine in Ubach, Germany. A stamp on the back of the photograph indicates the image was approved by the E.T.O. [European Theater of Operations] censor on April 23, 1945, and warns "Not for Publication."

"District Quartermaster's office and Old Glory in Kaefeld, Germany, on March 5, 1945" is the inscription on the back of a photograph taken by Downey. He identified the jubilant flag-waver as Cpl. Jack Boyle.

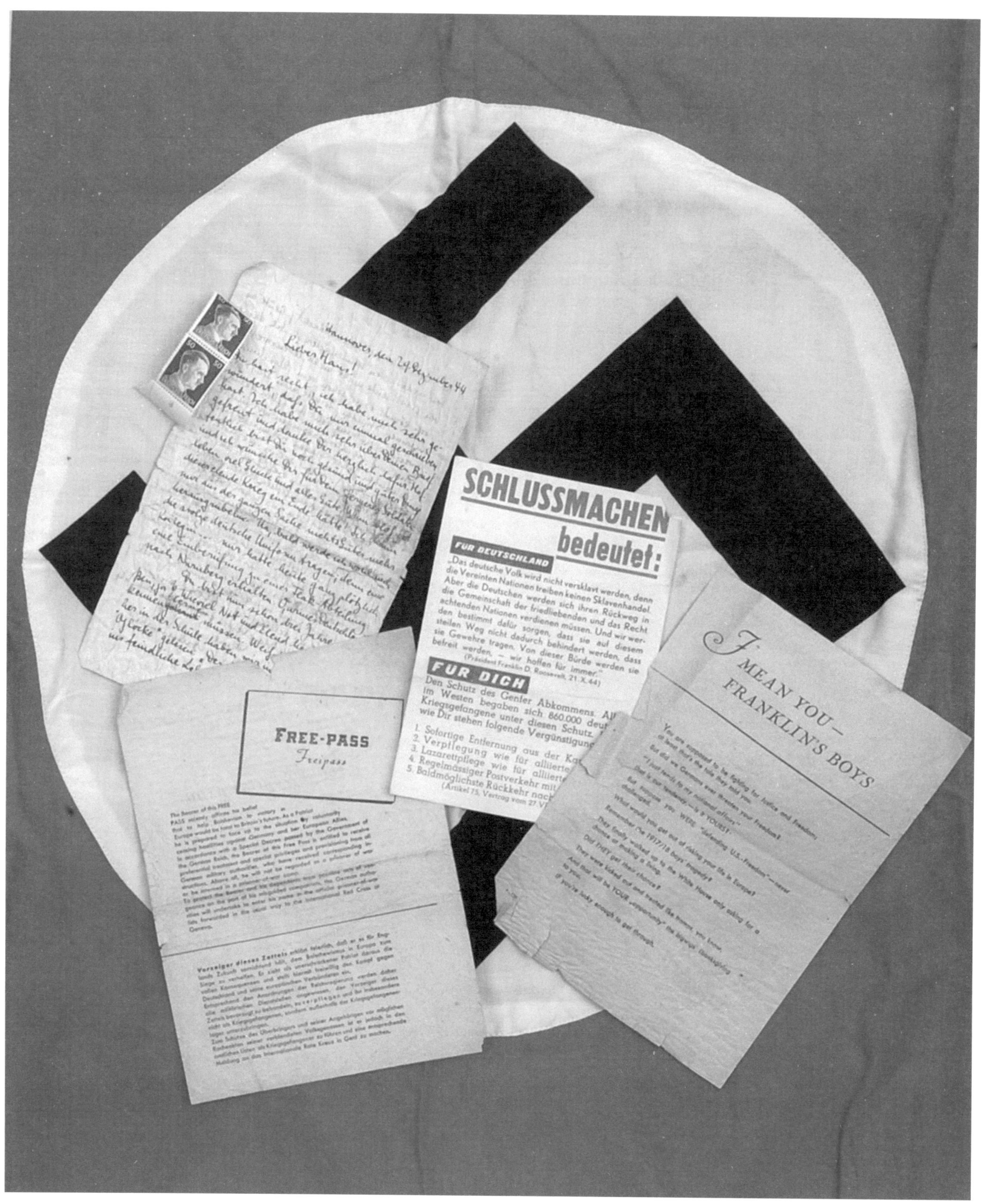

Downey returned with a Nazi flag and an assortment of enemy propaganda that was distributed behind American lines in an attempt to persuade U.S. troops to surrender. The collection also includes countervailing American Army leaflets, distributed within German ranks, explaining to soldiers what their surrender would mean "for Germany" and "for you."

Downey was among the group of soldiers from the 102nd Infantry Division who came upon the smoldering remains of a barn near the town of Gardelegen where 1,016 political and military prisoners were burned to death by German soldiers on Friday, April 13, 1945.

The prisoners were locked inside the barn and the structure was torched. Those who attempted to escape the flames were shot by German soldiers. Downey's division discovered the crime two days later, before German troops could hide the evidence. The division's commanding officer ordered the townspeople of Gardelegen to exhume the bodies the German soldiers had hastily buried in a mass grave, and rebury them in individually marked graves. A sign (left), erected by American soldiers, calls attention to the atrocity that took place only a few weeks before the end of the war in Europe. The site is now a national cemetery.

(Photographs and memorabilia courtesy of Patricia Martin, Charles L. Downey's daughter)

Snapshot of marked graves at Gardelegen Military Cemetery.

Passierschein

Der deutsche Soldat, der diesen Passierschein vorzeigt, benutzt ihn als Zeichen seines ehrlichen Willens, sich zu ergeben. Er ist zu entwaffnen. Er muß gut behandelt werden. Er hat Anspruch auf Verpflegung und, wenn nötig, ärztliche Behandlung. Er wird so bald wie möglich aus der Gefahrenzone entfernt.

Dwight D. Eisenhower
OBERBEFEHLSHABER
der alliierten Expeditions-Armeen

Englische Übersetzung nachstehend. Sie dient als Anweisung an die alliierten Vorposten.

SAFE CONDUCT

The German soldier who carries this safe conduct is using it as a sign of his genuine wish to give himself up. He is to be disarmed, to be well looked after, to receive food and medical attention as required, and to be removed from the danger zone as soon as possible.

Dwight D. Eisenhower
SUPREME COMMANDER,
Allied Expeditionary Force

Safe Conduct Pass (above) for German soldiers, honored by American and British forces, signed by Dwight Eisenhower, Supreme Commander, Allied Expeditionary Force.

Wilbur E. Huntzberry — Army — WWII

Wilbur E. Huntzberry joined the Army in 1944 and completed basic training at Camp Croft in South Carolina, sending the souvenir hat (lower right) to his wife. He later mailed a 1-cent post card showing Army jeeps under a 48-star American flag from Camp San Luis Obispo, California, to his daughter, Nancy. On the card he expressed the hope that Nancy and her baby brother "Buck" weren't fighting. "Don't forget to be a good girl," he wrote, signing the card, "from your Daddy."

Photograph of Huntzberry believed to have been taken in Germany. The specific details of his service have been lost to memory. Family members believe Huntzberry was a prisoner of war for a time during WWII, based on stories in which Huntzberry talked about how his German captors were puzzled by his Germanic surname — not believing Sgt. Huntzberry could be an American soldier. "They thought he was German," said Huntzberry's grandson, Curtis E. Shives.

(Photographs and memorabilia courtesy of Curtis E. Shives, Wilbur E. Huntzberry's grandson)

Howard H. Small — Army — WWII

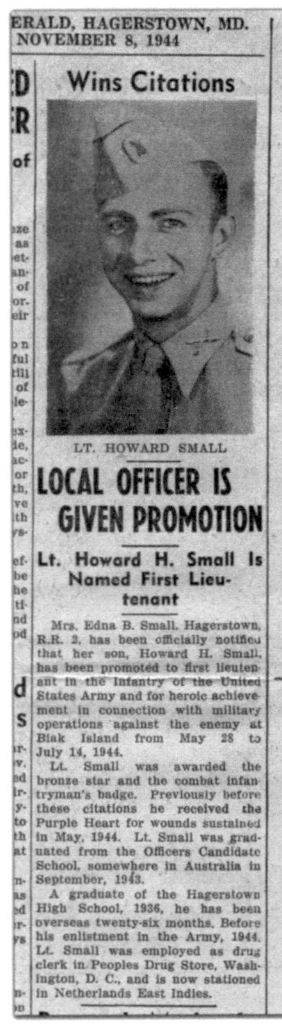

ERALD, HAGERSTOWN, MD.
NOVEMBER 8, 1944

Wins Citations

LT. HOWARD SMALL

LOCAL OFFICER IS GIVEN PROMOTION

Lt. Howard H. Small Is Named First Lieutenant

Mrs. Edna B. Small, Hagerstown, R.R. 2, has been officially notified that her son, Howard H. Small, has been promoted to first lieutenant in the Infantry of the United States Army and for heroic achievement in connection with military operations against the enemy at Biak Island from May 28 to July 14, 1944.

Lt. Small was awarded the bronze star and the combat infantryman's badge. Previously before these citations he received the Purple Heart for wounds sustained in May, 1944. Lt. Small was graduated from the Officers Candidate School, somewhere in Australia in September, 1943.

A graduate of the Hagerstown High School, 1936, he has been overseas twenty-six months. Before his enlistment in the Army, 1944, Lt. Small was employed as drug clerk in Peoples Drug Store, Washington, D. C., and is now stationed in Netherlands East Indies.

Howard H. Small, a Hagerstown High School Class of 1936 graduate, had been overseas for 26 months at the time of his promotion. The Hagerstown native had graduated from Officers Candidate School in Australia and was promoted to 1st lieutenant in 1944.

Among the medals Small received for his service in WWII were the American Defense Service Medal (left), the Purple Heart (center) and the World War II Victory Medal (right). Small was awarded the Purple Heart for wounds he received in May 1944 on the South Pacific island of Biak.

(Memorabilia courtesy of Rose Sweeney, Howard H. Small's sister-in-law)

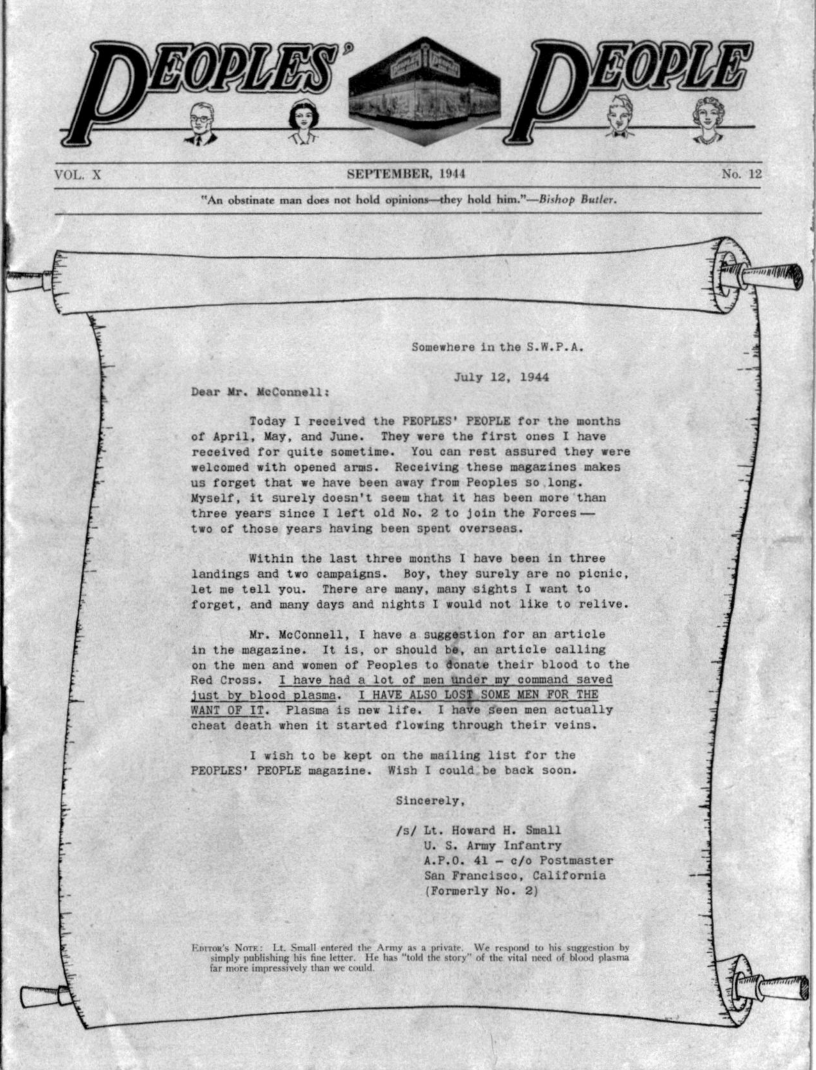

PEOPLES' PEOPLE

VOL. X | SEPTEMBER, 1944 | No. 12

"An obstinate man does not hold opinions—they hold him."—*Bishop Butler.*

Somewhere in the S.W.P.A.

July 12, 1944

Dear Mr. McConnell:

Today I received the PEOPLES' PEOPLE for the months of April, May, and June. They were the first ones I have received for quite sometime. You can rest assured they were welcomed with opened arms. Receiving these magazines makes us forget that we have been away from Peoples so long. Myself, it surely doesn't seem that it has been more than three years since I left old No. 2 to join the Forces — two of those years having been spent overseas.

Within the last three months I have been in three landings and two campaigns. Boy, they surely are no picnic, let me tell you. There are many, many sights I want to forget, and many days and nights I would not like to relive.

Mr. McConnell, I have a suggestion for an article in the magazine. It is, or should be, an article calling on the men and women of Peoples to donate their blood to the Red Cross. I have had a lot of men under my command saved just by blood plasma. I HAVE ALSO LOST SOME MEN FOR THE WANT OF IT. Plasma is new life. I have seen men actually cheat death when it started flowing through their veins.

I wish to be kept on the mailing list for the PEOPLES' PEOPLE magazine. Wish I could be back soon.

Sincerely,

/s/ Lt. Howard H. Small
U. S. Army Infantry
A.P.O. 41 - c/o Postmaster
San Francisco, California
(Formerly No. 2)

EDITOR'S NOTE: Lt. Small entered the Army as a private. We respond to his suggestion by simply publishing his fine letter. He has "told the story" of the vital need of blood plasma far more impressively than we could.

*Prior to entering the Army, Small had worked as a clerk at Peoples Drug Store in Washington, D.C. The September 1944 edition of the company newsletter, **Peoples' People**, carried this letter from Small encouraging "the men and women of Peoples to donate their blood to the Red Cross." Small went on to say that "I have a lot of men under my command saved just by blood plasma. I HAVE ALSO LOST SOME MEN FOR THE WANT OF IT. Plasma is new life. I have seen men actually cheat death when it started flowing through their veins."*

Lt. Small Gets Hero's Medal

Bronze Star Medal Is Awarded County Boy In Southwest Pacific.

Lt. Howard H. Small, son of Mrs. Edna B. Small, Hagerstown Rt. 2, has been awarded the Bronze Star medal for personal valor and a deep devotion to duty on the field of battle, according to a special dispatch to the Daily Mail from headquarters of the 41st Division, Southwest Pacific.

The decoration was bestowed upon Lt. Small, a platoon leader, by Maj. Gen. Jens A. Doe, commander of the famed infantry division.

The special dispatch states that "during a phase of most recent operations against the Japs, they struck Small's battalion on a flank where only one platoon was deployed. With alarcrity, the Marylander, collected his men and moved across a fire-flaked area to the aid of the hard-pressed defenders.

"On the scene, Small coordinated the defense, deftly spread his men into the proper formation and the foe was repulsed with heavy losses. By his courageous action and leadership the battalion was spared what might have turned into a serious predicament had the Japs broken through."

Details of Howard H. Small's heroic service against enemy operations on the island of Biak from May 28 to July 14, 1944, were big news back home. He was serving with the 3rd Platoon, 41st Infantry Division of the 162nd Infantry in the South Pacific.

Jack Schaffer — Army — WWII

Jack Schaffer served with the 90th Infantry Division and participated in the D-Day invasion. The photograph (above) was taken in Detroit, Michigan, just before he went overseas in 1943. He would survive the D-Day invasion and his division's march through Europe. The end of the war found Schaffer in Klatovy, Czechoslovakia (below). He served in the Army of Occupation in Germany until his unit was returned to the States and he was discharged in December 1945. He would rejoin the Army in 1947.

Schaffer, a member of 2nd Platoon, Company A., strikes a relaxed pose near a bridge over the Rhine River in Germany. As part of its sweep through Europe, the 90th Infantry Division crossed dozens of rivers and liberated hundreds of towns and several million people from German control.

Schaffer, who had celebrated his 19th birthday in a foxhole, was in Germany when he was wounded in action on Oct. 5, 1944. He was on patrol in no man's land stringing barbed wire when he tripped the wire to a booby trap.

Schaffer was only 18 at the time of the D-Day invasion. His first exposure to continental Europe was spilling out of landing craft in the English Channel positioned too far away from shore "with water up to your neck." He was carrying six .81 mm mortars to shore. Heavy in their own right, they became even heavier as they filled with water. He made his way to the shore and quickly dug a foxhole. On D-Day + 1, Schaffer moved forward as part of his unit's objective to take St. Lo, when he came across a group of 19-20 bodies laid out on the ground. "They were burned so badly that they had shrunk to about half the size of normal," Schaffer said. They had been in a farmer's field when they were hit by a flame-thrower.

The Normandy landing took place on June 6, 1944, and Schaffer's division pressed on to St. Lo, a target that was expected to be captured in days but was only secured after weeks of deadly fighting. He did not have a hot meal until July 15, nearly six weeks after the invasion.

A TRIBUTE TO THE 90th DIV.

"Sometimes I think you don't know how ... . good you are. You are the best soldiers in the world. It was a great honor to command you."

GEN. GEORGE S. PATTON

Weiden, Germany July 13, 1945

Third Army commander Gen. George S. Patton's words of praise, expressed in July 1945, were treasured by members of the 90th Infantry Division, which held the distinction of having at least one unit in contact with the enemy every day from D-Day to VE-Day.

The Third Army's 90th Infantry Division, known as the "Tough 'Ombres," had more days in combat than any other division in the European Theater. Originally the red "T" and the "O" stood for Texas and Oklahoma, since the majority of the division was made up of men from those two states, but eventually its ranks were filled by soldiers from across the country. Members of the "Tough 'Ombres" ("T" and "O") earned their reputation fighting their way through Europe.

The Division earned the Invasion Arrowhead and all five battle stars for the campaigns in Normandy, Northern France, Ardennes (Battle of the Bulge), Rhineland and Central Europe. Its members were also awarded the French Croix de Guerre. The 90th Infantry Division liberated Flossenburg concentration camp and captured the Merkers Salt Mine intact. It was the salt mine northeast of Frankfurt where the SS and Nazis stored gold from the Reichsbank, 400 art treasures from Berlin museums, and gold and personal possessions belonging to Nazi concentration camp victims. The 90th forced the surrender of the German 11th Panzer Division en masse and met Russian troops in Czechoslovakia.

Schaffer remembers liberating a hospital near Czechoslovakia and trying to persuade one of the nurses to play ***Tales from the Vienna Woods*** *by Johann Strauss. But she refused to play it because Strauss was a Jewish composer.*

Schaffer was one of a 12-member squad patrolling through a farmer's yard, when they received word that the war in Europe was over. The farmer invited them in and served veal cutlets and mashed potatoes and gravy — Schaffer's "first good meal" since landing in Normandy nearly 11 months earlier. It was then only a matter of days before the 90th Division met the Russian troops in Czechoslovakia.

Schaffer commemorated the end of the war in Europe by having his photograph taken with two women from the village in Czechoslovakia where his unit had moved in May 1945. Schaffer, in full combat gear, stands next to a brunette, who was married to a lieutenant in the Czech army. In the second photo, Schaffer is standing next to the blonde-haired, blue-eyed daughter of the farmer who provided shelter for Schaffer's squad in his barn, during the two weeks Schaffer's unit was in Czechoslovakia. "The farmer and his wife were a nice couple," Schaffer recalled, "but he watched me like a hawk. He knew I was about the same age as his daughter."

A record of Schaffer's service during WWII is recorded in this framed assortment of ribbons and insignia. At the top is the Combat Infantryman Badge with ribbon rack representing medals Schaffer was awarded for his service in WWII. The ribbons include (top down from left to right): The Bronze Star; Purple Heart; Good Conduct Medal; European-African-Mediterranean Campaign Medal; WWII Victory Medal; Army of Occupation Medal (Germany) and the French Croix De Guerre. At center, is Schaffer's Airborne Wings. Below, at left, is Schaffer's 82nd Airborne Division patch; Honorable Discharge Pin; Presidential Unit Citation, and his 90th Infantry Patch.

Schaffer displays a Nazi flag that was confiscated in Germany following WWII.

(Photographs and memorabilia courtesy of Jack Schaffer)

With the end of the war in Europe on May 8th, Schaffer took time to send a customized Mother's Day greeting home to his mother in 1945. He had sent to her a Christmas card six months earlier.

Amberg, Germany
June 6, 1945

Dear Mother and Dad,
Here goes my anniversary letter to you if you know what I mean. In other words today marks 365 days ago that my combat started. General Eisenhower proclaimed a legal holiday for the Army. I don't know how it was with you. Yes a year ago tonight I was in a foxhole with all that load that we were carrying and about a mile in shore. About this time they were dropping paratroopers and the sky was quite active with ack-ack.

That was quite an experience to have. I'm glad that one was done. That was some night in that foxhole and our clothes were all wet and I'm telling you, that we were cold. Here mother is the whole thing that I did since I left England.

When we got to England we wentto a part of Wales and there we stayed in those big tents. We trained a little but nothing to give us an idea then, that we were going to be in on the invasion. The place that we stayed at was called Berrington Park. Some big limey owned it. After being there for about a monthand a half we all moved to a camp that they called Camp 87. There we got new clothes and had everything inspected so we thoug that something would happen. We were there for about five days and one night we were on guard when they came down and wanted our platoon only to go back to the barracks. When we got there we were told to get ready to move out. In all we moved with the first battalion, third battalio regimental headquarters , and our platoon.

In this camp that we moved to they called it Syon Abbey. It was in southern England, about twenty miles from Plymonth. I never did get to Plymonth but the guys say that it was a nice place. At that camp they gave us

(2)

different kind of new equipment and we knew that we would be in on the invasion but we didn't know that it would be so close. Boy we had atime in that camp. We went to town all the time and it was pretty good. We didn't have any training to do but after being there for a few days they restricted us and three mornings before we left they told us that we would land on the coast of France.

Now you know that I'm in an Antitank Co. but I'm in the fourth platoon which is the mine Platoon. We take out mines and lay mines. This is the first time that I have ever told you what our duties was but thats it. We messed around wi with mines. Our duty was too carry mortar ammunition for the heavy weapons company of our third battalion. We hadsix mortars each and were they heavy. Well the sec ond morning before we left we thought we were going and they had us load up and do everything just like the orriginal would be. You know that the Army calls this dry run. Well we came back after beingpretty mad and won dered how many times that they would do this. The next morning we did the same thing only this time it was real We got on trucks and they took us to Plymouth. We had to walk quite a ways with that load and we boarded some small boats that took us out to the LCI in the harbor. We were on LCI 350. I think that the day was June 2. We were on it until June 6. On the LCI they told us That we would land on the coast of France on the Cherbou penninsula. Our duty would be to cut the Cherbourg penn in half and take Cherbourg. Our small part of the 90 th. would land at noon and support the 4th. division. The assembly point for our regiment would be a small hamlet called St. Germain de Veirvelle. Well the real day was to be June 5 but that night we had a bad storm so they postponed the whole thing.

(3)

At that time we were laying off the coast of England. So we layed around all day on June 5 and they said it would come off on June 6 , which it did,

When we got up in the morning it was a swell day and up on deck we watched the battle ships pound the shore. During the night we had moved to a transport area off the coast of France about 11 miles. I guess they had trouble cause we didn't load on a small invasion boat until 3 that afternoon. They were shelling the shore and the Germans were throwing shells out into the water. They let us offin the water about five hundred yards from the shore and they were glad to get rid of us. The water was up to our chests and they let about ten of us off and took the rest back out for a better land ing. I made it to shore but I don't know how . The other two boys who landed before me aren't aroundnow so I'm now the first one in the platoon who landed. Theres only fifteen of us left. Anyway we made it two this place that I mentioned in the first of my letter where we watched the paratroopers land. Finnally the whole pla toon made it but we were all over that beach.

The next morning we got to the assemby area and got rid of our mortars .Aboutten days later the company joined us and we got down to bussiness. I think that I'll get off that subject.

We had our first hot meal July 15 and was in a place until July 25 when we broke out of the penninsula. On July 24 they bombed the Germans with everything and thats where General McNair was killed. After the penn insula we drove to Le Mans and turned back to go to the Falaise Gap. It took a few days to finnish off the Ger man Seventh Army and a British outfit came in to releive us. Then wemoved south of Paris and past Reims to Metz.

(4)

We were there for two months while they prepard for the seige of Metz. A few days before Metz fell we moved back for a four day rest. Then we crossed that Mosselle River. That was quite a crossing. The river was swelled and we couldn't get anything back or forth.

It was November 29 that we entered Germany. We got to th Saar Riverand had to stop. The Germans broke through and we had to go to Luxembourg. Thats when we were in Belgui for a couple days. From the bulge we went to the Seig friend Line again and I went to the hospital. When I came back we were in Central Germany around Erfurt. We fought to the Border of Czech and then headed south along the border. On May the 6 our regiment entered Czech and was there when the peace was signed.

I forgot to tell you when we were in England, General Collins (seventh corp. commander) General Burton (fourth division commander) and General Patton, our commander were there at various times to see us.

I remember General Patton, there watching our platoon drill. Thats why we thought something would happen if all those big boys would come down and see us,

Well mother I've made quite an account of myself for the past few days.

No mail today from anybody .I must have hurt my foot because it pains tonight. I think that I'll go to the medics tomorrow and see what they ca n do with it.

Well thats all .

Your son,
Jack

Schaffer typed this account of his service from D-Day to the end of WWII, in this first anniversary letter written to his mother, Mrs. John Schaffer, in Detroit, from Amberg, Germany, June 6, 1945 — exactly one year after the Normandy Invasion.

Samuel J. Geiser Jr. — Army — WWII

Francis W. Geiser — Army Air Forces — WWII

Smithsburg brothers Samuel J. Geiser Jr. and Francis W. Geiser both served in the military in WWII. One came home, and one did not.

An Army infantryman, Samuel Geiser served in General George S. Patton's 6th Armored Division and saw action in France during the European campaign. He was actively engaged in the battle for Brest, France, and was in the vicinity of Nancy, France, when he was killed in action on Nov. 11, 1944. His last letter home told of being in Nancy on a few days' leave shortly before he was killed.

Samuel began his military service on March 23, 1942, at the age of 33. A 1928 graduate of Smithsburg High School, he had been employed for a brief period at the Barnhart & Clopper clothing store in Smithsburg. He then went to Washington, D.C., where he worked at a laundry before beginning his military tour of duty. He went overseas in February 1944.

Brother Francis W. Geiser served in the Army Air Forces as an engineer/gunner on a B-24 "Liberator," nicknamed "Termite Chaser." A member of the 15th Army Air Force, he flew 50 missions over enemy territory with a B-24 Liberator group, operating from an advanced air base in Italy. His group actively participated in air assaults on industrial and communication targets in Southern Germany, France, Northern Italy and the Balkans.

Tech Sgt. Francis Geiser received the Air Medal with three oak leaf clusters for "meritorious achievements while participating in sustained operational activities against the enemy." He was involved in some of the 15th Army Air Force's most successful missions, including aerial assaults over Steyr, Austria; Regensburg, Germany; and the oil fields in Ploesti, Romania.

(Photos and memorabilia courtesy of Robert C. Geiser, brother of Samuel J. and Francis W. Geiser)

Smithsburg Boy Killed In Action

Samuel J. Geiser, Jr., Meets Death While Fighting With Patton.

Samuel J. Geiser, Jr., technician fourth grade, son of Mr. and Mrs. S. J. Geiser, Smithsburg, was killed in action in France on November 11, according to a War Department telegram received by his parents.

Thirty-five years of age, the Smithsburg soldier was with Patton's army, participated in the battle for Brest and was in the vicinity of Nancy, France, when he was killed. His last letter told of being in Nancy on a few days leave before he was killed.

A graduate of the Smithsburg High school, class of 1928, he was employed for a brief period at the Barnhart and Clopper clothing store here before going to Washington, where he had been employed with a laundry before entering the service on March 23, 1942. He had been overseas since February, 1944.

Besides his parents, three brothers, Francis W., who is back at Langley Field, Va., after 50 missions in overseas action; Richard, Washington, and Robert, at home, survive.

THE CHIEF OF STAFF
WAR DEPARTMENT
WASHINGTON, D. C.
OFFICIAL BUSINESS

WASHINGTON, D.C. DEC 7 4-PM 1944

PENALTY FOR PRIVATE USE TO AVOID PAYMENT OF POSTAGE, $300

Mrs. Vera B. Geiser
Smithsburg, Maryland

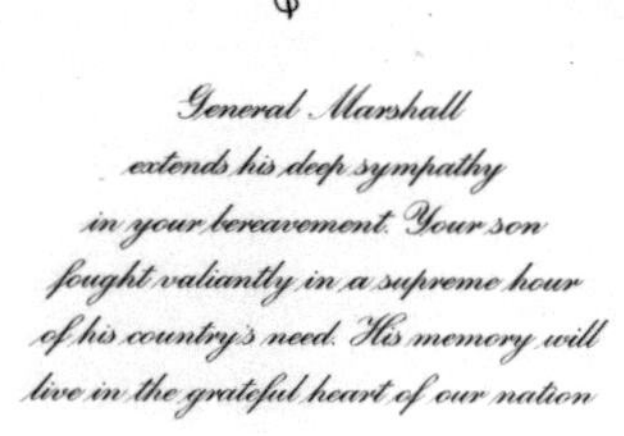

General Marshall
extends his deep sympathy
in your bereavement. Your son
fought valiantly in a supreme hour
of his country's need. His memory will
live in the grateful heart of our nation

Tech 4 Samuel Geiser Jr. (above) was killed in action in Nancy, France, on Nov. 11, 1944. A card of condolence was sent to his mother in Smithsburg by the Chief of Staff, War Department, Washington, D.C.

Smithsburg Boy On 50 Missions

Sergeant Geiser Operated From Base In Italy.

Fifteenth Army Air Force, Aug. 7 —Technical Sergeant Francis W. Geiser, son of Mr. and Mrs. S. J. Geiser, Smithsburg, Maryland, has flown fifty missions over enemy territory as an engineer-gunner in a 15th Army Air Force B-24 Liberator group operating from an advanced air base in Italy. This group has actively participated in

Technical Sergeant Francis W. Geiser beside the propeller of his B-24 bomber.

the recent air assaults upon industrial and communications targets in Southern Germany, France, Northern Italy, and the Balkans.

He is the recipient of the Air Medal and the first three Oak Leaf Clusters "for meritorious achievement while participating in sustained operational activities against the enemy."

Sergeant Geiser has flown on some of the most successful missions ever made by the 15th Army Air Force. Some of these include the aerial assaults over Steyr, Austria; Regensburg, Germany; and the Ploesti, Rumania, oil fields.

His wife, Mrs. Margaret Geiser, resides at Smith... Maryland.

Sergeant M...

Tech. Sgt. Francis Geiser of Smithsburg flew 50 missions with a B-24 Liberator group operating out of Italy during WWII. He was a member of the crew of The Termite Chaser #1, B-24 Liberator, with the 450th Bomb Group, 722nd Squadron. Pictured in the front row, from left, are: Sgt. Donald C. Hines, crew chief; Sgt. Walter J. Kostro, gunner; Sgt. John P. Connor, radio operator; Sgt. Charles R. Warren, radio operator; Sgt. Francis W. Geiser, engineer; Sgt. Baltizai C. Balazic, assistant radio operator; and Sgt. Glen K. Platt, gunner. In the back row, left to right, are: Lt. Marion D. Medley, co-pilot; W. J. Hodges, navigator; Lt. William H. Glavin, bombardier; and Lt. Walter J. Sharff, pilot.

Sgt. Francis W. Geiser is presented with a medal from Major Orris, in Manduria, Italy, on March 30, 1944, for completion of 28 missions with a B-24 Liberator group.

Paul H. Barr Jr. — Navy — WWII

Paul H. Barr Jr. was a riveter at Fairchild Aircraft when he joined the Navy in July 1943. He would spent most of the war in the South Pacific in New Guinea and the Philippines as a Navy Seabee.

Barr brought back this heart-shaped, mother-of-pearl pendant for his mother, but he also came back with a case of malaria, courtesy of the jungles of the South Pacific islands.

(Photograph and memorabilia courtesy of Rose Sweeney, Paul H. Barr Jr.'s sister)

Denzil E. Viands — Army — WWII

One of the most cherished possessions of service-members near the end of WWII was their military separation and discharge papers. The personalized, leather-bound portfolio (below) was presented to Denzil E. Viands (above) of Hagerstown by the Western Maryland Railway.

(Photograph and memorabilia courtesy of Rose Sweeney, Denzil E. Viands' sister-in-law)

Richard Grumbacher — Army — WWII

Richard Grumbacher works at his desk (below) somewhere in Italy during WWII. Born in York, Pennsylvania, Grumbacher was drafted into the Army Air Corps in the summer of 1941. After training in Texas and Florida, he was sent to Europe, where he served as a squadron commander in England, North Africa, Sicily and Italy. He returned to the States in April 1945 and prepared to be sent to the Pacific. But after V-J Day, he retired from the Army Air Forces as a captain in September 1945. The next year he married, and he and his wife, Marjorie, moved to Hagerstown in 1948, where he managed Eyerly's Department Store.

Women served as nurses in the military starting in 1901, when the Army established the Army Nurse Corps. The Navy followed suit in 1908, with the Navy Nurse Corps. Nurses held the insignia of rank but lacked full military status. In World War I, approximately 34,000 women served as nurses in the various branches of the military.

After the bombing of Pearl Harbor in WWII, largely to free up men for combat duty, Congress created the Women's Auxiliary Army Corps (WAACS) on March 15, 1942, and on July 30 authorized the Navy's Women Accepted for Volunteer Emergency Service (WAVES) and the Marine Corps Women's Reserve.

During WWII, an estimated 140,000 women served in the Women's Army Corps and 60,000 in the Army Nurse Corps. There were 100,000 Navy WAVES and 14,000 members of the Navy Nurse Corps. Approximately 23,000 women served in the Marine Corps Women's Reserve (MCWR), and close to 13,000 in the Coast Guard (SPARS). Altogether, more than 400,000 women served in the U.S. military during WWII.

Marjorie Grumbacher — WAVES — WWII

Marjorie Cohen Grumbacher in her WAVES uniform (below) during basic training in Northampton, Massachusetts, in 1942. A Pennsylvania native, Grumbacher was attending law school in Boston when she enlisted in the Navy on Oct. 6, 1942. "The men were leaving, and I wanted to do something for our country, too," she said. In the Navy, she became a member of the first class of WAVES [Women Accepted for Volunteer Emergency Service], which had been authorized by Congress on July 30 of that year.

The women were not being trained for combat but instead as cryptographers, freeing up men to fight. "Just about everyone in the first class was trained in communications," she said, "because they figured women could type."

The 1,000 WAVES were sent to Smith College in Northampton, Massachusetts, for three months of training. From there, Grumbacher went to the Philadelphia Navy Yard. Like most of her colleagues, she worked in communications, coding and decoding messages.

Due to her year of law school, Grumbacher was moved to the Legal Office the following year as an assistant to a District Legal Officer. "The Marines took care of disciplinary matters," she said. "I worked for three different Marine majors there."

During her last year and a half in the Navy, Grumbacher worked as a prosecuting attorney, with the Judge Advocate General's Corps, popularly known as a JAG.

"It was a good experience," Grumbacher said. "I enjoyed the Navy."

(Photos courtesy of Marjorie Grumbacher)

James Charles Mongold — Marine Corps — WWII

When James Charles Mongold left Maryland in 1943 to serve in the Marines in WWII, he took two things with him — a picture of Jesus and a camera. He carried them both with him for two years, and captured on film some of the most dramatic fighting of the war in the Pacific.

"He wasn't supposed to take photos," said his son, Dennis Mongold. "He carried that camera and another one under his tunic. They would have confiscated them if they'd found them."

As a mechanic with a Marine aviation unit, James Mongold saw action in places including the Marianas, Kwajalein in the Marshall Islands and Okinawa.

Dennis Mongold said, "He didn't talk about the war until late in his life. Then he spoke of the 24-hour shelling of everything made to man, and hiding in a cave to escape it. He talked about landing in Kwajalein as ground support with the air group, and he mentioned the terrible fighting in Okinawa. But just as he started to open up, he had a stroke."

Shown below are several of James Mongold's photos, most of them taken by him. All are believed to be taken during or after the invasion of Okinawa.

Picture of Jesus carried into war by James Charles Mongold. In a letter to his family from Okinawa, he wrote:

"It's terrible to see people kill each other like this. Thanks to the Lord, I am still living."

James Charles Mongold stands at far right in the upper row with other members of his Marine ground support unit, VMF 224, which was responsible for aircraft maintenance and the condition of airstrips. Mongold told his family he was one of six members of the group who survived the fighting during the invasion of Okinawa.

(Photos courtesy of Dennis Mongold, son of James Charles Mongold)

In a letter Mongold sent home from Okinawa, he described the tough battle on the Japanese island:

"When all those ships started spitting fire, a Jap plane doesn't have a chance. I never dreamed I would get this far from home and see what I have seen. It's terrible to see people kill each other like this. Thanks to the Lord, I am still living."

An expert rifleman and gunner, MP Richard William Smith fought at Guadalcanal, where he earned a Bronze Star and also caught malaria and spent eight months in the hospital. Years later, Smith marked his copy of *Young American Patriots*, a commemorative chronology of WWII, published by National Publishers, Inc., with

dates and notes that pertained to his service. He presented the book to his son, Gregory, on Dec. 10, 1950. The photos on these pages show Richard William Smith and some of his buddies on Guadalcanal, along with his helmet and canteen belt. (Photos and memorabilia courtesy of Gregory Smith, son of Richard William Smith)

Four Brothers — E. Ross Cline — Army — WWII

Ross Cline was a 19-year-old farmhand in Smithsburg in October 1944 when the Army called him to fight in WWII. Born in Downsville into a family of 13 children, Ross was one of four brothers who served in the military during and after WWII. A private 1st class, he served in Company D, 255th Infantry Regiment. He said his most memorable experience was the time his 1st sergeant was hit by gunshot and the two lay in a foxhole all night. The next morning they found the body of the German who had done the shooting, lying only a few feet away.

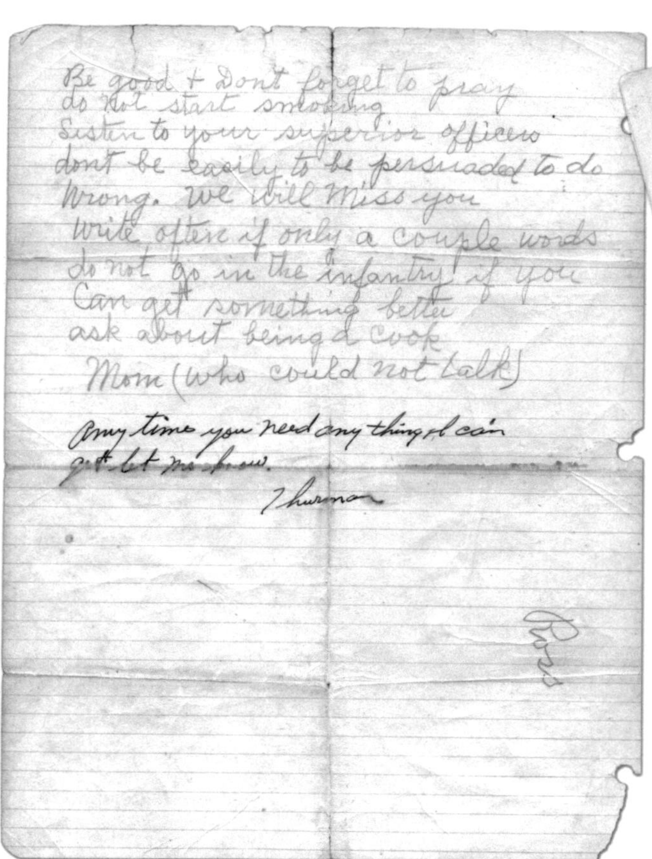

Be good + Dont forget to pray
do not start smoking
Listen to your superior officers
dont be easily to be persuaded to do
wrong. We will Miss you
write often if only a couple words
do not go in the infantry if you
Can get something better
ask about being a cook
Mom (who could not talk)

Any time you need any thing I can get let me know.
Thurman

Ross

Ross Cline's mother packed this note in his suitcase when he left for the Army in WWII. She wrote: "Be good + don't forget to pray. Do not start smoking. Listen to your superior officers. Don't be easily persuaded to do wrong. We will miss you. Write often if only a couple words. Do not go in the infantry if you can get something better. Ask about being a cook. Mom (who could not talk)." Ross' brother Thurman, who had just been honorably discharged from the Army for medical reasons, added the note: "Any time you need anything I can get let me know."

As a member of the 63rd Infantry Division under Gen. George S. Patton, Ross Cline "marched from Le Havre nearly all the way to Berlin" and fought in the Central Europe Campaign. Along the way he witnessed destruction caused by American bombs and passed the German Siegfried Line.

Ellis T. Cline — Army — WWII

The U.S. had not officially entered WWII when 22-year-old Ellis T. Cline left his job as a knitting machine operator and joined the Army in March 1941. Employed as a supply clerk with the 38th Ordnance Company, he served in Africa and Italy.

Thurman P. Cline — Army — WWII

Thurman P. Cline's service in the military was cut short after only seven months when he was honorably discharged for medical reasons at Camp Shanks, New York. The Downsville man was drafted in March 1943 in the midst of WWII. Pvt. Cline worked as a utility repairman with the 452nd Quartermaster Laundry Company.

(Photos and memorabilia courtesy of E. Ross Cline)

Walter L. Cline — Air Force — Libya, Cold War

Walter L. Cline spent much of his time in the Air Force at Wheelus Field in Libya. Though close to the shores of the Mediterranean Sea, the climate there was anything but pleasant. Cline, an aircraft mechanic, said, "It was so hot you could fry eggs on the wings of the planes," and whenever possible pilots would fly at night because it was so hot during the day.

This photo shows Cline in Libya on the wing of a F-84 Thunderjet — a turbojet fighter-bomber on which he served as crew chief. Cline said his four years in the Air Force "helped me in the long run. I got to travel, plus I was trained and able to get a good job."

Harry C. Grove Jr. — Army Air Forces — WWII

After Dr. Harry C. Grove Jr. joined the Army in 1942, he swore he would never again sign up to join anything once he got out.

He had his first heart attack while serving his country as an Army Air Forces dentist. He died ten years after being discharged from military service. A graduate of the University of Maryland Dental School, he had been engaged in the private practice of dentistry in Hagerstown for three years when the Japanese bombed Pearl Harbor. He enlisted ten months after that infamous attack, leaving behind his wife Beatrice. He eventually served as a prosthodontist on Okinawa and in Fukuoka, Japan, during the American occupation.

In Japan, Grove's duties expanded to constructing full dentures, partial dentures and stationary bridgework. One of the prized keepsakes he brought home from the war was a wood sign saying "Harry Grove - Dentist" in Japanese, which matched its English counterpart. During his time in Japan, Grove and two fellow officers entered a Japanese officers' patrol post during the night. He acquired two Japanese officers' swords and a large silk Japanese flag. They remain in his family's possession today.

As a dental officer with the rank of captain, Grove examined, diagnosed and treated hundreds of military personnel. In addition, he served as a mentor and teacher, giving young recruits advice on proper dental care and training technicians in the duties of dentist's assistant. He took his own dental equipment with him when he enlisted in October 1942, along with his favorite pair of eyeglasses.

Dr. Harry Grove collected numerous Army Air Forces patches and insignia during his military service. He enlisted in October 1942 and was assigned to Mitchel Field, New York, upon activation to commissioned service. He served overseas from July 25, 1945 to March 4, 1946.

(Photographs and memorabilia courtesy of Nancy Foltz and Harry C. Grove III, children of Dr. Harry C. Grove Jr.)

William H. Ruck Jr. — Army — WWII

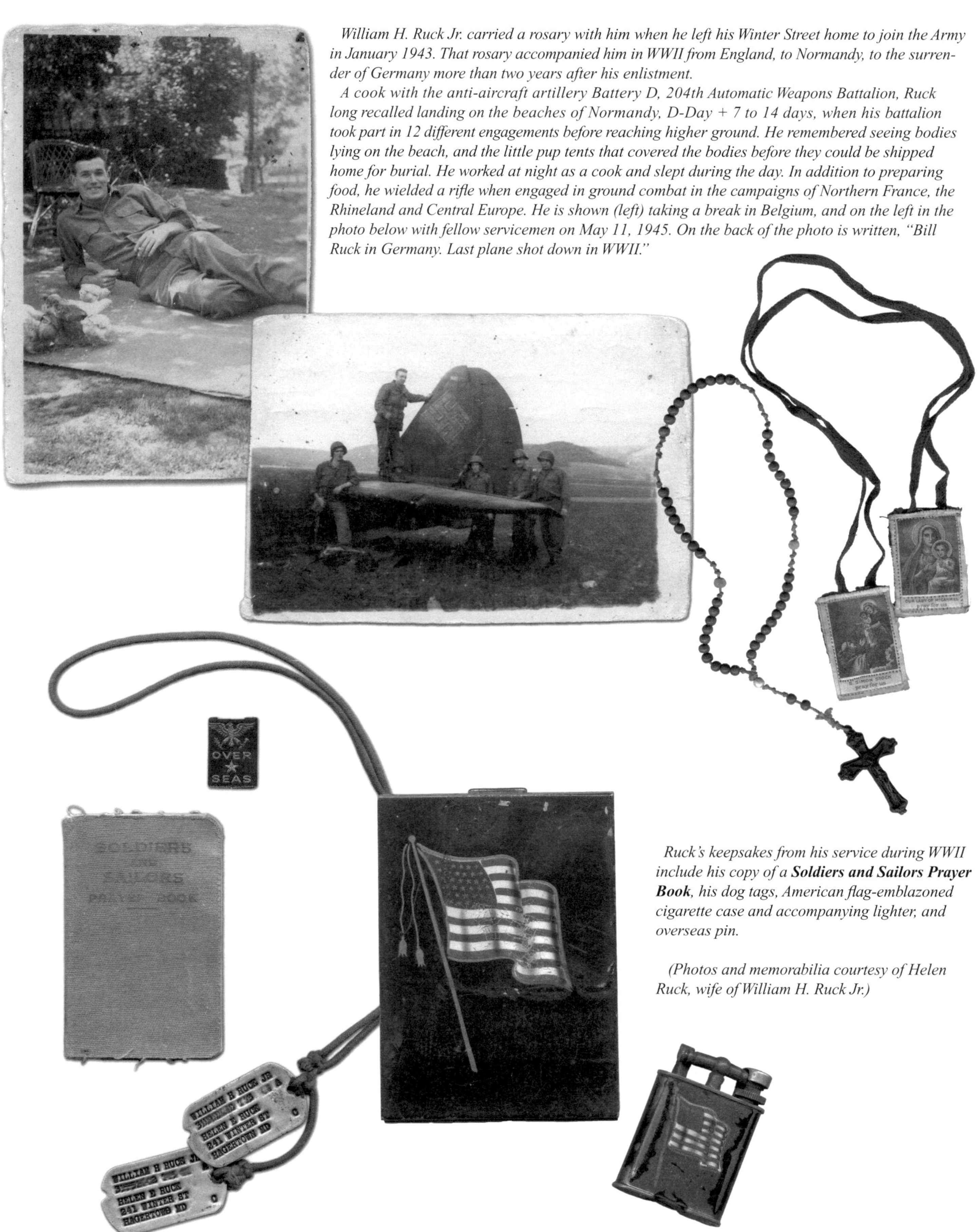

William H. Ruck Jr. carried a rosary with him when he left his Winter Street home to join the Army in January 1943. That rosary accompanied him in WWII from England, to Normandy, to the surrender of Germany more than two years after his enlistment.

A cook with the anti-aircraft artillery Battery D, 204th Automatic Weapons Battalion, Ruck long recalled landing on the beaches of Normandy, D-Day + 7 to 14 days, when his battalion took part in 12 different engagements before reaching higher ground. He remembered seeing bodies lying on the beach, and the little pup tents that covered the bodies before they could be shipped home for burial. He worked at night as a cook and slept during the day. In addition to preparing food, he wielded a rifle when engaged in ground combat in the campaigns of Northern France, the Rhineland and Central Europe. He is shown (left) taking a break in Belgium, and on the left in the photo below with fellow servicemen on May 11, 1945. On the back of the photo is written, "Bill Ruck in Germany. Last plane shot down in WWII."

Ruck's keepsakes from his service during WWII include his copy of a ***Soldiers and Sailors Prayer Book****, his dog tags, American flag-emblazoned cigarette case and accompanying lighter, and overseas pin.*

(Photos and memorabilia courtesy of Helen Ruck, wife of William H. Ruck Jr.)

A V-mail sent by William H. Ruck Jr. to his wife, Helen, in April 1944. V-mail, commonly used in WWII, was written on preprinted envelope sheets that were photographed and transferred to microfilm. As a result, one mail bag could carry the equivalent of 37 sacks of regular mail, with a reduction in weight from 2,575 to 45 pounds.

Proudly wearing new Army stripes, William H. Ruck Jr., (right), celebrates the end of WWII with buddies after their return to Camp Shanks, New York. The Army provided returnees with detailed information about adjusting to life in the U.S.

Samuel Ray Rhodes — Army — WWII

Samuel Ray Rhodes of Big Spring served in WWII as a military policeman with the 17th Airborne Division in Central Europe.

As a military policeman attached to an airborne unit, Rhodes earned his paratrooper qualification and held glider qualification as well. Gliders were used in WWII to transport men and materiel in combat zones.

Bracelet inscribed with "Love, Mother & Dad" on the back that Rhodes wore throughout his time in the service. His sister, Barbara Rhodes Gaddis, remembers the day she and her father took Samuel to the railway station when he left for the service. His mother was unable to accompany them and they "all cried for three days" after he left.

When the war with Japan was finally over, the family rejoiced that he would not be sent from Europe to fight in Japan, but he wasn't completely out of the woods. On his way home aboard ship, Samuel Rhodes was stricken with appendicitis, and was taken directly to a New York City hospital upon arrival. He recovered and was eventually reunited with his family.

(Photographs and memorabilia courtesy of Jay Dennis Rhodes, son of Samuel Ray Rhodes)

Rhodes arrived in Europe the day after the war in Europe ended. This photograph of Rhodes in helmet was taken in Nancy, France.

Jimmy Ridenour — Army — WWII

*Memorabilia collected by Pfc. Jimmy Ridenour include (lower right) a copy of **The Stars and Stripes** newspaper of May 8, 1945, announcing the surrender of Germany in WWII. To the right of the photo of Ridenour (below) are the patches of the 415th Regiment and the 104th Infantry "Timberwolf" Division, in which Ridenour fought. Above his photo is a book, **History of the 104th Infantry**, open to a page that shows him (second from left) carrying a Browning automatic rifle with his company in Duren, Germany, in 1945.*

A Downsville man, Ridenour was drafted into the Army in July 1944 and sent overseas to fight in Belgium and Germany. He said the 104th Infantry Division spent more time on the front lines than any other division. "Most of the 104th fighting was done at night," he said. "The Germans didn't like fighting at night."

Ridenour's most memorable experience of the war came on April 12, 1945, when he took part in the liberation of the concentration camp Dora at Nordhausen, Germany — also the site of the Nazis' V-2 rocket factory. He remembers the horrors he saw as he walked inside the buildings. A general told the division to get the townspeople to be litter carriers to get the bodies out of the building and bring them outside. The townspeople denied they knew anything about what was happening there, he said.

(Photos and memorabilia courtesy of Jimmy Ridenour)

*When Jimmy Ridenour was shot in the leg during reconnaissance in Bitterfield, Germany, the first thing he thought of, he said, was the famous WWI poem written by John McCrae, **In Flanders Fields.** McCrae was a Canadian physician who fought on the Western Front in 1914, then transferred to the medical corps to serve in a hospital in France. He died of pneumonia while on active duty in 1918. His volume of poetry, **In Flanders Fields and Other Poems**, was published in 1919.*

In Flanders Fields

In Flanders fields the poppies blow
Between the crosses, row on row,
That mark our place; and in the sky
The larks, still bravely singing, fly
Scarce heard amid the guns below.

We are the Dead. Short days ago
We lived, felt dawn, saw sunset glow,
Loved and were loved, and now we lie
In Flanders fields.

Take up our quarrel with the foe:
To you from failing hands we throw
The torch; be yours to hold it high.
If ye break faith with us who die
We shall not sleep, though poppies grow
In Flanders fields.

written by John McCrae

VE-DAY | New York · London Edition · Paris | VE-DAY

THE STARS AND STRIPES

Daily Newspaper of U.S. Armed Forces in the European Theater of Operations

TUESDAY, MAY 8, 1945

GERMANY QUITS

Today, May 8, is VE-Day, and will be officially proclaimed so by the leaders of the Big Three in simultaneous declarations in Washington, London and Moscow.

This was announced last night following unofficial celebrations yesterday afternoon throughout the world, inspired by a broadcast by Germany's new Foreign Minister that the Wehrmacht High Command had ordered its armed forces to surrender unconditionally, and by press reports, unconfirmed by SHAEF, that the Reich's capitulation to the Allies and Soviets had been signed early yesterday morning at Rheims, France, at a schoolhouse serving as Gen. Eisenhower's HQ.

Following publication yesterday afternoon of an Associated Press dispatch datelined Rheims and reporting that the surrender terms were signed by Lt. Gen. Walter Bedell Smith, Gen. Eisenhower's chief of staff; Russian Gen. Ivan A. Susloparov and French Gen. Francois Sevez, for the Allies and Russia, and Col. Gen. Gustav Jodl, new Wehrmacht chief of staff, for the Germans, the British Ministry of Information announced in London that today would be treated as VE-Day, ending the war five years, eight months and seven days after the Nazis invaded Poland on Sept. 1, 1939.

Prime Minister Churchill will broadcast the proclamation to the British at 3 PM in London today. Since the announcement will be made simultaneously by the Big Three leaders, this means that the statements by President Truman and Marshal Stalin ...

U.S. Really Let Go With Yells At (Unofficial) Peace News

NEW YORK, May 7—Clouds of torn paper and ticker tape swirled down on screaming crowds packed in the streets of New York this morning within a few minutes after news had been received that Germany had surrendered unconditionally.

London Shouts 'It's All Over'

THEY SIGNED

Passes, Furloughs Extended 48 Hours

Charles W. Riggs — Army Air Forces — WWII

Charles W. Riggs stands at the rear of his family's Maugansville home in 1943 in his Army Air Forces uniform.

Army Air Forces T/Sgt. Riggs (seated on the right second closest to the camera) meets with other members of his group at a periodic briefing at the air base in Natal, Brazil, in 1945, where he served as part of the South Atlantic Division, Air Transport Command during WWII. Natal was the easternmost tip of Brazil and, as the closest land point to Northern Africa, was a crucial jumping off point for many air transports heading to North Africa in support of the war in Europe.

(Photographs and memorabilia courtesy of Charles W. Riggs)

A few days before he returned to the United States, Riggs snapped this photo of Saturday morning parade at the edge of the airfield in Natal. Riggs was exempted from the exercises and able to take this photograph that day because he was leaving for the States two days later. "During the war, most Saturdays we had to get up, put on our Class A uniforms and go to the parade ground. We did not have a band of our own, so we had to rely on a Brazilian military band." The parades were doubly onerous for the men because Saturday would otherwise be a day off, and given the base's latitude in tropical Brazil, "it was summer there all year long."

This photograph of two Maugansville boys heading off to serve their country in WWII was taken in 1943 in Riggs' backyard, just before he and his friend, J. Robert Hyssong Jr., went overseas. Riggs headed to South America while Hyssong went to serve with the Army in Europe.

Hyssong participated in the invasion of southern France and said of WWII, "it cost four years of my life, but I was not injured, so I am thankful." Hyssong would later be called up to serve for a year, from September 1950 to September 1951, during the Korean War. He was a master sergeant assigned to train new men at Fort Meade, Maryland. "Again, I was lucky. I stayed at Meade the entire year," Hyssong said.

Riggs kept patches from his time in the Army Air Forces and Civil Air Patrol. The top patch is the insignia for the Air Transport Command. Center right is the Army Air Forces patch. At the bottom is the patch identifying the South Atlantic Forces in Brazil, featuring the stars of the Southern Cross, the most familiar constellation in the Southern Hemisphere. The patch at center left is the insignia for the Civil Air Patrol, the official auxiliary of the United States Air Force.

Riggs was a member of the Civil Air Patrol even before he went into the service. He didn't do any flying but he learned about first aid procedures and close-order drill and was ahead of the curve when he went off to basic training. The volunteer organization, established Dec. 1, 1941, still provides 95 percent of the continental U.S. inland search and rescue missions at the direction of the Air Force.

Riggs did not rejoin the Civil Air Patrol after the war. Instead, he used the GI Bill to pay for his education. He went to the University of Maryland and graduated with a degree in business administration.

The Air Transport Command patch, worn by members of several services assigned to South America during WWII, is a relatively unfamiliar insignia. But a clever unknown artist, with time on his hands, created an amended, unofficial symbol, ingeniously incorporating a cartoon version of pinup girl Betty Grable's famed legs into the emblem.

TO
PIGEONS, PILOTS, PASSENGERS, PIXIES
and all other habitants of the ozone
GREETINGS:
know ye by these presents,
by all the winds that blow from the four quarters of the earth whether from Grid North, Solid South, Near East or Mae West, by the stratosphere, the troposphere and the tropopause, the thunder, lightning and the rainbow, that

has on this______day of______19__
at Longitude 50° West, and at
LATITUDE 0° 00′ 00″
CROSSED THE EQUATOR, BY AIR
in view of which, hear ye:
I,
MERCURY,
godlike gremlin of the Greeks,
Jupiter's flying flash,
most high and mighty winged heel,
DO HEREBY AWARD HIM
One bag of select, tropically-warmed, Amazonian hot air, for use in describing his experiences on return to the States, and initiate him into the
TRUSTY ORDER OF FEATHERBACKS,
Equatorial Chapter,
and to all rights and privileges therein.

Signed and sealed:
MERCURIUS NUNTIUS AERIALIS
Chief Featherback.
Asst. Chief Featherback and Pilot:
Air Transport Command

Riggs brought home this souvenir pamphlet commemorating his crossing of the Equator by air. The certificate, addressed to all "Pigeons, Pilots, Passengers, Pixies and all other habitants of the ozone," from the winged Roman god Mercury, and signed by the captain flying the plane, is not unlike the Ancient Order of the Deep card given to those crossing the Equator by sea, only without buckets of fish guts and dunkings in sea water. "Flying at 10,000 to 15,000 feet above the Equator, there wasn't much of a ceremony," said Riggs.

HEADQUARTERS BULLETIN, Hq SATD-ATC, 7 August 1945, continued.

UNOFFICIAL:

RADIO NEWS - 0700 o'clock

ATOMIC BOMB: The Army Air Forces has released on the Japanese an atomic bomb containing more power than 20,000 tons of TNT, which produces more than 2000 times the blast of the largest bomb ever used before. Announcement of the development was made in a statement by President Truman, aboard the cruiser "Augusta", and released by the White House. The Bomb was dropped yesterday on Hiro Shima, important Japanese Army Base. The President said the bomb has "added a new and revolutionary increase in destruction. It is an atomic bomb. It is a harnessing of the basic power of the universe. The force from which the sun draws its power has been loosed against those who brought war to the Far East".

The President disclosed that the Germans worked feverishly in search of a way to use the atomic energy in their war effort, but failed. Meantime, American and British scientists studied the problem and developed two principal plants and some lesser factories for production of power. The President disclosed that more than 65,000 persons are now working in great secrecy in these plants, adding, "We have spent two billion dollars in the greatest scientific gamble in history, and we have won. We are now prepared to obliterate more rapidly and completely every productive enterprise the Japanese have above ground in any city. We shall completely destroy Japanese power to make war".

The President noted that the Big Three ultimatum issued July 26th at Potsdam intended to spare the Japanese people from added destruction, but that Japanese leaders rejected it. The atomic bomb now is the answer to that rejection, the president said. He stated, "They may expect a rain of ruin from the air, the like of which has never been seen on the earth".

The President stated this discovery may open the way for an entirely new conception of force and power, forecasting that sea and land forces will follow up this air attack in such numbers and power as the Japanese have never before witnessed.

*** *** ***

Senator Hiram Johnson, veteran California legislator, died at a Naval Hospital today at the age of 79.

125 B-29's, escorted by fighters, bombed Toyokawa, on Honshu.

Word of the dropping of the atomic bomb on Hiroshima reached Army Air Forces Tech Sgt. Charles W. Riggs in Brazil via a Headquarters Bulletin on Aug. 7, 1945. The Radio News announcement read in part:

"The Army Air Forces has released on the Japanese an atomic bomb containing more power than 20,000 tons of TNT, which produces more than 2000 times the blast of the largest bomb ever used before."

President Harry Truman was quoted as saying the bomb has "added a new and revolutionary increase in destruction. It is an atomic bomb. It is a harnessing of the basic power of the universe. The force from which the sun draws its power has been loosed against those who brought war to the Far East."

With the war in Europe over and the fight against Japanese troops still raging, Riggs and servicemen and servicewomen in Europe and elsewhere were fully expecting orders for the Pacific. When the surprise announcement came, Riggs recalls the "elation" that everyone felt that the war was effectively over. "It was a really happy event," Riggs recalled, "because we felt it would hasten our return to civilian life."

(Contributed by Charles W. Riggs)

(Contributed by Marie V. Zeigler)

Robert Benson Miller — Navy — WWII

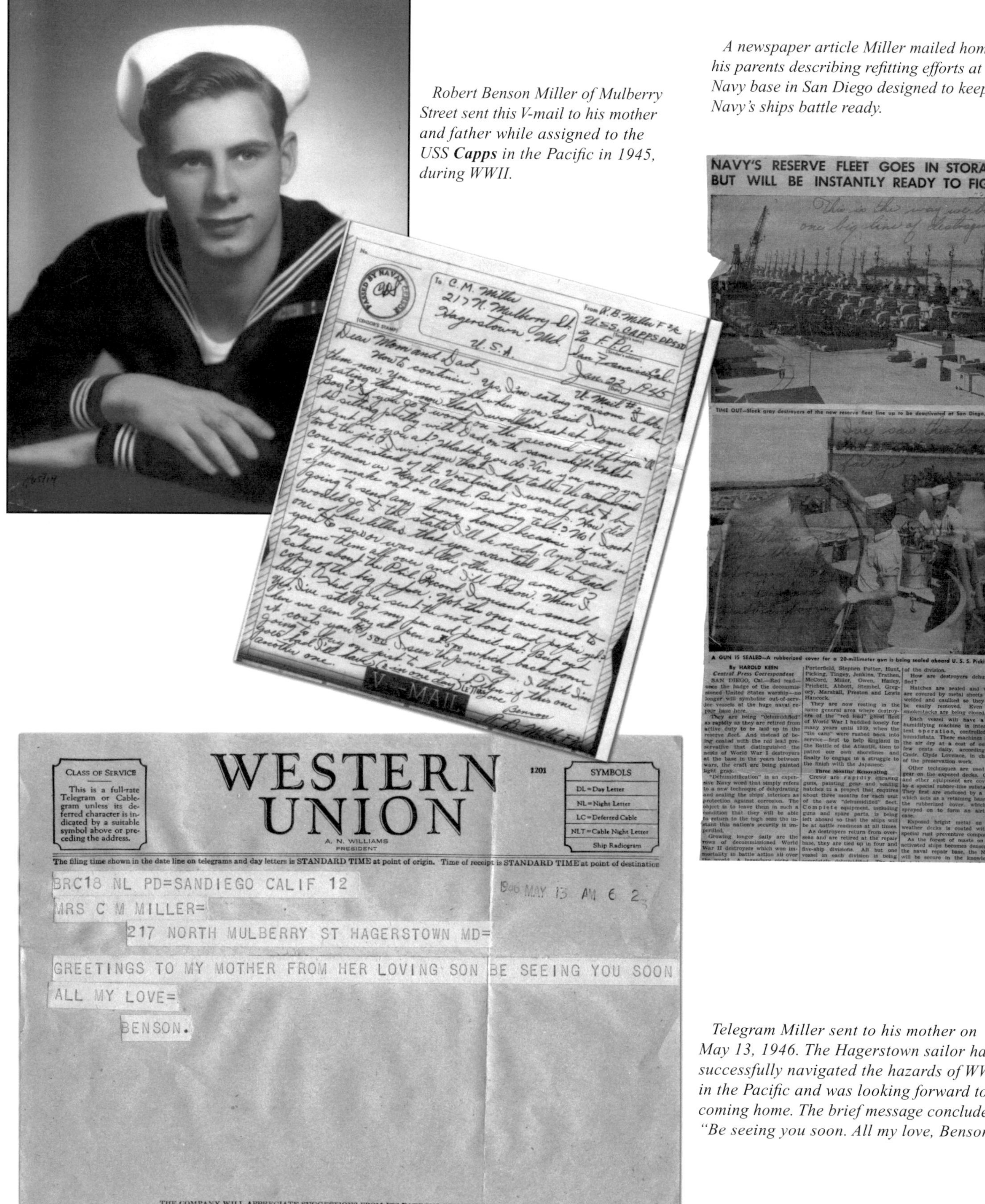

Robert Benson Miller of Mulberry Street sent this V-mail to his mother and father while assigned to the USS **Capps** in the Pacific in 1945, during WWII.

To C. M. Miller
217 N. Mulberry St.
Hagerstown, Md.
U.S.A.

From R. B. Miller
U.S.S. CAPPS DD550
F.P.O.
San Francisco, Cal.

Jan. 22, 1945

V-Mail #7

Dear Mom and Dad,

Love
Benson

V-MAIL

A newspaper article Miller mailed home to his parents describing refitting efforts at the Navy base in San Diego designed to keep the Navy's ships battle ready.

NAVY'S RESERVE FLEET GOES IN STORAGE BUT WILL BE INSTANTLY READY TO FIGHT

TIME OUT—Sleek gray destroyers of the new reserve fleet line up to be deactivated at San Diego, Cal.

A GUN IS SEALED—A rubberized cover for a 20-millimeter gun is being sealed aboard U. S. S. Picking.

By HAROLD KEEN
Central Press Correspondent

SAN DIEGO, Cal.—Red lead—once the badge of the decommissioned United States warship—no longer will symbolize out-of-service vessels at the huge naval repair base here.

They are being "dehumidified" as rapidly as they are retired from active duty to be laid up in the reserve fleet. And instead of being coated with the red lead preservative that distinguished the nests of World War I destroyers at the base in the years between wars, the craft are being painted light gray.

"Dehumidification" is an expensive Navy word that simply refers to a new technique of dehydrating and sealing the ships' interiors as protection against corrosion. The object is to leave them in such a condition that they will be able to return to the high seas the instant this nation's security is imperilled.

Growing longer daily are the rows of decommissioned World War II destroyers which won immortality in battle action all over the world. A legendary ... Porterfield, Stephen Potter, Hunt, Picking, Tingey, Jenkins, Trathen, McCord, Miller, Owen, Hailey, Prichett, Abbott, Stembel, Gregory, Marshall, Preston and Lewis Hancock.

They are now resting in the same general area where destroyers of the "red lead" ghost fleet of World War I huddled lonely for many years until 1939, when the "tin cans" were rushed back into service—first to help England in the Battle of the Atlantic, then to patrol our own shorelines and finally to engage in a struggle to the finish with the Japanese.

Three Months' Renovating

Crews are rapidly encasing guns, painting gear and sealing hatches in a project that requires about three months for each unit of the new "dehumidified" fleet. Complete equipment, including guns and spare parts, is being left aboard so that the ships will be at battle readiness at all times.

As destroyers return from overseas and are retired at the repair base, they are tied up in four and five-ship divisions. All but one vessel in each division is being ... of the division.

How are destroyers dehumidified?

Hatches are sealed and vents are covered by metal sheets tack welded and caulked so they can be easily removed. Even the smokestacks are being closed.

Each vessel will have a dehumidifying machine in intermittent operation, controlled by humidistats. These machines keep the air dry at a cost of only a few cents daily, according to Cmdr. Clyde Lovelace, in charge of the preservation work.

Other techniques are used for gear on the exposed decks. Guns and other equipment are covered by a special rubber-like substance. They first are enclosed by a web which acts as a retaining base for the rubberized cover, which is sprayed on to form an airtight case.

Exposed bright metal on the weather decks is coated with a special rust preventive compound.

As the forest of masts on deactivated ships becomes denser at the naval repair base, the Navy will be secure in the knowledge ...

CLASS OF SERVICE
This is a full-rate Telegram or Cablegram unless its deferred character is indicated by a suitable symbol above or preceding the address.

WESTERN UNION
A. N. WILLIAMS
PRESIDENT

1201

SYMBOLS
DL=Day Letter
NL=Night Letter
LC=Deferred Cable
NLT=Cable Night Letter
Ship Radiogram

The filing time shown in the date line on telegrams and day letters is STANDARD TIME at point of origin. Time of receipt is STANDARD TIME at point of destination

BRC18 NL PD=SANDIEGO CALIF 12

1946 MAY 13 AM 6 2

MRS C M MILLER=
217 NORTH MULBERRY ST HAGERSTOWN MD=

GREETINGS TO MY MOTHER FROM HER LOVING SON BE SEEING YOU SOON ALL MY LOVE=
BENSON.

THE COMPANY WILL APPRECIATE SUGGESTIONS FROM ITS PATRONS CONCERNING ITS SERVICE

Telegram Miller sent to his mother on May 13, 1946. The Hagerstown sailor had successfully navigated the hazards of WWII in the Pacific and was looking forward to coming home. The brief message concluded: "Be seeing you soon. All my love, Benson."

Brandenburg Brothers — Army — WWII

Hagerstown brothers Max and Kenneth "Buzz" Brandenburg posed for the camera for this WWII-era photograph. Both men were attached to Army Motor Pool units — Max in Germany and "Buzz" at Fort Jackson, South Carolina.

In this happy homecoming photograph, Buzz Brandenburg is surrounded by his family with wife, Dorothy "Tutty" Brandenburg, holding their 2-year-old son Kenneth "Lee" Brandenburg II, and 11-year-old daughter Barbara in 1945.

In a scene repeated across the country, returning GIs were embraced by their families following WWII. A proud, and, no doubt, relieved mother, Annie Brandenburg, sits between her two uniformed sons on the porch of her Jefferson Street home with Max A. Brandenburg (left) and Kenneth L. "Buzz" Brandenburg (right).

(Photographs courtesy of Barbara Reeder)

Homeward Bound — WWII

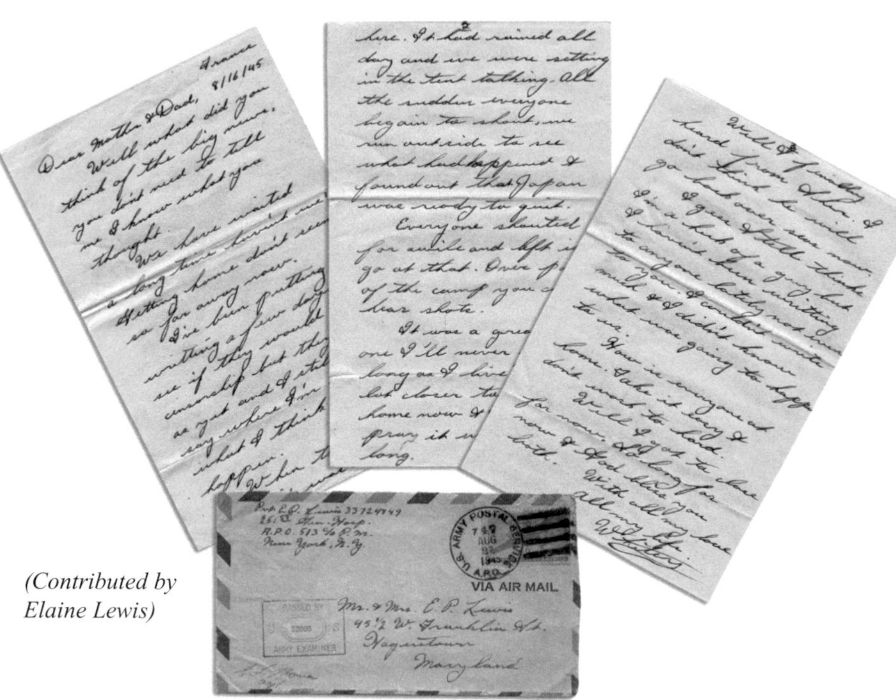

(Contributed by Elaine Lewis)

Joyful letter written by Elmer O. "Whitey" Lewis to his parents on Franklin Street in Hagerstown on Aug. 16, 1945, reflects the excitement of American servicemembers worldwide upon "the big news" that "Japan was ready to quit."

The famed "Ruptured Duck," or the Honorable Service Discharge patch or pin, was awarded to military personnel who were about to be released from military service with an honorable discharge. This cloth patch, an alternate form of the gold-plated brass or plastic pin awarded to servicemembers, features an eagle emerging from a wreath.

Because of clothing shortages, the emblem could be worn on uniforms up to 30 days following discharge. The pin recognized a servicemember's honorable discharge, but, more importantly, alerted Military Police officers that they were in transit and not AWOL [absent without leave].

The award was presented to more than 12 million American servicemembers between Sept. 8, 1939, and Dec. 31, 1946. It earned its distinctive nickname because many thought the eagle more closely resembled a duck. (Contributed by Elaine Lewis)

He signed his letter, "God bless you both. With all my love all my life. Whitey"

Charles Berry — Navy — WWII

A happy homecoming was the dream of most men and women in uniform during WWII. Charles R. Berry of Hagerstown is shown in the family photograph with wife, Marie, infant son, Michael (sporting a small sailor's cap) and daughter, Donna, in 1944, during Berry's first leave home. Berry went into the Navy one day and his son was born the next. It would be nine days before he learned he had a son and three months before he was able to rejoin his family and finally hold him.

Berry and his brother-in-law, Warren Conner, who both entered the Navy late in the war, were more fortunate than most, serving all of their time in the Navy relatively close to home. Both men completed boot camp together at Camp Peary, near Williamsburg, Virginia. Berry then served at Bainbridge Naval Training Station in Maryland, while Conner was assigned to Camp Shelton, near Norfolk, Virginia.

(Photograph courtesy of Marie Berry, widow of Charles R. Berry)

Home at Last!

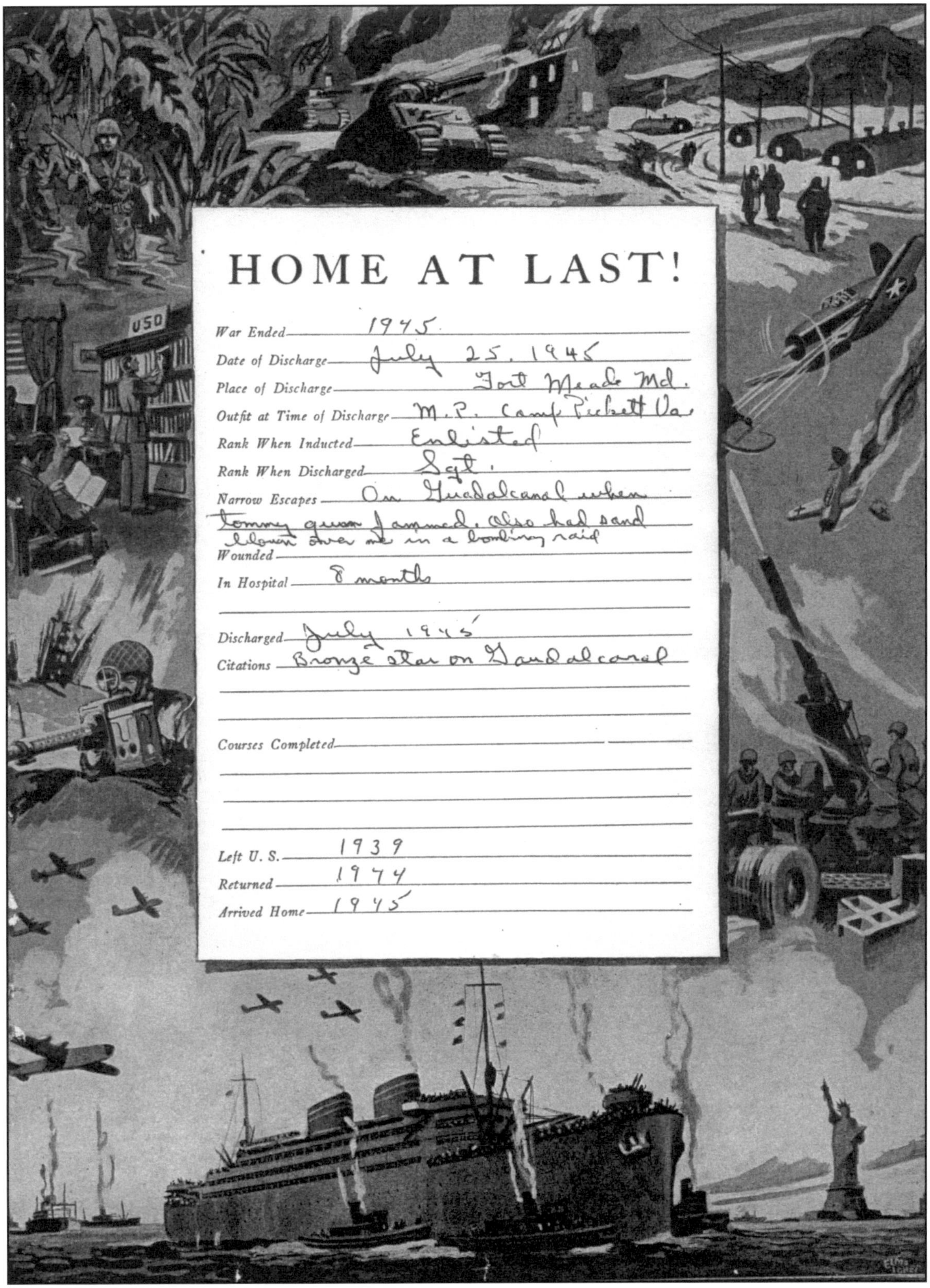

HOME AT LAST!

War Ended 1945

Date of Discharge July 25, 1945

Place of Discharge Fort Meade Md.

Outfit at Time of Discharge M.P. Camp Pickett Va.

Rank When Inducted Enlisted

Rank When Discharged Sgt.

Narrow Escapes On Guadalcanal when tommy gun jammed. Also had sand blown over me in a bombing raid

Wounded

In Hospital 8 months

Discharged July 1945

Citations Bronze star on Guadalcanal

Courses Completed

Left U. S. 1939

Returned 1944

Arrived Home 1945

The sentiments of countless servicemembers are reflected in this graphic from the publication *Young American Patriots: The Youth of Maryland and Delaware in World War II*, by National Publishers, Inc., Richmond, Virginia. Entries on the page are by Richard William Smith, who served at Pearl Harbor and on Guadalcanal.

(Contributed by Gregory Smith, son of Richard William Smith)

Ralph C. "Dutch" Hoover — Army — WWII, Korea, Cold War

Ralph "Dutch" Hoover brandishes a pistol in 1945 in the Philippines — just one stop during his 23-year-long, varied career in the Army. The Hagerstown man was 18 when he was drafted on March 29, 1943, and sent into combat duty in the South Pacific as a rifleman, machine gunner, anti-tank gunner and scout with the 6th Infantry Division. He returned to the U.S. a sergeant, after 29 months in Hawaii, New Guinea and the Philippines. He was honorably discharged on Dec. 15, 1945.

For a while he worked as a salesman for the DuPont Paint Company, but his heart was still in the Army. And he was inspired by the examples of his father, Edgar R. Hoover Sr., who served in France in WWI with the 78th Infantry Division, and his brother, Edgar R. Hoover Jr., who fought in WWII with the 204th Combat Engineers in Europe. So in 1948, he joined the Maryland National Guard and was called to active duty several months later.

He spent the next two years escorting the remains of servicemen killed in battle home to their families. In 1950 he returned to the Pacific, for 17 months of active duty in the Korean War. A master sergeant assigned to 21st Infantry Regiment, 24th Division, he saw combat as an infantry platoon sergeant, leader of a demolition platoon involved in demolition and mine-sweeping operations. In 1951, he received a battlefield commission as a second lieutenant.

Stateside again, he began a chain of assignments that took him all over the U.S. and Europe. He attended infantry school at Fort Benning, Georgia. He was basic training company commander with the 2nd Infantry Division at Indiantown Gap, Pennsylvania. In 1953 he was sent overseas again, this time to Germany. For the next three years he received, dispatched and delivered classified material throughout Europe, North Africa and the British Isles. Back in the U.S. in 1956, he trained soldiers at Fort Benning while waiting to attend the Infantry Officers Advanced Course there. His next stop was Fort McClellan, Alabama, as assistant post operations and training officer, from 1960 to 1963. Then it was back to Germany, as headquarters commandant in Nuremberg. Back home once more, he was a recruiting officer and commanding officer in Montgomery, Alabama, and in 1966 he graduated from the Command and General Staff College at Fort Leavenworth, Kansas. He finally retired as a major on Jan. 1, 1968, and in civilian life he worked for almost 16 years as executive director of Associated Builders and Contractors in Hagerstown.

In 1948 and 1949, Ralph Hoover was stationed at the Army's Fort Hayes in Columbus, Ohio. There his job was escorting the remains of war dead home to their families throughout the northeastern U.S. The remains were of servicemen killed in WWII — mostly in Europe, but also some from the Pacific — whose bodies had been located or disinterred. He escorted 37 bodies in all. He met the families, presented them with an American flag and expressed the appreciation of the nation for their sacrifice. "It was difficult until you got used to it," he said. At top, Hoover (left) and a sailor stand on either side of the coffin of Pfc. Stephan Nagy in Whitaker, Pennsylvania, on Dec. 20, 1948. The two lower photos show Hoover at a funeral in Kentucky, saluting (center) as the coffin is carried from a church, and presenting the American flag to the serviceman's family.

(Photos courtesy of Ralph C. "Dutch" Hoover)

Paul W. Rodeffer — Navy — WWII

Paul W. Rodeffer of Hagerstown was 18 when he left school in November 1944 to join the Navy and serve in WWII. He returned to school when he came home two years later and continued his education. He became active as a member of the American Legion, Morris Frock Post 42, which he served twice as commander.

"I wouldn't have changed the experience," he said.

(Photos courtesy of Paul W. Rodeffer)

Rodeffer served in the honor guard at the first WWII military funeral held in Hagerstown, at Rose Hill Cemetery, in 1946. Three local servicemen were buried on the same day. Rodeffer is at front left of the photo; the sailor to his left is unidentified. The Rev. Berry Plummer is officiating at center, and at far right is John Marshall Sr., father of sailor John Marshall Jr., who was killed aboard ship, though not in battle. The Marshalls owned Marshall Hatchery, on Memorial Boulevard, across from Memorial Stadium in Hagerstown. To the left of Marshall, from left, are Andrew Luther and Leonard Huber.

Seaman 1st Class Paul Rodeffer (right) and shipmate Louis Kensek on board the engine repair ship USS ***Kermit Roosevelt*** *at harbor in Tsingtao, China, in 1945 or 1946. Rodeffer was a deck hand and drove a motor launch during his service in the Pacific Theater. His most vivid memory is when the ship was sailing from Saipan south to Indochina and got caught in a big typhoon. "Our captain had converted all the heat to air conditioning," he said. "While at sea, they changed our orders and we were sent to Tsingtao instead. When we arrived, it was 6 degrees Fahrenheit. It took three days to reconvert to heat, and for three days, it was really cold."*

Richard H. Grimes — Army — WWII, Korea

The Philippine Liberation Medal was awarded to those who participated in landing operations on Leyte and adjoining islands from Oct. 17 - 20, 1944, or those who served on ships in Philippine waters or were members of airplane crews involved in the push to dislodge the Japanese from the Philippine Islands.

"I wouldn't take a million dollars for the experience, but I wouldn't give $5 to do it again."

Richard H. Grimes of Williamsport took a Bible and a care package presented by City Hall with him when he went to the Philippines in WWII. He came back with malaria and lots of memories. "I wouldn't take a million dollars for the experience, but I wouldn't give $5 to do it again."

On his arrival in Luzon by landcraft in 1944, Grimes remembers being greeted by a swarm of Filipino boys all clamoring for cigarettes as they approached the GIs who had come to wrest the Philippine Islands from Japanese control. "They learned to say 'Cigarette, Joe?' in perfect English," Grimes recalled.

Grimes was just two days shy of expiration of his Army Reserve status when he was called up for duty with the outbreak of the Korean War. Congress authorized President Truman to call up volunteer and inactive reservists on June 30, 1950. Within the first few weeks of the war, the president called up 25,000 reservists to rebuild the Army which had been sharply downsized following WWII. More than 10,000 of those recalled were junior officers and NCOs [non-commissioned officers] whose combat experience was sorely needed by the depleted armed forces. By the time the Korean War had entered its second year, another 135,000 reservists would be called up.

Grimes was one of 240,000 servicemen and servicewomen who served in WWII to be recalled to active duty with the outbreak of the Korean War in 1950.

Army of the United States

Honorable Discharge

This is to certify that

RICHARD H. GRIMES. 33 067 334, STAFF SERGEANT.

21ST REPLACEMENT DEPOT.

Army of the United States

is hereby Honorably Discharged from the military service of the United States of America.

This certificate is awarded as a testimonial of Honest and Faithful Service to this country.

Given at SEPARATION CENTER, FORT GEORGE G. MEADE, MARYLAND.

Date 30 DECEMBER 1945.

Henry M. Smick

HENRY M SMICK
LT. COL. CMP

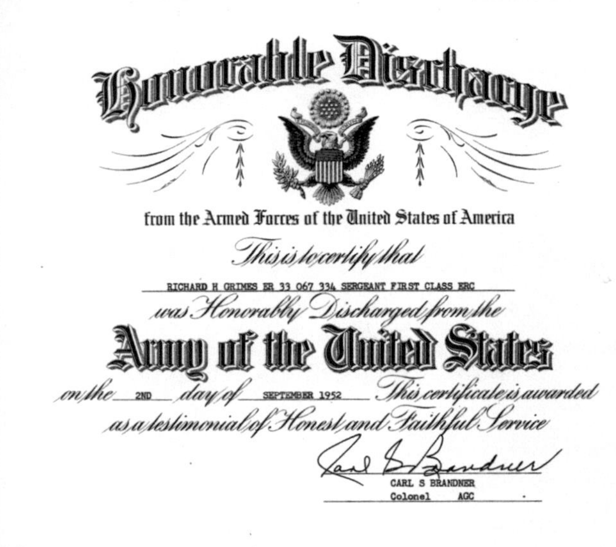

Honorable Discharge

from the Armed Forces of the United States of America

This is to certify that

RICHARD H GRIMES ER 33 067 334 SERGEANT FIRST CLASS ERC

was Honorably Discharged from the

Army of the United States

on the 2ND day of SEPTEMBER 1952 This certificate is awarded as a testimonial of Honest and Faithful Service

Carl S Brandner

CARL S BRANDNER
Colonel AGC

Grimes received this honorable discharge certificate following his service in WWII. Little did he know that less than five years later, America would be involved in yet another conflict and he would be in uniform again, this time serving for two years in the mess department at Fort Meade, Maryland.

(Photographs and memorabilia courtesy of Richard H. Grimes)

William E. Daley — Navy — WWII / Army National Guard — Cold War

William E. Daley was just 17 years old when he enlisted in the Navy at the induction center in Baltimore in 1945. He thought he would have time to return to his North Prospect Street home to pack, but the Navy was so shorthanded that he was immediately put on a train bound for Hunters Point Naval Shipyard in San Francisco. His training as a cook began the moment he set foot on the train. He learned to cook en route to California by reading a cooking manual. The self-taught chef would later became an award-winning military cook in the Army National Guard.

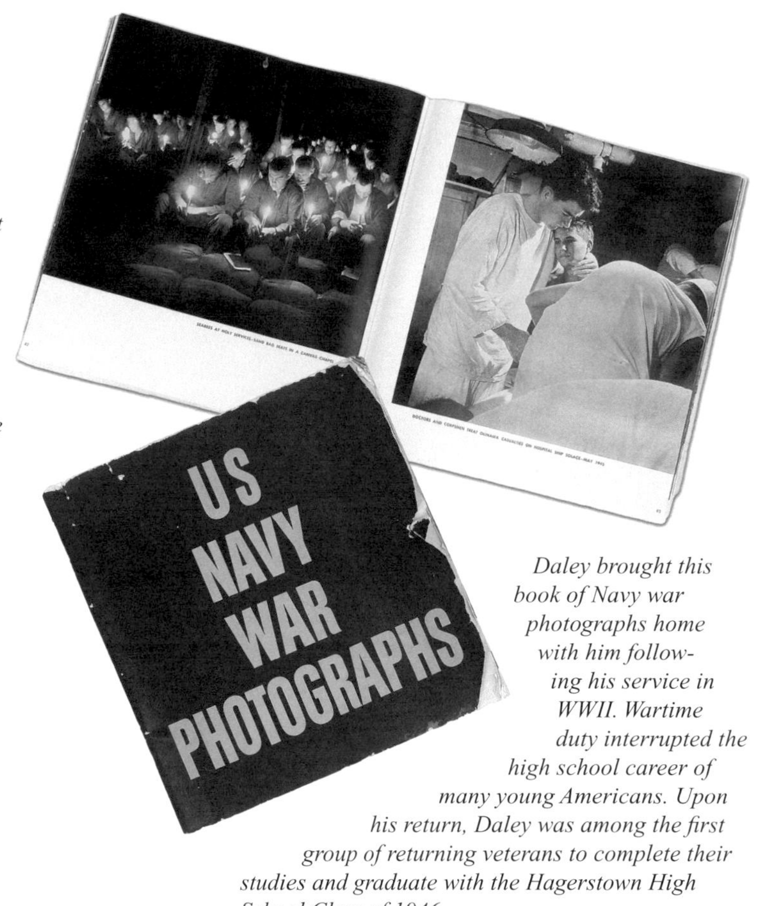

Daley brought this book of Navy war photographs home with him following his service in WWII. Wartime duty interrupted the high school career of many young Americans. Upon his return, Daley was among the first group of returning veterans to complete their studies and graduate with the Hagerstown High School Class of 1946.

*Daley was assigned to the commissary aboard the destroyer USS **Lavalette** for duty in the South Pacific. The ship was just 63 hours away from Hawaii on its trip from San Francisco to Okinawa when it hit a mine. Daley was asleep on board when the explosion occurred. The ship's galley was heavily damaged and the vessel was forced to make its way to Pearl Harbor for repairs. None of the ship's cooks were working in the galley at the time of the blast.*

Following WWII, Daley would go on to serve his country for several more decades in a reserve capacity — first with the Naval Reserve and then with the Army National Guard in Hagerstown.

During Cold War duty with the Army National Guard, Daley was called in to feed troops in 1964 who were searching the mountains near Cumberland for the wreckage of a B-52 believed to be carrying nuclear weapons. He fed the troops and assisted in successful efforts to locate the debris. It was never disclosed if the plane was actually carrying nuclear weapons.

Three years later, he was called upon to feed troops responsible for providing security for the armories and bridges during the 1967 riots in Baltimore, Cambridge and Salisbury. Daley can be found in the first row, far right, in this 1955 photo of his National Guard unit, 115 B Infantry Regiment.

(Photographs and memorabilia courtesy of Connie Daley, William E. Daley's wife)

Elwood B. Sterling — Army Air Corps — WWII / Air Force — Cold War

Capt. Elwood B. Sterling takes his place at the controls of an F-86 Sabre jet — one of the many planes he flew for the Air Force during his career as a military pilot that extended from WWII to the jet age.

The Hagerstown native was inducted into the Army in September 1941 and began training for the infantry. But he didn't stay there for long. He was sent to Texas and was in the 45th "Thunderbird" Division.

According to his wife, Jayne, "Elwood was upset with the infantry because the Air Force was using them for target practice, dropping bags of flour on them. He decided then that he wanted to be in the planes and not on the ground. He shook his finger at the sky and said, 'I am going to be up there.' And he was."

Within six months, Sterling had been accepted into the Army Air Corps and graduated from flying school in March 1943. Now a second lieutenant, by July he was with the ATC [Air Transport Command], European Division, flying B-24s, B-25s and B-17s out of Scotland, England and Ireland, delivering the planes to strategic areas in Africa and Europe.

He retired from active duty in February 1946 and began 25 years of service in the reserves. He served in the 9511th Army Reserve, where he was promoted to captain in 1956 and worked as squadron recruiting officer. In 1958, he transferred to the 167th Fighter Squadron of the West Virginia Air National Guard in Martinsburg, where he flew F-86's and broke the sound barrier.

The F-86 Sabres were the first American-produced swept-wing jets — an innovation that made the new craft aerodynamically superior to a straight wing jet. Following its initial flight in 1947, the jets were rushed into production with the outbreak of war in Korea. By the end of the Korean War, F-86 pilots had shot down 792 Russian MiGs.

In addition to his flight time with the West Virginia Air National Guard's fighter squadron, Sterling served as base engineer and chief executive officer to the base commander. Promoted to major and then lieutenant colonel, he was in the reserves until his death on July 31, 1971.

"He saw the world," his wife said, "flying to Africa, France, England, wherever they needed him. He said he learned a great deal and enjoyed the service."

THE WOLF

IF HE PARKS HIS LITTLE FLIVER
DOWN BESIDE THE MOONLIT RIVER
IF YOU FEEL HIM ALL AQUIVER
BABY, HE'S A WOLF.

IF HE SAYS YOUR A GORGEOUS LOOKER
AND YOUR DARK EYES SEND HIM COOKIN
BUT YOUR EYES AIN'T WHERE HE'S LOOKIN
BABY, HE'S A WOLF

WHEN HE SAYS YOUR AN EYEFUL
BUT HIS HANDS BEGIN TO TRIFLE
AND HIS HEART JUMPS LIKE A RIFLE
BABY, HE'S A WOLF.

IF BY CHANCE WHEN YOUR A KISSIN
YOU CAN FEEL HIS HEART A MISSIN
AND YOU TALK AND HE WON'T LISTEN
BABY, HE'S A WOLF.

IF HIS ARMS AS STRONG AS SINEW
AND HE STIRS THE GYBSY IN YOU
AND YOU WANT HIM CLOSE AGIN YOU
BABY, YOUR A WOLF.

(Photos and memorabilia courtesy of Jayne Sterling, widow of Elwood B. Sterling)

The Wolf *— a poem that Elwood B. Sterling sent to his wife, Jayne, when he was serving in Europe during WWII. "It was a satire of American servicemen," Jayne said. "They were sending them to all the girls."*

When he entered the service, Elwood B. Sterling took these photos (below) of his future wife, Jayne Fernsner, and always carried them with him.

While Elwood was overseas, Jayne was active with the USO in Washington County at the YMCA on North Potomac Street, organizing dances and other events for local servicemen home on leave. She was employed as a telephone operator at the C&P Telephone Co.

"I met him [Elwood] when I was 14 and in the 8th grade at Woodland Way," Jayne said. "I was walking to school on a very, very rainy day. He stopped his truck and asked me if I wanted a ride. I sure did! He took me to school, where he was delivering milk. That's how we met. Then when he found out where I lived, he would stop and talk and leave the engine running until it would run out of gas. This happened several times! His father was maintenance supervisor for Superior Dairy and rescued him with gas. He said 'this is kinda funny that you always run out of gas at the same place.' When he found out what was happening, he said, 'turn off the engine.' Elwood proposed to me on his birthday, April 21, 1940, up in the watchtower on Bloody Lane at the Antietam Battlefield. We were married on Sept. 12. When he was in the service, we corresponded all the time and I visited him when possible. He was cautious and thought things through. He had a good mind which helped him through the war.

"He looked ahead, he planned, he figured things out. He passed away in 1971 due to heart problems. I could never understand it. I was only 49 and never remarried. I could never find another Elwood."

The photo (above left) shows Elwood and Jayne in 1942 in Massachusetts, when he was on leave during basic training.

EUROPEAN DIVISION
AIR TRANSPORT COMMAND
1402nd
GREETS YOU

Program from Elwood B. Sterling's days with the European Division of the Air Transport Command.

DATE	AIRCRAFT FLOWN: MAKE OF AIRCRAFT	CLASS	TYPE	CERTIFICATE NUMBER	MAKE OF ENGINE	H. P.	REMARKS OR INSPECTOR'S SIGNATURE CERTIFICATION NUMBER AND RATING	CROSS COUNTRY: FROM	TO	TIME: INSTRUMENT RADIO OR HOOD	CO-PILOT: DAY (AS INSTRUCTOR)	NIGHT (AS STUDENT)	1ST PILOT: DAY	NIGHT	DAILY TOTAL TIME
12-27-43	AIRSPEED OXFORD	—		TWIN ENG.	CHEETAH-10			LOCAL			3 00				3 00
12-28-43	"	"		" "	"			"			2 30		2 35		5 05
12-30-43	DOUGLAS	C	53	" "	PRATT			ST. MAWGAN ENG.	PRESTWICK SCOTT.		1 30				1 30
1-6-44	"	"	"	" "	"			PWK. SCOTT.	ST. MAW. ENG.		3 50				3 50
1-20-44	NORTH AMERICAN	B	25-G	" "	R-2600			LOCAL			30				30
2-11-44	BOEING	B	17-F	FOUR "	WRIGHT CYCLONE		{2nd. CROSSING}	ST. MAWGAN	GIBRALTAR		6 00				6 00
2-12-44	"	"	"	" "				GIBRALTAR	ALGIERS		3 00				3 00
2-25-44	OXFORD	—		TWIN ENG.	CHEETAH-10			LOCAL					1 40		1 40
2-27-44	BOEING	B	17-F	FOUR "	WRIGHT CYCLONE			NUTTS CORNER	PRESTWICK + RETURN		1 15				1 15
3-2-44	OXFORD	—	—	TWIN ENG.	CHEETAH-10			LOCAL					1 35		1 35
3-3-44	"	—		" "	"			NUTTS CORNER	LONDONDARY RETURN				2 30		2 30
3-4-44	"			" "	"			LOCAL					1 50		1 50
3-5-44	"	—		" "	"			"					2 10		2 10
3-6-44	"	—		" "	"			NUTTS CORNER	ST. ANGELO + RETURN				2 25		2 25
3-7-44	"	—		" "				" "	LIMAVAUDY				2 15		2 15
3-10-44	CONSOLIDATED	B	24-H	FOUR "	PRATT + WHITNEY			LOCAL			1 00				1 00
									TOTAL		22 35		17 00		39 35
									AMT. FORWARD	25 50	6 05		51 25		96 25
									TOTAL TO DATE	25 50	28 40		68 25	30 40	13[illegible] 00

I HEREBY CERTIFY THAT THE FOREGOING ENTRIES ARE TRUE AND CORRECT.

SIGNED Elwood B. Sterling

Log book kept by Elwood B. Sterling when he was flying missions from the British Isles to points in Europe and North Africa from 1943 to 1945.

Charles R. Gehr Jr. — Navy — WWII, Korea

Charles R. Gehr Jr. left Hagerstown and joined the Navy in September 1943. He served for much of WWII on the troop transport ship USS *Gen. H.W. Butner*. He was discharged in December 1945 but rejoined the Navy during the Korean War.

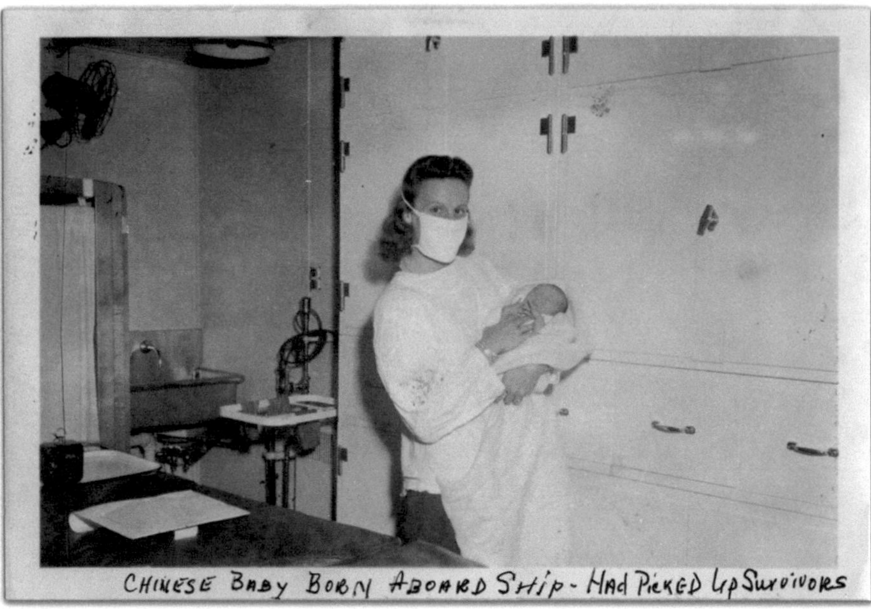

A Navy nurse on the USS ***Gen. H.W. Butner*** *holds a baby that was born to a pregnant Chinese woman, one of a group of survivors picked up by the ship.*

(Photos courtesy of Nancy Gehr, widow of Charles R. Gehr Jr.)

In lighthearted tradition, crewmen including Charles Gehr celebrate their initiation into the Ancient Order of the Deep as the USS ***Gen. H.W. Butner*** *crossed the Equator during WWII.*

The ***Butner*** *was one of two different ships that Gehr served on — in two different wars during two separate enlistments in the Navy. The first one began when he joined the Navy in September 1943. During WWII, he transported troops to and from operations aboard the* ***Butner****. The ship's war cruising record shows stops at ports including Baltimore, Casablanca, South Africa, Equatorial Africa, India, Australia, New Hebrides, New Guinea, Philippines, Panama Canal Zone, Marshall Islands, Caroline Islands and Okinawa.*

Gehr's most memorable experience was when he was in the engine room with two buddies and they heard a thud and scraping — the sounds of a "dud" torpedo that had struck the ship.

Gehr left the Navy in December 1945, but re-enlisted in November 1950, after the country became involved in the Korean War. This time he served on the destroyer USS ***Wedderburn****, seeing action off the Korean coast. He preserved a newspaper clipping that describes the time "the US cruiser* ***Toledo*** *and destroyer* ***Wedderburn*** *hit '16 large groups of Red soldiers' along the east coast with 23,000 pounds of high explosives." Gehr died in February 1997.*

Leon G. Ecton — Army — WWII, Korea, Cold War

Leon Ecton (standing at right) and an unidentified buddy with their tank during maneuvers in Grafenwoehr, Germany, in 1947.

Born near Sharpsburg in 1921, Ecton enlisted in the Army in June 1942. He was sent to Europe as a light-tank crewman (later a tank commander) with Company A, 630th Tank Destroyer Battalion. He served in the Northern (Normandy) and Southern France campaigns and fought in the Battle of the Ardennes, more commonly known as the Battle of the Bulge, and in the Rhineland Campaign. His twin brother, Thomas, was killed while serving in the Army in the Philippines in 1945.

(Photos courtesy of Brigitte Ecton)

The photo at right shows Leon Ecton and Brigitte Heintz in Germany on Dec. 31, 1946 — New Year's Eve, the day after Brigitte's 22nd birthday.

Leon met his future wife in 1945 in Oberauerbach, where her uncle owned a restaurant. Brigitte, a beautician, happened to be there, cutting her cousin's hair, when Leon and two other American servicemen came in for a meal. She overheard Leon asking for an extra glass, and the next thing she knew, he was offering her a drink of wine. She declined, but seeing his rifle next to him, "I thought I'd better say yes," she said. Two glasses of wine later, she was sick to her stomach and Leon was apologizing to her.

But the road to romance was not easy, since military authorities prohibited contact between Germans and American servicemen, and the Germans, likewise, didn't approve of contact with the enemy. "The German people hated me," Brigitte said. "We weren't allowed to see each other, but we found ways. My parents helped; they liked Leon a lot."

But Leon's tour in Germany came to an end, and he was sent home in November 1945. "I didn't think he was coming back," Brigitte said. "They all said they'd come back, but they didn't." But Leon did go back ... and back ... and back.

"He kept re-enlisting so he could come back," Brigitte said. Leon was stationed in Germany in 1946, though far away from Brigitte — in Augsburg. But they still managed to see each other. Not every assignment took him to Germany, however. Leon also served in Texas during the Korean War, training soldiers due to be sent overseas.

Leon and Brigitte finally were able to marry, and they had a son, Harry. In the photo above left, the family celebrates Christmas in Augsburg in 1950. It was still many years before Brigitte could get a visa to move to the U.S., however. She arrived in Washington County in 1956 and became a U.S. citizen three years later.

Leon finally decided to stop re-enlisting, and he retired from the Army in March 1963, after 21 years of service. After his discharge, he worked as parts manager at an auto dealer in Frederick and in janitorial work at Fort Detrick until his department closed. He also performed maintenance work on the C&O Canal during warm weather, before his death in 2001.

John Beair — Army, Army Reserve — WWII, Korean War

Cpl. John L. Beair Jr., 2nd Platoon, Company E, Gen. Douglas MacArthur's Honor Guard, on duty at the entrance to the Finance Building in Tokyo, Japan, March 1946

He was terribly seasick while aboard a troopship headed for Japan and slept in a sleeping bag atop the snow in Korea, but the hardships Staff Sergeant John L. Beair Jr. endured during military service in two wars didn't take the shine off his service as a member of Gen. Douglas MacArthur's Honor Guard.

The Hagerstown resident began his military service on Jan. 25, 1945, as an infantryman in the Army and served two years in the Pacific. He was recalled to military service in Korea in 1951 as a member of the Army Reserve and served as a communications sergeant in the 25th Signal Company.

"I credit my faith in God for my good fortune to return safely from two wars," he said.

Beair served with occupation forces in Japan after the Japanese surrender in August 1945, which put him in the right place at the right time for assignment to Gen. MacArthur's Honor Guard in Tokyo. But that came after 32 days on a troopship, seven of them "very seasick," and mopping up operations with the 27th Infantry Division to secure the Japanese island of Okinawa.

Beair's World War II troopship left port in San Francisco in June 1945 and anchored in a bay in the Caroline Islands 32 days later. "We were waiting for assignment to Army units, and a lot of supply ships were gathering for the expected invasion of the Japanese mainland," he said. "After several days our ship moved out, and on Aug. 22 we landed on Okinawa."

He was assigned to the 27th Infantry Division and participated in the final stages of the horrific battle for the Pacific island, which proved to be the last major battle of WWII.

"In early September 1945, I left Okinawa by C-47 for the occupation of Japan," he said. "I landed in a town about 90 miles north of Tokyo and spent the next several weeks searching homes for weapons. The Japanese people were very frightened of the American soldiers, but we did our best to calm them."

The official patch of Gen. MacArthur's Honor Guard also had its Japanese counterpart, which Beair said members of his platoon collected.

In November 1945, Beair said, "we received word the 27th Division was going home. The replacements, such as I, would be transferred to other units. I was fortunate enough to be sent to Tokyo, where I joined with Gen. MacArthur's Honor Guard." Assigned to the 2nd Platoon with quarters in the Finance Building, he said, "We were located about one mile from the Imperial Palace which faced across a moat to the Dai Ichi Building, which was Gen. MacArthur's headquarters."

Selection criteria for members of the Honor Guard were exceptionally high, as members of the guard were responsible for the security of the Dai Ichi Building and the safety of Gen. MacArthur, Supreme Commander of Allied Powers in the Far East, his wife Jean, and his son, Arthur.

"I joined the honor guard on Dec. 2, 1945, as a private first class and after 10 months of duty was released to return home on Sept. 12, 1946, as a staff sergeant," he said.

When he arrived at Fort George G. Meade, Maryland, he was approached to enlist in the inactive Army Reserve. "Having just reached my 20th birthday and with the rank of staff sergeant, I figured the Army would recall me fast if an emergency arose, so I enlisted to hold my rank."

Beair said he spent the next four years enjoying his job at the downtown A&P store and "seriously dating" his future wife, Betty Powles. Then came call-up for service in Korea in September 1950. He put an engagement ring on Betty's finger and reported for duty at Fort Campbell, Kentucky. At Fort Campbell, he discovered there had been many changes in the Army, particularly weapons, since 1946, and he had to learn them fast.

After just seven weeks of refresher training, his outfit was sent by troop train to Fort Lawton in Seattle, Washington. "We embarked by troopship several days later and arrived in Yokohama, Japan, about the tenth of December," he recalled. "There we got off the ship for 24 hours, during which we were interviewed and issued our weapons."

Sadly, the gunsight on the carbine issued to Beair was damaged, "So, I couldn't hit a target. I was told 'don't worry, you'll get a replacement weapon in Korea.'

"Back on the boat the next morning and sailing for Korea, I had a damaged rifle to protect myself and a summer sleeping bag for shelter in the middle of December," he said. "When we rounded the southern tip of Japan and headed for Korea, it was the coldest weather I had ever experienced. We hit the landing boats at Inchon on Dec. 18, 1950, and on the 19th I joined the 25th Division."

Beair was assigned to the 25th Signal Company, whose responsibility was to keep communications open to the front-line units of the division. "With snow all around and sleeping on the hard ground in a summer sleeping bag, it could not have been much more depressing," he said.

The signal company used radio, telegraph and messenger runs by jeep to communicate with and deliver information to troops at the front.

In the months ahead, the division moved north above the 38th parallel and "then the Chinese entered the war and we moved back below Suwan, south of Seoul." When spring finally came and with it the thawing of the rice paddies, "it was either deep mud or dust," Beair said.

Beair snapped a photo of fellow Honor Guard member Donald Patterson at attention as Gen. Douglas MacArthur left his headquarters in Tokyo during the American occupation of Japan. The general regularly arrived at the Dai Ichi Building at an early hour each day, and departed for his home at the American Embassy late in the day.

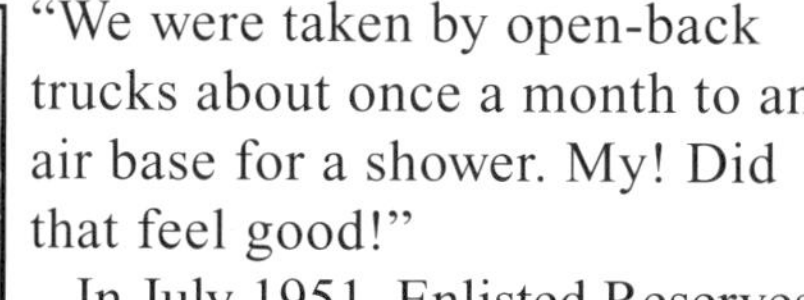

"We were taken by open-back trucks about once a month to an air base for a shower. My! Did that feel good!"

In July 1951, Enlisted Reserves were replaced by regular Army personnel, and Beair came home. He was reassigned to the Inactive Reserves on Aug. 21, 1951. Altogether, he served in the military eight years, one month and 27 days.

When he came home from Japan at the end of WWII, he brought with him three Japanese rifles. In later years, he gave a rifle to each of his children.

Of all his military service, he said the "most memorable" was his time with Gen. MacArthur's Honor Guard, marching in ceremonial events and participating in the formal retreat ceremony at the close of the Army day.

Beair said his military experience "changed me very much. I was a backward child, but the military taught me to come out of myself, to be with other people, and to be responsible."

Beair captured this photo of generals Douglas MacArthur and Dwight Eisenhower as they arrived at MacArthur's headquarters in the Dai Ichi Building in Tokyo in 1946.

Beair sailed home from Yokohama, Japan, aboard the ***Joseph P. Martinez*** *in September 1946. There were 700 troops aboard the ship, which came home to Seattle, Washington, via the Aleutian Islands.*

(Photographs and memorabilia courtesy of John Beair Jr.)

Sgt. John Beair Jr.. (middle of back row in photo at left) and fellow members of the 3rd Squad, 25th Signal Company, 25th Infantry Division, take a short break from duty in front of the message center in Suwan, South Korea, in 1951. He said children always gathered on the outskirts of Suwan looking for candy from the American troops. On the back of the photograph, he wrote: "Yours truly on one of those little details that keep popping up to keep us busy."

THE DAILY MAIL, HAGERSTOWN, MD., WEDNESDAY, MAY 29, 1946.

In Memoriam

Washington County Casualties

According to records, 228 Washington Countians paid the supreme sacrifice in World War II. The following list of casualties has been compiled by the Maryland Veterans Commission:

Altenderfer, Willis L., Jr.
Anderson, Eugene
Annan, William M.
Armstrong, Ralph E.
Baker, Edward
Beard, Roy B.
Bennett, Chester L.
Bingaman, Howard
Biser, Charles L., Jr.
Bishop, Harvey C.
Blickenstaff, Paul W.
Bohman, Jr., George M.
Bowers, Howard J.
Bowser, Ernest N.
Bowser, Roger Wm.
Boyle, James C.
Briscoe, Wilmer M.
Brown, Harry W.
Bruce, 3rd., William M.
Bryan, Albert R.
Buchanan, Ralph H.
Bussard, Harold E.
Bussard, John F.
Byrd, Robert L.
Campher, Phillip S.
Canfield, Gay
Carbaugh, Ray R.
Carpenter, Charles L.
Carpenter, Marshall E. A.
Carruthers, Elmer I.
Clayton, Lewin B.
Cline, Stewart P., Jr.
Clopper, Millard C.
Coffman, Elwood
Cohill, Benjamin M.
Colflesh, Ralph M.
Collette, Jack
Cooper, John F.
Cottrell, Richard L.
Crampton, Merle O.
Crouse, John C.
Curry, Leon
Dagenhart, Harold
Danner, Bruce W.
Daugherty, Irvin W.
Davies, Magnus
Davis, Ellsworth A.
Deavers, Emmert
Diehl, David R.
Dixon, Clyde W.
Dorsey, Roger M.
Doub, Jr., Harry G.
Drury, Walter V.
Dutton, Benjamin B.
Easterday, Roger
Eavey, Ernest L.
Ebersole, Irvin W.
Eckis, Jr., Samuel K.
Ecton, Thomas A.
Eichelberger, Earl
Elliott, Charles F.
English, George R.
Ernst, Jr., J. William
Eyler, Llewellyn C.
Eyler, Vance W.
Faith, Christie
Fearnow, Melvin C.
Fiery, Charles D.
Fletcher, Ernest R.
Foreman, Jr., Harry
Fost, Herbert L.
Fox, Jay H.
Frock, Vernon R.
Frush, John R.
Fry, Phillip A.
Gardner, Garland G.
Garman, John P.
Gatrell, Ralph G.
Gearhart, Lester B.
Geiser, Jr., Samuel J.
Gerber, Cecil M.
Getridge, Marion A., Jr.
Gigous, George L.
Gish, Leonard N.
Glesner, William A.
Gouker, Charles V.
Grab, Robert P.
Gray, Ralph S.
Griffith, James O.
Gross, Leland R.
Grove, Charles R.
Guessford, Earl M.
*Guessford, Lloyd T.
Hamilton, Roy
Hammaker, Atlee
Harbaugh, Jr., Marshall E.
Harne, Jack O.
Harness, Keith
Herbert, Joseph (first casualty before declaration of war).
Hessong, Arthur J.
Hessong, Robert L.
Hewett, James F.
Higgins, Russell L.
Hill, Raymond E.
Hixon, Earl S.
Hockman, Ernest L.
Hottel, Maurice C.
*Huffman, Raymond
Huntzberry, Richard W.
Hurd, Luther T.
Hutzell, Leroy A.
Itnyre, Karl W.
Jamison, Harvey L.
Jenkins, Jr., George D.
Johnson, George W.
Jones, Jay
Jones, Melvin L.
Judd, Fred L.
Keefer, Paul W.
Keplinger, Howard D.
Keplinger, Rudolph L.
King, Charles A.
Kinsell, Richard E.
Kline, Carroll M.
Koerner, Paul J.
Kriechbaum, Phillip E.
Landers, Harry R.
Lapole, Gardner E.
Lefever, Nelson D.
Lemen, Jr., Joseph L.
Lewis, Jr., John S.
Lewis, Robert L.
Lindsay, Robert H.
Lippman, Harold
Lowery, Francis E.
Lumm, Charles O.
Lutz, Frank T.
McAdams, Mervin L.
McClelland, Russell L.
Marshall, John Henry
Martin, Edward G.
Mason, Jr., Walter N.
Mauck, George M.
Mears, Raymond G.
Mentzer, Daniel A.
Mentzer, Earl W.
Miller, Chester A.
Miller, Gerald N.
Miller, Glenn A.
Miller, Harry T.
Miller, Kenneth E.
Miller, Paul V.
Miller, Richard R.
Miller, William H.
Moss, Carroll E.
Mosser, Glenn
Munday, Wilbert I.
Myers, Harold L.
Mulligan, John L.
Neikirk, Robert A.
Nick, Gilbert L.
Norford, Robert N.
Orndorff, James M.
Paden, Mervin W.
Palmer, Harry R.
Pappas, Thomas C.
Peer, Joseph C.
Pierce, Charles R.
Poffenberger, Harry
Powles, John B.
Rang, Francis B.
Reedy, Angus L.
Remsburg, Clayton I.
Rhinehart, Paul F.
Richard, Burton R.
Richardson, Paul E.
Rickard, Richard M.
Ridenour, Edward E.
Ringer, Joseph E.
Robinson, Guy F.
Roth, Warren N.
Schetrompf, Charles E.
Schindel, James W.
Schnebly, Andrew
Selby, Donald
Shackleford, Donald E.
Shaffer, William E.
Shank, Harold I.
Shantz, Jr., George
Sharar, John
Shifflett, Forrest D.
Shifflett, William J.
Shipley, Irvin H.
Skelton, Albert C.
Smith, Eugene G.
Smith, James R.
Smith, Omer L.
Smith, Robert McL.
Snowden, Shull V.
Snyder, Raymond E.
Spielman, Philip B.
Springer, Earl B.
Startzman, Vernon N.
Stine, Jack B.
Stone, Harry W.
Stottlemyer, Guy
Stouffer, Elvin E.
Summers, Glenn E.
Swain, Maxwell L.
Swisher, Bernard E.
Tagg, Ralph S., Jr., (first casualty after declaration of war).
Talhelm, Roy L.
Tedrick, Leon A.
Thomas, Charles W.
Thomas, John L.
Troxell, Ernest L.
Trout, William C.
Vance, Harold
Walker, James K.
Walters, Abner W.
Waters, Charles R.
Weller, Geary E.
Williams, Clarence B.
Wingert, Charles I.
Wolfe, Theodore
Wolford, Harry
Yonker, Lauvon H.

Of the casualties mentioned, 30 died in training camps or accidents not the result of enemy action.

Also, 3 died in enemy prison camps.

First Prisoner Of War

According to the records, T/Sgt. Wyatt Warrenfeltz was taken prisoner in March, 1942, by the Japs.

First Casualty of War (Peacetime)

According to records S/Sgt. Joseph Herbert, Clearspring, Md., was killed at Pearl Harbor, Dec. 7, 1941, by enemy action, peacetime.

First Casualty of War (Wartime)

According to records Pfc. Ralph S. Tagg, Jr., Hagerstown, Md., died in Jap prison camp, after the death march on Bataan, June 3, 1942, after declaration of war.

Total casualties, 228.

* Casualties so marked more information is desired. Contact Ralph S. Tagg, Assistant State Service Officer, Maryland Veterans Commission, 126 North Potomac street, Hagerstown, Md., or phone 2191. Anyone having knowledge of other casualties not listed please notify the same office.

A listing of Washington County's war dead appeared in the May 29, 1946, copy of *The Daily Mail*. Included on the list is Samuel J. Geiser Jr., who was killed in action in France on Nov. 11, 1944.

(Contributed by Robert C. Geiser, brother of Samuel J. Geiser Jr.)

WE REMEMBER

Those we left there in the cold
We remember, we remember
Have no fears of growing old
Oh do we remember

Those who fell in prison yards
We remember, we remember
Savage weather savage guards
Oh do we remember

Those who died face down in mud
We remember, we remember
Asian soil Yankee blood
Oh do we remember

— Excerpt of poem by M. Garvey, a Vietnam War veteran who wrote this tribute to those who served in the Korean War for the dedication of the Korean War Veterans Memorial in Washington, D.C., in 1995.
(Korean War Project
http://koreanwar.org/html/units/frontline/we_remember.htm)

Korean War

1950-1953

Prison Camp in Pusan, Korea. (Contributed by John C. Koontz Sr.)

Ernest R. "Dick" Rider — Marine Corps — Korea

Ernest R. "Dick" Rider is bundled up against the cold during duty watch in Seoul, Korea, in 1952. The frigid temperatures are what many Marines and other servicemen remember about their time in Korea.

(Photographs and memorabilia courtesy of Sylvia and Ernest R. "Dick" Rider)

Marine Corps Sgt. Rider leans casually against bags of gunpowder stacked under camouflage netting during a break in fighting during the Korean War.

When Ernest Rider was home on leave in Hagerstown during the Korean War, his family captured this photo of Rider men who fought in three wars: Ernest R. "Dick" Rider (left), Korean War; his father, Ulysses Grant Rider (center), WWI; and his brother, Thurman Rider (right), WWII, all of Hagerstown.

Embroidered scarf commemorating the service of the 1st Marine Division during the Korean War in 1953 with some of Ernest Rider's medals, including (left to right) the United Nations Medal, the Republic of Korea Service Medal and the Republic of Korea War Service Medal. Rider also received a certificate of recognition "for service during the period of the Cold War (Sept. 2, 1945 - Dec. 26, 1991) in promoting peace and stability for this Nation."

Sgt. Rider, in a quiet moment on the Korean War front in 1953, reading a letter from home.

Rider poses with Japanese school children on a 1953 trip to Japan during a break in his service in the Korean War.

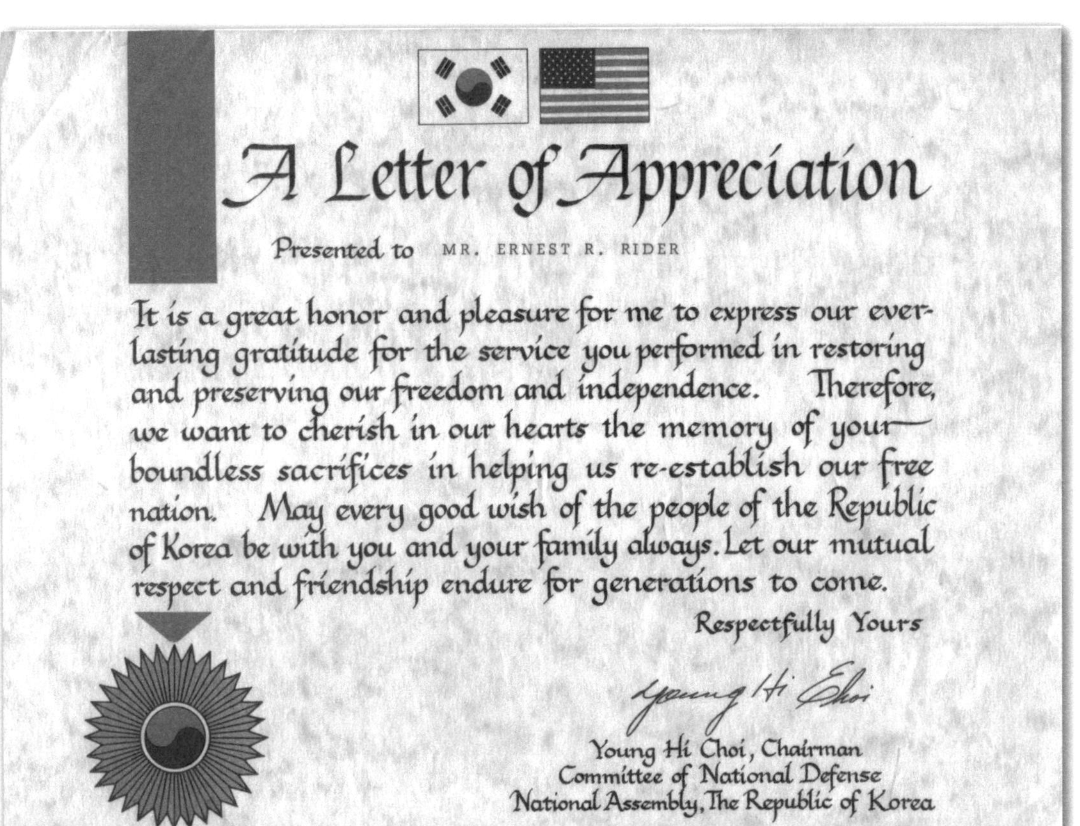

A Letter of Appreciation

Presented to MR. ERNEST R. RIDER

It is a great honor and pleasure for me to express our everlasting gratitude for the service you performed in restoring and preserving our freedom and independence. Therefore, we want to cherish in our hearts the memory of your boundless sacrifices in helping us re-establish our free nation. May every good wish of the people of the Republic of Korea be with you and your family always. Let our mutual respect and friendship endure for generations to come.

Respectfully Yours

Young Hi Choi

Young Hi Choi, Chairman
Committee of National Defense
National Assembly, The Republic of Korea

Troops serving in Korea during the Korean War received this letter of appreciation from the National Assembly of the Republic of Korea for their "boundless sacrifices in helping us re-establish our free nation."

Edward Kendall — Navy — Korea

The same month the U.S. entered the war in Korea, June 1950, Edward Kendall entered the Navy. He became a communications technician in Yokosuka, Japan, a naval base that was highly fortified with large caves for protection. As an intercept operator, his job was providing intelligence about Korea for the National Security Agency. The photo below shows him with some Japanese friends in Yokohama in January 1953.

One time Kendall was serving on a ship that was in drydock in Pearl Harbor, next to the battleship USS ***Arizona****. This was in 1952, before a memorial had been built to honor the sailors killed on Dec. 7, 1941. He remembers that the colors were raised each morning on the ship's superstructure as a tribute.*

In August 1952, Kendall's ship stopped at Midway Island — a name marking the naval battle that was the turning point of the war in the Pacific in WWII. On the back of this photo Kendall wrote: "A goony bird and myself on Midway. Me on the right."

(Photographs courtesy of Edward Kendall)

Thomas F. Kline — Navy — Korea

Thomas F. Kline had just turned 18 years old when he left his Locust Street home and joined the Navy in January 1949. After attending boot camp at the Great Lakes Naval Station in Illinois, he went to Norfolk, Virginia, where he was assigned to the heavy cruiser USS ***Albany*** *for one year. He was released to inactive duty, but was later reactivated and sent to Charleston, South Carolina, as a member of the crew and commissioning honor guard to assist in re-commissioning the destroyer escort USS* ***Otterstetter****. He was later sent to Newport, Rhode Island, where he served aboard the USS* ***Otterstetter*** *from April 1952 until December 1953, as a fire control technician.*

One of his most memorable experiences was visiting St. John in Newfoundland and crossing the Arctic Circle on board the USS ***Albany*** *on Nov. 12, 1949 — a feat which earned him a certificate commemorating his admission into the "Royal Order of Bluenoses." He also enjoyed his time cruising the warmer waters of the Caribbean. In this photo he is on the chilly deck of the USS* ***Albany*** *while it is being refueled at sea.*

"The Navy," he said, "instilled in me a sense of discipline and self-worth and made it easy to interact with others both as individuals and as part of a team. It also gave me pride and love for my country."

(Photograph courtesy of Thomas F. Kline)

David L. Murray — Air Force — Korea

David L. Murray of Hagerstown said he "learned to love America more" when he served in the Air Force in Japan during the Korean War.

The Hagerstown man was 20 when he joined the Air Force on July 5, 1951. He was stationed for two years at Hitachi, Japan — radar site for the Japan Air Defense Force, 41st Air Division. Working in radio communications, he was in charge of telephones at the base. Afterwards he served one more year stateside, and was discharged on Independence Day, 1955. In this 1953 photo (below) he stands in front of a Japanese WWII suicide bomber plane called the "Baka" ("crazy") bomb in Hitachi, Japan.

(Photographs courtesy of David L. Murray)

Jack A. Zirkle — Army — Korea

Hagerstown GI Killed In Korea

The first death of a Washington County soldier in Korea was reported here over the week-end.

Mrs. Elsie Zirkle, 221 West Howard Street, was notified by the War Department Saturday that her son, Pfc. Jack A. Zirkle, 19, was killed in action July 27.

PFC. JACK A. ZIRKLE

Jack enlisted in the Army last September and went to Japan in January of this year where he served in the U. S. Army of Occupation. He was with the First Cavalry Division in Korea, and apparently went to Korea about July 15.

He attended schools in Baltimore and Hagerstown before enlisting.

Besides his mother, he is survived by his father, Robert Zirkle of Martinsburg; sisters, Mrs. Peggy Smith, Baltimore, and Miss Roberta M. Zirkle, this city; brother, William Zirkle, Baltimore.

Since the outbreak of hostilities in Korea, there have been two other Washington Countians missing and three wounded in action.

*Readers of Hagerstown's **Daily Mail** learned of the first death of a Washington County soldier in Korea in July 1950. In the newspaper account, Pfc. Jack A. Zirkle, whose mother lived at 221 W. Howard St., had been killed in action on July 27, 1950, 12 days after arriving in Korea from Japan.*

The 19-year-old soldier enlisted in September 1949 and had been stationed in Japan before being sent to Korea. He was serving with D Company, 7th Cavalry Regiment of the 1st Cavalry Division. The 1st Cavalry had been ordered to shore up the Pusan perimeter.

At the time Zirkle's death was reported, two other Washington County servicemembers had been reported missing and three others wounded. After the war, unofficial tallies indicated that 31 Washington County residents gave their lives in combat during the Korean War.

(Contributed by Ron F. Hovis)

Distinctive gold and black shoulder patch identifying members of the 1st Cavalry Division.

The patch consists of a "sunset" yellow triangular Norman Shield with rounded corners 5 1/4 inches in height. A black diagonal stripe extends over the shield from upper left to lower right. In the upper right, a black horse's head, cut off diagonally at the neck, appears within 1/8 inch of an Army Green border. The traditional Cavalry color of yellow and the horse's head are symbolic of the original organizational structure of the cavalry, while the color black is symbolic of iron — an allusion to the organizational transition from mounted horses to tanks and heavy armor.

Glenn Edwin "Pete" Younker — Army — Korea

Born in 1932 in Big Pool, Pete Younker joined the Army in November 1952 and drove a jeep for two years during the war in Korea. A MLR [main line resource] driver for Headquarters Company, 3rd Battalion, 25th Infantry Division, Younker hauled mortar shells and rations up to the front line, mostly at night. "We called them cat eyes," he said. "We couldn't use regular lights, so we had special ones. Our windshields were always angled down so they wouldn't reflect light. When you drove, you just had to remember where the road obstacles were."

Driving down the mountain from the lines one time, however, "we hit something that flipped the jeep, and I busted my right eardrum. I have some hearing loss, but I feel lucky to only have that problem. It was a great experience."

A hospital in Korea where Younker spent time when suffering from malaria. He was in Korea 14 months, until March 1954, when he returned home and served five years in the Army Reserve at Fort Myer in Arlington, Virginia. There he went on TDY [temporary duty] with another company, hauling guns from Virginia to Bethlehem Beach, New Jersey. He retired from the Army as a corporal on Dec. 5, 1960.

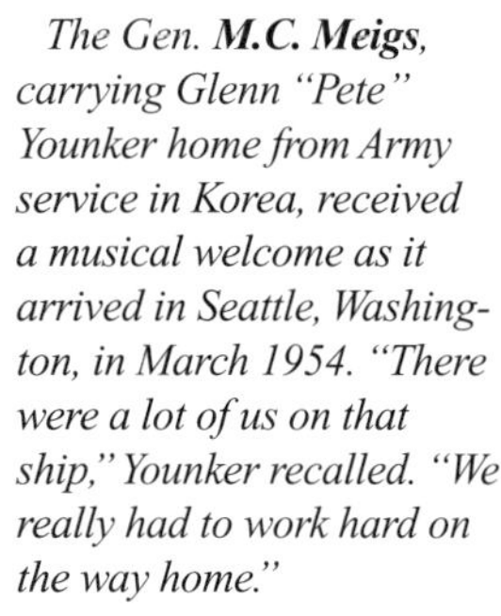

The Gen. ***M.C. Meigs****, carrying Glenn "Pete" Younker home from Army service in Korea, received a musical welcome as it arrived in Seattle, Washington, in March 1954. "There were a lot of us on that ship," Younker recalled. "We really had to work hard on the way home."*

(Photos courtesy of Glenn E. Younker)

Leon Jones — Army — WWII — Korea

Leon Jones served in the Army twice, in two different wars. The Boonsboro man, a member of the Maryland Minutemen (Army Reserve) since he was 16, was drafted on June 27, 1945, just after turning 18. The date was exactly midway between V-E Day [May 7-8] and V-J Day [Aug. 15]. He worked on ships on both the Atlantic and Pacific oceans that were carrying American troops and German POWs [prisoners of war] to and from the U.S.

The POWs were taken to Texas, where they worked on sugar beet farms, in PX's, and in NCO and USO clubs. They were distinguished by wearing shirts with PW written on them. Jones said he thought "that was not a good deal, to have the POWs pampered while our men were freezing in Germany."

He left the Army in December 1946, but couldn't stay out for long, and he re-enlisted in June 1950 and was sent to Fort Knox, Kentucky, for training. "There wasn't a war on," he said, "but after a couple of days in Fort Knox, there was a guy going around with a newspaper in his hand that said war was declared."

But instead of going to Korea, Jones found himself in Germany, working as an artillery mechanic and vehicle and track mechanic with Company F of the 14th Armored Cavalry, 2nd Battalion, until his honorable discharge in June 1953.

This photo shows him at Fort Knox in 1951, where he was sent back for training on maintenance of T-41 "Truman" tanks.

Leon Jones wasn't the only family member in uniform during these years. In WWII, one of his brothers, Gerald, was in Germany with the 8th Air Force. During the Korean War, his brother Harold was with the Air Force in Alaska, his brother Frank with the Army in California, and his brother Lewis Jr. with the Army in Korea.

(Photo courtesy of Leon Jones)

"P.S. It's not real," Younker assured his parents on the back of this photo he sent home from R&R [rest and relaxation] in Tokyo in December 1953. "We went to town the other night," he wrote. "This is what happens. Ha ha. There is a lot of stuff like this in this little town." Younker remembered earning $74 a month in Korea, paid in cash monthly. "When the paymaster came around you could mark the pay sheet with an X and they would hold your pay. When we'd go on R&R we would collect several X's to send home."

Pete Younker also did duty digging foxholes on the Korean front. Here he sits at the entrance to one of them with "my buddy, Tenagli. He was Italian, from New York. All those guys from New York were Italian." On the back of the photo he wrote, "How would you like to sleep in here?"

Younker spent as many as 20 days at a time on the line, and he said he "lost a lot of friends."

Wallace T. Minnich — Army — WWII, Korea

Staff Sgt. Wallace T. Minnich (right) celebrates with fellow officers and guests at an enlisted men's club in Occupied Germany in the late 1940s, midway in an Army career that took him from fighting on the battlefields of Italy in WWII to being killed in action in the Korean War.

Wallace Minnich was one of three sons of Walter and Lillie Minnich of Hagerstown. All three — Wallace, James and Daniel — served in the military, but Wallace was the only one of the three who didn't come home.

He enlisted on March 9, 1943, at the height of WWII, and was sent into action in Italy with Company B, 797th Military Police Battalion. Wounded in action at Anzio on June 3, 1944, he was awarded a Bronze Star. On June 16, after being wounded again, he received a Purple Heart. He was discharged on Oct. 5, 1945, but the Army was in his blood, and he re-enlisted. He served in Occupied Germany near Nuremberg, where he was connected to the wartime trials there that began in 1945.

Twice more he received honorable discharges — in August 1948 with the rank of sergeant and in May 1950 as sergeant 1st class — and twice more he re-enlisted. The last time was in Okinawa "for an indefinite period" beginning May 20, 1950. He headed to Korea for combat with "Charlie Company," 1st Battalion of 23rd Infantry Regiment, 2nd Infantry Division. This was the unit that almost single-handedly slowed the Aug. 31, 1950, invasion by three North Korean divisions (up to 20,000 men) across the Naktong River in a push to take Pusan. The only thing in the way were the men of Company C and other elements of the 2nd Infantry Division. The North Koreans pushed forward some 10 miles, but failed to drive the Americans off the peninsula. When the fighting let up, at least 120 of the original 200 members of the company were dead. Minnich was helping carry wounded soldiers off the battlefield. He returned to rescue more, and was never seen again by his comrades. He was determined to have been killed in action on Sept. 5, 1950, and was posthumously awarded a second Purple Heart on Nov. 16. He is shown here with his wife, Naomi.

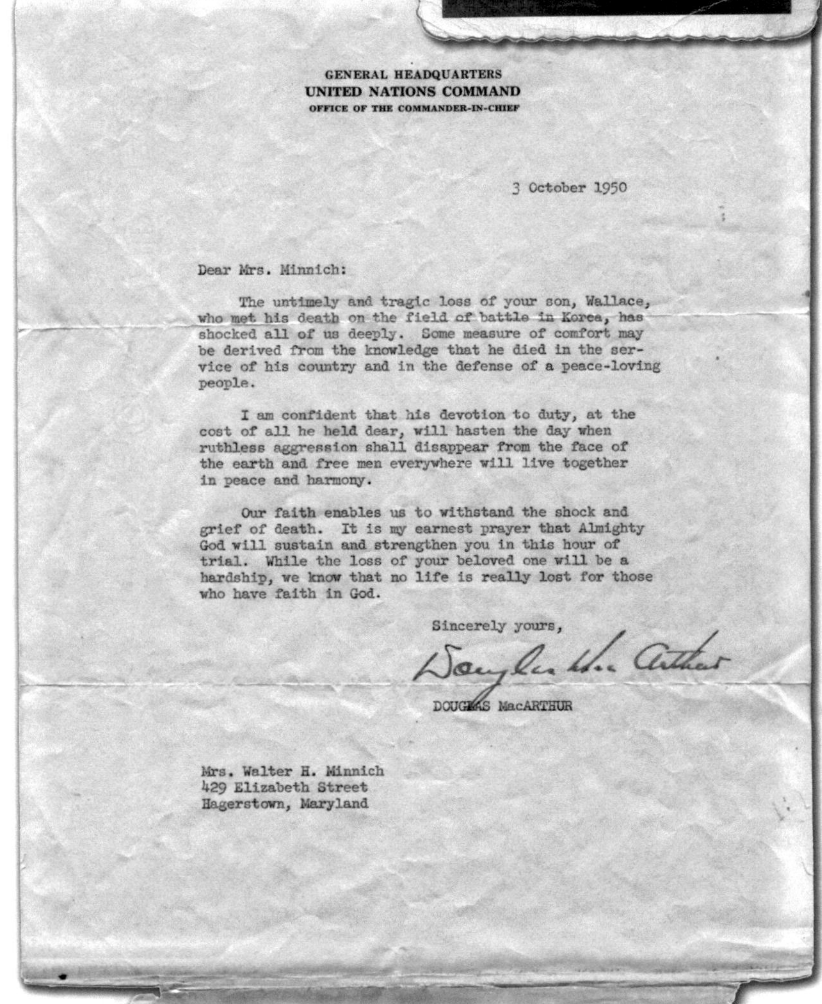

GENERAL HEADQUARTERS
UNITED NATIONS COMMAND
OFFICE OF THE COMMANDER-IN-CHIEF

3 October 1950

Dear Mrs. Minnich:

The untimely and tragic loss of your son, Wallace, who met his death on the field of battle in Korea, has shocked all of us deeply. Some measure of comfort may be derived from the knowledge that he died in the service of his country and in the defense of a peace-loving people.

I am confident that his devotion to duty, at the cost of all he held dear, will hasten the day when ruthless aggression shall disappear from the face of the earth and free men everywhere will live together in peace and harmony.

Our faith enables us to withstand the shock and grief of death. It is my earnest prayer that Almighty God will sustain and strengthen you in this hour of trial. While the loss of your beloved one will be a hardship, we know that no life is really lost for those who have faith in God.

Sincerely yours,

Douglas MacArthur

DOUGLAS MacARTHUR

Mrs. Walter H. Minnich
429 Elizabeth Street
Hagerstown, Maryland

Letter from Gen. Douglas MacArthur to the mother of Wallace T. Minnich, who was killed in action in Korea on Sept. 5, 1950. (Contributed by Nancy Barnes, sister of Wallace T. Minnich)

James W. Minnich — Army — Korea, Cold War

As netting provides camouflage overhead, Army cook James W. Minnich stands on a mess truck during maneuvers with the 44th Field Artillery in Germany in 1954. Minnich became a cook after a more dangerous assignment. He joined the Army in November 1947, after the end of WWII, and served in Korea in 1948 and Japan in 1949 as a military policeman with the 7th Division.

When hostilities broke out in Korea in 1950, Minnich returned there and was injured in 1951. He spent three weeks on the hospital ship USS ***Consolation****, which later became widely known as the hospital ship SS* ***Hope****, and then two more weeks in a hospital on land before returning to his unit. He was one of the first American servicemen shipped home from the Korean front in the spring of 1951.*

Having been trained as a cook and baker in Japan in 1949, he served for the next three years as first cook and mess sergeant at Fort Meade, Maryland, and Camp Pickett, Virginia. Then he took his culinary skills to Germany, where he served for another year and a half at an Army post near Frankfurt. He returned home and left the Army in June 1955.

(Photos and memorabilia submitted by James W. Minnich and Nancy Barnes, Mary Jane Parrish and Dolores Keller, sisters of Wallace, Daniel and James Minnich)

Daniel J. Minnich — Navy — WWII

Daniel J. Minnich, far right, and his buddies stand next to a Quonset hut when they were being discharged from the Navy at the end of WWII, at Bremington Naval Base in Washington state. Minnich worked as an armed guard on the Merchant Marine ship ***Dolores****, crossing the Atlantic Ocean many times during the war, protecting merchant vessels from attack by German U-boats. Noting that the men in the Merchant Marine got higher pay than the Naval guards, Daniel liked to tell his family that "I do the hard work and they get the big pay."*

Daniel's sister Mary Jane remembers that when Daniel docked at the Brooklyn Navy Yard and came home to Hagerstown on leave, he would ask her to buy lipstick to take to France, since the women there couldn't get it during the war. She'd buy a lot of cheap lipstick, which was all that was available in the states at the time.

Born in Hagerstown on July 14, 1925, Minnich worked for the Pennsylvania Railroad before joining the Navy. He died in May 1977.

Bob "Moe" Powell — Navy — Korea

Bob "Moe" Powell, now of Long Beach, California, was living at the YMCA on North Potomac Street in Hagerstown when he joined the Navy in 1946. When he went to boot camp at a Seabee training camp in Virginia, Camp Perry, "I took only the clothes on my back," he said, "and I returned with only my uniform."

Bob Powell served as a Quartermaster 2nd Class in the Pacific on the USS *Topeka* (CH 67), a light cruiser, and on the battleship USS *Iowa* . He said his most memorable experience was departing Aqua Harbor, Guam, on the light cruiser during a typhoon.

He was discharged in February 1948, but re-enlisted for a second tour during the Korean War, serving from June 1950 to November 1951. During that stint, he was stationed in Little Creek, Virginia, and in the Caribbean, training Marines in amphibious landings.

Leaving the Navy again, he graduated from Shippensburg State Teachers College in 1953 and worked for Fairchild Aircraft as a technical writer and a quality assurance representative. He stayed in the aerospace industry, later working as a military subcontractor in aircraft and facility maintenance. "I was a camp follower, going to a lot of different places around the world," he said.

(Photograph courtesy of Evelyn Stape, Bob Powell's sister)

Walter J. Mason— Army — Korea

Walter J. Mason of Williamsport, a private 1st class in the Army, was killed in action in Korea on July 11, 1950. He was a member of the 34th Infantry Regiment, 24th Infantry Division. He was awarded the Purple Heart, the Combat Infantryman Badge, the Korean Service Medal, the United Nations Service Medal, the National Defense Service Medal and the Korean War Service Medal.

His brother, Elvin E. Mason, who enlisted in the Air Force three years after his older brother's death, would die in an automobile accident while serving in Germany in 1957.

(Photographs courtesy of Carol Alexander)

George A. Drake Sr. — Marines — Korea
William L. Drake — Army — Korea

William L. Drake and George A. Drake Sr. were brothers. William was born in Keedysville in 1928 and George in 1929. In their early 20s, William joined the Army and George the Marines. Both fought on the battlefields of Korea from 1951 to 1953.

The winter of 1951 was a bleak time in the Korean War. The conflict was at a stalemate, the front was stabilized, but combat continued even as peace negotiations dragged on and on. U.N. and South Korean forces were trying to recapture as much territory as possible before a political deal was reached. The North Koreans and Chinese were doing the same. The most brutal enemy facing both sides was the bitter Korean winter, and western servicepeople found joy hard to come by at Christmastime.

The Drake brothers lived through that winter, and when they returned home they brought memories, photographs and souvenirs including those on this page. At right are samples of propaganda distributed by both North Korean and Allied forces.

William was wounded in Korea and received a Purple Heart; both returned home alive. William retired a sergeant, George a staff sergeant. George died in 1980, William in 1999.

On the back of this photo (below center) of himself in Korea, William wrote, "Not the best picture I ever had taken, but I believe it would exterminate rats. See those hills, that's all that's here and those are babies you see here. William L. Drake, 1951, Korea"

(Photos and memorabilia courtesy of Pauline G. Norris, aunt of George A. Drake Sr. and William L. Drake)

A Christmas card sent home by George with best wishes in English and Korean.

George takes aim with a pistol in December 1951.

George stands out against the rugged and desolate landscape behind him in Korea.

Jim Smith — Air Force — Korean War

Jim Smith of Chewsville stands at ease near half-ton trucks in Okinawa in 1952. Smith provided clerical support for the 15th Weather Squadron, spending two of his three years in the Air Force on that southernmost Japanese Island.

He also completed temporary assignments at other weather squadrons based on the island of Formosa, on Guam and in the Philippines. "The best part of my time in the Army was meeting other soldiers," he said.

Jim Smith (second from the right in the front row) was a member of "the best softball team on the island," as part of the 15th Weather Squadron in Okinawa. Their team was the softball champion of 1952.

Most of the fellows on the team were meteorologists, working to help determine the most favorable weather conditions for bombing raids on Korea during the Korean War.

Servicemembers formed a softball league in an effort to combat boredom. "We played softball because there wasn't much else to do on that island," Smith said.

(Photographs courtesy of Jim Smith)

Thomas Shank — Army — Korea

The outbreak of the Korean War put many young men who thought of military service as something their fathers had done suddenly in uniform themselves. Warren Shirey and Thomas H. Shank of Hagerstown are shown below in 1951 in front of wooden Army barracks of Fort George G. Meade, Maryland. The two friends were drafted at the same time. Shank served in an anti-aircraft battalion assigned to protect New York City. The battalion was housed in tents placed in open fields on Staten Island, New York. Shirey was assigned to an anti-aircraft battalion tasked with providing comparable protection to Philadelphia.

(Photograph contributed by Marlene Shank, wife of Thomas H. Shank)

Lester F. Joy — Army — Korea

Hancock resident Lester F. Joy enlisted in the Army on May 16, 1950, and by the end of October of that year found himself in heavy fighting in the midst of the Korean War.

Joy, only 18 at the time, was wounded in action in Korea on March 2, 1951. He was treated in Japan, brought back to the United States on March 12, 1951, and recuperated at an Army hospital at Camp Pickett, Virginia.

Daily Mail.

HAGERSTOWN, MD., TUESDAY, FEBRUARY 27, 1951.

SINGLE COPIES, 5 CENTS.

Reds In Savage Counterattacks Sent Reeling

Five Pre-Dawn Assaults Hurled Back By Yanks

U. S. Second Division Battles Three Hours In Sharpest Action Of Week-Old U.N. Offensive.

Hancock Soldier Is Called The Best Machine Gunner; Mowed Down Foe

Pfc. Lester Joy's Gun Got Too Hot, So He Took One From Enemy.

PFC. LESTER JOY

Senate Starting Debate On Draft Of 18-Year-Olds

Hold Boy For Slaying Parents

New Order Aims At Guaranteeing Needed Supplies

All Businesses And Institutions Come Under Plan.

Boy Who Killed Parents Facing Murder Charges

Assembly Told Truck Loads Are Too High

BULLETIN

Front-page headlines note the 2nd Infantry Division's fierce winter fighting in the face of communist counterattacks. Joy had only been in Korea for four months when he helped thwart a massive attempt by Chinese troops to break through United Nations lines at Chipyong. Joy and fellow Hancock soldier Pfc. Boyd Fletcher were in a dug-in position when Chinese troops struck at 10 p.m. on Valentine's Day 1951. The two men, from the same hometown, had taken basic and infantry training together and ended up sharing the same foxhole in Korea.

(Photographs and memorabilia courtesy of Ramon Joy, Lester F. Joy's brother)

—Heroic 2nd Division—

One of the best things about the new and victorious advance in Korea is the way the gallant 2nd Division has staged a comeback. Last November, in the tragic retreat from Korea, the 2nd Division took the heaviest punishment of all. It was given the tough assignment of holding off the enemy while the rest of the 8th Army pulled back below the 38th parallel.

This resulted in some bitter, bloody punishment, with casualties so heavy that General MacArthur cabled Washington that the 2nd Division was "unfit for further combat."

However, the 2nd Division has now staged one of the most magnificent comebacks of the Korean war. [illegible] way. It went back into the line along the Taebak mountains in the bitterly contested Wonju area and heroically stopped a North Korean end run around the U.N. right flank.

Then the 2nd Division reversed the tables, pulled back 12 miles, drew the North Koreans into a trap, hit the trapped Communists on their flank and wiped them out. It was a brilliant maneuver, proving that this division, with an outstanding record in two previous wars, is now carrying on its tradition as proudly as ever.

—Washington [illegible]

Storm Heartbreak Ridge

On the ground, Allied forces stormed again at Heartbreak Ridge in east-central Korea. They were carrying on their five-weeks old drive to take the height commanding a key Communist supply area.

Only Tuesday American and South Korean infantry had seized towering "Kim Il Sung" Mountain, a peak named for the Red Korean premier. It is southwest of Heartbreak Ridge.

The famed U. S. Second Division's 23rd Regiment with its French battalion was carrying the ball on the bitter fight for Heartbreak Ridge. The Ninth Regiment, also attached to the Second Division, was helping out.

The ridge is north of Yanggu and about 30 miles inland from the Sea of Japan.

Sept 26 - 1951

Copy of newspaper clipping, kept by Lester Joy's family, recounting the heroic service of Joy's 23rd Regiment of the 2nd Infantry Division which fought with valor and exceptional sacrifice in Korea.

John C. Koontz Sr. — Army — Korea

John C. Koontz Sr. carries a field map near the 38th parallel dividing North and South Korea in 1953. Koontz was in North Korea when the truce was signed ending the conflict on July 27. Koontz was 20 when he was drafted into the Army in 1952. He was sent to Inchon, Korea, in the spring of 1952 with the Army's 101st Airborne Division. After receiving special training in Japan, he returned to Korea, this time based in Pusan with the 24th Infantry Division. He served in various jobs that ranged from training with interpreters to guarding POWs, and spent several days in North Korea. He returned home and was discharged as a technical sergeant in November 1954.

The United Nations Memorial Cemetery in Pusan, South Korea, in October 1953. More than 2,000 servicemen from UN countries are buried at the site.

A temporary "transfer station" for North Korean prisoners of war located between Pusan and Seoul, South Korea. Koontz worked there guarding prisoners after the truce was signed ending the war on July 27, 1953. He assisted MPs as POWs were being loaded and unloaded on their way to being repatriated. Koontz remembers one occasion when he was guarding a prisoner who kept silent during two days of questioning. Only later did the interrogator realize that he was deaf.

Two South Korean girls peer through barbed wire into the POW station where Koontz worked in 1953.

Lewis E. Jones Jr. — Army — Korea

Army Cpl. Lewis E. Jones Jr., of Boonsboro, learned a thing or two as a medic in Korea during the Korean War. He was photographed in 1952 on the tarmac in front of a B-29, one of the bombers used in the war.

Jones, not unlike thousands of other American men, was drafted into the Army with the outbreak of the Korean War. "I was a mechanic, so they made me a medic," Jones said.

During his time in Korea, he worked at a field hospital and then at an evacuation hospital, driving ambulances and assisting with medical services. "They were really hurting for medics at the time," Jones said.

His service "made me more aware of the responsibility of life."

(Photograph courtesy of Lewis E. Jones Jr.)

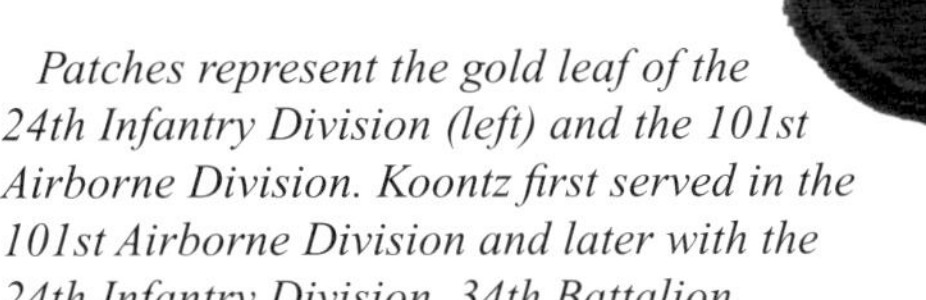

Patches represent the gold leaf of the 24th Infantry Division (left) and the 101st Airborne Division. Koontz first served in the 101st Airborne Division and later with the 24th Infantry Division, 34th Battalion.

John C. Koontz Sr. and his wife, Anna Jean, at home before he left for Korea in 1952. Almost every day, John received a letter from his wife, who was pregnant with their first child when he left. John Koontz Jr. was 18 months old when his father first saw him. At one point in Korea, Koontz was moving so fast he didn't get any letters for 48 days. "It was a bit hellish," he said. "Anything can go through your mind." Finally he was told there was mail call for him, and he found 48 letters and five packages waiting for him. "One had homemade fudge," he said. "It was moldy, but we scraped it off and ate it anyway."

Alvey C. Moser — Air Force — Korea

Alvey Moser was raised in Boonsboro but "grew up in a hurry" during his time in the Air Force. Coming from a small town in a rural setting, "I soon learned what it was like to live and work with people of different backgrounds." He received training in Texas and Mississippi and served in Japan and Korea. He believes his time in uniform was "in all a good experience."

With the exception of a few photographs, Moser took very little with him on his overseas assignment. He came back with something special though — an engagement ring he purchased in a PX [post exchange] in Japan and carried in his top shirt pocket the whole way home. The ring was for Arlene "Deanie" Rhodes, "my wife of now 54 years ... She obviously said 'Yes'," Moser said.

Emblem of the Fifth Air Force which was called into service during the Korean War. Moser, who was a staff sergeant in a support capacity providing food service for Air Force personnel, still carries the memory of seeing jet fighters in action in Korea and the customary air shows returning pilots would put on overhead to celebrate their 100th mission.

One of the highlights of Moser's time in the Air Force was running into two other Boonsboro men at an air base in Fukuoka, Japan, in October 1952. The friends spent three days together before returning to their assignments.

Boonsboro Boys Meet In Japan

It was like old times for three Boonsboro youths when they met recently at an advanced air base in Japan. They spent three days together.

They want to hear from their friends. They are, left to right:

Pfc. Lewis F. Jones, Jr., U. S. 52003891, 21st Evan. Hosp., APO 301, care Postmaster, San Francisco, Calif.

A/2c Jesse F. Kephart, AF 13362-335, 850th AC and W Sqdn., Box 41, APO 929, care Postmaster, San Francisco, Calif.

A/1c Alvey C. Moser, AF13360040, 58th Fd. Sv. Sqdn., Det. 1, APO 929-2, care Postmaster, San Francisco, Calif.

*The photo from their meeting was published in the Nov. 7, 1952, **Morning Herald**, with a story detailing the event and identifying the three uniformed service members. They are Airman 2nd Class Jesse F. Kephart (left), Private 1st Class Lewis F. Jones Jr. (center) and Airman 1st Class Alvey Moser.*

(Photographs and memorabilia courtesy of Alvey C. Moser)

Ed Peters — Army — Korea

Ed Peters thought he might be a mechanic when he was drafted in October 1952, but the Army had other plans for him.

"They were looking for men over 6'2" with some college education," he said. "I was almost 6'4", so they decided I was going to be an MP [military policeman]."

Soon he found himself on Yeongdo Island in the harbor of Pusan, the second-largest city in South Korea. He was with the 58th Military Police Company, part of the 7th Transportation Military Port. He worked in shifts, eight hours a day, seven days a week, both night and day. His work took him to some interesting places.

"There were 1,200 registered houses of ill-repute in Pusan at the time," he said. "For some reason, the commanding general made them off-limits to American servicemen. Our job was to police that. I was always with a Korean policeman. He and I couldn't talk, but we communicated. He'd take care of the Koreans and I comunicated with the Americans. I always said I was in every brothel in Pusan, but that wasn't true."

But Peters had no enthusiasm for this part of his job. So ...

"The alleys in Pusan are very, very narrow," he said. "I patrolled in a jeep with low range, four-wheel drive. When we got near a brothel, I'd put it in low range and it would sound like an airplane. We took our time, and by the time we got inside they'd gone over the back fence or got out some other way. I never caught anybody."

(Photographs courtesy of Ed Peters)

After the armistice on July 27, 1953, Peters was re-assigned to the 91st MP Battalion in Pusan, where one of his jobs was directing traffic on city streets. "Korean drivers wouldn't move unless you gave them specific directions," he said. "They'd just sit there."

Making his job more difficult was his location, standing on a large can between trolley tracks, as seen in the photo above. "Each time a trolley came from one direction, I had to get down and move the can and then put it back," he said. "When one came from other direction, I had to do the same thing. It's not easy to direct traffic when you're doing that. Also, I had to salute all officers, American and Korean. The Korean officers really insisted, and they'd report you if you didn't salute them. Often I couldn't see if they were officers or not, so I had to salute anything that came along."

After a huge fire in 1953 destroyed a large part of Pusan, Ed Peters and some friends went into the city to survey the damage. "People were milling around homeless, trying to salvage things," he said. "I stood up on a pedestal and one of my buddies took my picture."

Heading to Japan for a seven-day R&R, American troops prepare to board a plane at Taegu Military Airport in 1952. "As our bus approached the airport, I noticed our plane was a Fairchild C-119, built in Hagerstown," Peters said. "I felt really proud and told my buddies. But before we boarded the aircraft, they made us put on parachutes. Then the plane shook, rattled and rolled all the way to Japan and back. And here I'd been bragging about it. But it was a sturdy and reliable airplane."

John C. Frye — Army — Korean War

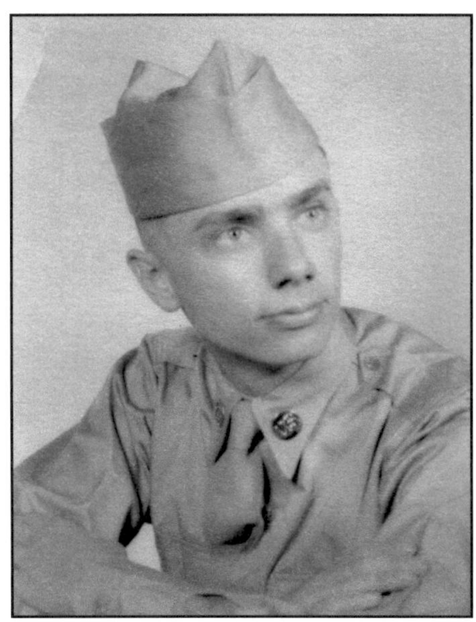

John Frye strikes a somber pose in this photograph taken during Army basic training in 1953.

Frye, of Hagerstown, enlisted in July 1953 "at the tail end of the Korean War. It was either enlist or get drafted," Frye said. "I was never gung-ho about the service. I was in because I was forced in. A lot of guys enjoyed their time in the service. I was there because I had to be there and I did what they told me to do."

After a battery of tests for which the military is famous, Frye was assigned to the Army Security Agency (ASA), one of a select group of recruits chosen for their ability to decipher code, to train and work for the highly secure communications agency. After being given a security clearance — the result of FBI agents and counterintelligence officers looking into his background and interviewing those who knew him — Frye was sent to Camp Gordon, Georgia, to be trained in all aspects of communications available to the military at that time.

Soldiers selected to attend the intensive six-month school mastered every form of radio, voice and teletype communications that the Army used at that time. "We even learned Morse code. Can't say that I enjoyed it [the schooling]," said Frye, "but I did graduate first in my class."

"A lot of guys enjoyed their time in the service. I was there because I had to be there and I did what they told me to do." ——John Frye

Frye was preparing to embark on a career in cryptology — the art and science of codes and cyphers — when his father, Harry Frye, died unexpectedly at 53. He was transferred from the regular Army to the Army Reserve to allow him to be closer to his widowed mother. With no equivalent ASA position nearby, he was transferred to the Signal Corps and trained in Hagerstown to be a combat correspondent, serving in a reserve capacity for eight years.

"I received good journalistic training at a time when few reporters had trained in journalism," Frye said. The military retained a cadre of uniformed journalists to write for the *Stars & Stripes*, a widely distributed newspaper for military personnel abroad, and instructed the correspondents how to rapidly produce dispatches and how to work with censors in times of war. "It was good training," said Frye, who noted the most valuable aspect of his ASA training was "learning how to type." The closest Frye ever came to serving overseas was when President Dwight D. Eisenhower sent troops into Lebanon in 1958. "I was at Fort Meade (Maryland) at the time and we were told to get ready to move out. Not a shot was fired, so we didn't have to go."

John Frye, holding the large pot on the right, and a buddy, Dan Hawk, perform one of the most dreaded assignments in the military — KP or kitchen patrol — hours spent working in the military mess, helping with preparation of food, cooking and serving meals, and the inevitable cleaning up. "It was unpleasant," said Frye, who recalls "the heat, noise and steam" associated with washing the oversized pots, utensils and dinnerware. The two soldiers appear to be in surprisingly good spirits for the camera as they performed this essential duty during basic training at Fort Knox, Kentucky, in 1953. "You had to clean every one of those pans, everything was highly sanitary," Frye recalled.

"It was a long, hot day. You had to prepare and clean up for three complete meals, plus scrubbing down the dining room," said Frye, recounting having to get up at 4 a.m. to work the breakfast shift and staying on duty until 8 p.m. "If you happened to have leave, it didn't matter. Once your name was posted on the bulletin board, you couldn't get out of it." Frye said that KP duty was not a punishment for transgressions, but was part of the routine operation of a military installation, with KP, at least theoretically, assigned on an equitable basis. Still, it got to be kind of an unfunny joke: "Every time I turned around it seemed as though I was assigned to KP duty. I even got pulled for KP when we were in the field," Frye said.

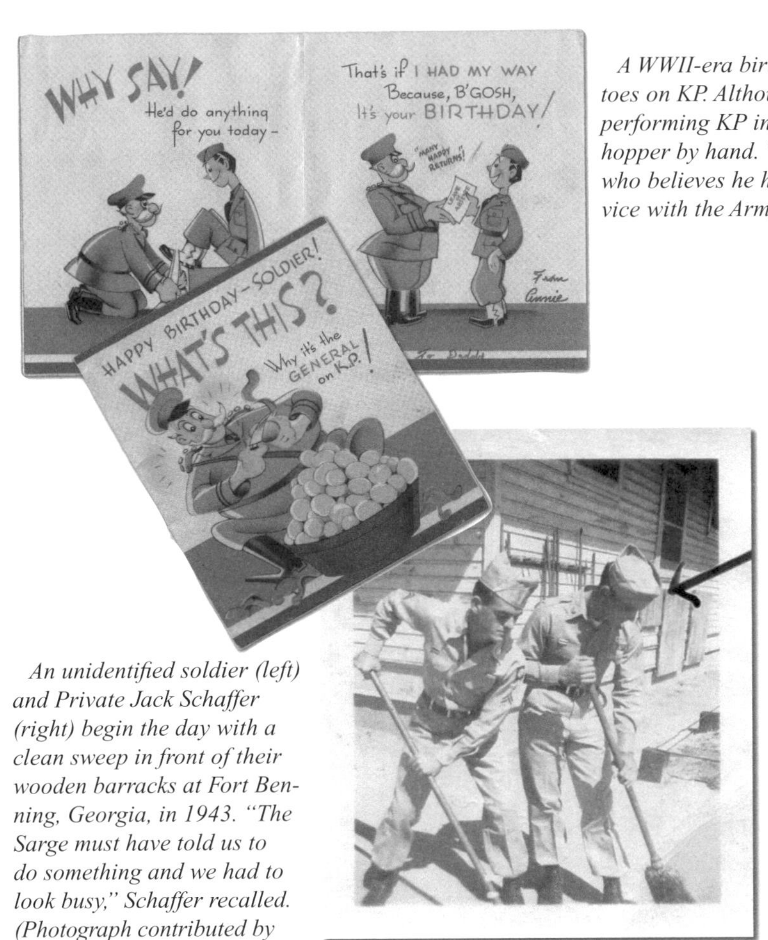

A WWII-era birthday card with an improbable depiction of a general peeling potatoes on KP. Although automatic potato peelers had come into use by the time Frye was performing KP in the 1950s, the bushels of potatoes still had to be fed into the machine's hopper by hand. "A general doing KP! Now that would be something to see," said Frye, who believes he had more than his share of kitchen duty during his brief stateside service with the Army during the Korean War. (Contributed by Betty Spence)

An unidentified soldier (left) and Private Jack Schaffer (right) begin the day with a clean sweep in front of their wooden barracks at Fort Benning, Georgia, in 1943. "The Sarge must have told us to do something and we had to look busy," Schaffer recalled. (Photograph contributed by Jack Schaffer)

Post cards such as this one were designed to shed light on the less glorified aspects of soldiering. The card, showing a soldier doing laundry, was mailed on July 8, 1944, to Sgt. Robert H. Kelsh of Hagerstown, who was assigned to the adjutant general school at Fort Washington, Maryland. (Contributed by Janice Kelsh, daughter of Robert H. Kelsh)

Warren V. Middlekauff — Army — Korea, Vietnam

Clear Spring resident Warren V. Middlekauff Sr., shown here with his Army-issued rifle, was drafted in 1952. He completed eight weeks of basic training at Fort Eustis, Virginia, and completed an additional 16 weeks of training with the 169th Transportation Company at Fort Story, Virginia — including eight weeks of stevedore training. He had only been at Fort Dix, New Jersey, one week before being shipped to Korea in early 1953.

Middlekauff drove trucks carrying ammunition along the hazardous roadways in Korea, hauling the much needed ammo to the front lines. He returned to the United States in 1954 and joined the Army Reserve. In 1968, his transportation unit was called to active duty. Middlekauff served as a motor sergeant in Vietnam. He returned home in 1969 and eventually retired in 1989 with 35 years of military service.

(Photographs courtesy of Warren V. Middlekauff Sr.)

The Nightmare Never Ends

www.angelfire.com

Close your eyes and go to sleep,
My poor, haunted soldier man.
I'll try my best to keep you safe,
In any way I possibly can.

Cradled there in my loving arms,
He drifted off to Vietnam once more.
I tried my best to soothe him,
But he was already back in the war.

His body's tense and twitching,
As he dreams of yesteryear.
I call out his name in vain,
Just trying to ease his fear.

But the battle is already brewing,
He's in the midst of a fire fight.
And for what seems like an eternity,
My soldier thrashes in the night.

And it's too late to bring him home,
He's fighting alongside his brothers.
He hears his comrades cry out in pain,
And call out for their mothers.

He's soaked in sweat as he jumps about,
He feels the bullets whizzing by.
His body's numb as he checks himself,
He's so certain he's gonna die.

No, not today my brave hero,
Though you've lost so many friends.
He opens his eyes as the dream has passed,
But the nightmare never ends.

Chris Woolnough
11/1/03

Vietnam War

1962-1975

Vietnam photograph contributed by Larry Michael
Vietnam Service Medal (opposite page) contributed by Jerry Violet

Dennis E. Reeder — Marine Corps — Vietnam

Dennis E. Reeder had just graduated from boot camp at the Marine Corps Recruit Depot in San Diego, California, in 1967, and was all of 18 years old when this photograph was taken. Within weeks of completing his training he found himself far from his Locust Street neighborhood, patrolling the jungles and rice paddies of Vietnam.

Reeder is wearing the jacket and cover from the Marine Corps dress uniform for this photograph, but he never got to own one of the distinctive Marine dress uniforms himself. At the time of his service, the uniforms were not issued to recruits. Marines had to purchase the uniforms themselves. Less than six months after completing basic training, Reeder was in the hospital recuperating from his Vietnam War injuries. He was honorably discharged four years after this photo was taken, without ever having the need or opportunity to purchase the uniform of "The Few. The Proud."

Cpl. Reeder was assigned to the 2nd Battalion, 1st Marines in Vietnam. He was armed with an M-79 grenade launcher, the next to the last in line as part of the five-man patrol in jungle terrain, 14 miles south of Danang, when he was injured. The men were participating in a routine night patrol and the contingent was looking for enemy movement. One of the Marines ahead of him hit the trip wire to an explosive device. The booby trap exploded directly beneath Reeder. Four of the five members of the patrol were injured, but Reeder was the most badly hurt. A Navy corpsman, whose name (Ronnie Brookshire) Reeder will never forget, rushed to his side and stayed with him until he could be evacuated by helicopter. Shown here are Reeder's dog tags (right), a medallion commemorating his battalion (lower left) and the Marine Corps Good Conduct Medal (center). Reeder was also awarded a Purple Heart and a Combat Action Ribbon.

Reeder readily admits "I was scared to death" when he got off the bus at boot camp. "When I first met the drill instructor, my knees started knocking and I thought, "My God, what am I getting into?" The training was "pretty brutal," but didn't last long. He went into the Marine Corps in November 1966 and was on the ground in Vietnam in April 1967, only five months later. Not unlike other young Marines, Reeder purchased this commemorative cigarette lighter bearing the Marine Corps emblem, but he learned early in his career that there was no benefit to smoking. His drill instructor had a unique way of encouraging the leathernecks to give up the habit. During training, the drill instructor would assign additional PT [physical training] exercises to those who smoked. "I quit," said Reeder, who gave up smoking for good, but kept the lighter.

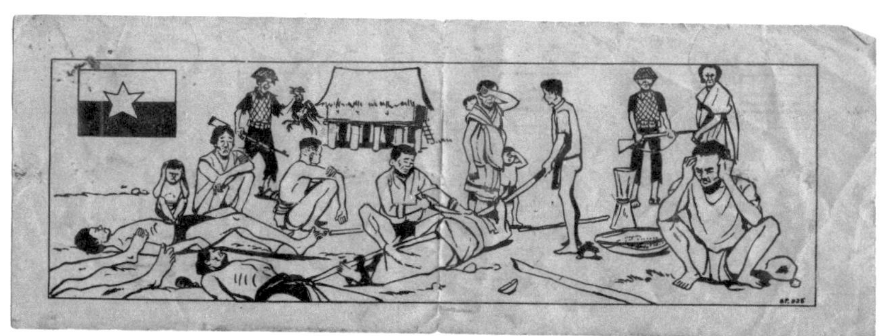

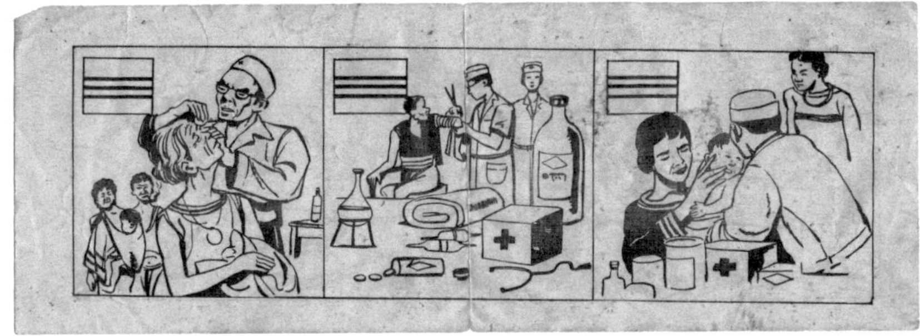

In an effort to discourage support for the North Vietnamese and Viet Cong fighters, leaflets such as these were distributed in areas known to be frequented by the enemies of the South Vietnamese government. One side of the panel shows Viet Cong and North Vietnamese troops killing villagers and stealing a rooster, while the panel on the other side shows South Vietnamese medical personnel treating the elderly, injured and young children.

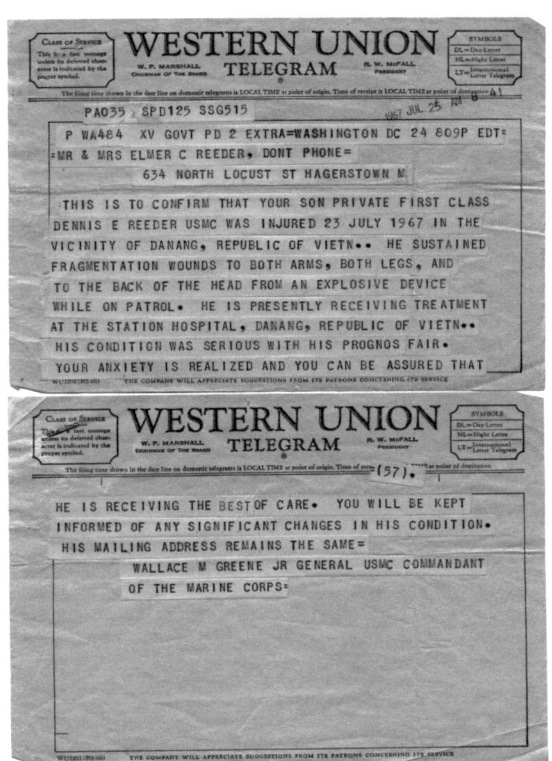

WESTERN UNION TELEGRAM

PA035 SPD125 SSG515 1967 JUL 25 AM 8 41

P WA484 XV GOVT PD 2 EXTRA=WASHINGTON DC 24 809P EDT=
=MR & MRS ELMER C REEDER, DONT PHONE=
634 NORTH LOCUST ST HAGERSTOWN M

THIS IS TO CONFIRM THAT YOUR SON PRIVATE FIRST CLASS DENNIS E REEDER USMC WAS INJURED 23 JULY 1967 IN THE VICINITY OF DANANG, REPUBLIC OF VIETN.. HE SUSTAINED FRAGMENTATION WOUNDS TO BOTH ARMS, BOTH LEGS, AND TO THE BACK OF THE HEAD FROM AN EXPLOSIVE DEVICE WHILE ON PATROL. HE IS PRESENTLY RECEIVING TREATMENT AT THE STATION HOSPITAL, DANANG, REPUBLIC OF VIETN.. HIS CONDITION WAS SERIOUS WITH HIS PROGNOS FAIR. YOUR ANXIETY IS REALIZED AND YOU CAN BE ASSURED THAT

WESTERN UNION TELEGRAM

(57).

HE IS RECEIVING THE BEST OF CARE. YOU WILL BE KEPT INFORMED OF ANY SIGNIFICANT CHANGES IN HIS CONDITION. HIS MAILING ADDRESS REMAINS THE SAME=
WALLACE M GREENE JR GENERAL USMC COMMANDANT OF THE MARINE CORPS=

Marine Corps officials didn't pull any punches in the July 25, 1967, telegram informing Mrs. and Mrs. Elmer C. Reeder of Hagerstown that their son had been badly wounded in the vicinity of Danang. The telegram advised his parents that Reeder had "sustained fragmentation wounds to both arms, both legs and to the back of the head from an explosive device while on patrol ... His condition is serious with his prognosis fair."

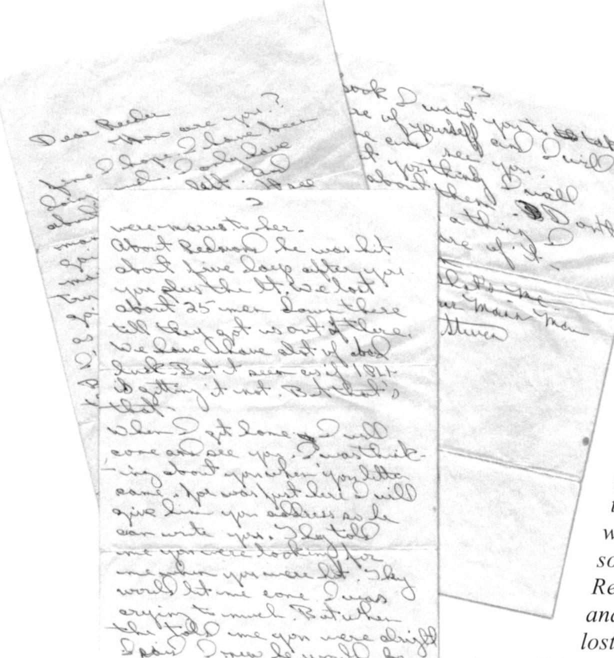

Reeder received the following letter from a buddy, Cpl. Stephen Green, from Michigan, when he was in the hospital in Bethesda. Green gave Reeder news of the unit, reporting the wounding of another soldier five days after Reeder was injured and reporting that "we lost about 25 men down there till they got us out of there. We have have [had] a lot of bad luck ... But that's that ... They told me you were looking for me when you were hit. They would[n't] let me come. I was crying to[sic] much. But when they told me you were alright I said I knew he would be."

Reeder, who was born on the 4th of July, said he had "a lot of good care" in the immediate aftermath of his injuries. "The Lord was on my side. I have been pretty well blessed." Reeder concedes that many others were not quite so lucky, describing those with more horrifying injuries as "the real heroes." But wounds don't have to be visible to be real. "A lot of guys didn't get hurt physically, but they saw a lot of things. Some of them are screwed up for life and very few will talk about it," Reeder said.

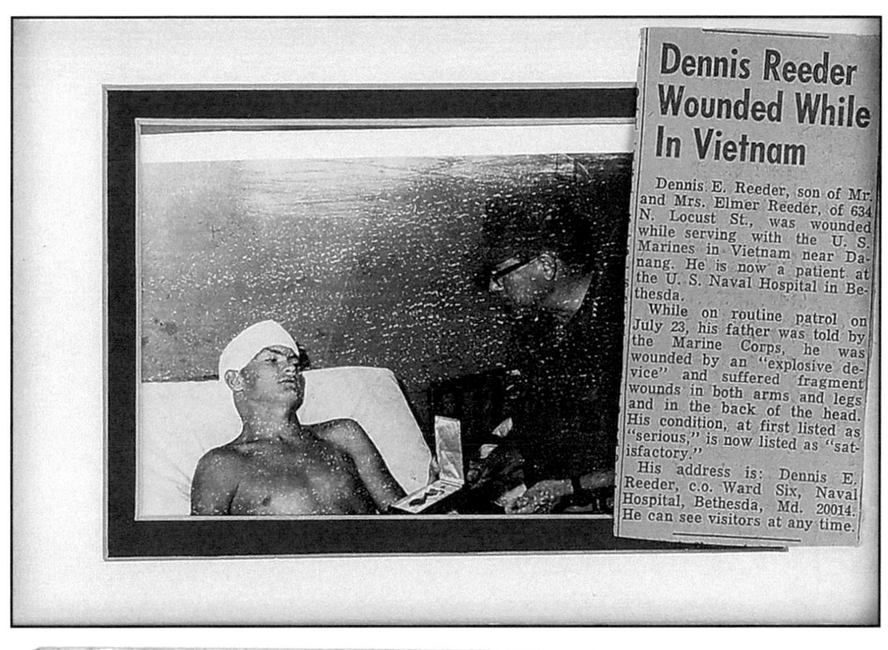

Dennis Reeder Wounded While In Vietnam

Dennis E. Reeder, son of Mr. and Mrs. Elmer Reeder, of 634 N. Locust St., was wounded while serving with the U. S. Marines in Vietnam near Danang. He is now a patient at the U. S. Naval Hospital in Bethesda.

While on routine patrol on July 23, his father was told by the Marine Corps, he was wounded by an "explosive device" and suffered fragment wounds in both arms and legs and in the back of the head. His condition, at first listed as "serious," is now listed as "satisfactory."

His address is: Dennis E. Reeder, c.o. Ward Six, Naval Hospital, Bethesda, Md. 20014. He can see visitors at any time.

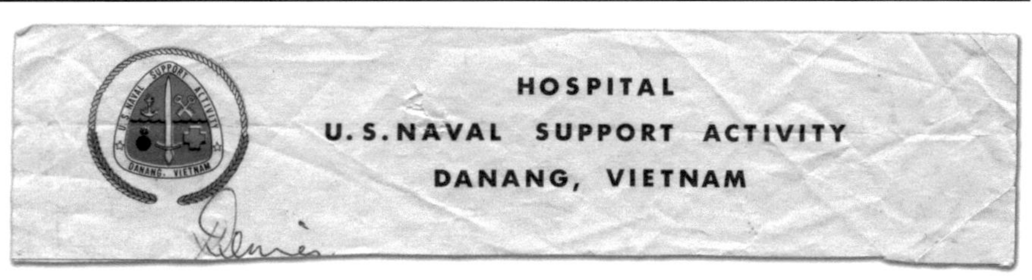

Reeder spent one year at the U.S. Naval Hospital in Bethesda recuperating from his wounds. The Vietnam War's biggest impact on Reeder was not the time he spent overseas, but his exposure to other wounded veterans during his recovery at the famed naval hospital. Seeing all the other Marines and sailors who were hurt worse than he was, was a humbling experience. Reeder was transported from a field hospital to the hospital in Danang, and was evacuated to the United States only after his condition had stabilized. Reeder has no memory of Gen. Green presenting him with the Purple Heart, an event captured in this photo taken at the hospital in Danang not long after he was wounded.

Service in the Marine Corps "turned my life 100% around. It made me look at everything differently," Reeder said. Despite the visible scars he carries on his legs, skull injuries and hearing loss in his right ear, Reeder has nothing but praise for the Marine Corps and the medical care he received during and after his time in Vietnam.

Reeder's wife, Cheryl, assembled this shadowbox that includes her favorite photo of Reeder (in combat helmet in the lower right), the Marine Corps medallion (left) and a snapshot of Reeder in his Marine Corps uniform next to his mother-in-law's Pontiac (at the top of the frame).

(Photographs and memorabilia courtesy of Dennis E. Reeder)

Purple Heart (above) and Marine Corps commemorative knives (below) from the Vietnam War from Dennis Reeder's collection.

Dennis Reeder's wallet was in his back pocket when he was hit by shrapnel from a booby trap. The wallet, visibly damaged in the blast, absorbed some of the shock and at least one of the pieces of shrapnel that cut into Reeder's body that day. Hc didn't realize what a help the wallet had been until his personal belongings "caught up with me" when he was recuperating at Bethesda Naval Hospital.

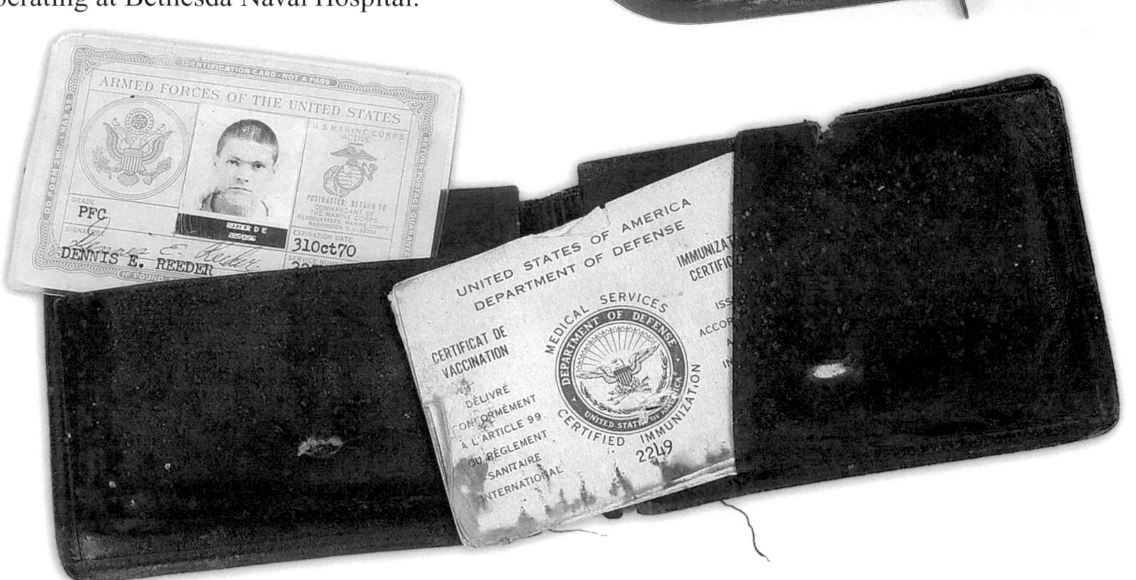

Harry J. "Blackie" Layman — Marine Corps — Vietnam

Harry J. "Blackie" Layman and his father, Harry Layman, share a quiet moment at Parris Island, South Carolina, following Layman's graduation from boot camp in August 1968. He had only been in the Marine Corps for four months before landing in Vietnam. Layman served in the Marine Corps from 1968 to 1970. The elder Layman had served in WWII as a crewmember on a B-24 "Liberator" bomber, part of the 99th Bomb Group in Europe.

Lance Cpl. Layman, sits outside his wooden barracks in 1969, near Con Thien, near the DMZ [demilitarized zone] separating North and South Vietnam, his ever-present M-16 by his side. The region was the site of fierce combat between North Vietnamese regulars and U.S. Marines. On the back of the color snapshot sent to his family in Frostburg, he wrote in large letters: "I think you know who this homesick kid is."

Among Layman's most memorable experiences in Vietnam were his interactions with the children who lived in a nearby orphanage. Layman and other members of the 3rd Marines routinely took food and medical supplies to the orphanage run by Buddhist monks and nuns in nearby Gio Linh. One of the children, a little girl named Mai Ling, approximately 5 years old, made an impression upon him. "I wanted to adopt her and bring her back to the States, but I was only 19 at the time," Layman said. Mai Ling is standing to the left of Layman in this photograph taken in 1969.

When the 3rd Marine Division pulled out of the region, after Layman had rotated back to the United States, he learned that North Vietnamese Army troops overran the compound and killed all the staff members and children at the orphanage.

(Photographs courtesy of Beth Layman, wife of Harry J. "Blackie" Layman)

Barry Melvin "Rick" Cunningham — Army — Vietnam

Cunningham was proud to have served with the 25th Infantry Division, which is assigned to the Pacific region. The 25th Infantry Division was activated on Oct. 1, 1941, at Schofield Barracks, Hawaii, and saw its first combat during the attack on Pearl Harbor. The division engaged North Korean troops in the Korean War and became fully involved in Vietnam in 1966.

Barry Melvin "Rick" Cunningham of Williamsport was a 19-year-old "tunnel rat," assigned to the 14th Battalion of the 25th Infantry Division during the Vietnam War. The 25th Infantry Division, nicknamed "Tropic Lightning," was the largest division in Vietnam, fighting the North Vietnamese and Viet Cong north and west of Saigon. Between April of 1966 and 1972, the 25th Infantry Division fought some of the toughest battles of the war.

As a "tunnel rat," Cunningham was trained to penetrate unexplored tunnels dug by Viet Cong fighters. Construction of the tunnels began during the First Indochina War, in the days following the end of World War II. They were used as bomb shelters and weapons storage in the guerrilla war against the French. In their most elaborate form, the tunnels included kitchens, sleeping rooms, hospitals and ammunition depots. Viet Cong and North Vietnamese soldiers also relied on the complex network of tunnels to provide safe passage in their later war against American and South Vietnamese troops. When American or Allied troops passed overhead, fighters would either hide in the tunnels or use them to launch surprise attacks.

Barry Melvin "Rick" Cunningham was surrounded by his family the day they took him to Dulles Airport in 1966 for his assignment to Vietnam. Shown from left to right are: his older brother, Larry "Butch" Cunningham, his mother, Kathryn Cunningham, his brother George, his sister, Lois Hawbaker South, and Lois's daughter, Sherri Hawbaker.

The Army flew Cunningham to Vietnam because he refused to go on the troopship. According to Lois, Cunningham "was terrified of the water."

In some of the most daring and dangerous assignments of the Vietnam War, these specially trained soldiers risked their lives by crawling alone into the well-disguised tunnels to determine where they led. Because Vietnamese fighters were generally smaller than the average U.S. soldier, Cunningham's spare build was an advantage in his daring missions into the oftentimes deadly tunnels.

The largest of these tunnel complexes was at Cu Chi, 45 miles north of Saigon, where Cunningham was assigned. The network of multi-level tunnels covered more than 155 miles and encompassed air shafts, underwater entrances and sentry posts. Some of the rooms even had electricity. Cunningham was part of the massive effort to eliminate the tunnels as a base for enemy operations.

Armed with a .45-caliber pistol, a knife and a flashlight, the soldiers would squirm their way through the dark passages, not knowing if enemy fighters would be waiting for them. Firearms were of little value since bullets did not travel far before becoming embedded in the winding tunnel walls.

For tunnel rats, military-issued all-black knives, known as "Ka-Bars," provided the best defense. Tunnel rats also employed code words to let each other know if an area was booby trapped. Often before entering a tunnel, a tunnel rat would toss in a tear-gas canister, hoping the noxious gas would overcome Viet Cong sentries in the twisting tunnels.

While on an extended "search-and-destroy mission" by the Saigon River on Aug. 18, 1967, Cunningham was badly injured when he tripped a booby trap at the entrance to a tunnel from which he had just emerged. The coded call alerting the men to the presence of these deadly explosives had just gone out when he was thrown into the air.

Photo of Cunningham (right) in Vietnam and a buddy named "Smitty" taken not long after he was wounded for the first time in Vietnam.

Cunningham received multiple fragment wounds and lay on the ground for nearly eight hours before he could be taken to a field hospital. Enemy fire had pinned down the soldiers and it was too dangerous to attempt an evacuation in daylight. "Medics kept coming to his side giving him shots of morphine until it was dark and they could carry him out of there," said his widow, Karon Cunningham. "He described his leg as looking like raw hamburger," she recalled. Four days after he arrived at a field hospital, Cunningham underwent a below-knee amputation of his left leg.

Cunningham might have been considered the "lucky one." Of the three men injured on that patrol, the first was killed and the second lost both legs.

The very morning he was wounded, Cunningham's mother, Kathryn, was awakened from a terrible dream in which she heard her son crying and calling her name. "She was so upset that she telephoned her daughter to come over. Lois had not been at the house very long before the early morning telephone call came saying Cunningham had been injured. Later that evening, a soldier was dispatched to the house to give them additional information.

One of two Purple Hearts Cunningham was awarded for wounds he received during the Vietnam War. He lost his left leg in 1967 as a result of a booby trap.

When he returned to the States, Cunningham shared a vivid memory with his family of the day he was wounded. According to Lois, the last thing her brother remembered before the blast was catching sight of "the most beautiful bird he had ever seen. He called it the bird of paradise. [After the explosion] He knew that he was hurt bad, but he said he knew he would be OK. The memory of that bird stayed with him."

Upon his evacuation back to the United States, Cunningham spent much of the next two years in and out of hospitals — first, Walter Reed Army Hospital, and then, the veterans' hospital in Martinsburg, West Virginia, where he learned to walk all over again.

Not long after his return to Washington County, Cunningham, who had not yet received his prosthetic leg, was making his way on crutches to a Hagerstown pharmacy for pain medicine, when a woman walked up to him and called him a "baby killer." Cunningham and other soldiers discharged from the hospital in 1967 had been cautioned not to wear their uniforms in public. Cunningham now knew why.

The lightning bolt is the readily identifiable insignia of the 25th Infantry Division, nicknamed "Tropic Lightning."

Particularly hurtful, according to Cunningham's family, was the refusal of the American Legion to admit him in 1968 because Vietnam wasn't considered a "real war." Although the Legion's official policy at the time would have included him, Cunningham was apparently told he could only join as the son of a WWII veteran, but not in his own right. Cunningham later joined the Veterans of Foreign Wars.

Cunningham's family reported that he often had to fight to get medical attention and assistance once he returned from Vietnam, including the special socks he wore over the stump of his leg.

Despite his injuries, Cunnningham was determined to regain his mobility. "He had such a good attitude," said

Karon, who said Cunningham once told her, that of the group of soldiers who went to Vietnam with him, only three came home from Vietnam alive.

"He was so glad to have made it back."

His motivation for entering the military was no different than that of many young men at the time. He wanted to serve his country and to send money home to his mother to help support his younger brothers, Bob and George.

Cunningham died unexpectedly on April 16, 1997, almost 20 years after his service in Southeast Asia, from what was believed to have been a heart attack. A piece of shrapnel from the booby trap had been lodged in his lung since the instant of the explosion and he had been advised that if the fragment of metal ever moved, "it would kill him."

(Photographs and memorabilia courtesy of Karon Cunningham, widow of Barry Melvin "Rick" Cunningham)

Cunningham's Airborne beret and his camouflage fatigue jacket from his service during the Vietnam War.

An all black "Ka-Bar" combat knife was an indispensible part of a "tunnel rat's" weaponry during the Vietnam War. (Contributed by Dennis E. Reeder)

Stephen C. Haines — Army — Vietnam

"The real heroes are in Arlington Cemetery."

Lt. Haines came home in August 1971 with a number of decorations and insignia. Pictured here at the top (left to right) are his lieutenant and captain's bars with infantry insignia. On either side of his ribbon rack in the center are 25th Infantry Division patches, one illustrating the division's slogan, "Follow Me," and the other, its nickname, "Tropic Lightning."

On the bottom row between his Bronze Star and Army Commendation Medal is the 101st Airborne Division patch with Ranger insignia. When he went to war, Haines carried a cross and a picture of his first-born son, Stephen.

(Photos and memorabilia courtesy of Stephen C. Haines)

After serving one year in Vietnam, Lt. Stephen C. Haines said people here don't know what a bad day is. The Hagerstown resident was commander of his infantry company, responsible for about 150 men, while serving in the Vietnam War. A 20-year-old Haines is pictured here on a bunker beside his M16 rifle reading a letter from home. He had just completed an all-day search mission in Tay Ninh, Vietnam, when this photo was snapped by an Army photographer in October 1968. Haines said there were enemy attacks, mostly at night, on a weekly basis in this location, and time for relaxation was rare.

When he thinks he's had a bad day at work at Mack Truck, he said, "I always remember what a bad day really was in Vietnam. I tell myself I'm not sleeping in the mud, I'm not being shot at, and everyone is coming home today. This always changes my perspective on a bad day.

"It was a different time and a different place," he said. "You have to leave the baggage behind and go on with life." Haines acknowledged he's lucky he came home alive. "The real heroes," he said, "are in Arlington Cemetery."

He also said he's proud of the fact that the military weapons of today, which all allow a much smaller loss of life during war, were developed after the Vietnam War "with input from those of us who experienced it."

William F. Carpenter — Army — Vietnam

Not long after William F. Carpenter graduated from South Hagerstown High School, he found himself in the Army, fighting in Vietnam with the 1st Infantry Division. A clerk-typist, mail clerk and supply clerk, he was also a "tunnel rat." A newspaper article about Carpenter after his return called this "one of the dirtiest, nastiest, fighting jobs in that dirty, nasty war."

The job, it said, was "to crawl on your stomach down a narrow, dark tunnel, just big enough for a small man, never knowing when you might crawl straight into the barrel of a Viet Cong gun." Carpenter recalled the time his outfit approached a Viet Cong tunnel. One of his buddies stepped on a mine, and five of them were killed.

HIS JOB – ONE OF THE NASTIEST

'Tunnel Rat' Bill Carpenter Hunted Cong

By FAIN MILLER

Call most men a "rat" and you're likely to get a punch in the nose.

Call William Carpenter a "rat" and his chest swells with pride.

But we wouldn't advise you to use the term with him unless you put the word "tunnel" in front of it.

That's because Carpenter has just returned from Vietnam, where he was, among other things, a "tunnel rat" — one of the dirtiest, nastiest fighting jobs in that dirty, nasty war.

How would you like to crawl on your stomach down a narrow, dark tunnel just big enough for a small man, never knowing when you might crawl straight into the barrel of a Viet Cong gun?

That's what William Carpenter did.

How would you like to search that tunnel, never knowing when that innocent looking object left behind might contain a booby trap ready to blast any careless American?

That's what William Carpenter did.

He can smile about it now as he relaxes with his wife, Dolores, and his parents, Mr. and Mrs. Aden Carpenter, 832 Virginia Ave.

But the memories will always be with the 20-year-old graduate of North Hagerstown High School.

Memories like the time he was with a First Infantry outfit approaching a Viet Cong tunnel. Someone stepped on a mine. Five of Carpenter's buddies were killed.

Pfc. Carpenter never did encounter any Viet Cong in the elaborately constructed tunnel networks.

But he did find lots of documents, radios, weapons — and even some VC pajamas.

While most of the tunnels were only high enough to permit crawling or sliding through on the stomach, they found a room in one of them which was high enough to allow standing. The room had been used as a hospital.

When Carpenter wasn't on "tunnel rat" missions, he served his company at different times as a clerk typist, mail clerk and supply clerk.

"We also worked with the 'little people' helping them to make bunkers, fill in ditches and dig latrines," Carpenter said, as he explained that the Vietnamese are referred to as the "little people."

Aside from the differences in the food, customs and clothing from that of the United States, Carpenter said he found the Vietnamese "very nice people to work with, despite the language barrier and they did the job required of them."

When asked the inevitable question about the morale of the men stationed in Vietnam, he replied, "It's really not bad, the stopped there, it could happen here."

On the question of draft card burners, Carpenter said "if they could be over there to see what is going on, they wouldn't be so happy."

As for the general concensus of the men in Vietnam he said they didn't think too much of it either.

"They know what we must do if we want to be free of communism. I have seen what the Communists do and I'm glad I can say I'm an American and I can do and say as I want," Carpenter said.

For his efforts in Vietnam, Carpenter was awarded the Army Commendation Medal for, in the words of Nathanial Morse, his NCO, "outstanding courage while operating as a member of the Di An Base Rapid Reaction Force."

Morse said in a letter to the Morning Herald, "Time and men know they are over there for a job which they would rather fight over there, than here.

"They also know if it's not time again he (Carpenter) has placed his life in danger while protecting or rescuing the lives of other soldiers. Showing no concern for his own safety he has always acted swiftly and professionally and insured that his mission was accomplished.

"The professionalism, dependability, aggressiveness and courage shown by Pfc. William F. Carpenter . . . is in the finest tradition of the 1st Infantry," Morse concluded.

Although he was supposed to return to the states in March, Carpenter said he really didn't mind waiting 'til May, although he did miss his family.

The North High graduate interrupted his education at LaSalle University of Chicago, which he is now continuing by correspondence, working toward a law degree.

'TUNNEL RAT' SOUVENIR
. . . Carpenter examines pj's

Carpenter in Vietnam with one of "the little people" — a term used to characterize the Vietnamese. Carpenter worked directly with Vietnamese laborers in manual work such as making bunkers, filling in ditches and digging latrines. He said, "they are very nice people to work with, despite the language barrier and they did the job required of them."

(Photos courtesy of David Carpenter, nephew of William F. Carpenter)

Ray L. "Jimmy" Haines Jr. — Army — Vietnam

Pfc. Ray L. "Jimmy" Haines Jr. leans against a family car for a photograph taken before he headed for Vietnam. Haines was a radio operator in Ahn Khe, where his platoon and two platoons of Korean soldiers ran a fuel pumping station. He was there during the Tet Offensive of 1968 and was wounded in his arm by shrapnel. "In a situation like this," Haines told his aunt, Rose Sweeney, "when you are fighting for your life, your buddies and the freedom of others ... it's a good feeling fighting for a just cause."

Somber photos of Ray L. "Jimmy" Haines Jr. with his parents taken before he left for Vietnam in 1967. In the family snapshot on the right, Jimmy stands with his father, Ray "Jim" Haines Sr., in front of Army barracks, and in the photo at left he is shown with his mother, Thelma Barr Haines.

(Photographs courtesy of Rose Sweeney, Ray L. "Jimmy" Haines Jr.'s aunt)

Charles Kent Wyndham — Army — Vietnam

Charles Kent Wyndham didn't talk about his service in Vietnam, according to his wife, Darlene.

"The first 15 years of our marriage I had to wash the sheets every day because of his night sweats," she said. "But he didn't talk about it ... only once, with Freddie."

Born July 8, 1943, in Martinsburg, West Virginia, Wyndham graduated from high school in Bellefonte, Pennsylvania, and went to Slippery Rock State College, north of Pittsburgh. There he played football and wrestled and got his B.S. in Health Education in January 1966, planning to be a gym teacher.

But U.S. involvement in Vietnam was escalating, and Wyndham felt he had to be there.

"He was an only son. He didn't have to go. But he wanted to go to Vietnam," Darlene said.

Four months after graduation, on April 8, 1966, Wyndham joined the Army. After graduating from Infantry School at Fort Benning, Georgia, and taking a course on Vietnam at the Army Civil Affairs School at Fort Gordon, Georgia, Second Lieutenant Kent Wyndham found himself serving in the Infantry in Vietnam.

He had scarcely arrived there before his mother died, and he came home for her funeral. Returning to Vietnam, he found himself at My Lai.

The My Lai massacre was the killing of hundreds of unarmed Vietnamese civilians, mostly women and children, by U.S. soldiers on March 16, 1968. It prompted widespread outrage around the world and reduced American support at home for the war in Vietnam.

My Lai was in an area where the Viet Cong were deeply entrenched. Troops of the Army's Americal Division, involving C Company under the command of Lt. William Calley, entered the village poised for engagement with the enemy. The "search and destroy" mission degenerated into the massacre of more than 300 apparently unarmed civilians.

Wyndham, second from right, with members of his company in Vietnam

Kent Wyndham (right) with his gunner and best buddy, Freddie Hagendorn, in Vietnam.

A military investigation resulted in Calley's being charged with murder. At his trial, he testified that he was ordered by a superior to kill everyone in the village, but there was enough evidence to convict only Calley of murder. He was sentenced to life in prison, but President Richard Nixon arranged to have the sentence reduced to 20 years and granted Calley parole after he had spent only three days in prison. After being discharged, Calley went into the insurance business.

Kent Wyndham never told his wife what he experienced at My Lai, but she said, "He would never watch pictures on TV of women and children in war situations."

Wyndham came home from Vietnam a first lieutenant with a Bronze Star, awarded for the period December 1967 to November 1968. But felt his job was not through. He wanted to go back to Vietnam.

In June 1969, he commenced eight weeks of combat training at the Army Training Center, Infantry, at Fort Bragg, North Carolina, and two months later emerged as Captain Wyndham, Commander, Company D, Eighth Battalion, Second Brigade.

Soon he was back on the battlefields of Vietnam, where he was exposed to Agent Orange — a herbicide used as a defoliant in widespread deforestation of the countryside. He developed "a disease of unknown origin" and was sent home, this time to stay. He was released from active duty in February 1970, and after two years in the Army Reserve, he

Capt. Kent Wyndham in Vietnam

received an honorable discharge on April 30, 1972.

"He decided he wasn't going to make a life of it," Darlene said. Returning to the Tri-State area, he settled in Williamsport and began a different kind of career, with the U.S. Postal Service in Hagerstown, where he worked as a clerk for the next 30 years.

"At work they called him 'Commander'," Darlene said. "And after he went grey they called him 'The Grey Fox.' He was named employee of the month so many times."

But in all those years, he never talked about to her his experiences in Vietnam. She knew he had strong feelings about what happened at My Lai, however. He submitted written comments and testified before Congress in support of Lt. Calley. "He didn't agree with Calley being imprisoned ... not at all," Darlene said. "All he would say was, 'the Commander-in-Chief is aware of everything.' That's it; that's all he'd say."

After his death, Darlene found a newspaper clipping that Kent had taped to the back of the frame of a collection of photos taken during his time in Vietnam. Dated April 16, 1995, the article from the Associated Press was titled, "McNamara's confession stirs anger in veterans."

In it, AP National Writer Robert Dvorchak wrote: "Like a tripwire, [former secretary of defense] Robert McNamara's belated admission that U.S. persistence in Vietnam was 'terribly wrong' has opened old wounds among those who battled in the jungles, rice paddies and tall grass of America's longest war.

"McNamara said he concluded the war was unwinnable in the mid-'60s, yet he did not speak out and continued to dispatch troops into combat, in part because he feared that the apearance of weakness by the United States could have emboldened the Soviet Union and created the risk of war.

"The vast majority of the 58,196 names etched in the somber black granite on the Vietnam Memorial are those of people who died after 1965."

Wyndham made one thing very clear to his wife. "He always said if we had a son, he'd never go in the service. Kent had too many friends MIA [missing in action]. He said no child of ours would ever go into the military, because there was no guarantee he wouldn't end up a POW [prisoner of war]."

Wyndham's exposure to Agent Orange "was also an issue with us," she said. Dioxins in the herbicide had been implicated in the occurrence of birth defects in the children of parents who had been exposed to it. The couple had no children.

There was one time that her husband did talk about Vietnam, Darlene said.

"He had lost touch with his comrades in Vietnam," she said. "They thought he'd died.

"But one day in 1996, I answered the phone and a man asked if my husband had been a commander in Vietnam. I said yes, and on the other end of the line I heard someone shout, 'I found him!'

"That was Freddie Hagendorn, his best buddy in Vietnam, his gunner. Kent was the captain, Freddie was the radio guy, he had to be right beside Kent, so he could give orders. He really loved Freddie.

"Freddie said he called every Wyndham in the country to find Kent. Then he came out here from Portland, Oregon, and the minute he walked in the door, they started talking. They talked and talked, and they drank a lot of beer, and they went down to the wall [the Vietnam Veterans Memorial wall] together. Freddie came back again, about five years ago. He knew he was dying then, and he did die, three months later."

Freddie Hagendorn, Kent's buddy in Vietnam.

In December 2006, Kent Wyndham died instantly from a massive heart attack, 10 months after retiring from the Postal Service. There had been warning signs, but "he would never go to a doctor," Darlene said. "Never!"

U.S. Army Freedom Team Salute Certificate of Appreciation (right) that accompanied an Army lapel pin awarded to Kent Wyndham.

Second Lieutenant Kent Wyndham

(Photos and memorabilia courtesy of Darlene Wyndham, wife of Kent Wyndham)

Freedom Team
SALUTE

Certificate of Appreciation

is awarded to

Kent Wyndham

For outstanding service to the Nation as a United States Army Soldier. You are being recognized for your patriotism and continued support of the Army family. Your legacy is today's Army and the values Soldiers exhibit while fighting the Global War on Terrorism. Their efforts are a direct reflection of your service, and the United States Army and a grateful Nation thank you.

Peter J. Schoomaker
General, United States Army
Chief of Staff

U.S.ARMY

Francis J. Harvey
Secretary of the Army

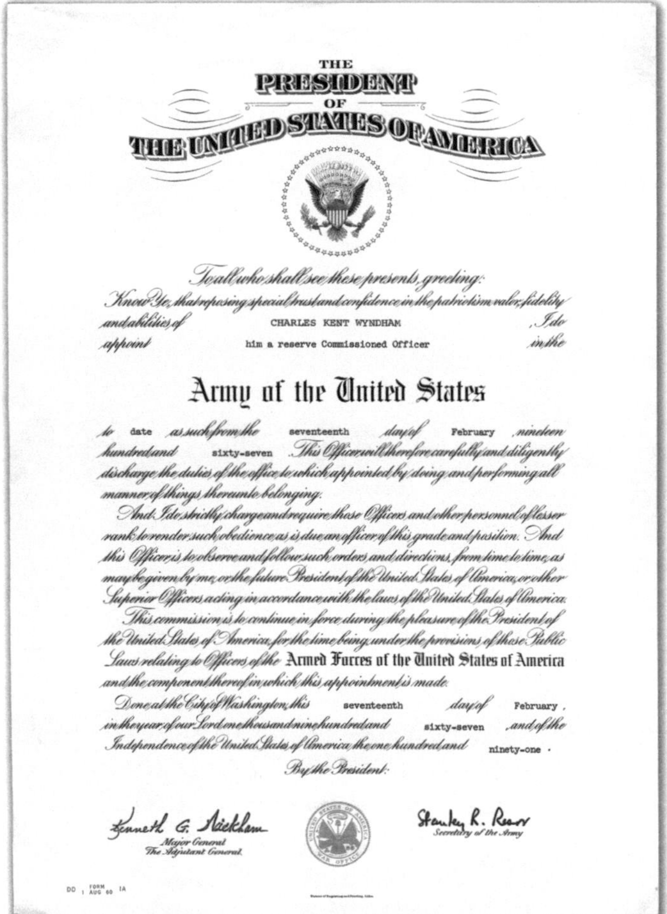

THE
PRESIDENT
OF
THE UNITED STATES OF AMERICA

To all who shall see these presents, greeting:

Know Ye, that reposing special trust and confidence in the patriotism valor, fidelity and abilities of CHARLES KENT WYNDHAM, I do appoint him a reserve Commissioned Officer in the

Army of the United States

to date as such from the seventeenth day of February, nineteen hundred and sixty-seven. This Officer will therefore carefully and diligently discharge the duties of the office to which appointed by doing and performing all manner of things thereunto belonging.

And I do strictly charge and require those Officers and other personnel of lesser rank to render such obedience as is due an officer of this grade and position. And this Officer is to observe and follow such orders and directions, from time to time, as may be given by me, or the future President of the United States of America, or other Superior Officers acting in accordance with the laws of the United States of America.

This commission is to continue in force during the pleasure of the President of the United States of America, for the time being, under the provisions of those Public Laws relating to Officers of the Armed Forces of the United States of America and the component thereof in which this appointment is made.

Done at the City of Washington, this seventeenth day of February, in the year of our Lord one thousand nine hundred and sixty-seven, and of the Independence of the United States of America the one hundred and ninety-one.

By the President:

Kenneth G. Wickham
Major General
The Adjutant General

Stanley R. Resor
Secretary of the Army

Presidential appointment of Kent Wyndham as a Reserve Commissioned Officer, Feb. 17, 1967

Cover of a book produced for Company D, Eighth Battalion, Second Brigade, at the U.S. Army Training Center in Fort Bragg, N.C. Kent Wyndham trained there in 1969.

Harry L. Ecton — Army — Vietnam

An unidentified Army colonel (right) presents medals earned by Harry Ecton, the only child of Leon and Brigitte Ecton, to the family in their Boonsboro home in March 1968. From left are Leon Ecton, Brigitte Ecton and Brigitte's parents, Otto and Amalie Heintz. Among the medals are a Bronze Star and a Purple Heart. Brigitte said, "At Harry's funeral I cried, but Leon couldn't. He said to me, 'I heard Harry standing behind me, and he said, don't cry, I did it for my country'."

Brigitte said, "Harry was a very loving son. I have only good memories. I was blessed with a wonderful loving husband and son."

(Photos and memorabilia courtesy of Brigitte Ecton, mother of Harry L. Ecton)

Harry L. Ecton in a tank in Vietnam during the three months he served in that war, before his death in battle on Jan. 31, 1968 — the second day of the Tet Offensive. Born in Germany in 1947 to an American serviceman and his German wife, Ecton came to U.S. in 1956 and graduated from Boonsboro High School in 1965.

After graduation, he worked for State Farm Insurance in Frederick until he was drafted into the Army on June 1, 1967. After training at Fort Bragg, North Carolina, and Fort Knox, Kentucky, he was sent to Vietnam on October 24. While doing reconnaissance with the 9th Infantry Division, 5th Cavalry, he was killed by hostile fire at Bien Hoa a little more than three months later.

"He was in Vietnam for three months and never had one day off," said his mother, Brigitte Ecton of Boonsboro. "He kept writing that there'd be relief the next day, but there never was." Harry's father, WWII veteran Leon Ecton, regretted the fact that his son had received only eight days of jungle training. An Army trainer during the Korean War, Leon Ecton "recognized the value of training. He was a great trainer," Brigitte Ecton said.

The Republic of Vietnam Gallantry Cross and the Republic of Vietnam Campaign Medal awarded to Harry L. Ecton by the government of Vietnam for his service during the Vietnam War.

Douglass C. Reed — Marine Corps — Vietnam

Douglass C. Reed of Hagerstown was only 18 when he enlisted in the Marine Corps.

After boot camp, he was assigned to the 2nd Marine Division, based in Camp Lejeune, North Carolina. He was involved with a battalion that underwent two years of advanced jungle warfare training throughout the Caribbean and at the Jungle Warfare School at Fort Sherman, Panama.

After a short stay at the Navy Yard in Washington, D.C., Reed arrived in Vietnam Oct. 31, 1968. By Nov. 3, 1968, he was in I Corps serving with the infantry during Operation Taylor Common, a major offensive against a critical staging area for the North Vietnamese Army (NVA) which resulted in the capture of huge quantities of ammunition and supplies.

In February 1969, he volunteered for and was assigned to the III Marine Amphibious Force (III MAF) 3rd Combined Action Group, 5th Company, 4th Platoon CAP 3-5-4.

The Combined Action Program [CAP] was instituted in 1965 in Hue and Phu Bai as a viable alternative to the "search and destroy" strategy of Commanding General William C. Westmoreland. CAP was a Marine Corps pacification initiative that combined a Marine rifle squad with a platoon of South Vietnamese Popular Forces (PFs), basing its strategy on undermining the infrastructure and support an agrarian population gave to the guerrilla fighters. The two groups of soldiers lived together within a particular village, getting to know its people and the terrain, combining protection and public service. As part of his service with the CAP, Reed completed a one-month intensive Vietnamese language course from which he graduated first in his class. Reed command CAP 3-5-2.

According to Marine Corps historian Curtis L. Williamson III, the CAP, which never grew beyond 2,500 men and 114 platoons, "achieved unsurpassed success towards providing security for the populace, threatening the guerrilla infrastructure, empowering the local and regional leaders to govern, and killing the enemy. Additionally, all attempts by senior Marine leaders to convince Gen. Westmoreland of the CAP's validity as a fitting strategy for all ground forces failed to overcome his conventional inclination towards the nature of the war."

According to Al Hemingway, author of *Our War Was Different: Marine Combined Action Platoons in Vietnam,* the mission of the CAP was to:

- neutralize the VC threat in the village or hamlet
- provide security and help maintain law and order
- protect local Vietnamese authorities
- guard important facilities and lines of communication
- conduct combined operations with other allied forces
- participate in civic-action and psychological operations
- assist in economic and social development
- provide military training to Popular Forces (PF) soldiers, and
- collect intelligence

Reed gingerly takes a B-40 RPG [rocket propelled grenade] from a gunnery sergeant, who was unaware that the aluminum tip at the point of the device was so sensitive it would detonate instantly if its trigger mechanism were depressed. "I thought he knew about rockets," said Reed, alarmed at the cavalier handling of such a deadly munition. Reed said the confiscated rocket grenade was later safely exploded by his squad.

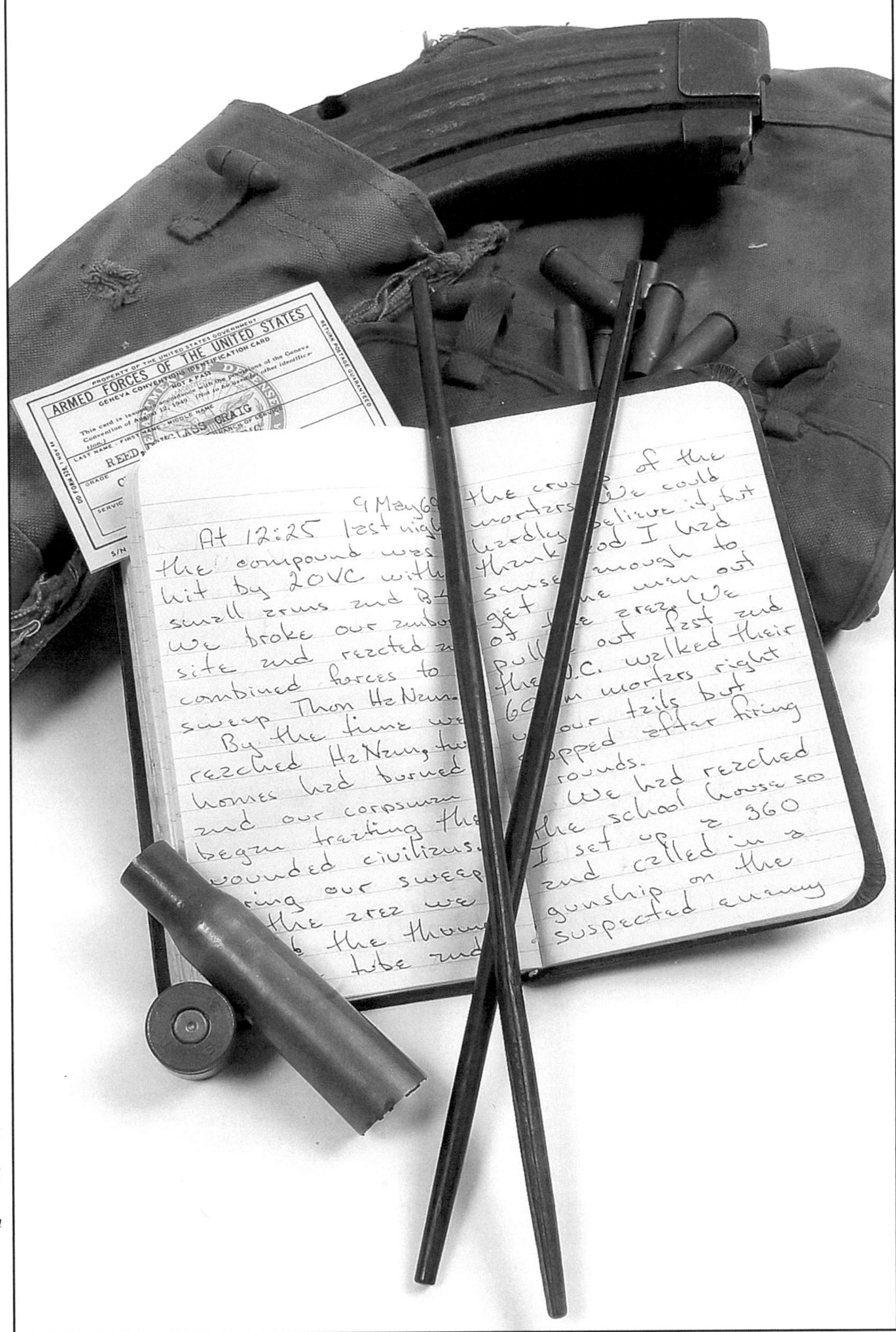

Reed's 30-round "banana" (ammo) clip for an AK-47, ammunition pouches, Geneva Conventions card, AK-47 shell casings, diary, the chopsticks he carried with him, and a spent .50-caliber machine gun shell casing from his days fighting in the Vietnam War.

As an interpreter-translator, Reed spent much of his time in Vietnam in Thua Thien Province in villages located approximately eight miles south of Phu Bai. His small band of eight to 12 Marines was constantly on the move and relocated approximately every 12 hours.

Trained in stealth fighting, Reed and his rifle squad lived among the villagers in an effort to protect them from infiltrating Viet Cong fighters. The men carried their own chopsticks "because spoons made so much noise." Sometimes, when ammunition was available, the Marines abandoned their U.S.-issued M16s in favor of what Reed believes were the far superior Czechoslovakian-made AK-47s. North Vietnamese and Viet Cong fighters used the AK-47s, which were easier to reload and did not jam as frequently as the M16s.

On rare occasions, Reed and his men would lie submerged in rice paddies for short periods of time with only a narrow reed for a breathing tube, waiting to ambush an enemy patrol. Use of the enemy's weaponry gave the Marines a "one- to two-second advantage," Reed said. Enemy soldiers would hesitate for a split second, thinking the sound of the discharging weaponry was from "friendly" fire, Reed said. Sometimes the slight advantage was the difference between living and dying. "It gave us a psychological advantage."

During a particularly rough period in 1969, when Reed's squad was cut off from supply sources, he wondered what it would be like to have a hot bath and warm food. Years later he was reading the WWII diary his father, Roderick Reed, kept during fighting in Italy, when he came across this wistful entry: "Oh, what it would be like to have a hot bath and warm food" — an entry made almost 25 years to the day Reed wrote his own chronicle of deprivation in a far different war.

The elder Reed, who flew to Dulles Airport from his home in Birmingham, Alabama, the day Douglass left for Vietnam, gave his son the New Testament [featured in the WWII section] that he had carried with him to Europe. "The Bible was in two wars," said Reed, who theorizes the only way it survived was that it remained safe inside his father's footlocker. "It was in such good shape, he couldn't have kept it with him," Reed said. "And if I had carried the little Bible with me in the jungle, it would have been destroyed the first week."

While commanding a Combined Action Program [CAP] team in Thua Thien Province, Reed recorded this matter-of-fact diary account of a Viet Cong attack on the evening of May 8, 1969, near Thon Ha Nam. As the mortars came in, Sgt. Reed wrote: "Thank God I had sense enough to get the men out of the area. We pulled out fast and the V.C. walked their 60mm mortars right up our tails but stopped after firing 13 rounds."

Sometimes Reed and his squad would get trapped behind enemy lines. "We hardly ate," he said. "Once, the unit went four days without food."

A Jan. 21, 1969, entry records a happier event — coming in from the field for a USO show featuring "four girls from the Philippines." He and his platoon "got more beer, fried steaks and beans." They also got hot showers, new clothing and new boots.

After a firefight one night, this simple Viet Cong medical kit and poncho were found near the body of a dead Viet Cong fighter. The blood-stained bandages had been carefully re-rolled for future use and carried inside a light shoulder-slung pouch by the fast-moving Viet Cong fighters. The kit carried no medications of any kind, but contained a pack of monosodium glutamate to flavor food.

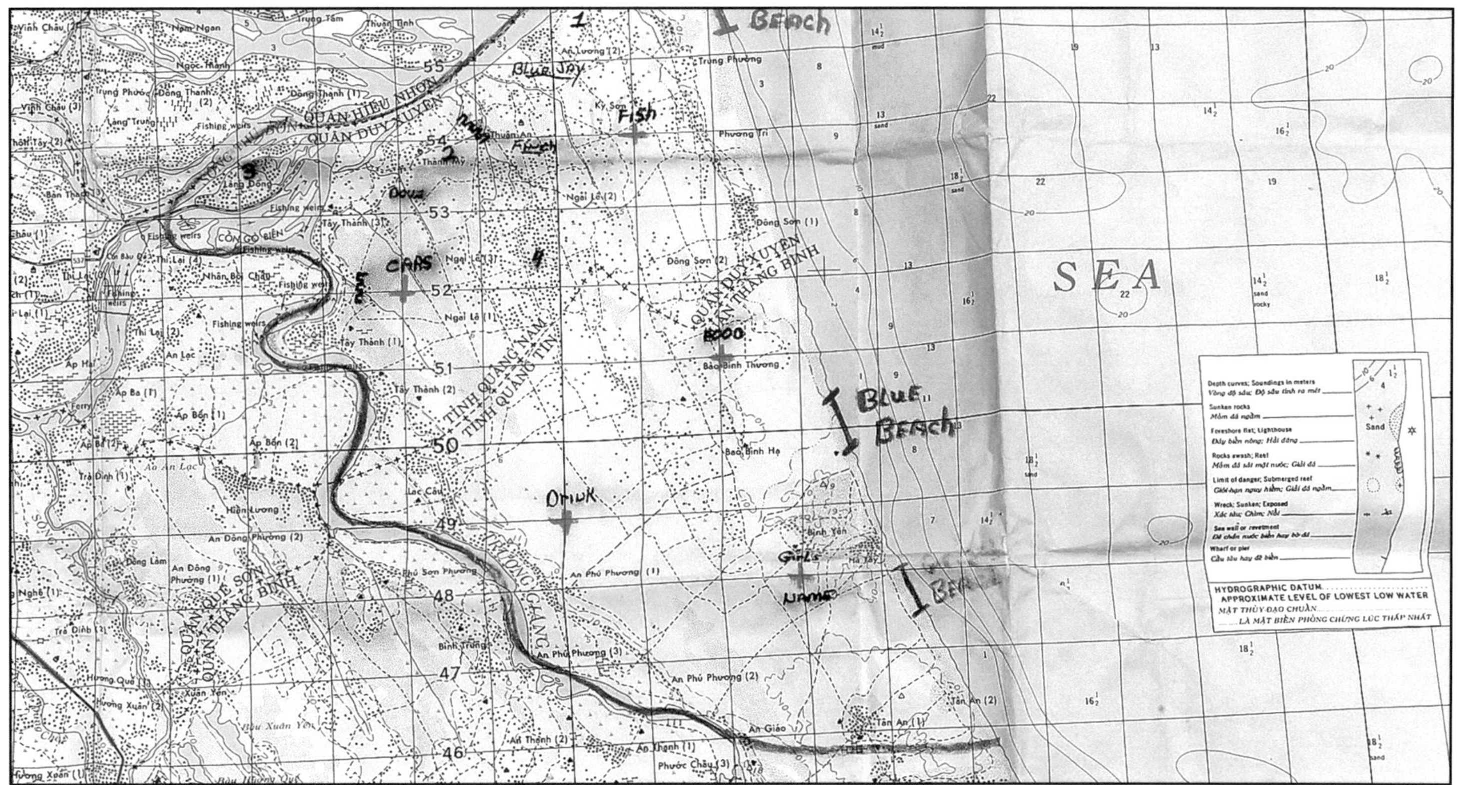

Map of the area where Reed engaged the enemy as a Marine Corps sergeant during the Vietnam War. In addition to ambushing enemy fighters and protecting villages, Reed participated in efforts to provide medical assistance such as typhoid vaccinations, in what CAP members would remember as MEDCAP operations. "I gave thousands of booster shots," Reed said.

In the preface to the Naval Institute Press's ***Our War Was Different***, historian Al Hemingway wrote of the CAP Marines: "They did an outstanding job. They were thrust into an alien culture to live work, fight, and — in many cases — die. They are intensely proud of their CAP service in spite of the outcome of the Vietnam War."

North Vietnamese regular's bayonet and scabbard, belt with NVA [North Vietnamese Army] belt buckle and rifle sling that Reed brought back from his time in Vietnam. "He didn't make it, I did," Reed said.

On April 1, 1969, Cpl. Reed had his photograph taken with Nguyen Che at Suho Dung, in Loc Dien Province, the day Reed got his sergeant's stripes. "I watched out for him and he watched out for me. He was the best friend of the Americans in this village. He kept us alive," Reed said.

In his younger days, Nguyen Che (shown in a photo taken in the 1950s) was a prominent Vietnamese freedom fighter, defending what was then French Indochina from the Japanese invaders, and then, later, fighting with the Viet Minh in its campaign for independence from the French.

The Viet Minh, Vietnamese for "League for the Independence of Vietnam," was established as a revolutionary movement by Ho Chi Minh in 1941. Nguyen split with Ho Chi Minh over the leader's communist ideology and later fought alongside the Americans in defense of a democratic South Vietnam.

"I'm quite sure the conquering North Vietnamese and Viet Cong killed him and his family too," Reed said, referring to the eventual abandonment by American troops and the 1973 North Vietnamese takeover. Reed, who assisted with the birth of Nguyen's 11th child in 1969, believes his friend saved the lives of the men in his platoon many times over.

A bad case of hepatitis sidelined Reed when he was evacuated from his CAP unit to a hospital in Japan for recuperation. While he was gone, his patrol was under the command of Jay Sacks, an experienced corporal, who had survived the harrowing defense of Khe Shanh in 1968. The unit had become accustomed to the intelligence support of a member of a Popular Force platoon they nicknamed "Mousey." While on patrol in Reed's absence, though, Mousey, who turned out to be Viet Cong, shot Cpl. Sacks through the back of his head. "Sometimes I feel guilty about that," said Reed. "I should have been there."

Sacks left behind a Vietnamese girlfriend, who ran a Coke stand in one of the villages. Reed still has a copy of a letter in Vietnamese the young woman wrote to the fallen Marine.

Reed said for the most part Vietnamese villagers were "friendly to your face," but that the Marines could trust no one. "You would be walking along the road in front of a row of bamboo stick hooches and you could hear the mama sans counting off the number of men and types of weapons under their breath as we walked by." Reed disguised his knowledge of the language, and Viet Cong fighters could not figure out how the patrol's intelligence was so good. One day, though, he discerned an imminent attack and shouted a warning to his men and the Popular Forces (PF) fighters. "I blew my cover," said Reed. "That's when the enemy knew I understood the language."

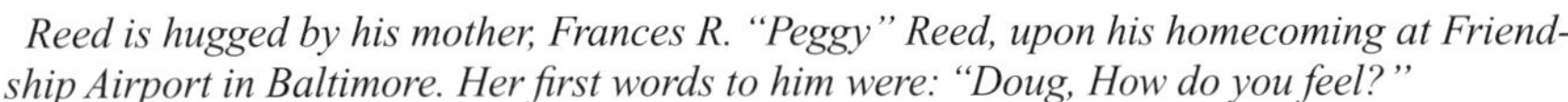

Reed is hugged by his mother, Frances R. "Peggy" Reed, upon his homecoming at Friendship Airport in Baltimore. Her first words to him were: "Doug, How do you feel?"

"Gosh, it was good to be home," Reed recalled, looking at the long-ago candid snapshot. His brother, Murray Reed, who took the photograph that day, remembers his younger brother stepping off the plane in his Marine Corps uniform and a small group of passengers in the terminal applauding — an unexpected phenomenon, when at other times and places during that unpopular war, returning servicemen were sometimes spat upon.

Of his Vietnam War experience, Reed said he is a "much stronger person. I try to live each day so those who died beside me get a chance to live through me."

(Photographs and memorabilia courtesy of Douglass C. Reed)

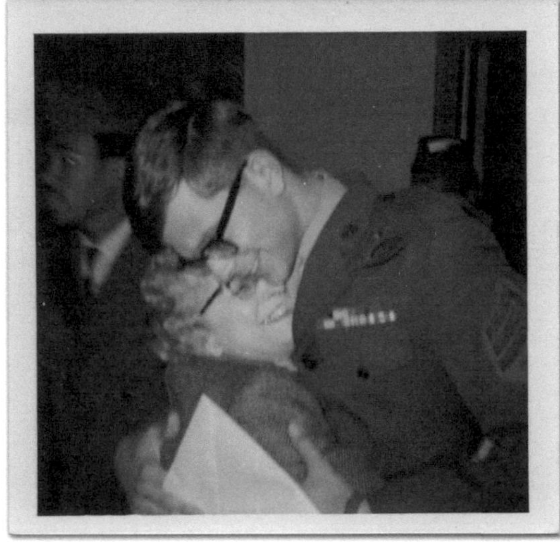

James "Dale" Mongold — Marine Corps — Vietnam

James "Dale" Mongold (second from left) and four classmates from South Hagerstown High School during Marine Corps basic training at Parris Island, South Carolina, in 1965. The five joined the Marines under the buddy system that allowed them to stay together at least until the completion of training. When the group was split up, Dale and his best friend, Jack Deavers (fourth from left), went to Vietnam together. Dale was devastated later when he learned of Deavers' death. The men, all from Washington County, are (from left): Doug Cornell, Dale Mongold, Dave Itnyre, Jack Deavers and Dennis Domer.

Dale, who was stationed with MABS [Marine Base Squadron] II at Danang Air Base, returned home safely from the war. But according to his brother, Dennis, "the war ate him away inside. He wouldn't talk about it, but his most memorable recollection was the shock of learning about his best friend's death."

Dale was discharged as a corporal on May 1, 1970. Afterwards, Dennis said, "he did whatever he could for all veterans. He dressed neat, he respected others, he loved life, he was happy and loving outside. He loved his country and he was a leader for all veterans. He made a goal of being voted commander of American Legion Post 42." Dale Mongold died on Nov. 24, 1994, while he was holding that office.

(Photo courtesy of Dennis Mongold, brother of James "Dale" Mongold)

Kenneth L. "Lee" Brandenburg — Army — Vietnam

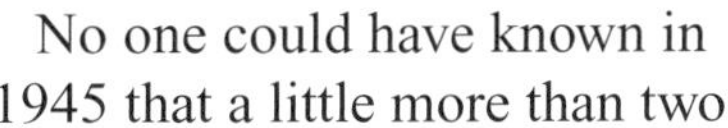

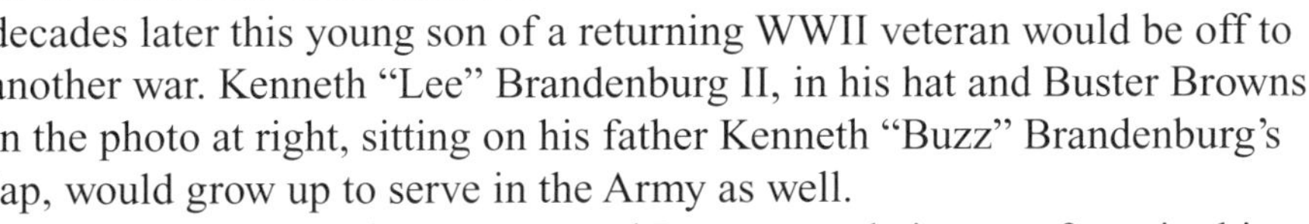

No one could have known in 1945 that a little more than two decades later this young son of a returning WWII veteran would be off to another war. Kenneth "Lee" Brandenburg II, in his hat and Buster Browns in the photo at right, sitting on his father Kenneth "Buzz" Brandenburg's lap, would grow up to serve in the Army as well.

In the 1967 photo above, Buzz and Lee put on their game faces in this Kodak moment following the younger Brandenburg's graduation from Marine Corps boot camp at Parris Island, South Carolina, before 22-year-old Lee went off to Vietnam.

(Photographs courtesy of Barbara Reeder, daughter of Kenneth L. "Buzz" Brandenburg and sister of Kenneth L. "Lee" Brandenburg II)

Eleanor G. "Ellie" Briggs Bowles — Army — Vietnam

Eleanor G. Briggs Bowles graduated from nursing school in 1961 and had been working as a nurse in an Ohio hospital when she enlisted in the Army. Her reason: "Patriotism." The war in Vietnam was heating up and the military was experiencing a tremendous need for skilled nurses — particularly nurses who were willing to serve in combat zones.

Bowles, at 26, was more mature than many nursing recruits, and her time as an intensive care and emergency room nurse and work as head of a psychiatric unit provided a wellspring of experience for what she would soon encounter in Vietnam. She served with the 2nd Mobile Army Surgical Unit (MASH) with the 1st Air Cavalry in Ahn Khe in the highlands of South Vietnam and later at Chu Lai on South Vietnam's northern coast from October 1966 until October 1967. She was one of the estimated 6,000 women nurses from the Army, Air Force and Navy who served in Vietnam.

"The recruiter was very impressive," said Bowles, who signed on the dotted line only on the condition that she would be sent to Vietnam. "I told them Vietnam was the only possibility for me," Bowles said. The Army accommodated her request, first sending her to Officer Candidate School at Fort Sam Houston, Texas, where she became a "90-day wonder," emerging with the bars of a first lieutenant. "The military was all new to me," said Bowles, who recalls that in addition to field training, the nursing recruits had to "learn to march and how to polish boots."

She flew from San Francisco to Saigon and then to Ahn Khe in the Central Highlands where the nurses were housed in newly-constructed Quonset huts — a big improvement from the canvas tents her predecessors had used. While at "Camp Radcliffe," the nurses quickly became accustomed to the daily and nightly mortars that would be lobbed at the camp. The first time a mortar round came in, "I remember thinking it was fireworks," said Bowles, who describes the younger version of herself as "being young and invincible."

Winter and summer nursing caps designed to accompany Bowles' Class-A uniform. The winter cap bears Bowles' captain's bars. Much of her work in Vietnam, however, was performed in scrubs and fatigues.

Bowles stands in front of rows of containers for water and gasoline. In the distance is the tented structure that housed her MASH unit in Ahn Khe in 1966.

Patch identifying Bowles as a member of the 2nd Mobile Army Surgical Unit. The MASH unit's motto was "Second To None."

Bowles took this snapshot of a "chopper" leaving the landing pad near the hospital at Ahn Khe. Great progress in trauma medicine had been made during the Korean war with the use of medivac helicopters airlifting wounded soldiers to field hospitals, something not possible in previous wars.

The Vietnam War brought further advances in evacuation, triage techniques and treatment that would save the lives of many more combat wounded. "Field techs would dress the wounds in the field or on the chopper," Bowles said. Sometimes a note would accompany the wounded with an explanation of their specific injuries. More often than not, receiving nurses had to determine the severity of the wounds themselves. At Chu Lai, Bowles was in charge of "receiving," and her aggressive stance in insisting upon treatment came close to getting her court-martialed several times.

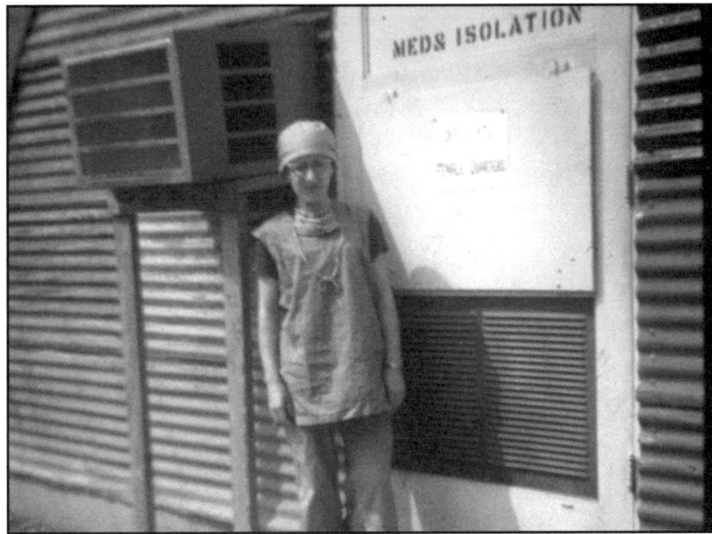

A diminutive Bowles stands outside a field Quonset hut at Ahn Khe, where doctors and nurses routinely operated on soldiers brought in from the field. When the hospital came under frequent mortar attacks, medical personnel stayed at the operating tables until the operation was over — shelling or no shelling — and routinely worked around the clock treating waves of soldiers in the aftermath of major offensives. "When you got started, you worked until you were done," said Bowles, who was assigned to the operating room at the mountainside outpost.

Bowles' private little corner of the world was space she shared with three other nurses in a Quonset hut. It consisted of a bed, footlocker and table.

One of the biggest challenges of Bowles' time in Vietnam would be the relocation of the entire field hospital to Chu Lai, 60 miles south of Danang, where she would be placed in charge of the receiving area. Nurses and staff had to pack up the hospital in its entirety, load the equipment and supplies on huge C-130 cargo planes and set the entire facility up in its new location. The move was partially predicated on a hoped-for rescue of American prisoners of war held by the North Vietnamese. The staff was preparing for a massive influx of seriously ill and injured captives, but the anticipated recovery of the American captives never occurred.

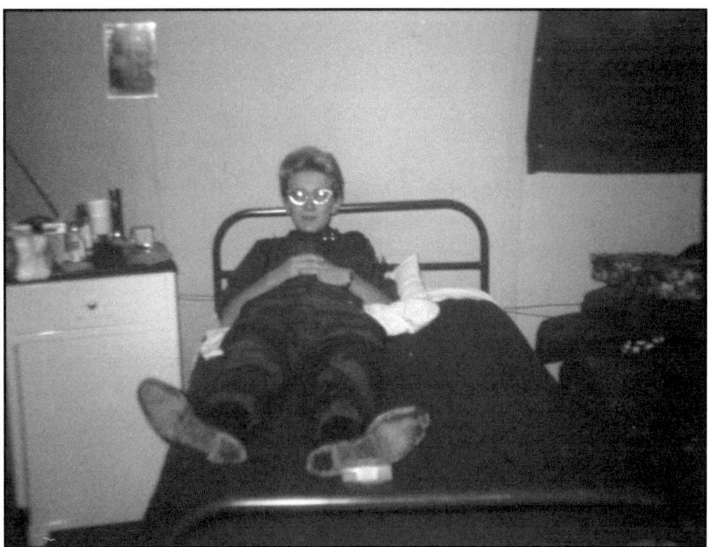

During her time at Chu Lai, wounded soldiers would pour into the receiving area in the wake of military offensives. Heartbreaking decisions about who was treatable and who was not proved the most agonizing part of her service as a nurse in Vietnam. One day a young soldier arrived with his head bandaged and no obvious clue as to his condition. "His head was wrapped and I insisted that the corpsman unwrap it," said Bowles. "That was a mistake. He was not savable. Sometimes the hardest decisions to live with are the ones you learn to make quickly at the time."

Shelves with modest supplies line the open-air receiving station in Chu Lai, where the wounded would be taken from the helicopters and placed directly on the stretchers for immediate evaluation.

Even in combat zones, paperwork was an ever-present part of nursing in 1967 in Vietnam.

"The 19th Hole" was a canvas tent-turned-cantina where doctors and nursing staff would relax at the end of a hard day. "I never drank beer until I went over there," said Bowles, who reports that the antics of the MASH unit depicted in the popular television series about a MASH unit in Korea bore little resemblance to the long days and hazards of her experience in a wartime field hospital.

A few of the more adventurous USO entertainers would venture out to the remote outpost at Ahn Khe to visit with patients and staff during the war in Vietnam. Bowles snapped this photo of Roy Rogers (right) and his wife, Dale Evans (left), in late 1966 in the chapel at Ahn Khe. Other visitors included Robert Stack and Henry Fonda, who stopped "in our hooch to have a beer with the girls."

Shoulder patch for the Americal Division to which Bowles was attached during the Vietnam War. The Americal Division was reactivated in 1967 and operated in Vietnam until 1971. The Division was made up of brigades from the 25th Infantry Division, the 101st Airborne Division and the 1st Marine Division.

Bowles was awarded the Vietnam Campaign Medal with 1960 device, the Vietnam Service Medal and the Bronze Star for her service in Vietnam. The "1960" device displays the date of 1960 followed by a dash and a blank space. The South Vietnamese government hoped that the bar would show the dates of the Vietnam War from start to finish, with the ending date placed on the 1960 bar after the South Vietnamese had triumphed over North Vietnam. Because South Vietnam fell, and the government ceased to exist, an ending date for the 1960 bar was never established.

When the nursing staff wasn't treating the wounded, they would often venture into nearby villages to provide public health services. Bowles was a source of fascination to the Vietnamese children and adults because of her blond hair — a rare sight in 1960s Vietnam.

The children were a delight, but American servicemen and servicewomen learned to be wary of them, after several incidents where children — strapped with explosives or booby-trapped — came in proximity to American servicemen, resulting in the death of the child and the American servicemen.

At the field hospital, the staff had occasion to remove the tumor from the tongue of a young Montagnard girl, who would likely have died without medical attention. The Montagnards, the indigenous tribal peoples in the hills of Vietnam, were staunch supporters of the American military. Bowles recalls that the family would not leave the girl in the Americans' care unless the entire family could be by her side. As a result, a good portion of the hospital was filled with the crouching forms of the young girl's kinsmen. In appreciation, the tribesmen presented Bowles with one of the Montagnards' famed crossbows and a quiver of razor-sharp bamboo arrows.

On off-duty hours, but always in the company of armed soldiers, Bowles and other nurses would venture into the villages on market day. "But it got to be too dangerous," said Bowles, who said the novelty of a woman in uniform with blond hair attracted far too much attention.

Bowles and her fellow nurses treated wounded Viet Cong and North Vietnamese regulars as well as American servicemen. "It didn't make any difference." During an interrogation of one prisoner in her receiving area, Bowles actually "pulled rank" to order an end to a much-too-rough interrogation of an enemy captive. "It didn't happen very often, but sometimes it did," Bowles said.

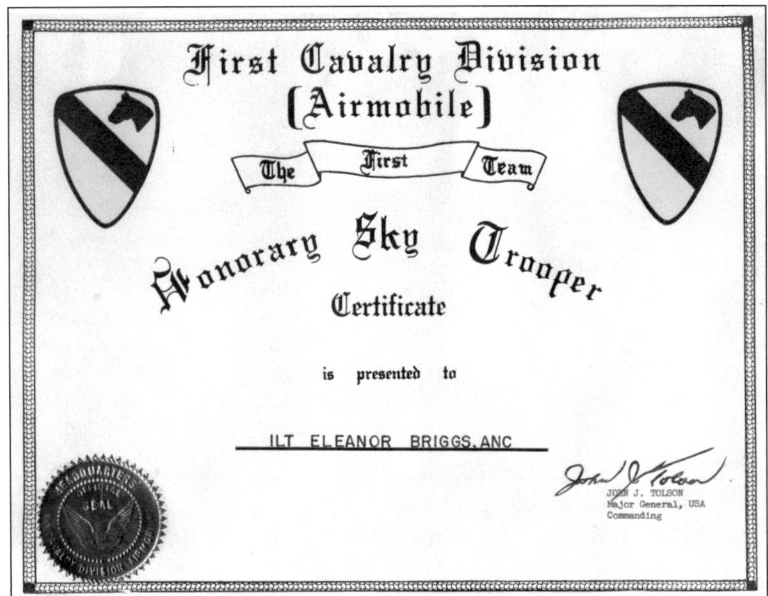

First Cavalry Division
(Airmobile)

The First Team

Honorary Sky Trooper
Certificate

is presented to

1LT ELEANOR BRIGGS, ANC

JOHN J. TOLSON
Major General, USA
Commanding

Bowles holds the rare distinction of being named an Honorary Sky Trooper with the First Cavalry Division (Airmobile).

Bowles is presented a Bronze Star by the commander of Kirk Army Hospital, in recognition of her service in Vietnam. Bowles was assigned to Kirk Army Hospital at Aberdeen Proving Grounds upon her return to the States.

In 2006, Bowles, shown here on her Harley-Davidson "2000 Sportster 883 Hugger" motorcycle in front of the Pentagon, participated in her first "Rolling Thunder" ride, an annual Memorial Day event in which thousands of Vietnam veterans ride their motorcycles to the Vietnam Veterans Memorial in Washington, D.C.

When asked about her Vietnam experience, Bowles doesn't usually say very much, remembering the antipathy that confronted returning Vietnam War veterans in the 1960s. "When I came back, they advised us to change clothes, not to travel in our uniforms. When I came back they were spitting on veterans. You didn't want to deal with it, so you didn't talk about your service."

Bowles married the year after she returned to the States, with little outward sign of the lingering effects of having served in combat. She began to do some public relations for the military until her husband advised her to stop. "You're having nightmares and I can't wake you up," he told her.

Her time in Vietnam didn't come up again until her son, Shannon Christopher Bowles, who is now 37, asked her to speak to his sixth grade Clear Spring Elementary School class about her wartime service.

Although Post-traumatic stress disorder (PTSD) is a phenomenon about which society is becoming increasingly aware, Bowles' only clue that she might somehow be affected was on a family outing to a Gettysburg Battlefield re-enactment. "I didn't think anything about it, until the cannon went off, and I started to run. I just heard it and it started getting to me, and I took off," Bowles said. "So I can understand when some of the guys experience this. I think it is part of the fight or flight instinct we all have."

Even so, "we don't go to re-enactments anymore," Bowles said.

(Photographs and memorabilia courtesy of Eleanor G. "Ellie" Briggs Bowles)

Orville Lee Knight — Army — Vietnam

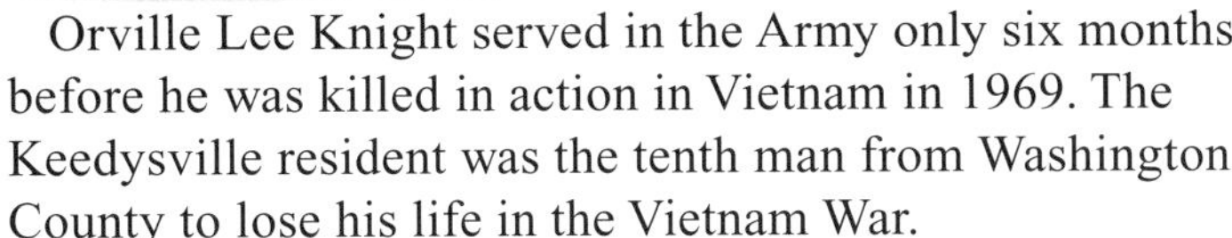

Orville Lee Knight served in the Army only six months before he was killed in action in Vietnam in 1969. The Keedysville resident was the tenth man from Washington County to lose his life in the Vietnam War.

Cpl. Knight was serving as a radioman in Company B, 2nd Battalion, 16th Infantry, 1st Infantry Division in Vietnam. He had been in the country only weeks before his death on April 8, 1969, in Bien Hoa. He was on patrol when he heard enemy fire, turned around, and stepped on a land mine.

In letters home to his family, Cpl. Knight described the impenetrable jungle terrain of Vietnam and often wrote that "if the snakes don't get me, the water will." Digging a trench was one of many chores in the infantryman's life. Time out with a buddy was rare.

Knight was just 20 years old and a recent graduate of Boonsboro High School when he was drafted. Married prior to his induction, he became the father of a daughter while taking basic training and was granted one week of leave to see his newborn child before shipping out. He never saw his daughter again. She died at the young age of 37.

Knight's wife, Sarah, and his parents, Mr. and Mrs. Francis Knight, were notified of his death on April 12, 1969. He was promoted posthumously to corporal.

(Photos courtesy of Whylmenia Knight, mother of Orville Knight)

Thurman W. "Sonny" Divelbliss Jr. — Army — Vietnam

Thurman W. "Sonny" Divelbliss Jr. served with the Army as an infantryman and machine gunner in Vietnam from March 1968 until April 1969, with the 1st Battalion, 18th Infantry of the 1st Infantry Division, in the vicinity of Saigon.

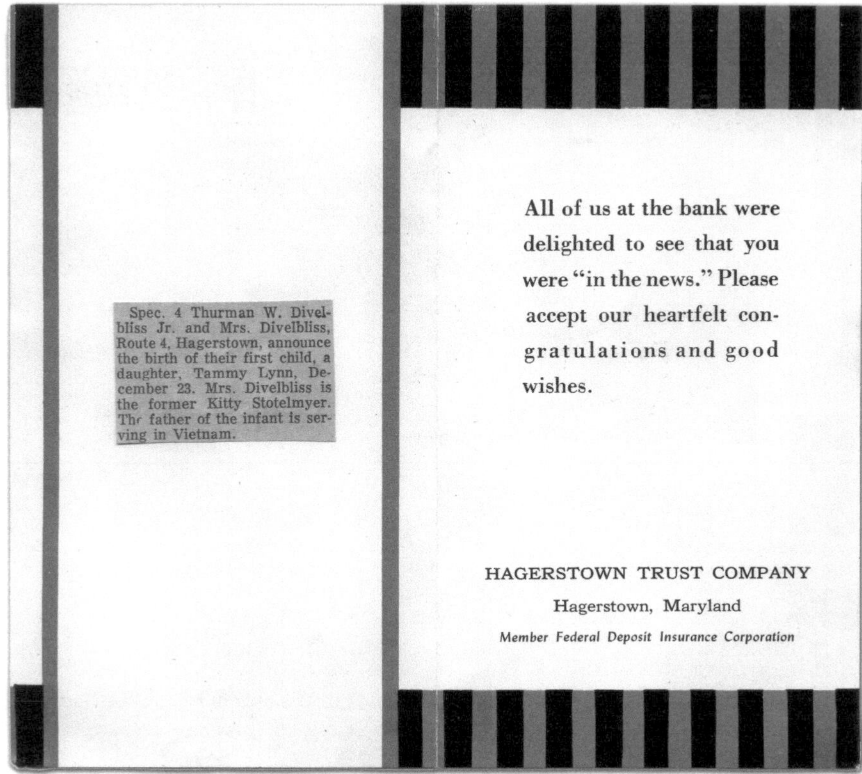

Spec. 4 Thurman W. Divelbliss Jr. and Mrs. Divelbliss, Route 4, Hagerstown, announce the birth of their first child, a daughter, Tammy Lynn, December 23. Mrs. Divelbliss is the former Kitty Stotelmyer. The father of the infant is serving in Vietnam.

All of us at the bank were delighted to see that you were "in the news." Please accept our heartfelt congratulations and good wishes.

HAGERSTOWN TRUST COMPANY
Hagerstown, Maryland
Member Federal Deposit Insurance Corporation

Pfc. Divelbliss of Hagerstown left for Vietnam on Sunday, March 31, 1968 — his first wedding anniversary. He left behind his bride, the former Kitty Stotelmyer, who would deliver their first child, Tammy Wynn, on Dec. 23, 1968, while he was in combat in Vietnam. Kitty received a newspaper clipping of their daughter's birth announcement and a congratulatory card from Hagerstown Trust Company.

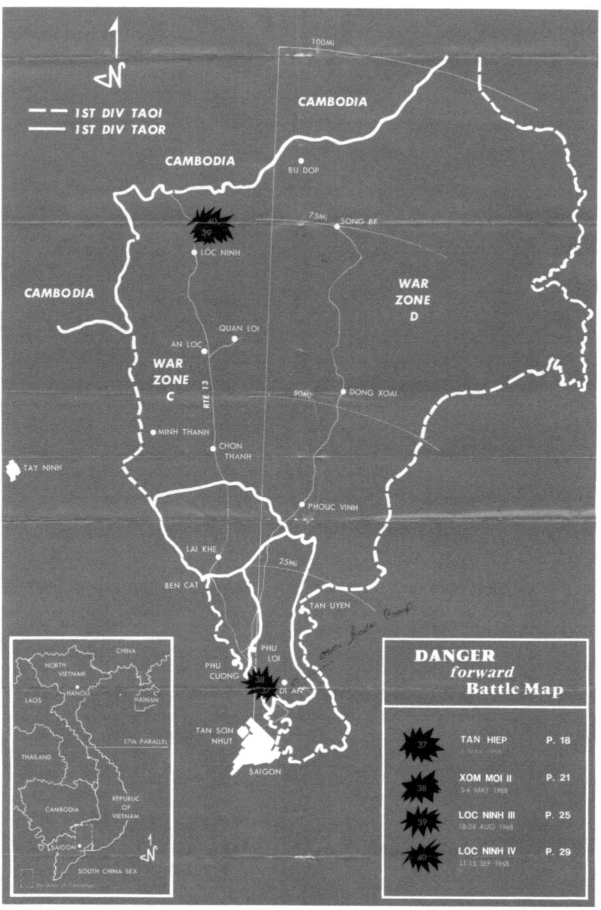

Battle map of South Vietnam where Divelbliss served with the 1st Battalion, 18th Infantry, as part of the 1st Infantry Division. The 1st Infantry Division, known as the "Big Red One" because of the insignia on the shoulder patch, is the oldest organized division in the Army, having been organized in 1917.

The 1st Infantry Division fought in Vietnam from 1965 until 1970. In April 1968, while Divelbliss was assigned there, the division participated in the largest operation of the Vietnam War — Operation Certain Victory. More than 3,000 soldiers of the Big Red One died in action during its five years of service in Vietnam.

THE UNITED STATES OF AMERICA

TO ALL WHO SHALL SEE THESE PRESENTS, GREETING:

THIS IS TO CERTIFY THAT
THE PRESIDENT OF THE UNITED STATES OF AMERICA
AUTHORIZED BY EXECUTIVE ORDER, MAY 11, 1942
HAS AWARDED

THE AIR MEDAL

TO

SPECIALIST FOUR THURGEN W. DIVELBLISS, US67003755
UNITED STATES ARMY

FOR
MERITORIOUS ACHIEVEMENT
WHILE PARTICIPATING IN AERIAL FLIGHT
IN THE REPUBLIC OF VIETNAM DURING THE PERIOD 28 APRIL 1968 TO 18 NOVEMBER 1968

GIVEN UNDER MY HAND IN THE CITY OF WASHINGTON
THIS TWENTY FIFTH DAY OF FEBRUARY 1969

Orwin C. Talbott
ORWIN C. TALBOTT
Major General, USA
Commanding

Stanley R. Resor
SECRETARY OF THE ARMY

Divelbliss was awarded the Air Medal for his service in Vietnam. Because of the expanse of jungle and lack of roadways, infantrymen were transported to battle zones in Vietnam by helicopter. The Vietnam War is sometimes called the "Helicopter War" because redesigned "choppers" gave American and South Vietnamese soldiers an advantage over North Vietnamese troops that operated without helicopters. In this 1969 photo, Divelbliss stands next to a helicopter used to transport soldiers and supplies, which bears a painted rendering of the battalion's mascot, the Looney Tunes cartoon character "Yosemite Sam."

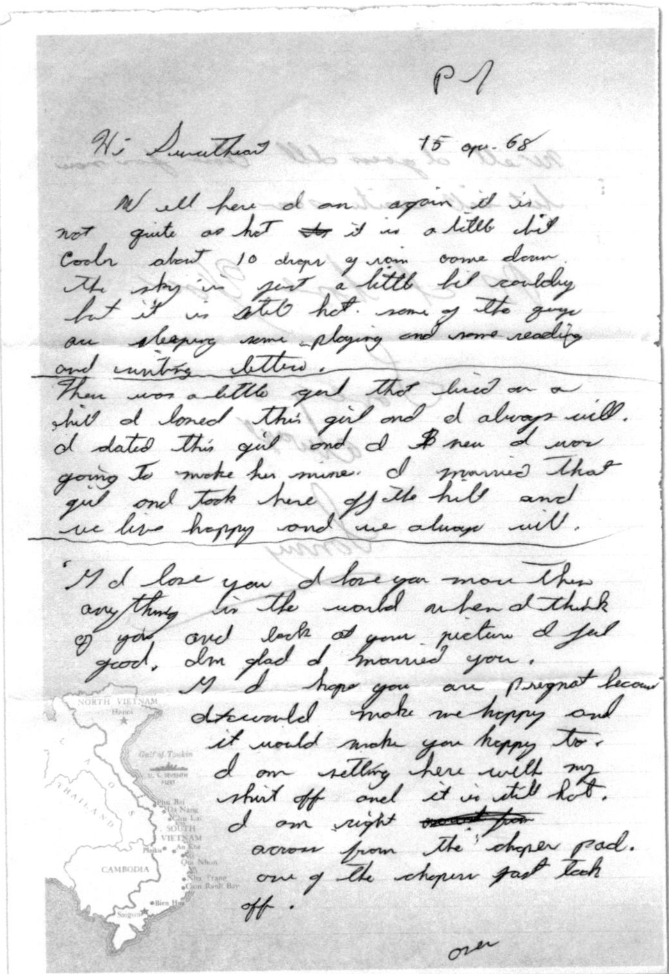
P 1

Hi Sweetheart 15 apr. 68

Well here I am again it is not quite as hot as it is a little bit cooler about 10 drops of rain come down. The sky is just a little bit cloudy but it is still hot. some of the guys are sleeping some playing and some reading and writing letters.

There was a little girl that lived on a hill I loved this girl and I always will. I dated this girl and I knew I was going to make her mine. I married that girl and took here off the hill and we live happy and we always will.

Hi I love you I love you more then anything in the world when I think of you and look at your picture I feel good. I'm glad I married you.

Hi I hope you are pregnat because it would make me happy and it would make you happy to. I am setting here with my shirt off and it is still hot. I am right across from the choper pad. one of the chopers just took off.

over

Letter from Divelbliss to his wife, Kitty, written on April 15, 1968, from Vietnam. "I love you more than anything in the world when I think of you and look at your picture I feel good. I'm glad I married you." He ends the letter, "Love always, Sonny."

According to Kitty, her husband would often include a poem in his letters as seen in the one at left. The poem he most often included was:

GI love you
GI do
GI'm glad I married you.

The Hagerstown couple have two daughters and have been married 39 years.

Snapshots from his days in Vietnam include "Sonny" Divelbliss (upper left) sitting on top of sandbags holding an M16 rifle. The photograph in the center is of a bunker soldiers would fashion out of sand bags and ammunition boxes. They would stretch ponchos over them to make a roof under which they could sleep. The soldiers would also place five-gallon drums of water on top of the bunkers to be heated by the sun, and then pour the water into a bucket outfitted with sprinkler holes, so they could take a hot shower at the end of the day. The third photo shows Divelbliss (without helmet), holding an M60 machine gun, crouched on patrol in the dense underbrush outside Saigon.

One of the most heartbreaking stories he shared with his family was the story of a young Vietnamese war orphan — a girl approximately 4 or 5 years old — who he wanted to wanted to adopt. One day she came into camp with a bomb strapped to her. The bomb was detonated and "it killed a lot of men in the camp."

Vietnamese bank notes, coins and cigarette pack Divelbliss slipped into the letters he mailed home from Vietnam in 1968 and 1969.

(Photographs and memorabilia courtesy of Kitty Divelbliss, Thurman W. "Sonny" Divelbliss Jr.'s wife, and Kelly Cline, his youngest daughter)

Elwood "Woody" Moats — Ronald J. McNeer — Army — Vietnam

Dear Lee:

I was so pleasantly surprised to see so many of Woody's kin and friends at the funeral home tonight. We spoke often of our hometowns and families.

No one but another soldier can truly understand what being in a war is like, or how it affects one afterwards. You dream of home constantly, and what all you'll do when you get home. But on your return, it seems everyone and everything has changed. Unfortunately, after years and years, you realize you're the one who has changed, and not always for the better! In fact, it's always for the worse – or at least that's the way it seems.

I once told Woody I believed the good Lord watched over me for a special reason. That He had plans for me to do something great and deserving of His shielding me in Vietnam – while some of my friends went home early in body bags or with missing limbs.

As of yet, I haven't performed anything worthy of His great compassion. Maybe…just maybe… it was to be a comforter to my fellow soldier's sister by the name of Lee, whom Elwood Moats loved dearly and trusted beyond all. He looked forward to Saturdays and your visits.

Woody's friend,

Ron

Elwood "Woody" Moats

Ronald J. McNeer

Elwood "Woody" Moats and Ron McNeer didn't know each other when they served in the Army in Vietnam. Both returned home, but suffered from illnesses. They met while being treated at the VA Hospital in Martinsburg, W.Va. They "clicked," said Woody's sister, Lee Jenkins, and became the best of friends. Ron visited Woody — among many other veterans — faithfully when Woody was hospitalized, and several months before he died, fulfilled one of his last wishes by taking him fishing for a day. Elwood died in November 2005 from lung cancer resulting from exposure in Vietnam to the controversial herbicide Agent Orange. On the day of Woody's funeral, Ron handed this letter to Lee. Since then, he visits Woody's grave regularly and makes sure the flag is still there and upright.

(Photos and letter courtesy of Ronald McNeer and Lee Jenkins, sister of Elwood "Woody" Moats)

Dwayne R. Ebersole — Army — Vietnam

When Dwayne R. Ebersole of Maugansville joined the Army in 1966 at 18, he took his first trip on an airplane to Lai Khe, where he was based with the 1st Infantry Division, known as "The Big Red One" or "The Fighting First."

This photo was taken after Operation Cedar Falls, a multi-division search and destroy mission in January 1967 in Vietnam's Iron Triangle. He drove a supply truck armed with a gunner onboard. He also participated in Operation Junction City, and in his work as a supply man he often traveled Highway 13 or "Thunder Road" as it was known, because of the nightly planting of mines by the Viet Cong.

When he arrived in Lai Khe, Ebersole found that his sergeant, Richard Dowler, was also from Hagerstown. They became friends and their families met at picnics after the men returned home. Ebersole left Vietnam in November 1967 and served stateside at the Aberdeen Proving Ground, Maryland, until his discharge in 1969. Dwayne married the former Joyce Shipley of Funkstown and they had two sons, Steven R. Ebersole and Kevin D. Ebersole. He died at age 41 in 1989.

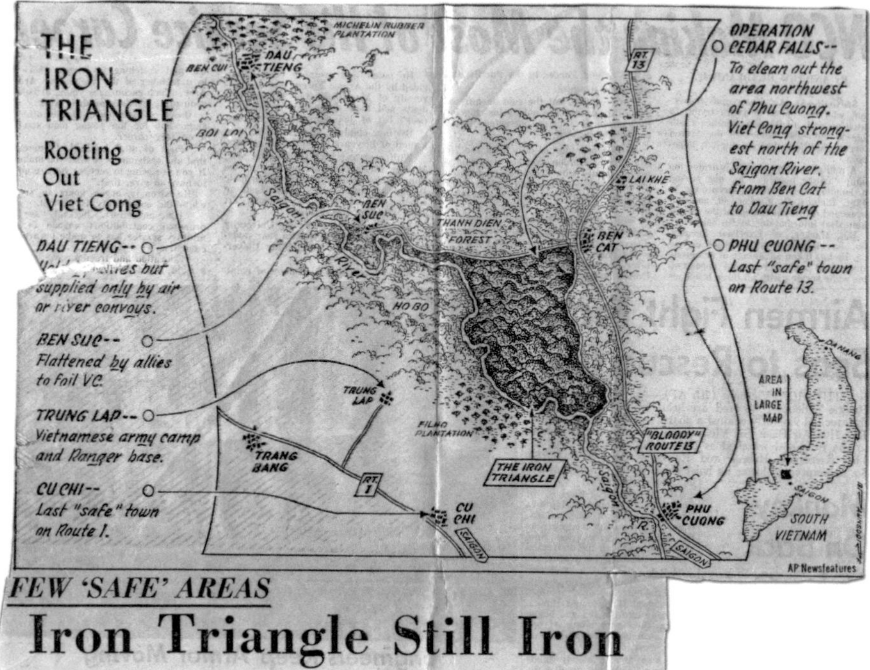

The infamous "Iron Triangle" in Vietnam, long a stronghold of the Viet Cong, was situated 30 miles north of Saigon between two strategic highways. During Operation Cedar Falls, civilians were removed to refugee camps and their villages were destroyed. Viet Cong camps were raided and the entire area was searched. Then a wide path was bulldozed, creating a large "free-fire zone" devoid of civilians, in which anything that moved would be shot.

Dwayne with his pal Nuey (left), a 10-year-old Vietnamese boy who was adopted by the company after his family disappeared. Dwayne gave Nuey the watch he is wearing here before he returned to the States. He said it was difficult to leave him behind, knowing he would never see him again.

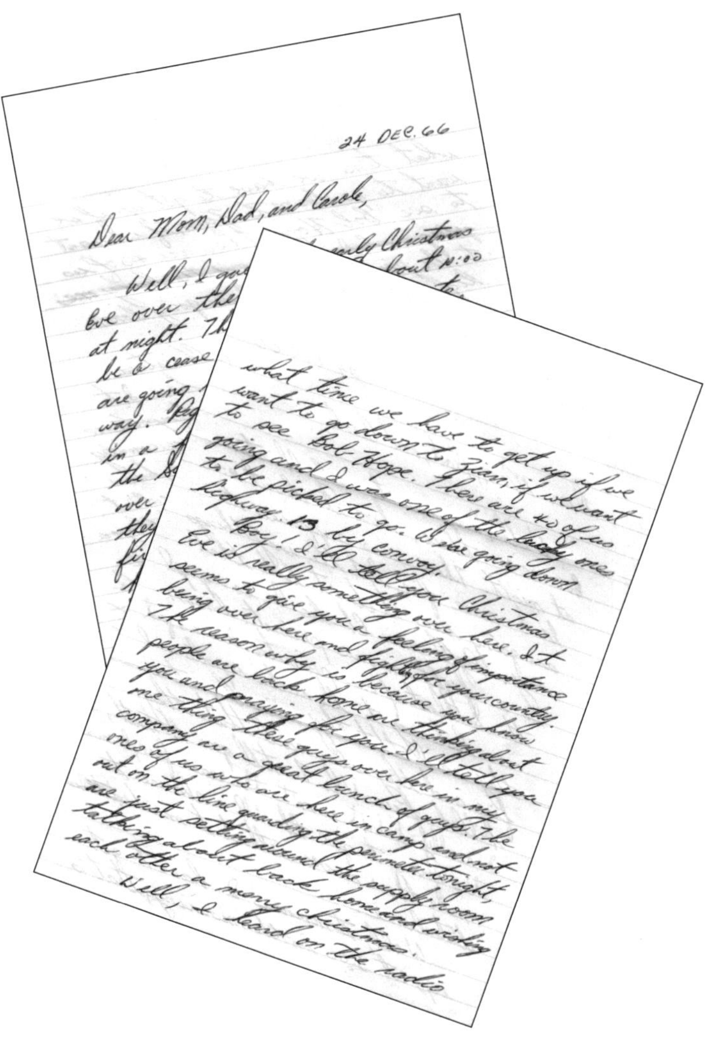

24 DEC. 66

Dear Mom, Dad, and Carole,

Well, I ...

what time we have to get up if we want to go down to Zian, if we want to see Bob Hope. There are 40 of us going and I was one of the lucky ones to be picked to go. We're going down Highway 13 by convoy.

Boy! I'll tell you Christmas Eve is really something over here. It seems to give you a feeling of importance being over here and fighting for your country. The reason why is because you know people are back home are thinking about you and praying for you. I'll tell you one thing these guys over here in my company are a great bunch of guys. The ones of us who are here in camp and not out on the line guarding the perimeter tonight, are just setting around the supply room talking about back home and wishing each other a merry christmas.

Well, I heard on the radio

Harold R. Ebersole, Dwayne's father, bought two tape recorders when his son went to Vietnam. The Ebersole family kept one and they sent the other to Dwayne, so they could keep in touch by mailing recorded messages to each other. His sisters, Joyce Ebersole Finniff and Carole Ebersole Clark, especially liked to record messages for him. At one point, his two-year-old niece, Deborah Finniff, referred to the tape recorder as "Uncle Dwayne." The Maugansville Fire Department, where Dwayne served, also recorded tapes. The family also exchanged letters, such as this one Dwayne wrote on Christmas Eve 1966.

"I have to get up at 5:00 in the morning, that's what time we have to get up if we want to go down to Zian, if we want to see Bob Hope. There are 40 of us going and I was one of the lucky ones to be picked to go. We're going down Highway 13 by convoy.

Boy, I'll tell you Christmas Eve is really something over here. It seems to give you a feeling of importance being over here and fighting for your country. The reason why is because you know people back home are thinking about you and praying for you. I'll tell you one thing; these guys over here in my company are a great bunch of guys. The ones of us who are here in camp and not out on the line guarding the perimeter tonight, we're just sitting around the supply room talking about back home and wishing each other a Merry Christmas."

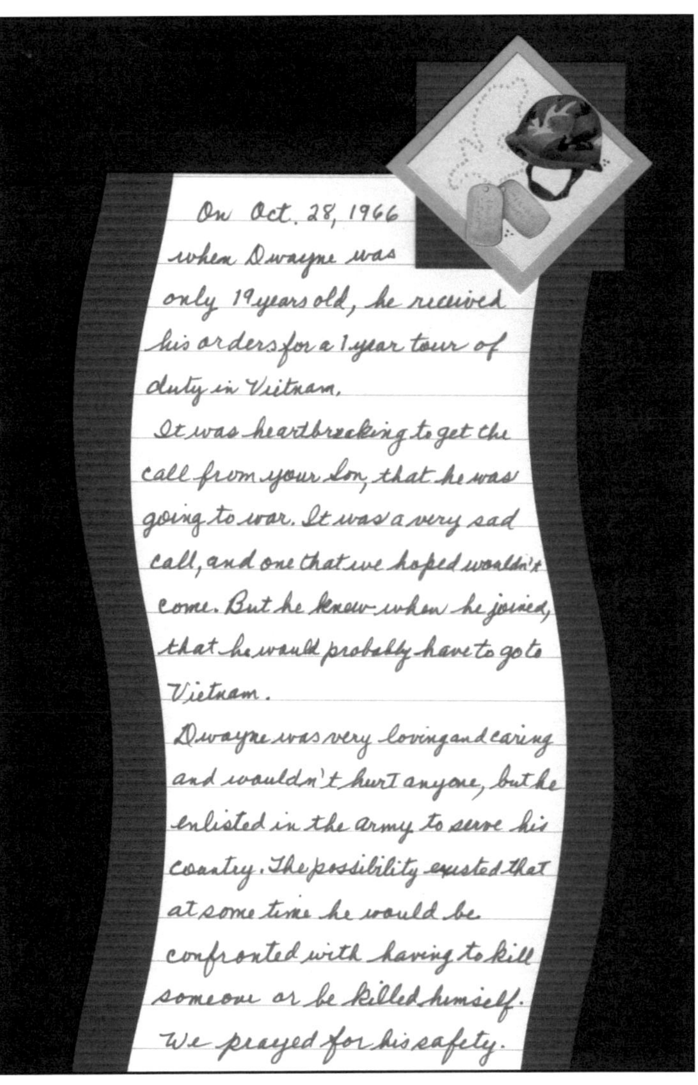

On Oct. 28, 1966 when Dwayne was only 19 years old, he received his orders for a 1 year tour of duty in Vietnam.

It was heartbreaking to get the call from your son, that he was going to war. It was a very sad call, and one that we hoped wouldn't come. But he knew when he joined, that he would probably have to go to Vietnam.

Dwayne was very loving and caring and wouldn't hurt anyone, but he enlisted in the army to serve his country. The possibility existed that at some time he would be confronted with having to kill someone or be killed himself. We prayed for his safety.

An entry in a scrapbook kept by Dwayne's mother, Helen, when her son was in Vietnam. A member of the North Hagerstown High School Class of 1965 and an employee of Mack Truck, Dwayne enlisted in the Army in June 1966. He was sent to Vietnam that November. At the advice of a friend, Helen nailed a pair of Dwayne's shoes to the floor in the attic, facing the direction from which he would return home. Her friend had done the same thing for her brothers who fought in WWII, and they all came home safely. Dwayne also had his good-luck charm: a bullet that narrowly missed hitting him. While sitting by his locker at Lai Khe in Vietnam, a bullet passed through the back plate of the locker, but only dented the door on the inside. If it had pierced the door, it would have gone through his back. From then on he carried that bullet for good luck.

(Photos and memorabilia courtesy of Helen Hurd Ebersole Myers, mother of Dwayne R. Ebersole)

Larry F. Michael — Army — Vietnam

Staff Sgt. Larry Michael of Clear Spring in combat gear in Vietnam in February 1969. He spent much of his time on search and destroy missions in the "Iron Triangle." The Iron Triangle was a Viet Cong stronghold in a 60-square mile area between the Saigon River and Route 13, 25 miles north of Saigon. Michael served with the 2nd Battalion, 16th Regiment, 1st Infantry Division, the "Big Red One," operating out of an Army base camp near Phu Loi Army Airfield, west of Bin Hoa, northeast of Saigon.

Phu Loi was the scene of fierce fighting between American forces engaging North Vietnamese and Viet Cong fighters in the unexpected Tet Offensive of 1968. The area around the airfield was the setting for raids on American and South Vietnamese installations in the vicinity of the South Vietnamese capitol. Troops braced for a second major offensive during the same holiday period while Michael was there in 1969, but a repeat of the dramatic massive assault on the scale of the prior year did not materialize.

A mustachioed Michael in a photo taken in Phu Loi on Nov. 7, 1968, "just before 'Bush.'" In the brutal lexicon of the Vietnam war, the word "Bush" could be used as a noun or a verb, referring in the context of combat to either a destination — the jungle, or the verb — to ambush. "Sometimes, words can have a lot of meaning," Michael said.

Someone took this photograph of Michael reading a letter from home. Written on the back of the Kodacolor print is: "Nov. 68 Torch Hill Vietnam. Torch Hill" was the name given to a Night Defensive Perimeter — an elaborate description for an area no larger than half a football field with modest bunkers, sandbags and canvas for shade, designed to give troops some cover. The soldiers, who were constantly on the move from one defensive perimeter to another, gave names to humble stations scattered throughout the dense undergrowth. The patrols would be in the jungle days at a time. "You rarely took your boots off, much less took a shower," Michael said. "Lots of times we would have to wash in river water and you could go weeks without bathing," not to mention a hot meal.

Michael said he and his fellow soldiers relied on "Army bug juice" to ward off mosquitoes in the humid terrain, and had to contend with leeches as long as four or five inches and fire ants that made their lives miserable.

Makeshift showers such as this one were luxury to Michael and other soldiers returning from the field. Vietnam veteran Ron McNeer contributed this photograph of a shower where 55-gallon drums, mounted on a bamboo framework, provided "nothing but cold water."

Despite the hardships, Michael recalls the beauty and depth of the night sky over Vietnam, and the multitude of meteor showers that streaked the darkness above the jungle canopy.

Christmas 1968 was memorable for Larry Michael, not so much for what happened as what didn't happen that day. Michael recognized that his "Christmas Story" is hard for people to understand if they weren't there. Events unfolded this way:

Michael spent that Christmas Eve sitting on a bunker, sharing a Tiger Beer with a couple of his men. One of them had been carrying the beer in his pack for just such an occasion. They talked about what they would be doing if they were back in the "world" — their term for the U.S.A. The night was uneventful and they rested well.

Close to noon the next day a helicopter flew in with Christmas dinner — hot turkey, quite a change from the cold C-rations to which they had become accustomed. In late afternoon, they were given the order to "saddle up" in preparation for an ambush. By nightfall, they had reached their destination and set up a three-point ambush on the corners of a rice paddy.

Michael was on first watch, staring out into the darkness while the other three men slept. He thought of home, where it was 8 a.m. Christmas morning. He wondered what his family and friends were doing, and he felt the warmth of Christmases past with his mother and dad and family. But his solitude was about to end.

He saw enemy soldiers climbing up a big dike to his left, walking toward his machine gun position. He knew he had a serious dilemma, and a thousand thoughts ran through his mind. There was supposed to be a Christmas truce in effect, but he could see that the enemy was not honoring it, and he knew he might be forced to break the terms of the cease-fire.

Enemy soldiers were "silhouetted against the sky, and they were only 30 feet away," he said. "It was my duty to kill them, but I didn't want to be reminded every Christmas morning (if I made it home) that I killed all these men. I also was thinking that this could be my end and my family would have to mourn my death instead of celebrating Christmas. It's amazing what can go through your mind in such a short time. I was hoping the machine gun would open fire and take all these decisions away from me."

But Michael knew that the turkey dinner and fatigue had put his buddies to sleep, so he made a snap decision — to push the enemy to the other side of the dike by firing at their feet.

They reacted as he anticipated. But there was no guarantee they wouldn't return fire, and he knew he would have no choice but to fight.

There was a tense moment when they did start to fire, but no one was hit, and then the enemy ran.

Michael never reported that his buddy, who was supposed to be awake, had fallen asleep.

"He knew what he had done and I knew he would never fall asleep on ambush again. Nothing more was said about that night. But it still gives me cause to ponder, did I make the right decision?"

Michael personalized his helmet cover with a series of slogans penned into the thick canvas covering: "A man hasn't lived until he felt he was about to die; USA God's Country; Peace or We'll Kill You; Somebody up there likes me" (drawn with an upward pointing arrow); "Come on July," a reference to Michael's departure date; "God is my Pointman; Maryland Land of Pleasant Living," and "War is Hell, Vietnam 68 - 69."

"Everyone personalized their helmets," Michael said. "That's just what we did. Sometimes the covers wore out, but soldiers were often reluctant to part with them, almost as if they were totems, keeping them from harm."

Michael is reflective about his experiences "both good and bad" in Vietnam. His time in combat in Vietnam "gave me a whole new appreciation for life."

Michael was lucky in the sense that he only had to serve 10 months of a typical 12-month combat tour. He had been wounded and was sent to a hospital in Vietnam to recuperate. One month later, he was patched up and back in the field. While he was in the hospital though, his unit was ambushed and suffered many casualties. "When I went back to my outfit, I was the only NCO," Michael said. "We were way down in numbers.

"You could say that someone was looking out for me," said Michael of his fortunate hospital stay, "but I feel a little guilty about not having been there. Guess you could say it was meant to be."

The suddenness of the transition from combat to the States was somewhat jarring. Michael was in combat one day, and 36 hours later he was on a jetliner back to "the world."

"When the orders came down and the chopper came in, you went. It was a quick goodbye," Michael said. Soldiers, who had trusted their lives to their comrades-in-arms, had to fight "a mixture of feelings" when their tour of duty was over. Michael said soldiers were always happy to be going home, but as they were whisked out of the combat zone and away from their buddies to be processed for the trip to the States, "you felt that you were abandoning them."

In Vietnam, more than in previous wars, the fighting man was treated as an individual — not as part of a cohesive fighting unit that trained, traveled, and fought together. Troops rotated in and out of combat on a continual, revolving basis. In most cases soldiers went to war in Vietnam alone and came home by themselves — if they were fortunate enough to come home at all.

Michael poses for the photo at upper right with a Kit Carson Scout in 1968 at Pagoda Inn (the name of another Night Defensive Perimeter erected around the ruins of a pagoda), near Phu Loi, Vietnam. Kit Carson Scouts were former Viet Cong fighters who, once repatriated, were retrained and served with American forces in Vietnam. The Kit Carson program was begun in November 1967 and by the end of the war, more than 7,000 had served with Army and Marine Corps units in Vietnam. They were valued as guides and for their knowledge of enemy tactics and procedures. Many would be executed or die in communist reeducation camps following the U.S. military's departure from Vietnam in 1975.

(Photographs and memorabilia courtesy of Larry F. Michael)

Going home was the one thing all soldiers in Vietnam wanted to do.

Kenneth L. Deavers Killed With Marines In Vietnam

By CYNTHIA MOLLE

The two officers offered their condolences, their eyes downcast, not knowing exactly what to say to the man who had just been told his son was dead.

They were all standing in the personnel office at Mack Trucks where Kenneth L. Deavers Sr. learned of the second terrible loss in his life brought about by war.

What is a man's reaction in that first awful moment?

"I was astonished and paralyzed for a minute. I was bewildered. I couldn't realize it was my son. I had served in World War II and lost a brother in it. I didn't want to realize this could happen in my family."

Deavers explained his feelings after he read the military telegram: "Lance Cpl. Kenneth Deavers Jr., U.S. Marine... Feb. 7, 1967, in the... Quang Tin, Repu... He was wou... in the ch... while...

...entered the Marines soon afterward. He trained at Parris Island and in California. He had been in Vietnam for 10 months.

He liked to wrestle and played the trumpet in the South High band, his father said. "And he loved the girls. He was gay... liked to have fun," hi... remembers.

"He was very... a Marine, he... be one..."

Douglas L. Tracy Is Killed In Vietnam

Greencastle Soldier Killed In Vietnam

Cpl. T. R. Cook Jr. ... Viet War Victim

Brothers Serve In Army

City Marine Dies In Action In Vietnam

Cpl. Ralph Flint

City Marine Wounded In Vietnam

Douglas Seller

Chief Diehl Becomes Retiree

IN VIETNAM — A1-C William Baer, son of Mr. and Mrs. Edgar Baer, 121 East Lee St., is currently serving a tour of duty with the U.S. Air Force in Vietnam. He is stationed at Tan Son Nbut Air Base near Saigon. He graduated from South Hagerstown High School in 1964. Friends may write to him at this address: A1-C William Baer, AF 13854465; Box 9840; 460 Field Main. Sqd.; APO San Francisco, Calif. 96307.

SERVING IN VIETNAM — Pfc. Guy L. Rudisill Jr., son of Mr. and Mrs. Guy Rudisill Sr., 811 Salem Avenue, is stationed in Da Nang with the Marines. He graduated from

IN GERMANY — Sp-4 Gary W. Spaid, son of Mr. and Mrs. Clyde Spaid, 352 Nottingham

PROMOTED — Kevin B. Judd, son of Mrs. Joan Judd, 301 Ross St., and Warren C. Judd, 319 Ridge Ave., has been promoted to private first class in the U.S. Army, and is stationed at Ft. Sill, Okla. His address: Pfc. Kevin B. Judd US51 663 853, "B"

ASSIGNED — Pvt. E-2 Lloyd C. Heiston Jr., son of Mr. and Mrs. Lloyd C. Heiston Sr., 439 Rhode Island Avenue, has been assigned to Brook Army Medical Center, Ft. Sam Houston, Tex. He completed nine weeks of basic training at Ft. Bragg, N. C. and nine weeks of special

Pages from a scrapbook kept by Diane Bartles of Hagerstown featuring news clippings about area servicemembers during the Vietnam War.

Eugene Y. Nakada — Army — Korea, Vietnam, Cold War

Eugene Y. Nakada survived life in wartime Japan to grow up to become an American Army officer who was drafted during the Korean War and served two tours of duty in Vietnam.

Eugene Y. Nakada's first exposure to American military might was seeing American fighter planes from aircraft carriers swoop across the skies over Tokyo in the closing days of World War II. As a child of 12 living in Japan during the war, "I would climb up on the rooftop and watch the fighters go by and I'd wave at the pilots." Nakada's Japanese father had been studying in the United States and was translating English hymns into Japanese just before WWII. In 1940, his father made the fateful decision to return to Japan. Six months after his father returned, Japan and the United States were at war.

"It was a tough decision. My Dad knew that things were going to be bad. If we had stayed in the United States we would have been put in concentration camps," Nakada said. "It was the old rock and a hard place." As it turned out, once in Japan, Nakada's family, who spoke English in their home, was accused of being American spies. Only the intervention of their friend and neighbor, a lawyer-turned-judge who eventually rose to the equivalent of Japan's attorney general during the war, saved them.

"He was a good man. Our family had known him for years. He was a great fan of the United States and had asked my father to bring American jazz records back with him," Nakada said. The minister of justice's protection was the only thing that kept them from being imprisoned.

Capt. Nakada was in Vietnam in 1965 at Cam Rahn Bay as a logistics officer for his first tour of duty in the war-torn country.

"It worked out," said Nakada, "especially for me."

By the time he was 14, Nakada who, thanks to his parents, spoke perfect Japanese and English, was traveling all over northern Japan with the 11th Airborne Division, part of the U.S. Army Occupation force tasked with the massive effort to confiscate weapons. Nakada, wearing a GI jacket "two sizes too big," served as an interpreter-translator for the troops, as he watched civilians turn over small arms, antique weapons and elaborate, but deadly, swords that had been in their families for generations. "There were stacks and stacks of weapons and swords that GIs were simply allowed to go in and pick out what they wanted to send home." Some of the swords are considered works of art and would be worth $10,000 or more today, Nakada said.

But in 1945, Nakada was still a kid, envied by the Japanese kids for his paid work with the U.S. military, and enjoying the adventure. "I learned to love C-rations," said Nakada. Each ration consisted of a canned entrée, a "B2 unit" that contained cheese, crackers and candy, and a canned dessert. The combat rations also contained an accessory pack with a can opener, a hot beverage mix, salt and sugar packets, a plastic spoon, chewing gum, a pack of four cigarettes and several sheets of toilet paper. Each complete meal provided approximately 1,200 calories. "The GIs were puking, but I thought C-rations were great! They were high in calories, and teenagers love that kind of thing."

Nakada came to the United States to attend college, but was drafted into the Army with the sudden onset of the Korean War. "Back then they grabbed any warm body they could." He was en route to combat in Korea when a personnel officer at the replacement depot at Fort Lewis, Washington, yanked his orders after recognizing Nakada's special ability — not his flawless Japanese, but rather, Nakada's ability to type 65 words a minute. Typists were in short supply and Nakada said the young officer knew a clerk-typist would be a valuable addition to his

Nakada, in helmet with sidearm, was never too far away from his machine gun when traveling the Mekong Delta region of Vietnam during his second tour of duty in that most unpopular of American wars. On the back of the photo of Nakada in an observation tower in Dong Tan, Vietnam, Nakada wrote: "This is where I pull 'duty officer's job.' It was creepy. Mortar rounds had hit only a few feet away from my bunker."

staff. He spent the duration of the Korean War at McChord Air Base in Washington State. "So I guess you could say, typing may have saved me."

Once the Korean War was over, a majority of soldiers were kept on reserve status. "You didn't have a choice," Nakada said. At the time, there were "rumors of war" and from his own life experience of just over two decades, he had come to believe another war was "inevitable." From his short time in uniform, Nakada reasoned that if he had to be in the military, and there was going to be another war, he would rather be an officer.

While in the reserves, Nakada was commissioned as a second lieutenant. Soon "it was one crisis after another," and he was back on active duty and sent to France during the Berlin Crisis in 1961, and then to Germany in 1962.

By 1965, Nakada was in Vietnam and again in 1969 in the Mekong Delta right after the Tet Offensive — the massive surprise assault on the U.S. and Allied positions during the Vietnamese 1968 New Year's holiday.

Even though the bold military offensive was successfully countered, the North Vietnamese and Viet Cong assault had the psychological effect of being the turning point of the war.

Nakada received two Bronze Stars with four campaign stars for his service in Vietnam with the 9th Infantry Division. Even so, Nakada is quick to say, "I am no hero."

Nakada noticed a decided change in the attitude of our troops in Vietnam between his two tours, only four years apart. "In 1965, it was all enthusiasm," he said, a feeling he thinks was fueled by the residual sense of infallibility of a military that had "won" WWII. By his second tour of duty, which started in 1969, "everyone was just ready to get out. Eventually, we turned everything over to the South Vietnamese Army, and when we left, it collapsed." Nakada also remembers the hostility during that time on the domestic front, with the turmoil on college campuses and in major U.S. cities. "Nobody wanted to be drafted. And one way to keep from being drafted was to end the war."

In 1970, while Nakada was stationed at Headquarters, U.S. Forces in Japan, Army Chief of Staff Gen. William C. Westmoreland made a trip to Japan to meet with his counterpart in the Japanese Defense Force in a bid to garner logistical support for the U.S. efforts in Vietnam. Westmoreland had previously served as commander of U.S. forces in Vietnam, and Nakada was now serving as his interpreter — providing simultaneous translations in Tokyo between senior officials at high-level meetings for the duration of the general's visit.

Nakada came to Washington County in the 1970s with an assignment to Site R — a secure underground military facility on the Pennsylvania-Maryland border, near Camp David. "It was all very hush-hush then, but everyone knew about it when the Cold War ended," said Nakada. By then, his two daughters were happily enrolled at Smithsburg High School and didn't want to move, so after a 25-year career in the Army, Nakada retired in 1977 and went to work for Fairchild Aircraft.

It wasn't long, though, before his language skills were called into service on behalf of the U.S. State Department and then, later on, with the FBI Language Services Section. Nakada has served as an interpreter-translator in a number of high-profile and low-profile cases that have bearing on world events today, but he is not allowed to provide details.

In one of the cases, which received wide publicity in *The New York Times*, Nakada was a translator during testimony against defendants charged in the 1998 bombing of the U.S. embassy in Nairobi, Kenya, in the days when al Qaeda was not yet a household word. The perpetrators of that harrowing attack were convicted in the spring of 2001. Months later, FBI Director Robert Mueller had only had the job for a short time before September 11, when jetliners were flown into the Twin Towers in New York City and the Pentagon, and a fourth plane was prevented from striking another Washington, D.C., target. In an effort to coordinate international anti-terrorism efforts, Mueller flew to Japan to meet with Japanese security officials, and Nakada went with him to serve as his interpreter.

In 1998, Nakada was summoned to Lebanon, where members of the nearly forgotten Japanese Red Army terrorist group, which had orchestrated hijackings, vicious assaults, bombings and kidnappings around the world in the 1970s and 1980s, were training in the Bakaa Valley. According to Nakada, members of the terrorist group had been living in the Middle East quite comfortably, preparing for unspecified terrorist attacks, when they were apprehended as a result of a traffic violation.

Maj. Nakada serving as an interpreter for Gen. William C. Westmoreland during his visit to Tokyo to meet with Japanese defense officials.

The Yomiuri Shimbun

Helping hands

National Public Safety Commission Chairwoman Kiyoko Ono shakes hands with U.S. Federal Bureau of Investigation Director Robert Mueller at the National Police Agency on Friday before discussing security affairs. Mueller, who is visiting Japan for three days from Thursday, also was to hold talks with NPA Commissioner General Hidehiko Sato and Metropolitan Police Department chief Masuo Okumura on the global security situation following the Sept. 11, 2001, attacks on the United States, as well as countermeasures for organized crime.

Not long after the Sept. 11, 2001, attacks on the World Trade Center and the Pentagon, newly appointed FBI Director Robert Mueller met with senior Japanese security officials, and Nakada provided the simultaneous translation/ interpretation.

A courtroom artist's rendering shows Nakada (far right), leaning near a key witness in the 2001 trial of Islamic fundamentalists who were later convicted of carrying out the bombings at the U.S. Embassy in Nairobi, Kenya. The four Al Qaeda suspects were convicted and are serving life sentences in the bombing that claimed 213 lives.

(Photographs courtesy of Eugene Y. Nakada)

FBI Language Services Section, Eugene Nakada, interpreting for Mr. Miyagi, Toyota Motor Company, at KENBOMB trial (Federal Court, S.D.N.Y.) Mr. Miyagi identified the exact model of truck used in the bombing from small fragments collected by the FBI at the U.S. Embassy, Nairobi, Kenya, leading to the arrest, conviction and life-sentence of four al-Qaeda suspects.

Albert L. Keyser III — Air Force — Vietnam

Albert L. Keyser III, who lived on Salem Church Road at the time he entered the Air Force, trained as a fire control systems operator for B-52Gs at Lowry Air Force Base in Denver, Colorado.

The B-52G "Stratofortress" was a long-range jet strategic bomber, designed to carry nuclear and conventional weapons.

During April 1972, a contingent of B-52Gs was sent to Southeast Asia to support the bombing campaign against North Vietnam.

Keyser was a member of the 416th Bombardment Squadron, based at Griffiss Air Force Base, Rome, New York, under the auspices of the Strategic Air Command.

His service in support of the Vietnam War, however, took place on the ground. As part of a "black ops" unit, Keyser was transported by helicopter from bases in Thailand for clandestine missions in Cambodia and Laos as part of U.S. and Allied combat efforts in the Republic of Vietnam. For 35 years, Keyser kept silent about the covert operations in which he participated in the jungles of Southeast Asia.

In advance of the missions, participants were instructed to remove their dog tags and anything that might identify them as Americans. In addition, members of the team of 10 to 12 men did not know each others' real identities, in the event of capture or disclosure. The teams were spirited into and out of Laos and Cambodia via unmarked helicopters, according to Keyser.

On one of his last missions, in December 1972, the team was preparing to withdraw when one of his counterparts, a young man Keyser knew only as "Jim," stood up and was hit by a bullet — a bullet intended for Keyser. In defiance of a protocol that dictated the injured were to be left behind, Keyser dragged his wounded comrade to the departing helicopter where the young man died in his arms. "I am only here because he saved my life," Keyser said.

(Photographs courtesy of Albert L. Keyser III)

The inability to speak openly about his experiences in Vietnam was a source of pain, but Keyser is reflective about the role he played in this most-tortured of American wars.

"There is no glory in war," said Keyser, who has ancestors who fought in every war from the Revolutionary War to Vietnam.

"I'm no hero, but I served with a lot of heroes. Only, some of those heroes didn't come back."

An armored fist clenching lightning bolts and olive branches is the symbol of the Strategic Air Command.

Bill Young — Army — Vietnam

Bill Young has served in two very different Vietnams, in two very different ways. In 1968, during the Vietnam War, he was a captain in the Army Judge Advocate General's Corp at Long Binh near Saigon. Since 2000, he has returned to Vietnam every year with his wife, Frances, to get to know the country and its people and work with them in community service projects.

Born in Hagerstown in 1940, Young joined the ROTC unit at Johns Hopkins University before entering the University of Maryland School of Law. After passing the state bar exam, he was transferred to the Judge Advocate General's Corps (JAG) — the Army's judicial arm. After training in Charlottesville, Virginia (where he met his future wife), he was assigned to the Fifth Army at Fort Sheridan, Illinois. From April 1966 to September 1967, serving as an Assistant and Deputy Judge Advocate, he worked as a prosecutor, defense counsel, advised clients, processed claims, and conducted investigations.

But the U.S. was becoming more and more involved in Vietnam, and in 1967 he got orders to join the 1st Cavalry in the Central Highlands near Pleiku. His departure was delayed by his final case and when he arrived in Vietnam, he was assigned to Saigon Support Command, an arm of the 1st Logistical Command at Long Binh near Bien Hoa.

"There were approximately 25,000 American service personnel, men and women, and about 22,000 Vietnamese workers at Long Binh each day," he said. "It was like a small town, with all the problems that exist in small towns." As the post Judge Advocate, Young was responsible for advising the post commander on legal matters, counseling service personnel on legal problems, conducting investigations on procurement and supply matters, and prosecuting and defending service personnel. In addition, Young and his colleagues were responsible for legal matters involving officers' clubs and messes, two hospitals, and the Long Binh Jail — commonly called "the LBJ ranch."

Young was serving at Long Binh during the Tet Offensive that began in January 1968, though his only direct exposure was the sound of shooting when Viet Cong attempted to penetrate the perimeter of the post.

He left Vietnam in October 1968 and was assigned first to the 3rd Armored Division in Frankfurt, Germany, and then to the USARE & 7th Army in Heidelberg as Deputy Judge Advocate for Administrative Law. He returned home long enough to get married to Frances Mulford in February 1969. He was released from active duty in 1971 and returned to private law practice in Hagerstown.

When Bill Young returned to Vietnam in 2000, he said, "I went back to find the Vietnam I knew, but it wasn't there. I discovered I didn't know Vietnam ... not at all."

He had been more fortunate than many Americans serving there in time of war, for he had gotten to know some Vietnamese civilians well. "I was adopted by a Vietnamese family," he said. The Muoi family, who owned a rubber plantation that became Long Binh, invited Young to a reception. Jean Muoi, a strong anti-communist, took Young under his wing and he became a regular Sunday guest at the Muoi residence in Ben Go, a small village outside the post. This was the start of a long friendship. Jean died before the fall of Saigon, but his wife and two daughters and a son-in-law fled during the fall of Saigon and were eventually united with a third daughter in the U.S. Madame Muoi and her daughters have visited the Youngs, who have established ties with Jean's other children and grandchildren in the Saigon area.

In spite of his personal involvement with a Vietnamese family, Young said he never wanted to go back to the country. But 32 years later, with the encouragement of his wife, he did return. Frances found a travel agent who specialized in Vietnamese travel, who planned the classical Indochina trip. When the couple went to Vietnam in 2000, they had a guide who sensed that they might be responsive to an in-depth look at the society, the culture and the people. So they saw more than Saigon, Danang, Hue and Hanoi. They also went into the hamlets and villages and saw the people and their needs — people living in poverty, orphans, disabled children, people living without adequate food, health care or housing. "We saw the needs," Young said, "and we felt moved to help."

Every year since, the Youngs have returned to Vietnam, and they have helped. Their help has included some physical labor such as painting, some teaching, and simply some holding and giving attention to orphans

starved for affection and human contact. They have also helped by serving as trustees on the Global Community Service Foundation, whose goal is to reduce poverty and make people self-reliant in Southeast Asia, "one village at a time." It raises money for badly-needed projects and deals with the paperwork, politics and bureaucracy that stand in the way of getting help where it is needed.

The photos at left and on this page show the Youngs and Vietnamese at various sites where they have worked together. They show beds in a Bahnar orphanage in Kontum, children at a house construction project in Danang, orphans in Pleiku and a free clinic in Quang Tri Province. Among the initiatives of the foundation is a "voluntourism program" that combines tourism and community service. Under this program, the Youngs have taken two groups of students from St. James School in Washington County to Vietnam. "It has been a life-changing experience for them," Young said. In 2008, they will take a third group on a voluntour that will include Saigon, Danang, Hoi An, Hue, Dong Ha, Hue and Hanoi. Students at St. James have also raised funds for the foundation's work.

Young said his passion for helping the Vietnamese doesn't spring directly from his wartime experience. "It could be Africa or it could be Washington County," he said. But it is his recent experiences in Vietnam that have helped shape Young's view of the world.

"Life experiences are a great teacher, and I have learned from them," he said. "What Vietnam has taught me is that the U.S. doesn't always know what's best for others. We are a great nation founded on principles of democracy, liberty and the rule of law. But not all of these principles work in other cultures. We should study the culture, the traditions and the history of other countries before we attempt to export our democratic system of government where such principles are almost unknown. We need to understand the incredible diversity that exists in the world and that people can find happiness in non-democratic political environments and in cultures that differ substantially from our own."

Young said he and his wife get "an overwhelming welcome" from the Vietnamese every time they visit the country. "They are so friendly. Many Americans are still scarred by the war; the Vietnamese have moved on."

(Photos courtesy of Frances and Bill Young)

And the rocket's red glare,
the bombs bursting in air,
Gave proof through the night
that our flag was still there.
Oh, say does that
star-spangled banner yet wave
O'er the land of the free
and the home of the brave?

—Excerpt from The Star-Spangled Banner,
written by Maryland native
Francis Scott Key in 1814

Cold War

1945-1991

(Contributed by Curtis E. Shives)

Ray L. Nalley — Army — Cold War

This photo of Ray Nalley was taken in Germany in 1950 and mailed to his parents back in Williamsport with "Lots of love." As with many young men and women who served in the military during the Cold War and in the years since, time in uniform away from home was the opportunity to gain experiences they would draw upon for a lifetime. Nalley credits the Army as giving him an opportunity to grow up. "It had a complete bearing on my outlook."

Soldiers slept in tents while on maneuvers in the German countryside during the Cold War. Nalley stands next to Konrad Kolloch, a DP, or "Displaced Person" from Poland, who worked as the unit's barber and helped with training missions by doing odd jobs. Displaced Persons were individuals driven from their homelands as a part of forced migrations — many of them had been inmates of Nazi concentration camps, labor camps or prisoners of war.

(Photographs and memorabilia contributed by Ray L. Nalley)

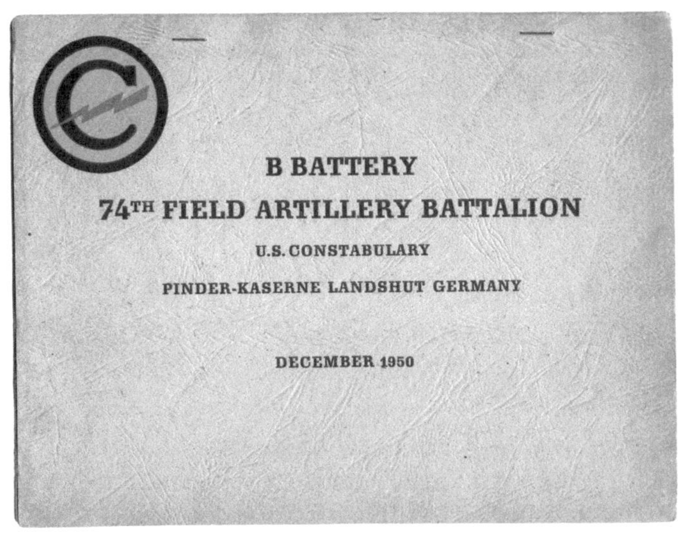

B BATTERY

74TH FIELD ARTILLERY BATTALION

U.S. CONSTABULARY

PINDER-KASERNE LANDSHUT GERMANY

DECEMBER 1950

Commemorative book from Nalley's tour of duty in Germany.

Nalley was a forward observer with Battery B of the 74th Field Artillery Battalion, based in Landshut, Germany. As a reconnaissance operative, Nalley manned an observation post recording map coordinates at the Artillery and Tank Training Center in Graffenwohr, Germany, in 1951.

Nalley and Wayne Poland, a fellow soldier and friend, pose for this photo on a 1945 Harley-Davidson motorcycle in Altstadt, Germany, in 1951.

For Nalley, portions of the Cold War were really cold, particularly during his time in the field in Germany. Nalley and fellow soldiers warmed themselves around an open fire while camping in a German forest in 1951. Part of Nalley's education was seeing the destruction caused by WWII and the struggle of civilians to survive in its aftermath.

Dennis Lynn Mongold

Navy — Cold War

During his four years in the Navy from 1970 to 1974, Dennis Mongold of Hagerstown said he "learned responsibility, learned to be respectful to others, made friends for life, and saw and did things that I will remember for life." He worked as a radioman at a naval communications station in Guam, where this photo was taken. He also traveled to Saipan, Tinian and the Philippines. But he described himself as a "land crab" — "I never saw a ship in four years."

His most memorable experience was "getting stuck on the side of an ocean cliff with two friends ... no one knowing we were out there." The men were hunting for war relics and found themselves trapped under a ledge about 10 feet from the top of the cliff. They finally managed to make their way to the top.

(Photo courtesy of Dennis Mongold)

Lewis Stanley "Pat" Rudesill Jr. — Navy — Cold War

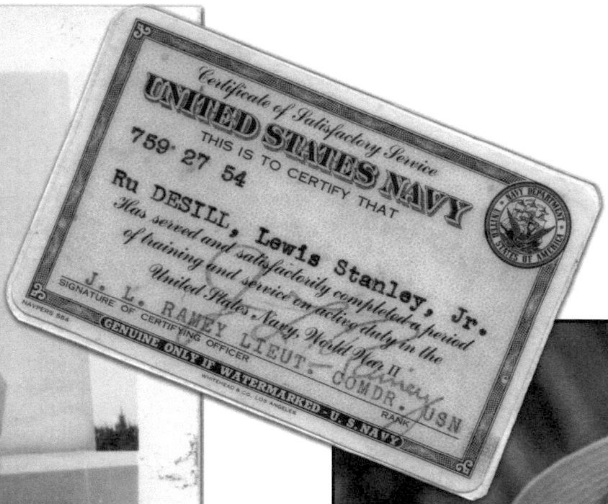

While serving in Hawaii, Rudesill was a model for Ray's photography studio in Honolulu. The large studio employed American servicemen as models for photographs used in advertising. Rudesill and his buddies earned some "fun money" for posing.

Lewis Stanley "Pat" Rudesill Jr. was in his senior year at Hagerstown High School when he joined the Navy in April 1945, and he didn't graduate with his class. After basic training at the Naval Training Station in Bainbridge, Maryland, he was assigned to San Diego and then to Hickam Field, the Air Force base in Honolulu, Hawaii. He was quartered at Schofield Barracks, which had been hit four years earlier during the Japanese attack on Pearl Harbor. He worked as a fireman, at the ready to extinguish fires on aircraft. He didn't talk much about his time in the service, according to his wife, Kathleen. But he would tell her how much he liked going to the landing field to see planes come in and talk to the pilots.

Rudesill did get his high school diploma; it was mailed to him from Hagerstown. And he got a good education from the military, taking advantage of the GI Bill to study engineering. He became a state highway engineer with the Maryland State Highway Administration, where he worked for 40 years in Frederick, Howard and Carroll counties.

(Photos courtesy of Kathleen Rudesill, widow of Lewis Stanley "Pat" Rudesill Jr.)

Bainbridge Naval Training Center was constructed in 1942 as a training facility for WWII Navy recruits. The center, located in Port Deposit, Maryland, overlooking the Susquehanna River in Cecil County, operated until 1976. During that time, more than 500,000 recruits were trained at the facility.

This post card was sent from Bainbridge by Washington County resident Jonas William "Buck" Zeigler, who trained there in 1944 before being sent to the South Pacific.

(Contributed by Marie V. Zeigler, widow of Jonas William "Buck" Zeigler)

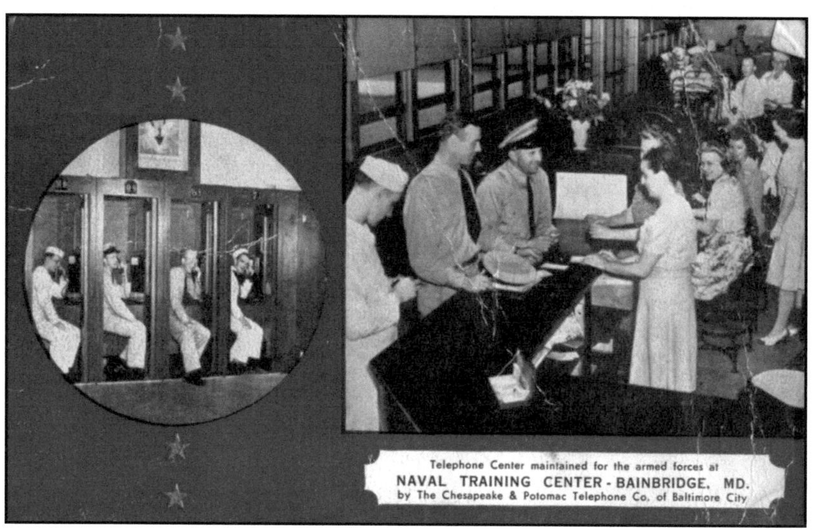

Homer Abbott — Army — Cold War

Four men from Washington County in 1957 at the completion of Army basic training at Fort Jackson, South Carolina. At top are Richard Cramer (left) and Homer Abbott. At bottom are Richard Mohn (left) and Gerald Hammond.

Homer Abbott in his guard uniform starts 24-hour guard duty in front of his barracks in Baumholder, Germany, in what was the headquarters of Field Marshal Erwin Rommel during WWII. His 24-hour shift consisted of alternating two hours on, four hours off. Abbott, of Sharpsburg, was a machinist at Fairchild Aircraft when he was drafted into the Army in 1957 at age 23. Trained in the use of a 105 mm howitzer, Abbott was sent to Germany with the 868th Field Artillery Battalion. Discharged from the Army in 1959, he was in the Army Reserve for two years, leaving the service in 1961. After two years in the garage business he got a job with Mack Truck, where he worked for the next 30 years. Abbott said of his service in the Army, "It was the most rewarding time of my life, a good experience. I wouldn't have changed it for the world. I think every young man should have two years in the military."

(Photographs courtesy of Homer Abbott)

Abbott and other American soldiers ferry a 280 mm "atomic cannon" across the Rhine River in Germany after laying tracks on pontoon boats. Abbott was trained to operate the 85-ton weapon, which was capable of delivering an atomic warhead 21 miles away. Fortunately, he never had to fire anything more powerful than high-explosive warheads.

Stanley T. Hoover — Air Force — Korea, Cold War

(Photographs courtesy of Stanley T. Hoover)

Stanley T. Hoover (indicated by arrow below) served as a mechanic with the Air Defense Command, providing critical maintenance for the 96th and 332nd Fighter Interceptor Squadrons at New Castle County Airport in Delaware. But when the base commander decided that the installation needed a marching band, Hoover was recruited to play the alto sax in addition to his other duties.

The Hagerstown native served from 1951 to 1955 "defending the home front during the Korean War." He remembers the camaraderie of his fellow airmen and still smiles at the memory of a not-so-welcoming sign he saw in a San Antonio yard, during his days of basic training at Lackland Air Force Base, Texas. The sign read: "Airmen and dogs — Keep off grass."

Hoover said the Air Force "made my life more regimented (neat and organized) and prepared me for life." The GI Bill, which provides educational benefits to veterans, helped Hoover earn a degree in business administration.

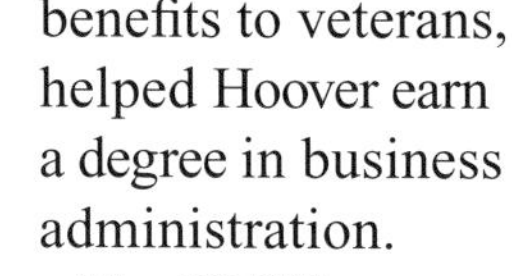

The GI Bill was one of the most revolutionary pieces of legislation to be approved by Congress. With millions of servicemembers returning from across the globe at the end of WWII, the government sought the means to absorb the massive influx of workers into a peacetime economy.

Educational benefits put a college education within the grasp of many who had never before had the opportunity to earn an advanced degree and chipped away at class barriers. In addition, preferential homebuyer loans helped returning servicemembers and their families purchase houses of their own, helping to fuel America's postwar economic boom. The GI Bill benefits veterans to this day.

Jayne C. Harple — Air Force — Cold War

WOMEN IN MILITARY SERVICE FOR AMERICA
MSgt Jayne Christine Harple USAF Ret

THE WOMEN'S MEMORIAL

Member 506529

HIGHEST RANK: MSgt

SERVICE: Air Force From Nov 11, 1965 to Jan 31, 1986

WAR/CONFLICTS: Vietnam War Serving in: Philippines

BORN: Jun 18, 1947
BIRTH PLACE: Hagerstown, MD
HOMETOWN: Hagerstown, MD
MAIDEN:
PREVIOUS:
NICKNAME:
AKA:
SERVICE NAME:
DECORATIONS: Meritorious Service Medal
Air Force Commendation Medal w/2 Bronze OLCs
Air Force Good Conduct Medal w/1 Silver OLC

MEMORABLE EXPERIENCES:
My entire time on Active Duty was memorable. I remember the first day of basic training in November 1965, until my retirement ceremony at Lackland Air Force Base, twenty years later. Looking back over those years, the most memorable time was my assignment to the 1961st Communications Group, Clark Air Base, Philippines, from September 1970 to January 1972. When I was a young twenty-three year old far away from my family, the reality of serving on Active Duty really hit home. The Vietnam Conflict was not far away, and the duties of controlling the critical message traffic into and out of the Pacific and Southeast Asia area made me realize the importance of serving my country. Even though I played a small role, I was still part of the big picture, and was and always will be proud to have served. I was known as a WAF when I enlisted in 1965. During my twenty years, I was fortunate to see the Air Force continually open its doors wider to women. When I retired, I was known as a Senior NCO who was not separate and distinct for being a woman.

REGISTERED BY:
HONORED BY:

(Memorial page courtesy of www.womensmemorial.org)

Jayne C. Harple's 20-year career in the Air Force is recorded at the Women's Memorial in Arlington, Virginia, part of an ongoing effort to recognize the contribution of women in uniform in the service of our nation. The Hagerstown native served at air bases throughout the United States and in the Philippines in support of the Vietnam War. "My entire career was memorable, but using my communication skills and training in support of the Vietnam War was the most memorable [experience] when I was only in my twenties," Harple said. The military "gave me education, opportunities and experiences which have made me a more grounded, confident, independent and dependable individual."

The Women In Military Service For America Memorial is located near the ceremonial entrance to Arlington National Cemetery. It was dedicated Oct. 18, 1997, and is the "only major national monument honoring all women who have defended America throughout history," according to the Women In Military Service For America Memorial Foundation. More than 200,000 visitors come to the monument each year.

(Contributed by Jayne C. Harple)

EUROPEAN EDITION

THE STARS AND STRIPES

Unofficial Publication of the U.S. Armed Forces in Europe

Weather Forecast

Cloudy with fog and haze in the Heidelberg, Wiesbaden, Kaiserslautern and Frankfurt areas. Maximum temperature 46 degrees, minimum 36.
—Air Weather Service

Late News

WASHINGTON, Nov. 14 (UP)—The Defense Department will recommend that the 3,500,000 men and women in the armed services be given Social Security coverage, the Army, Navy, Air Force Journal reported today.

Volume 12, Number 211 ✻ ✻ ✻ 5 cents a copy, $1.25 a month Sunday, November 15, 1953

Truman Says He Will Tell All Facts

NEW YORK, Nov. 14 (UP) Former President Harry S. Truman will give his side of the Harry Dexter White case to the American people Monday night in a radio broadcast and possibly on television too, he announced today.

"I'll make an all-out broadcast and answer all pertinent questions," that have been raised, the ex-President said. He added that he would take advantage of "any facilities, radio or TV," that are made available to him.

Mr. Truman announced his decision to reveal his role in the controversial White case about an hour before he left by train for his home in Independence, Mo.

The former Chief Executive said it was too early to announce the time of the broadcast or any other details except to say it would originate in Kansas City. He said he would "tell all the facts" about what he smilingly described as the "pending difficulties."

Earlier, Mr. Truman indicated he may have kept suspected-Commu-

Bulletins

TRIESTE, Nov. 14 (AP)—Riot police and some Allied troops went on the alert tonight for a possible new outbreak of violence in this troubled free port.

STRASBOURG, Nov. 14 (UP) Seven French political prisoners who spent several years in Soviet Russian concentration camps and were recently released arrived here today by train.

AMSTERDAM, Nov. 14 (AP)—Amsterdam's public prosecutor said today that capsules of arsenic mistakenly distributed as vitamins had killed two persons and left others partially paralyzed in several Dutch cities. Prosecutor Hollander said that a two-month investigation had traced the killer capsules to an Amsterdam pharmaceutical firm.

LATE SPORTS

Army 21, Penn 14
South Carolina 20, West Virginia 14
Navy 14, Columbia 6
Coast Guard 7, St. Michael's 6
Marquette 13, Holy Cross 7
Wesleyan 12, Trinity 7
Pitt 40, North Carolina State 6
Yale 26, Princeton 24
Fordham 28, Temple 0
Michigan State 14, Michigan 6
Harvard 27, Brown 20
Boston U 30, Villanova 19
Syracuse 34, Colgate 18
Lehigh 26, Carnegie Tech 13
Ohio State 21, Purdue 6
Rhode Island 19, Connecticut 13
Cornell 28, Dartmouth 26
Notre Dame 34, North Carolina 14
Wisconsin 34, Illinois 7
Penn State 54, Rutgers 26
Gettysburg 26, Bucknell 13
Iowa 27, Minnesota 0

Soviet Spies Threaten U.S., Canada, Ike Warns

She Steals the Spotlight

Urges Action In Ottawa Speech

OTTAWA, Nov. 14 (UP) President Eisenhower declared today that enemy espionage threatens both the U.S. and Canada and must be dealt with promptly. He also called on the Western world to reject Soviet "wile" lest Russian propaganda suck the democracies into "the suicide of nuclear war."

The President declared that "these days demand ceaseless vigilance," and added: "You of Canada and we of the United States can and will devise ways to protect our North America from any surprise attack by air.

"And we shall achieve the defense of our continent without whittling our pledges to Western Europe or forgetting our friends in the Pacific.

Joined by Geography

"Defense of our soil presents a

*A copy of the European Edition of the military newspaper **The Stars and Stripes** dated Nov. 15, 1953, captures the mood of the Cold War era.*

(Contributed by Ralph C. "Dutch" Hoover)

David F. Powell — Navy — Cold War

David F. Powell was under age when he joined the Navy at 16, and he was discharged. But he signed up again as soon as he could, in 1946. By the time of his discharge, 11 years later, he had attained the rank of Boatswains Mate 2nd Class and had spent many years as a salvage diver. "It was a good life. I liked being in the Navy," he said. "It had a profound effect on my life."

After boot camp at Bainbridge Naval Training Center in Perryville, Maryland, Powell was assigned to a ship out of Norfolk, the tanker USS ***Waccamaw****. But that was just a start. Before he left the Navy, he had served on seven different ships, including a net tender and a salvage lift vessel, USS* ***Windlass****.*

Powell said, "The Navy is different now. They don't have those kinds of ships any more."

He remembers serving with an auxiliary tug fleet (ATF) off Newport, towing a target "like a sled on the water." The target was used for training, as warships picked it up with radar and shot at it.

"You couldn't see the ships firing," Powell said. "Once, a six-inch projectile hit the wardroom. Fortunately, all the men were standing on the deck above."

After diving school, Powell remembers another time when he was working in salvage. "We raised a German U-boat in the Atlantic, and towed it to Piney Point [Maryland]. Then Naval intelligence came in, and we weren't allowed to get in it. Two years later, they towed it out to sea again. It was used for testing new weapons technology ... how it could penetrate, etc. Now it's at the bottom of the Potomac River."

(Photo courtesy of Evelyn Powell Stape, David Powell's sister)

David Powell hit the books while in diving school in Bayonne, New Jersey, in 1951. (Contributed by David Powell)

To keep them occupied during down time aboard ship, David Powell and his shipmates made handicrafts like this — one piece of rope formed into what was called a Napoleon's bend. Powell made full-size doormats the same way, all out of one piece of rope. (Contributed by David Powell)

David Powell in diving gear, complete with weighted boots, prepared for mine recovery on board the USS ***Waxsaw****, a net tender, on the Atlantic Ocean in 1951. (Contributed by David Powell)*

Lewis R. Watson — Marine Corps — Cold War

Sgt. Lewis R. Watson, who graduated from North Street School in Hagerstown, served with the Marine Corps from May 1954 until June 1960. Part of his time in the Marines was spent in Lebanon with Headquarters American Land Forces Middle East. When he returned to Hagerstown he owned and operated Watson's Funeral Home, 24 W. Bethel St., for 25 years before his death in July 2003.

According to his widow, Dr. Mary Watson, her husband was "very proud" of his service in the Marine Corps. "He used to celebrate the birthday of the Marine Corps in November every year."

Lewis was a member of the Montford Point Marine Association, a non-profit veterans association established to perpetuate the legacy of the first African Americans who entered the Marine Corps from 1942 to 1949 at Montford Point Camp, New River, North Carolina.

In 1942, President Roosevelt established a presidential directive giving African Americans an opportunity to be recruited into the all-white Marine Corps.

From 1942 to 1949, more than 20,000 African American recruits received basic training at a segregated boot camp at Montford Point Camp.

On July 26, 1948, President Truman signed Executive Order 9981 requiring full integration of all branches of the armed forces.

Lewis was also a 32nd degree Prince Hall Mason, with Masonic Lodge #99 in New York City. The Prince Hall Masons were the only Masonic order open to African Americans for many years. The fraternal order is named after Prince Hall, one of the original African American freemasons inducted into the fraternal order in 1775.

(Photo and memorabilia courtesy of Dr. Mary Watson, Lewis Watson's widow)

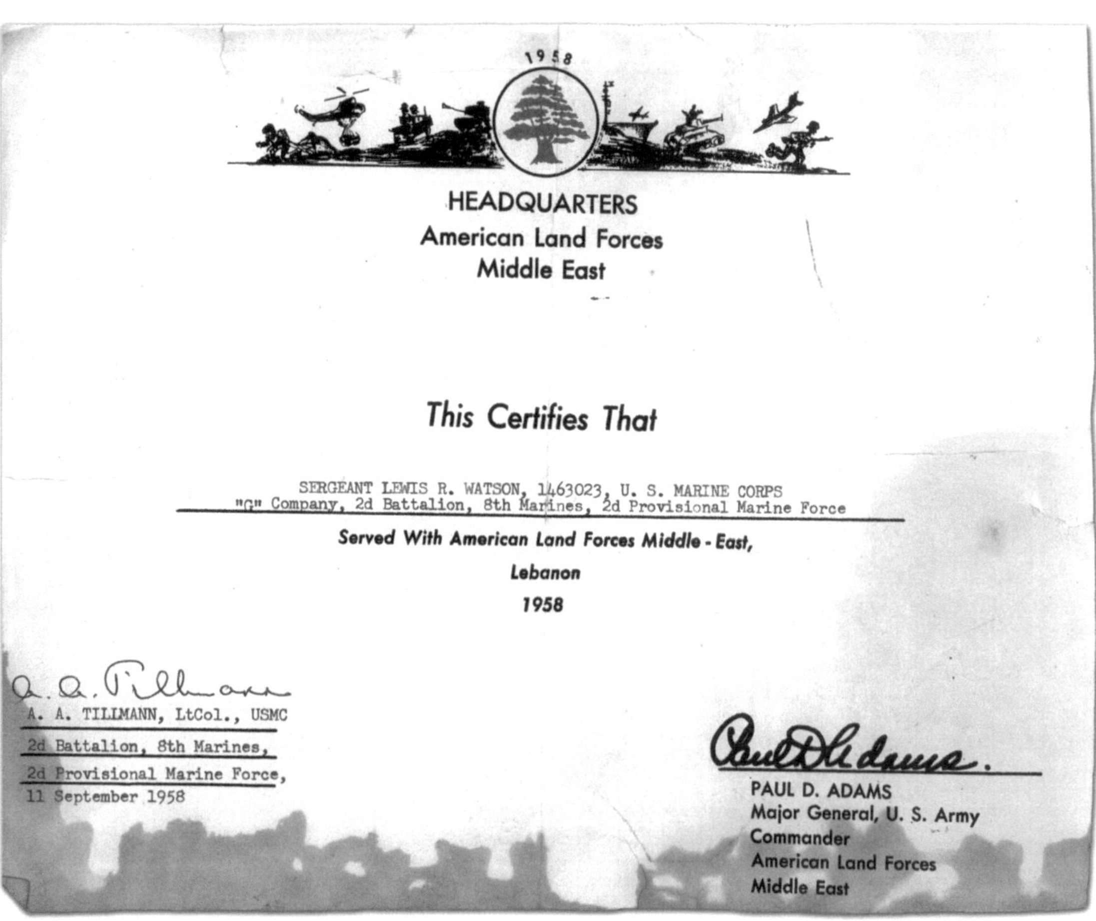

1958

HEADQUARTERS
American Land Forces
Middle East

This Certifies That

SERGEANT LEWIS R. WATSON, 1463023, U. S. MARINE CORPS
"G" Company, 2d Battalion, 8th Marines, 2d Provisional Marine Force

Served With American Land Forces Middle - East,
Lebanon
1958

A. A. TILLMANN, LtCol., USMC
2d Battalion, 8th Marines,
2d Provisional Marine Force,
11 September 1958

PAUL D. ADAMS
Major General, U. S. Army
Commander
American Land Forces
Middle East

Gisele Luipersbeck Klincewicz — WAVES — Cold War

Gisele Luipersbeck Klincewicz left her Hagerstown home and joined the WAVES [Women Accepted for Volunteer Emergency Service] in April 1947. After basic training at Hunter College in the Bronx, New York, she attended corpsman school at Bethesda Naval Hospital and served as a pharmacist's mate at the Naval hospital at Quantico, Virginia. "My military experience made me compassionate," she said. "It made me think of the sufferings of our service-people." Gisele's brother, Tony, was a master sergeant in the Army, and his wife, Marion, was in the WAF [Women's Air Force] after its inauguration in 1956. Gisele Luipersbeck Klincewicz is a charter member of the Women In Military Service For America Memorial at Arlington National Cemetery. She lives in Norristown, Pennsylvania.

(Photo courtesy of Gisele Luipersbeck Klincewicz)

WHAT PAY DOES A NAVY **WAVE** GET?

U.S. NAVY

RATE	Monthly Base Pay—Clear	Food Allowance*	Quarters Allowance*	Total Monthly Income
Apprentice Seaman	$50.00	$54.00	$37.50	$141.50
Seaman Second Class	54.00	54.00	37.50	145.50
Seaman First Class	66.00	54.00	37.50	157.50
Petty Officers	78.00 TO 126.00	54.00	37.50	169.50 TO 217.50

*(Unless food and quarters are provided by Navy)

PLUS $200. for clothing, the finest medical and dental care, special tax exemption, low-cost Government life insurance, and free mail, reduced rates on transportation, theater tickets, etc.

A WAVE recruiting poster produced by the Navy during WWII.

Ernest W. Martin Jr. — Marine Corps — Cold War

Ernest W. Martin Jr. of Maugansville still has his Marine Corps uniform from his service during the Cold War.

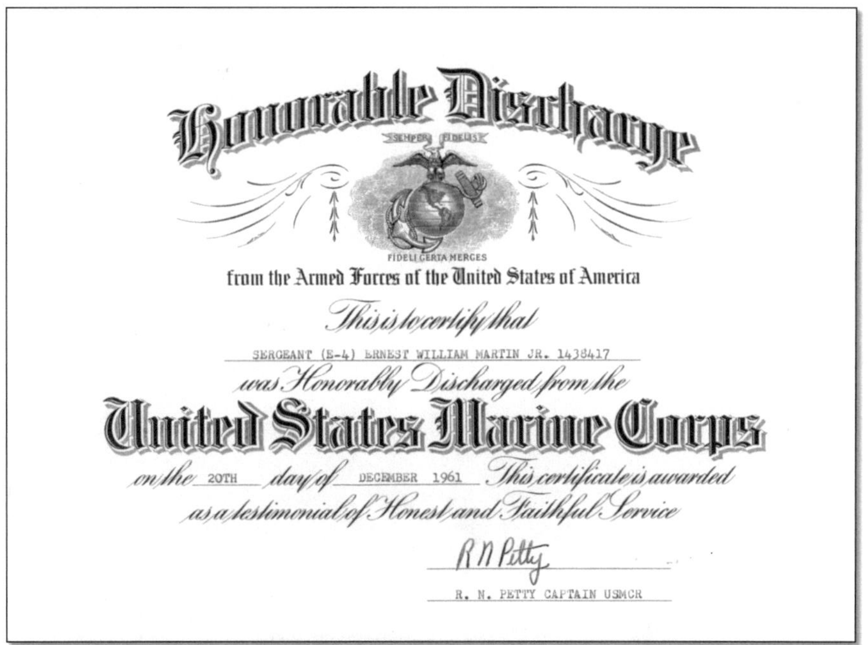

Honorable Discharge

SEMPER FIDELIS

FIDELI CERTA MERCES

from the Armed Forces of the United States of America

This is to certify that

SERGEANT (E-4) ERNEST WILLIAM MARTIN JR. 1438417

was Honorably Discharged from the

United States Marine Corps

on the 20TH day of DECEMBER 1961 This certificate is awarded as a testimonial of Honest and Faithful Service

R N Petty

R. N. PETTY CAPTAIN USMCR

Marine Corps Pfc. Martin served as a rifleman and automotive mechanic during his time at Camp Lejeune, North Carolina, from 1954 to 1957. "It was a great experience for a young guy. It created discipline and appreciation for what Mom did, washing clothes and everything," Martin said. The sober reality, though, came from Marine Corps instructors who told the young Marines "you are now professional killers."
(Photographs courtesy of Ernest W. Martin Jr.)

Martin is one of the freshly minted Marines in this March 26, 1954, boot camp graduation photograph taken at the Marine Corps Recruiting Depot at Parris Island, South Carolina. He is in the second row, third from the left.

Marine Corps boot camp was "three months of hell," according to Martin, who was 18 years old when he joined. "After that, it wasn't too bad."

Several other Washington County men are also included in the photograph of the Maryland Free State Platoon, Platoon 28. William Cianelli is fifth from the right in the fourth row back. Donald J. Cianelli, Ernest "Bill" Martin, Frank Merdebaugh, Frank Hiser and John H. Ganbe are also in the photo, but their mothers are probably the only ones who could pick them out of the rows of Marines at ramrod attention.

Russell B. Wingerd — Air Force — Libya, Cold War

Russell B. Wingerd's years in the Air Force took him from his hometown of Hagerstown as far east as Africa and as far west as Japan. Employed in munitions and weapons maintenance, he was stationed in Libya for a year and a half at a practice bombing range in the desert. Then came five months in Japan as the war in Vietnam was heating up, working on F-105 "Thunderchief" supersonic fighter-bombers. Known as "The Big Thud" by its crews, the F-105 was used to bomb North Vietnam. Returning to the U.S., Wingerd served at Seymour Johnson Air Force Base in Goldsboro, North Carolina, until his separation on Dec. 23, 1965. He then spent two years in the inactive reserves.

Wingerd sports a 20 mm ammo clip in Libya, where he was stationed for 18 months between July 1962 and January 1964. His work in munitions and maintenance involved various missiles and rockets as well as the F-100 Super Sabre jet fighter aircraft used by the Air Force from 1954 to 1971. It was the first of a series of U.S. fighters capable of supersonic speed in level flight.

THANKSGIVING Menu 1962

Wheelus Air Base
Usafe Weapons Center
Tripoli, Libya

TIP. AURORA - TEL. 32077

THANKSGIVING MESSAGE

Thanksgiving has a deep, special meaning for Americans. It reflects a firmly-rooted national reverence for the humility, strength and faith which enabled our forebears to survive harsh trials and establish the foundations of a great democratic society.

Today, in our present environment overseas, we are privileged to be not only the inheritors of this tradition but also its defenders and ambassadors. As part of the Free World forces dedicated to the deterrence of war, we stand for the preservation of those same principles of freedom, justice and humanity for which our forefathers braved a wild-rness.

In this role, we can give thanks -- both in the tional American way and in the larger sense of owship of free nations. Here, in Libya, we e our national and common goals by providing possible example of our American ideals. join with our host nation in a shared ratitude for the freedom we both enjoy.

IRWIN H. DREGNE
Colonel, USAF
Commander

Thanksgiving Meal

DINNER

Shrimp Cocktail w/ Cocktail Sauce
Lemon Wedges
Roast Turkey w/Giblet Gravy
Baked Ham
Bread Dressing
Cranberry Sauce
Mashed Potatoes
Buttered Corn
Candied Sweet Potatoes
Buttered Green Beans
Assorted Crisp Relishes
Parkerhouse Rolls Butter
Pumpkin Pie w/Whipped Cream or Mincemeat Pie
Fruitcake
Tea
Candy - Nuts
Coffee
Milk

The menu for Thanksgiving dinner in 1962 at Wheelus Air Base in Libya.

Frederick William Bolland Jr.
Army — Cold War

Frederick William Bolland Jr. was scarcely 18 when he joined the Army in 1963 and headed for jump school at Fort Benning, Georgia, where he is shown here. He worked as a mechanic in the motor pool of the 82nd Airborne Division, known as the "All-American" Division. He took part in Operation Power Pack from April to June 1965, when U.S. forces intervened in the Dominican Republic. Supported by the 82nd Airborne, more than 42,000 Marines and soldiers were dispatched to quell an uprising in the Caribbean island nation.

Bolland said his most memorable experience in the service occurred during a parachute jump over Vieques Island off Puerto Rico, when a "gore" [segment] of his parachute blew out while he was in midair. He hit the ground hard and was unconscious for several hours, but his only injury was a bruise that ran up his entire right side, foot to shoulder. "Every man should spend at least a year in the military," Bolland said. "It gives you focus and discipline."

(Photos and memorabilia courtesy of Pat and Frederick Bolland Jr.)

Patch of the El Uotia Bombing Range. Located approximately 90 miles from Wheelus Air Base, the range was used for bombing practice for pilots from Europe who came to Libya for a month's training. Any ideas the pilots and support crews might have had of a mild Mediterranean climate were soon dispelled by temperatures at the site, which in summer could reach as high as 120 degrees. Pilots were trained in air-to-air and air-to-ground gunnery and delivery of conventional ordnance and nuclear "shapes" at the weapons range. Russell Wingerd, who worked there, said pilots would aim at 20x20 foot canvas targets. The color of paint on the tips of their munitions would reveal where each pilot had struck.

Patch of the weapons center for USAFE — the Air Force component of the U.S. European Command. Russell B. Wingerd worked at the USAFE Weapons Center located at Wheelus Air Base in Libya, seven miles east of Tripoli on the shores of the Mediterranean Sea. First used by the Army Air Force in 1943 as a bomber base, Wheelus served primarily as a training site in the 1960s. It was used for month-long squadron rotations by the Europe-based tactical fighter wings. In addition, Strategic Air Command [SAC] bombers trained there in 45-day rotational deployments, and Wheelus served as a staging area for potential strikes against the Soviet Union.

With nearly 5,000 military personnel and dependents on the base, Wheelus was described as "a Little America." It remained in American hands until 1970, one year after Col. Muammar al-Gaddafi took power. While initially the U.S. wanted to hold on to Wheelus, its strategic value had declined with the development of nuclear missiles, which effectively replaced many bomber bases.

David Schwartz — Navy – Cold War

The Navy made good on its promise to show David Schwartz the world. The Hagerstown native was a graduate of Mercersburg Academy and Franklin & Marshall College when he went to Officer Candidate School in Newport, Rhode Island. He was commissioned as an ensign in the Naval Reserve in 1953. By the time he was discharged three years later, the lieutenant had served in the Pacific and the Atlantic and had visited more than 15 countries on four continents.

In 1953 and 1954, he served as communications officer, and later, navigator and operations officer aboard the USS *Kaskaskia*, an oiler cruising the Pacific. He concluded his naval career as a navigator and operations officer on the USS *Canisteo*, a fleet oiler which took him to Halifax, Nova Scotia; various Atlantic ports; Greece; Italy; North Africa and Cuba.

In the Pacific, Schwartz's ship was responsible for refueling vessels in the Western Pacific and the South China Sea. Schwartz's ship was sailing off thc coast of Indochina when the French outpost of Dien Bien Phu fell on May 7, 1954. After the surrender of the French and the signing of the 1954 Geneva Accords, which partitioned Vietnam, Schwartz's ship returned from Sasebo, Japan, later that summer to evacuate refugees fleeing the communist north for non-communist South Vietnam. French withdrawal from Indochina marked the beginning of U.S. military involvement in Vietnam.

(Photographs courtesy of David Schwartz)

*This emblem of the USS **Kaskaskia** features an image of the ship, along with a globe representing the worldwide mission of a fleet oiler. The Latin motto is translated: **"Best in the World"***

*Schwartz enjoyed his travels in the Mediterranean that took him from the open city of Tangiers in North Africa to France. His ship was responsible for transporting fuel to vessels in the Sixth Fleet, such as the aircraft carrier shown behind him in this photograph taken on the bridge of the USS **Canisteo** in 1956.*

*Schwartz got a view of Mount Vesuvius in the Bay of Naples in 1956 in Italy during his assignment as a navigator and operations officer on the Navy oil frigate USS **Canisteo**, during operations as part of the Sixth Fleet in the Mediterranean. The ship's motto could be applied to servicemen and servicewomen at duty stations around the globe during the Cold War: "If freedom were easy, we wouldn't be here."*

Robert E. Bruchey Sr. — Army — Cold War

Robert Eugene Bruchey Sr. of Hagerstown served two tours of duty with the Army during the Cold War years from 1950 to 1956, serving with the Military Police in the U.S. and overseas in Italy and Austria. Bruchey enlisted as an 18-year-old after working during his student years at Hagerstown High School as a pin boy for Eugene Rainey at Rainey's Coliseum bowling alleys in downtown Hagerstown.

Robert Bruchey served his first tour of duty with the 436th Military Police Company at Fort Lewis, Washington, and was retained an extra 116 days "for the convenience of the government." He re-enlisted on March 10, 1953, and was assigned to Company A, 701st MP Battalion. He attended MP School at Camp Gordon, Georgia, taking advanced military police training.

(Photographs and memorabilia courtesy of Pat Bruchey)

Murray Baechtel Reed — Air Force — Cold War

Reed's flight suit bearing the insignia of the 4750th Test Squadron of the Air Defense Command, with which Reed was stationed at the time of the Cuban Missile Crisis.

During the two weeks the world held its breath, the volume of traffic at Tyndall Air Base increased dramatically as the Air Force repositioned aircraft from northern bases to landing facilities in Florida to be closer to Cuba. "There was an awful lot of traffic during those two days (at the height of the crisis, when the United States' alert level was raised to DEFCOM 2) with squadrons coming and going. Our job was to get them in and get them out," Reed said. DEFCOM 2, only one level away from authorization of nuclear weapons, has occurred only that one time — during the Cuban Missile Crisis, Oct. 14 - 28, 1962.

In the midst of the heightened activity, there were casualties. Two pilots from Reed's squadron were lost on a night mission when their plane ended up in the Gulf of Mexico immediately upon takeoff. Both are buried at Arlington National Cemetery, Reed said. He believes the high volume of traffic at the air base contributed to the accident.

Murray Baechtel Reed was 19 when he joined the Air Force. After basic training at Lackland Air Force Base, San Antonio, Texas, he completed technical training at Fort Belvoir, Virginia. Then he was assigned to Tyndall Air Force Base, Panama City, Florida, where he worked as a classified support technician on the ground and in the air.

He was part of a team responsible for providing support services for F-102, Delta Dagger, and F-106 Delta Dart interceptors that flew to the busy base in Florida's panhandle. In the beginning, life was routine and the assignment wasn't too taxing. "That's where I learned to play bridge," Reed said.

But Reed and American military personnel around the globe got a real taste of what the Cold War was all about in the fall of 1962.

During the Cuban Missile Crisis in October of that year, ground and flight crews were on high alert with the looming confrontation between the United States and the Soviet Union over placement of nuclear missiles in Cuba.

Reed remembers being "scared to death" during the tense days when the world came as close at it has ever come to nuclear war. "We had pulled a lot of alerts and drills before that," Reed said. "But when they started fully arming our aircraft we knew something was going to happen."

Base personnel were issued ammunition for their side arms and rifles, and security was tightened as military installations went on high alert. "I personally thought that we were going to go to war," Reed said. "You never knew if the Big Button would be pushed or not."

Murray Reed, sporting his own set of wings, stands with his mother, Frances R. "Peggy" Reed, and WWII Army Air Corps Capt. Roderick C. Reed, in front of his mother's family's home at 1135 Potomac Ave., in Hagerstown, in 1942.

(Photographs and memorabilia courtesy of Murray Baechtel Reed)

Reed with his mother, Frances "Peggy" Reed, in Hagerstown, in late 1961. Reed, who was too young to vote for President John F. Kennedy in the 1960 election, had gotten a glimpse of Kennedy. His team put on a firepower demonstration for the young president, who was touring Eglin Air Force Base in nearby Fort Walton Beach, Florida. "I had so looked forward to voting for him," said Reed, who remembers exactly where he was when he heard the news of the President's assassination. "But I never got the chance."

Jacquelyn Sue Bartles

Army — Cold War

The death of a servicemember does not always come in battle; thousands have lost their lives over time in performance of other military duties, in ways often unexpected. But for loved ones, the deaths are no less painful.

Hagerstown's Jacquelyn Sue Bartles, an Army specialist 4th class, who served as a medical records courier in Germany, was killed in July 1987 in an automobile accident while transporting military records. The 583rd Medical Company and the 68th Medical Group at Wiesbaden Air Base held a memorial service in her honor on July 1, 1988.

The ceremony included the unveiling of a plaque honoring her service, and a tree was planted in her memory.

In a July 8, 1988, letter to Jacquelyn's parents, Clyde and Linda Bartles, Col. William L. Speer wrote that "Jackie was a special soldier who is greatly missed by the 583rd Medical Company (AMB) and the 68th Medical Group." He reported that in a tribute to their daughter, Ltc. Tyler, acting commander of the Medical Group, described "Jackie's energetic and professional nature," and said "she was a model soldier to emulate."

A wreath of flowers was placed near the plaque and taps was played while the unit presented arms. The ceremony concluded with a closing prayer by Chaplain Swedlund.

Bart Fraker — Navy — Cold War

Bart Fraker of Hagerstown had a 30-year career in the Navy, but he spent 14 of those years working with the Marines. That's because the Marines have no medical services of their own; they rely on Navy medical personnel. Fraker's training and expertise as a hospital corpsman was just what was needed, by the Marines as well as the Navy.

Born in Hagerstown in 1940, Fraker joined the Navy in 1958 and went to Great Lakes Naval Training Center, north of Chicago, Illinois, for boot camp and hospital corpsman school. He was stationed at Quantico, Virginia, from April 1959 to September 1962. Then he was assigned to the USS *Graffias* based in Sasebo, Japan, where he made regular trips to Vietnam between 1962 and 1965. Then he was transferred to Yokusuka, Japan, where he was regularly deployed to Vietnam between 1965 and 1967 with the Amphibious Construction Battalion #1 (the Navy's Seabees).

There he provided medical support for Seabees and Beachmasters, who manned the beaches when amphibious operations were being carried out. He and his buddies often found themselves under mortar fire in a ship moored off the coast or in a river, treating servicemen wounded during landing operations.

Back in the U.S., he studied at Independent Duty School in Portsmouth, Virginia, learning how to provide medical support in the absence of a doctor. His next assignment was at the Navy's Damage Control Training Center in Philadelphia, Pennsylvania, where he taught medical aspects of nuclear, biological and chemical warfare.

After attending Field Medical School at the Marines' Camp Lejeune, North Carolina, Fraker got orders to go to Danang, Vietnam. But the orders were modified at the last minute, and he found himself in Hawaii, at Kaneohe Marine Corps Air Station, where from 1970 to 1973 he started and directed a program to train corpsmen in taking advancement exams.

He spent the following three years in New York state, assisting the Marines in recruiting, and in 1976 was back at Camp Lejeune with the 2nd Marine Division as Medical Battalion Chief. His next move, in 1979, took him to the Naval hospital at Pensacola, Florida, where he was master chief from 1981 to 1984, running education and training programs. After a stint in Okinawa, Japan, as command master chief with the 3rd Marine Division, he moved for the last time in 1985, back to Pensacola, where he retired from the Navy in December 1988.

The next year he took on a civilian job that used many of the skills he learned in the Navy. He now works in the Industrial Hygiene Department of the Branch Medical Clinic at the Naval Air Station in Pensacola.

Bart Fraker with his wife, Betty, in Hawaii in the early 1970s on the aircraft carrier USS ***Coral Sea****. Fraker met Betty Stevens on a blind date when she was working with his sister Brenda as an operating room technician at Washington County Hospital.*

(Photos courtesy of Vicki Fraker Bard, sister of Bart Fraker)

John "Jack" Aubrey Hill II — Army — Cold War

John "Jack" Aubrey Hill II took his duffle bag and bowling ball with him when he left his Oak Hill Avenue home for the Army in February 1962, but had to leave his car and his best girl behind.

Hill was a former **Daily Mail** newspaper boy and a recognized athlete from the South Hagerstown High School Class of 1960, well known for his proficiency in golf, softball and baseball.

After one year at Frostburg State Teachers College he enlisted, and was sent to Fort Gordon, Georgia, for basic training, and later sent to Fort Meade and Edgewood Arsenal, Maryland, for specialized training as a radar operator. He used his skills while on active duty during the Cuban Missile Crisis in October 1962.

During his time in the military, Hill won his battalion's golf championship, when he was stationed at Edgewood Arsenal. He married his sweetheart, the former Carol Jean Eisiminger of Paramount, who is shown with him, bundled up on the February day Hill went off to the Army. The couple married and went on to have six children.

(Photographs courtesy of Carolyn Hill, mother of John "Jack" Aubrey Hill II)

Gilbert Ware — Army — Cold War

Gilbert Ware left his North Potomac Street home to attend Morgan State University and, upon graduation, was commissioned in the Army as a 2nd Lieutenant. He served in uniform until 1959 as an infantry company executive officer and a military police company executive officer and Provost Marshall.

Ware served at Forts Benning and Gordon, in Georgia, Fort Dix, New Jersey, and in the Bavarian town of Regensburg, Germany. His most interesting experience was serving as executive officer for a military police company on the Czech border during the Cold War.

But his most memorable experience was "living free of racism on military posts while submerged in it when off post." Ware said his time in the military "fueled the conviction that genuine racial equality could, should, and in meaningful measure, would be promoted, even appreciably achieved by blacks, whites and others — together."

(Photograph and memorabilia courtesy of Gilbert Ware)

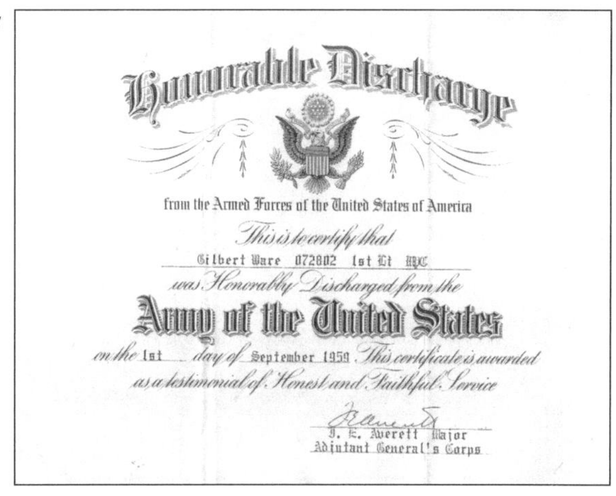

Honorable Discharge

from the Armed Forces of the United States of America

This is to certify that

Gilbert Ware 072802 1st Lt MPC

was Honorably Discharged from the

Army of the United States

on the 1st day of September 1959. This certificate is awarded as a testimonial of Honest and Faithful Service

J. E. Averett Major
Adjutant General's Corps

Following his honorable discharge, Ware earned a master's degree in 1961 and a Ph.D. in 1962 from Princeton University. He began his academic career at Drexel University in Philadelphia, advancing from assistant professor of political science in 1970, to professor in 1983, and professor emeritus in 1999. He also served as a research staff and assistant director, Federal Programs Division, U.S. Commission on Civil Rights, and as a program executive in the Maryland Governor's Office. He has also served on the senior research staff of The Urban Institute.

He is the author of **William Hastie: Grace Under Pressure** (Oxford University Press, 1985), **From the Black Bar: Voices for Equal Justice** (G.P. Putnam's Sons Inc., 1976) and numerous articles for professional and popular audiences.

Donald M. Ruth— Air Force — Cold War

Cpl. Ruth Is Awarded Honor

Claims Music Scholarship To Texas Christian University.

Corporal Donald M. Ruth, 17 East Irvin Avenue, has been awarded a special music scholarship to Texas Christian University in Fort Worth, Texas.

The scholarship also includes two advanced music classes each weekend at Southern Methodist University in Dallas, Texas.

CPL. DONALD RUTH

Cpl. Ruth is stationed with the 5485th Air Force Band at Carswell Air Force Base of the Strategic Air Command in Fort Worth. He is a trombonist in the concert and marching band at the base and also pianist and arranger in the dance orchestra. He is able to attend these classes during special off-duty hours.

"Don Ruth and the Carswell Air Base Dance Orchestra" are now appearing on a Southwest radio and television show originating from Dallas two Sunday nights monthly. Don is also writing several popular ballads which may be published at some future date.

In February of 1949, the young musician was winner in the Horace Heidt contest held in this city. Before entering the Air Force last January, he was assistant organist of the Church of the Brethren and also organist at the First Brethren Church for several months. He made many other musical appearances in this area.

At the present time, Cpl. Ruth is spending a holiday leave with his parents here.

Donald M. Ruth of Hagerstown, father of Brian D. Ruth, was a church organist before he joined the Air Force and found himself playing music to a different audience.

Stationed with the Strategic Air Command at Carswell Air Force Base in Fort Worth, Texas, Ruth performed with the 548th Air Force Marching Band, where he played the keyboard and the trombone. The article at right appeared in ***The Daily Mail*** *when he was on leave, visiting his East Irvin Avenue home in 1952.*

Music composed by Donald Ruth while a member of the Carswell Air Force Base Band. "Don Ruth and the Carswell Air Base Dance Band Orchestra" was broadcast on radio and television originating from Dallas, two Sunday nights monthly. Besides playing the piano and arranging music, Ruth also wrote popular ballads of his own.

Brian D. Ruth— Army — Cold War

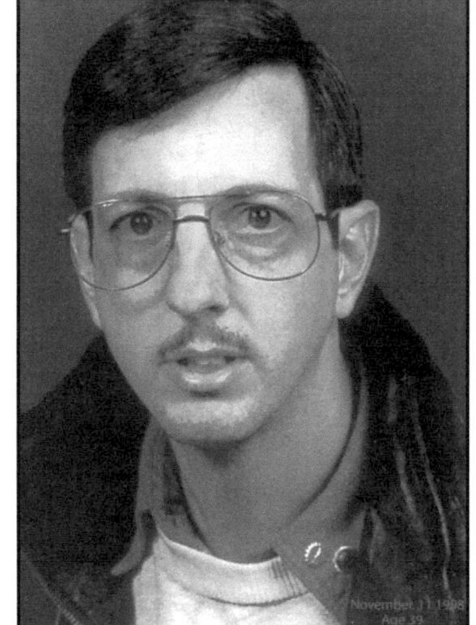

Brian D. Ruth of Hagerstown enlisted in the Army in 1987 just before the official end of the Cold War "because it was a family tradition."

During his 10-year military career, Brian Ruth, a specialist 4th class, served as a helicopter mechanic, tool room clerk and cook. He served stateside and on three other continents — Europe, Asia and Africa. Some of his time was spent in the field, participating in military exercises.

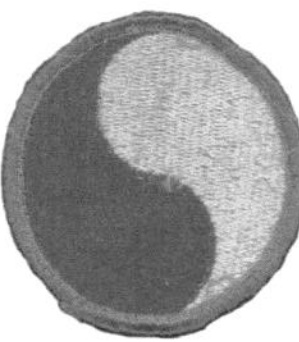

Patches in Ruth's collection include: 24th Infantry Division, 29th Infantry Division, 3rd Infantry Division and 2nd Infantry Division.

Brian Ruth and his father, Donald (right), who served as member of Air Force bands, shared an interest in music.
(Photos and memorabilia courtesy of Brian D. Ruth)

Knode Brothers — Four Brothers — Four Services — Cold War

During the Cold War era, which also encompassed United States involvement in Vietnam, four Williamsport brothers served in each branch of the armed forces during the 1960s. They were the sons of David Harry Knode and Amy Mentzer Knode.

In this photograph taken at the Wilmyer Studio in 1964, the brothers stand at attention (left to right): David H. Knode, a seaman in the Navy; Gary L. Knode, a corporal in the Marine Corps; Thomas M. Knode, an airman 1st class in the Air Force, and Harry E. Knode, a sergeant in the Army.

With his three older brothers in three different branches of the service, David, the youngest, decided to enter the Navy so each branch would be represented, according to Thomas Knode.

The Navy assigned David Knode to the aircraft carrier USS *Coral Sea*. There he ran utility boats for launches when the ships went into ports for liberty in the South China Sea during the war in Vietnam. He credits his Navy service with teaching him to accept discipline and giving him self-respect and confidence.

Gary Knode saw duty with the Marine Corps at Parris Island, South Carolina; Camp Lejeune, North Carolina, and at Marine Corps schools in Quantico, Virginia. His most memorable experience was serving guard duty at the Guantanamo Bay base in Cuba during the Cuban Missile Crisis.

During his Air Force service, Thomas Knode learned discipline and greater "respect for my country, its leaders and my fellow man." He spent much of his service between 1960 and 1964 at Shaw Air Force Base in Sumter, South Carolina, but in 1961 he was dispatched to Tampa, Florida, and was on standby following the Bay of Pigs invasion of Cuba.

Harry Knode, the oldest of the four brothers, was stationed with the Army at Wildflecken, Germany, with the 50th Infantry, 3rd Armored Battalion, assigned to patrol the border between East and West Germany during the Cold War. He was promoted to sergeant after only 20 months of service and was discharged in 1967.

Thomas Knode often kidded his mother about using carbon paper to send the same letter to each of her sons when they were all in the service at the same time. "But she wouldn't do that." Instead, she faithfully sent packages of cookies and other treats to their duty stations as a reminder of home.

Their father never got to see his sons in uniform. David Harry Knode died in 1959.

(Photograph contributed by Mr. & Mrs. Thomas M. Knode)

Robert Harding Miles — Army — WWII, Korea, Vietnam, Cold War

Clear Spring native Robert Harding Miles enlisted in the Army in March 1939 at Fort Myer, Virginia, and thus began a 30-year military career with the 3rd Horse Cavalry. The son of the late James Gardner and Evalyn Lucretia Swope Miles of Clear Spring served with distinction in three wars: WWII, Korea and Vietnam. As a mounted military policeman, the corporal was a familiar sight astride his horse "Remount" at the Virginia post in 1940.

During WWII, he was responsible for the care of Gen. George S. Patton's horse.

Robert Miles had advanced to the rank of Chief Warrant Officer 2 when he saw action in Korea in 1952 and 1953. He had advanced to Chief Warrant Officer 4 by the time he was on the front lines again in Vietnam in 1968. He retired from the military on Aug. 31, 1969 at Fort Benning, Georgia.

Miles died on Aug. 25, 1998, and was buried in the Fort Benning Cemetery. He was a member of The Retired Officers' Association and the U.S. Cavalry Association until his death.

(Photographs courtesy of Louise K. Miles, widow of Robert Harding Miles)

Gary McDonald — Air Force, Navy — Cold War, Gulf War

At the start of his two-service career in the armed forces, Gary Lynn McDonald (left) gets a visit from his proud mother, Lorraine, in Biloxi, Mississippi, in the summer of 1970. McDonald joined the Air Force a year after graduating from South Hagerstown High School in 1969. After basic training at Lackland Air Force Base in San Antonio, Texas, he was in technical school in Biloxi learning to intercept and copy Morse code.

For the next six years he worked as a Morse code operator in Alaska and Turkey, including a two-week TDY [temporary duty] in Danang, Vietnam, that turned into six months. He left the Air Force in 1976 and took a four-year break before joining the Navy in 1980.

McDonald served in the Navy twice, from January 1980 to November 1980, and from March 1985 to January 1998. After basic training at the Great Lakes Naval Training Center in Illinois and operation specialist school in Virginia, he was based in Little Creek, Virginia, and served on the USS *Harlan County* in the North Atlantic until November.

Joining the Navy again in March 1985, he served for another 13 years in Philadelphia, Pennsylvania, and Norfolk and Little Creek, Virginia, aboard the USS *Saipan* and the USS *Wasp*. He participated in four Mediterranean cruises, three Caribbean cruises and two cruises in Persian Gulf area. An operation specialist, he worked with radar and guidance of the ships, which were called "Gator Freighters" and carried Marines and helicopters and Harrier jets. He retired from the Navy in 1998 and returned to Washington County in 2005.

He said his most memorable experience was visiting his ancestral homeland (Ireland) in 1980 and "seeing most of Europe, places I wouldn't have seen if I wasn't in the service."

(Photographs courtesy of Lorraine McDonald, mother of Gary Lynn McDonald)

William C. Wolfinger — Air Force / Air National Guard — Cold War

Master Sergeant William C. "Bill" Wolfinger with his ever-present video camera equipment in 1993 in Savannah, Georgia. Wolfinger, a Hagerstown native, served a total of 33 years in the Air Force, 27 of those with the 167th Airlift Wing of the West Virginia Air National Guard. Wolfinger had duty assignments in more than 40 countries on five continents.

View of a UH-1 Army helicopter dropping water in a sling loading operation to help contain blinding dust kicked up during the U.S. Army's road-building effort in Honduras in 1988. Wolfinger flew 54 missions out of Panama into Honduras, Nicaragua and El Salvador in the 1980s. Although he served in Bosnia and in many other parts of the world, it was his experiences in Central America that proved the most memorable.

Snapshot of Wolfinger in front of barracks at Homestead Air Force Base in Florida in 1983, where he participated in cross-country training missions in air evacuation. A buddy said, "Hey, Bill, you're always taking pictures. Let's take one of you!"

(Photographs courtesy of William C. Wolfinger)

Nation-building and humanitarian relief efforts assumed a greater role for the U.S. military during the Cold War era. Wolfinger photographed a young Honduran girl who had received cough medicine flown into the country on C-130 transport planes during the February 1988 "Med Red" Operation, conducted by the United States as part of a Central American Medical Relief effort.

In this November 1967 photograph, Wolfinger captured the image of fuel trailers, personnel tents and American-built F-5 fighter planes on the island of Crete following the April 21, 1967, coup by Greek army colonels, which aggravated troubled Greek-Turkish-Cypriot relations. At the time, such photographs were strictly prohibited by the Greek government.

As a combat cameraman, Wolfinger participated in military operations, thinly described as training missions, during the El Salvadoran-Honduran-Sandinista conflict, in which the United States was not technically involved. As the cameraman in this February 1988 photograph with Army engineers in Honduras, he was the only person in camp without a weapon, at a time when "we heard gunfire every night."

Wolfinger later participated in combat and combat support missions with the West Virginia Air National Guard's 167th Airlift Wing in Bosnia in 1996.

Excerpt from:

Arlington

Recorded by Trace Adkins
Composed by Jeremy Spillman/Dave Turnbull

I never thought that this is where I'd settle down,
I thought I'd die an old man back in my hometown,
They gave me this plot of land, me and some other men,
for a job well done,
there's a big white house sits on a hill just up the road,
the man inside he cried the day they brought me home,
they folded up a flag and told my mom and dad,
we're proud of your son

And I'm proud to be on this peaceful piece of property,
I'm on sacred ground and I'm in the best of company,
I'm thankful for those things I've done,
I can rest in peace, I'm one of the chosen ones,
I made it to Arlington.

Desert Shield-Desert Storm

1991-1992

Global War on Terrorism

2001-2007

Operation Iraqi Freedom (Contributed by Daniel L. Watson Jr.)

Curtis E. Shives — Navy — Cold War — Desert Storm

When Boonsboro native Curtis E. Shives enlisted in the Navy in 1979, he might not have guessed that his Navy service would span 20 years, take him to 15 countries and provide a wealth of experiences — from meeting fellow naval officer Prince Charles in 1981 in Norfolk, Virginia, to intercepting weapons and contraband off the coast of Bosnia in support of NATO, to serving in the communications link in Washington, D.C., for Coalition forces' action against Iraq in Operation Desert Storm.

*During his time in the Mediterranean when there were tensions in the Balkans, the crew's mission was to board suspicious vessels and intercept weapons. The USS **Bainbridge** was routinely positioned only five miles off the coast of Bosnia. Shives' captain would often reassuringly advise the crew over the ship's intercom at "Lights Out" ... "Sleep tight, you could be hit in 60 seconds."*

*In his combined service at sea on the USS **Mount Whitney**, the flagship of the Navy's 2nd Fleet and the guided missile cruiser USS **Bainbridge**, Shives traveled to Denmark, Germany, Greece, Cuba, Italy, Crete, the Netherlands, Norway, Spain, England, France and Puerto Rico. He even completed two rotations of land-based assignments on the Indian Ocean island of Diego Garcia, as well as assignments in Adak, Alaska, and on Guam.*

*Enameled pin Shives wore on the pocket of his Navy uniform indicating his service in support of ACLANT, the acronym for the Allied Command Atlantic — a NATO command responsible for the area from the North Pole to the Tropic of Cancer and from the east coast of North America to the west coast of Africa. In 1993, the USS **Bainbridge** helped enforce United Nations sanctions against the former Republic of Yugoslavia. In the Adriatic, the USS **Bainbridge** distinguished herself by setting the single ship record for ship boarding inspections, with 104 boardings without a single incident. By the time the mission ended in August, the ship had sailed more than 40,000 miles in 183 days.*

*Shives served aboard the USS **Bainbridge** (CGN-25), the fourth ship to bear the name, from 1992 to 1996. The USS **Bainbridge**, a nuclear-powered guided missile cruiser, weighed 9,100 tons. The ship was the smallest nuclear-powered surface warship commissioned by any navy. Shives served a total of 50 months on board the USS **Bainbridge** over his 20-year career. He was the last sailor to leave the ship when it was decommissioned in 1996, in Portsmouth, Virginia. The ship had been in active service since 1959.*

Aerial photograph of the island of Diego Garcia, in the Indian Ocean, used as a refueling and resupply base for the Navy's Pacific fleet. Sailors refer to the 37-mile long island, only 22 feet above sea level, as "Fantasy Island."

*Patch from the USS **Bainbridge**.*

*The USS **Bainbridge** participated in NATO exercises in which some of the ship's SM-2 extended-range surface to air missiles were fired. The heat and fire generated in the launch were so intense that once the exercises were over, the deck of the ship had to be repainted, Shives said.*

CERTIFICATE OF APPRECIATION

FOR SERVICE IN THE ARMED FORCES OF THE UNITED STATES

RADIOMAN FIRST CLASS PETTY OFFICER
(ENLISTED SURFACE WARFARE SPECIALIST)
CURTIS EUGENE SHIVES

I extend to you my personal thanks and the sincere appreciation of our nation for your honorable service. You helped to maintain the security of the United States of America with a devotion to duty that is in keeping with the proud tradition of our Armed Forces.

I honor your service and respect the commitment and loyalty you displayed over the years.

My best wishes to you for happiness and success in the future.

Bill Clinton

Commander in Chief

President Bill Clinton signed this certificate, presented to Shives upon his retirement from the Navy in 1979, after 20 years of service. He also received letters from Maryland Sen. Paul Sarbanes and Gov. Parris N. Glendening. One of the most valued achievements for this highly decorated Boonsboro native, however, is the Military Outstanding Volunteer Award, which was presented in recognition of the more than 300 hours of volunteer service he rendered each year to a variety of organizations that included Special Olympics, programs that provide service to senior citizens, benefit concerts and the United Way's annual Day of Caring.

"I didn't smoke. I didn't drink. And I didn't swear. Some of the guys accused me of giving the Navy a bad name," Shives said.

(Photographs and memorabilia courtesy of Curtis E. Shives)

Gary Hayes — Air Force
Cold War, Operation Provide Comfort, Operation Northern Watch

The possessiveness of a jet aircraft's maintenance crew comes through in Williamsport native Gary Hayes' identification of this November 1987 photograph as "my airplane, my pilot and my assistant." Hayes was describing this snapshot, taken in Las Vegas, Nevada, during a huge Red Flag Exercise. Hayes' name and that of his assistant, Larry Steigerwald, are stenciled near the distinctive bubble canopy of an F-16. Hayes said it was rare to have a photograph of all three components — the pilot and his two maintenance crew chiefs — all together at the same time. "That was my plane," said Hayes. "The pilot just rented it for a few hours."

Hayes, who spent most of his Air Force career working on aircraft on the ground, had the opportunity to take his first ride in an F-16 in Las Vegas with Capt. Greg "Sledge" Hammer in November 1984. The Air Force has a limited number of F-16s with two seats that are used primarily for training.

The F-16 multiple jet fighter aircraft was developed by General Dynamics and Lockheed Martin and introduced in 1978. This was the first fighter built to sustain 9g turns. G-forces refer to the forces of acceleration that pull on a pilot's body when the plane of motion is changed.

"We took off and did a maximum climb straight up and went over the Grand Canyon," said Hayes. They were flying through the Grand Canyon when, at one point, the pilot flipped the aircraft over and they flew down over a plateau, only 500 feet from the surface. "The pilot did acrobatics and a loop and we pulled 9.1 g's before coming back to base," Hayes said. On the return home, an indicator showed that the landing gear was not "down and locked" and that they were running out of fuel. Their difficulties constituted an IFE, otherwise known as an "In-Flight Emergency," so fire department equipment was on hand to receive them. "Because you never know what can happen," Hayes said. Happily, "we landed uneventfully."

While stationed near Bitburg, Germany, in 1983, Hayes and his team of aircraft mechanics worked on the massive C-130 Hercules cargo planes which have been the workhorses of American military forces around the world for more than 50 years. The versatile cavernous aircraft are used to transport everything from soldiers and paratroopers to the equipment and supplies necessary for a global military force.

During a later assignment in Germany, Hayes and a friend were among the throngs of spectators watching the air show at Ramstein Air Force Base on Aug. 28, 1988, when Italian Air Force jet planes crashed in midair. Hayes said they felt the heat of the fireball as it passed over the crowd and he pushed his companion to the ground. When Hayes tried to rouse the fallen German man who had been standing next to them, Hayes discovered that the man was dead. "When you looked at him, he looked fine, but a mailbox-sized piece of debris from one of the jets struck him, and he was killed instantly."

What is regarded as the world's worst air show disaster claimed the lives of 72 people. Another 346 individuals were severely injured. An estimated crowd of 300,000 spectators witnessed the calamity.

"The worst two weeks of my life," according to Hayes, were spent in a "glorified tent" in Incirlik, Turkey, in 1991. Hayes, who was detailed as a visiting instructor, did not have high priority for the limited assignment. "They gave me a cot in the corner of the tent," he said.

The training session was in support of Operation Provide Comfort I, one of the initiatives that began immediately after the Gulf War. Hayes participated in Operation Provide Comfort II and III as well as Operation Northern Watch — part of the U.S European Command Combined Task Force charged with enforcing the United Nations mandated no-fly Zone above the 36th parallel in Iraq. The multi-national effort was an attempt to protect Iraqi Kurds from Saddam Hussein.

According to globalsecurity.org, from 1997 to March 1998, Operation Northern Watch rotated more than 40,000 troops in support of the mission and more than 36,000 sorties were flown. Operation Provide Comfort involved more than 42,000 sorties between 1991 and 1996.

Hayes is shown driving a "sand wagon" in Doha, Qatar, in 1993. Hayes was assisting the Navy and friendly forces in the desert kingdom as part of an exercise designed to improve flying skills of non-U.S. pilots and to encourage the sale of the Lockheed-produced F-16 fighter jets. The highly maneuverable fighter jets were known by pilots as "Vipers" because of their resemblance to starfighters on the popular television series ***Battlestar Gallactica****.*

On one of Hayes' overseas assignments to Bahrain in 1993, his team was staying in the capital, Manama, a 45-minute drive to the air base. On the long commute, "our biggest fear was running into camels" that roamed the desert landscape as they have for centuries. "They would look at you. You would look at them, and then you'd slow down," Hayes said.

Mobile barracks sprang out of the barren landscape near Doha, Qatar, where Hayes was detailed in 1993. The modular units were equipped with air-conditioners that provided a modicum of relief from the desert heat. The real treat, though, came from the water tanks atop the units, which supplied water for showers. Up on the rooftops, the water would be exposed to temperatures of 130 to 140 degrees. "You could turn on the cold water and scald yourself to death," Hayes said.

Desert sands posed a different kind of challenge to aircraft mechanics performing engine cleaning and maintenance on sophisticated F-16 jets in Doha, Qatar, in 1993.

Photo of an F-16 "Fighting Falcon" fighter jet loaded with AGM-88 HARM [high-speed anti-radiation missiles] as part of a "live fire" mission from Salt Lake City, Utah, where Hayes was a troop commander in 1997, to test new missile firing software. The purpose of the flight was to test new avionics equipment on board the jet and fire a few test rounds in the desert using the new software.

Hayes is presented with a Meritorious Service Medal at Spangdahlem Air Force Base, near Bitburg, Germany, in 1999, in recognition of his service with Operation Allied Force in Kosovo. This was the most memorable of Hayes' assignments, when he supported bombing missions over Yugoslavia from airfields in Albania and Italy during the Kosovo crisis. As part of the SEAD [Suppression of Enemy Air Defense] effort, F-16s would go in first and shut down all surface-to-air missile [SAM] sites. "They were always the first in and the last out," Hayes said.

Gary Hayes in his Air Force mess dress and his bride, Anna DeVere, a native of Ireland, at their Aug. 26, 1989, wedding at a castle in Ballina in the Republic of Ireland. Hayes said he "loved every minute" of his service during the Cold War. "It was a lot of work, but it was also a lot of fun."

(Photographs courtesy of Gary Hayes)

End of an Era

The fall of the Berlin Wall in November 1989 marked the beginning of the end of the prolonged standoff between the United States and the Soviet Union. The "official" end of the conflict was considered to be December 1991.

Certificates marking the end of the Cold War acknowledge the contributions of service members in the 46-year standoff between East and West superpowers. After 1991, U.S. military personnel would be involved in a series of conflicts around the globe.

The September 11, 2001, attacks on the United States would result in American troops in Afghanistan and a new round of U.S. fighting in Iraq.

(Certificate courtesy of Scott L. Port)

CERTIFICATE OF RECOGNITION

LANDON S. PORT

In recognition of your service during the period of the Cold War (2 September 1945 - 26 December 1991) in promoting peace and stability for this Nation, the people of this Nation are forever grateful.

William S. Cohen

SECRETARY OF DEFENSE

George F. McAllister Jr. — Army Reserve — Desert-Shield-Desert Storm, Operation Iraqi Freedom

Army Reservist George F. McAllister Jr. of Hagerstown has had the opportunity to serve his country in the troubled region of Kuwait and Iraq, not once, but twice — first in Operation Desert Shield-Desert Storm in 1991, and later in support of Operation Iraqi Freedom in 2003.

McAllister, an ammunition specialist, is shown in this 1991 photograph in the cab of 6,000-pound rough terrain variable reach forklift — heavy equipment used for loading containers of captured ammunition in a staging area in Saudi Arabia, on the border of Kuwait. Some of the captured ammunition was put into sea containers for transport while other confiscated ammunition was destroyed. Even though he was working in the desert region, McAllister is wearing a heavy camouflage jacket because it was cold in the desert region that winter of 1991.

McAllister is the driver of this fuel tanker, which was part of a military convoy delivering fuel to the International Airport in Baghdad as part of Operation Enduring Freedom in April 2003.

McAllister, having had two tours of duty to the region, is no longer in the Army Reserve. His son, Jesse Barrin, 20, a paratrooper with the 82nd Airborne, was sent to Iraq in June 2007 for a 15-month deployment.

Staff Sgt. McAllister found himself back in Iraq in support of Operation Iraqi Freedom in 2003, when he and another of his fellow reservists from the 309th Transportation Co., based in Greencastle, Pennsylvania, were attached to the 946th Transportation Company, based in Lewes, Delaware, for duty in Iraq.

McAllister, holding an M16, stands guard over his company's gear at a staging area in Kuwait en route to Iraq in April 2003. McAllister was a little taken aback that he would have been selected for the second detail to the region. "I had some misgivings and wondered why, at 42 years old, I was the going back over, but you deal with it the best you can," he said. When McAllister got the assignment, he had "no clue" how long the unit would be asked to serve. They were in Iraq for a year.

Oversized Christmas and New Year's greeting card presented to American servicemen at Camp Doha in Kuwait in December 2003 by Kuwaitis. The card was placed outside the camp's PX not long after the capture of former Iraqi leader Saddam Hussein on Dec. 15 of that year.

Iraq invaded Kuwait Aug. 2, 1990, precipitating Operation Desert Shield-Desert Storm, also known as the First Gulf War. American troops would once again occupy Iraqi territory as a result of Operation Iraqi Freedom, which began in 2003.

McAllister's mother, Vera, came across a photograph of a statue at the 4th Infantry Division's headquarters in Tikrit, Iraq, depicting an American soldier mourning the loss of a comrade. The form of a young Iraqi girl, comforting the soldier, stands to the side. The bronze statue, created by Iraqi sculptor Kalat, was made from two original statues of Iraqi leader Saddam Hussein that had adorned the gates to one of his many palaces. The statues were removed with explosives in 2004 and melted down to provide material for the new sculpture. The statue's final home will be the 4th Infantry Division Museum at Fort Hood, Texas.

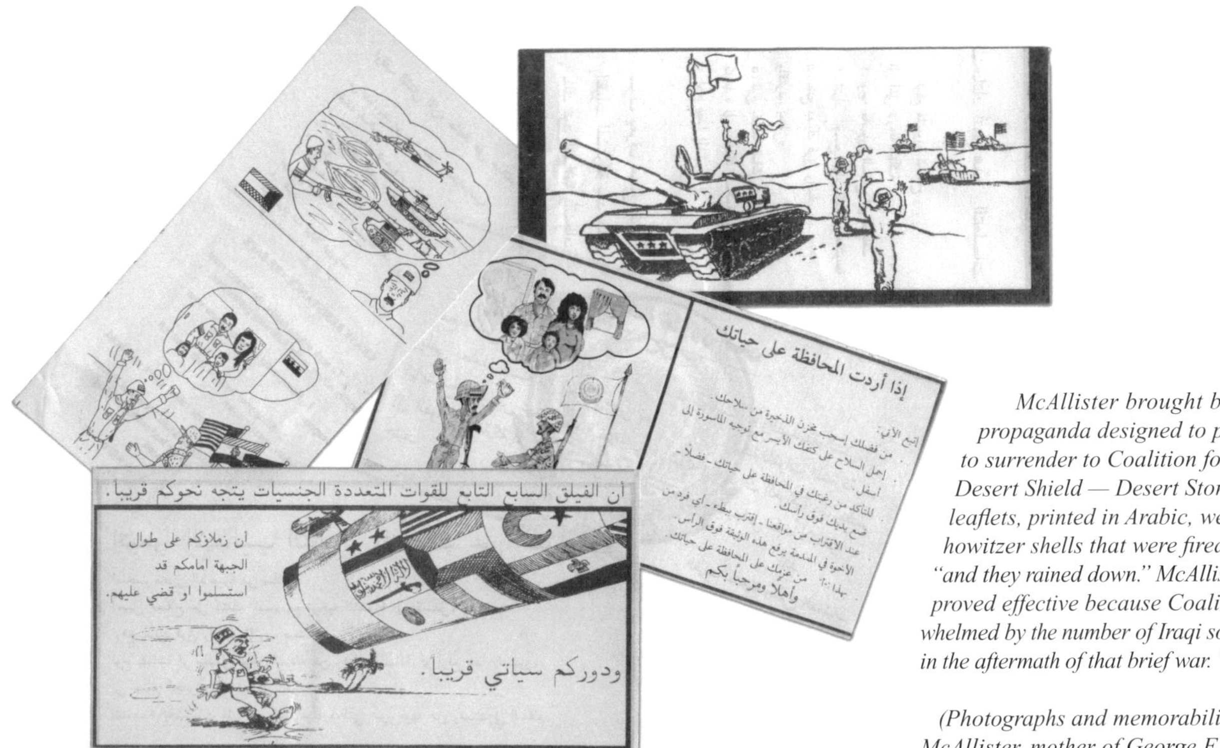

McAllister brought back copies of U.S. propaganda designed to persuade Iraqi troops to surrender to Coalition forces during Operation Desert Shield — Desert Storm in 1991. The leaflets, printed in Arabic, were placed in 155 mm howitzer shells that were fired over enemy lines "and they rained down." McAllister said the material proved effective because Coalition forces were overwhelmed by the number of Iraqi soldiers who surrendered in the aftermath of that brief war. "It caught us off guard."

(Photographs and memorabilia courtesy of Vera McAllister, mother of George F. McAllister Jr.)

Glenn S. Bolland — Army — Global War on Terrorism

Sgt. Glenn Bolland (center) of Boonsboro served in Iraq between 2003 and 2005 as a medic with the 173rd Airborne Brigade. He participated in both Operation Iraqi Freedom and Operation Enduring Freedom in Afghanistan. His service also has taken him to Italy, Kosovo, Hungary, Tunisia, Germany and Poland.

Members of the 173rd Airborne Brigade prepare to deploy to Iraq from Vicenza, Italy, during the start of Operation Iraqi Freedom on March 26, 2003. The 173rd Airborne Brigade, known as the "Red Devils," was based in Vicenza at the time but has since been reassigned to Fort Bragg, North Carolina.

Paratroopers get a final check before they board their aircraft prior to the jump over Iraq. This was the 173rd Airborne's first combat jump since 1967, during the Vietnam War, and the military's largest combat airborne operation since WWII. During the assault, 447 "Red Devils" jumped into Northern Iraq. Glenn said that jump was his most memorable experience in the service.

Glenn Bolland (left) in Iraq with two other members of the 173rd Airborne Brigade.

Glenn Bolland (center) is flanked by Iraqi medical personnel while coordinating the support and supply of medical services to an Iraqi hospital south of Kirkuk.

Sgt. Glenn Bolland, 3rd Platoon medic, Company B, 1st Battalion, 508th Infantry Airborne, served in Paktika Province in Afghanistan in 2006 as part of Operation Enduring Freedom. Bolland and other medics were recognized for saving the lives of Afghan civilians as well as Coalition soldiers. "It's our job to save lives whether they are American or Afghan," Bolland said. "Medics have an appreciation for the personal rewards of our work. It's fulfilling and then some. It's an empowering experience to save someone's life."

St. Michael medal carried by Glenn Bolland has on the reverse the insignia of the 1st Battlion, 508th Airborne Infantry ("Fury from the Sky"), based in Vicenza, Italy. Saint Michael is considered the patron saint of paratroopers.

Pat Bolland, mother of Sgt. Glenn Bolland, treasures a shadow box her son made for her in 2003 containing photographs and memorabilia of his service in the Army. Among the items included are a piece of a parachute Glenn used in his jump into Iraq; photos of paratroopers before, during and after their flight to Iraq; patch of the 173rd Airborne Brigade; patch of the 1st Battalion, 508th Parachute Infantry Regiment with the slogan "Fury From the Sky"; and patch depicting the American flag flying backwards. American soldiers would wear the backwards flag patch on their right shoulder — a symbol of soldiers who marched into battle carrying a flag so forcefully and bravely that the flag billowed out behind them. On the arm of American soldiers, the flag faces backward as if being carried into battle, blowing behind them. Pat Bolland said the shadow box was a big hit when it was displayed during a South Washington County Military Support Group holiday card fundraiser. She said it stirred up quite a bit of conversation among both young boys and veterans.

Fred Bolland pins a Parachutist Badge, known as "Jump Wings," on his son, Glenn Bolland, when Glenn graduated from jump school in 2001. The ceremony had special meaning for the family. Only a paratrooper can pin another paratrooper, and Fred Bolland was a paratrooper with the 82nd Airborne Division in the 1960s.

Jen Bolland, Glenn's wife, celebrates with him after his graduation from jump school in 2001.

(Photos and memorabilia courtesy of Pat and Frederick Bolland Jr., parents of Glenn S. Bolland)

Michael David Shobe — Army
Operation Enduring Freedom, Afghanistan, Kosovo

Army Sergeant Michael David Shobe graduated from St. James School in 1999 and attended the University of Maryland before entering the military. He graduated from basic training at Fort Jackson, South Carolina — something Shobe had in common with both his parents.

His late father, Joseph W. Shobe of Hagerstown, was an engineer at Fort Riley, Kansas, and served in Korea in the 1960s. His mother, Carol Easterday, served as a clerk-typist at Fort Lee, Virginia, in the 1970s. They are shown in the photos below.

At Fort Eustis, Virginia, Shobe received additional training as an Apache armament/avionics/electronics specialist. Shobe was stationed at Storck Barracks, Illesheim, Germany, as part of armament platoon with the 2nd Squadron of the 6th U.S. Cavalry, 11th Aviation Regiment. He completed a deployment to Afghanistan as part of Operation Enduring Freedom VI in 2006 and is currently serving in Kosovo with KFOR, the NATO-led Balkan peacekeeping force.

Shobe is part of the aircraft (AH-64D Apache helicopter) maintenance team. He makes certain that the complex weapons and electrical systems on board the helicopters are properly maintained and repaired — a responsibility that includes maintaining the avionics, flight controls, sensors, sighting systems, electronics and weapons systems.

(Photograph contributed by Mary Shobe, Michael David Shobe's grandmother)

Joseph W. Shobe

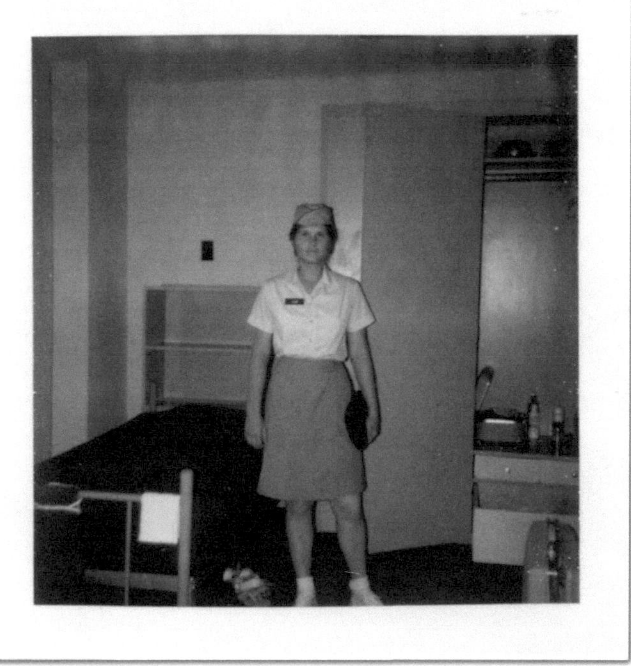

Carol Easterday

Shane M. Olden — Marine Corps — Operation Iraqi Freedom

Clear Spring High School track star Shane Olden left home to become a Marine in 2003. Months later he would find himself assigned to a small craft unit patrolling the Euphrates River in Iraq — the ancient legendary tributary he had only read about in his high school history classes.

In his four-year military career, he acquired the disciplined demeanor of a United States Marine, saw his training tested under fire and lost a comrade in battle — all before the age of 19.

Olden would go on to aid fellow citizens in hurricane-ravaged Mississippi and Louisiana in the wake of the most devastating natural disaster to strike the continental United States, and the first in which active duty servicemembers were called in to provide relief. While assigned to a ship in the Mediterranean in the summer of 2006, he would rescue American citizens from the shores of Lebanon. They were fleeing the exchange of missiles and killing fire of the Israel-Lebanon Conflict.

In an e-mail sent to The Herald-Mail Co. on Jan. 31, 2007, Olden wrote: "The Marine Corps affected me greatly both good and bad." His most memorable moment, according to Olden, was "when I was coming back from Iraq and I stepped off the plane, and as I was walking through the airport terminal in Bangor, Maine, I had older veterans greeting me, thanking me and shaking my hand for a job well done."

The older vets extended the welcome that only those who have been in combat can truly extend to another with shared experience — combat in a very different war, perhaps, but still the same deprivation and loss.

For much of his time in Iraq, Olden manned a SURC [small unit ravine craft], patrolling the Euphrates River. The highly maneuverable small craft, designed for speed and versatility, is a critical component to securing the waterways around the massive Haditha Dam. The mostly routine patrols on both the north and south sides of the dam were essential in the protection of the important hydroelectric facility and the threat of devastating flooding that would occur should the dam be damaged.

On New Year's Day 2005, Olden's eight-man team was scrambled after reports of small arms fire on the banks of the Euphrates River. The Marines raced to their boat to assist in the response. On land, patrolling the shore, Lance Cpl. Brian Parrello of West Milford, New Jersey, was badly wounded by an IED [improvised explosive device]. Despite the efforts of corpsmen on the ground, a speedy evacuation to a field hospital and then a helicopter transfer, the young Marine, the same age as Olden, died en route to a full-fledged medical facility. Four other Marines, including the unit's captain, were injured in the attack.

In a written account Olden prepared after the attack, he described the sequence of events. "The boats were beached a couple hundred meters north of the objective. Once all the GCE [ground combat element] was inserted and on land, all the Marines got on line to sweep the area heading south. The boats remained on the scene. Heading south Brian was to the left of me. Everything was going fine until we received contact on the ground. I heard an explosion and enemy gunfire, after that I heard screaming and yelling."

In the midst of the response, Olden wrote: "What hurt me the most was seeing Brian on the ground ... stripped of his flak jacket, kevlar and blouse so that doc could provide aid for him."

Olden was among those who helped carry his fallen comrade from the shore to the boat. Despite the speedy evacuation, Parrello died of internal injuries in the helicopter on his way to a military hospital. In an irony of warfare, it was supposed to have been Parrello's day off.

Photographic tribute to Olden's comrade-in-arms, Lance Cpl. Brian Parrello, 19, of West Milford, New Jersey, who was killed in action while on patrol in on Jan. 1, 2005, in Iraq. In an e-mail to Parrello's mother, Olden wrote: "Brian is an outstanding Marine and as an individual. He will be greatly missed by fourth platoon as well as small craft [company] and will be remembered in our hearts and minds. The Parrellos are in my thoughts and prayers ... God Bless, take care, and ***Semper Fi****," Olden wrote.*

"You see him one time and the next time, you don't see him," said Olden, who will never forget the events of that day.

Olden's more recent assignments included Hurricane Katrina relief in New Orleans in September 2005. He was among the first active duty military personnel in the history of the U.S. military to ever be called in to assist with a domestic natural disaster. Olden was assigned to a National Guard facility in Picayune, Mississippi. He remembers riding in a seven-ton MTVR [medium tactical vehicle replacement] through the storm-ravaged Mississippi Delta towns and having other vehicles on the road pull over and motorists and townspeople waving and cheering. "It was like being a celebrity," Olden said. During the two-week assignment, the Marines saw the devastation wrought by Mother Nature. Members of his unit were also the ones to make the grim discovery of the bodies of the 34 nursing home residents who drowned in St. Bernard Parish.

Weeks later, Olden's unit was also on a Navy supply ship that passed through Hurricane Rita in the Gulf of Mexico. The USS *Iwo Jima* navigated fierce winds and 20-foot swells in its effort to provide hurricane relief for the victims of the previous storm. "I didn't come out of my bed for two days," said Olden. Because his battalion went right through the eye of the hurricane, its members became known as "the storm chasers."

In July 2006, Olden served on board the USS *Nashville,* which was called in to evacuate American citizens displaced by the Israel-Lebanon Conflict. On board ship with no insight as to what was happening or where they were heading, the Marines tuned in to CNN and learned they were to be part of evacuation efforts off the coast of Lebanon. "If it wasn't for CNN, we wouldn't have known what we were going to be doing," Olden said.

"From the shores of Tripoli," a reference to Marine activity in Lebanon in the 1800s in the Marine Hymn, is a reminder of past military involvement in the Middle East. Olden and his fellow Marines were well aware that they were the first Marines to return to Lebanon since Marines pulled out years earlier. "My unit was there 20 years ago," he said.

"The good thing about the Marine Corps is that it made me a better person, it made me appreciate things around me more and taught me excellent leadership skills," Olden said. "It has been a stressful experience, but it is going to pay off. I definitely learned a lot."

Olden is photographed with a medium machine gun (M240G) which was mounted on his small craft. The 30-pound weapon can be shoulder-fired and is accurate up to 1,800 meters, Olden said. Given the sandy desert environment, "maintenance was a challenge."

Olden manned a SURC [small unit ravine craft], patrolling the Euphrates River, much of his time in Iraq. His small craft company patrolled as far north as Haditha Dam and as far south as Iskandariyah. It also served as a mobile unit to be employed on the Euphrates River anywhere at anytime. The highly-maneuverable small craft, not unlike the swift boats used in the dangerous Vietnamese waterways during the Vietnam War, are designed for speed and versatility. The small craft units are a critical component to securing the waterways around the Haditha Dam. The swift craft are small enough to get in close to shore and even have the capability of running directly onto the 10- to 12-foot banks if necessary. The daily and nightly patrols to the north and south of the dam were designed to keep intruders at bay. "We chased away a lot of fishermen who weren't too happy about being kept from their traditional fishing spots," Olden said.

Shane Olden's seven months with a small craft company in Iraq overlapped with Operation Phantom Fury [Fallujah]. The battle, later renamed al-Fajr (Arabic for dawn) by the Department of Defense, began on Nov. 8, 2004. An estimated 10,000 to 15,000 Americans were part of the operation, also known as the Second Battle of Fallujah. The assault on the city of approximately 300,000 inhabitants was an attempt to wrest control of the city from insurgents ahead of the Iraqi national elections in January 2005. Officials estimated that 2,000 to 3,000 hard-core insurgents were entrenched in the city at the time the assault began.

After two days of intense fighting, U.S. military officials announced they controlled 70 percent of the city. Newly captured sites included the mayor's office, several mosques, a commercial center and other objectives. During the first stage of the assault, a Marine unit and other troops seized two strategic bridges and a hospital situated on a peninsula formed by the Euphrates River leading to an area that was a possible fallback zone for insurgents driven out of central Fallujah.

The military later revealed that Jordanian Abu Musab al-Zarqawi, the Al Qaeda leader of the brutal insurgent faction in Fallujah, was believed to have fled the city in advance of the assault. Zarqawi was eventually killed in an air strike in Baghdad in June 2006.

Olden, shown here with a satellite telephone, was able to "phone home" as often as once a week during his time in Iraq, with the exception of periods of combat when satellite phone use was restricted.

During the Second Battle of Fallujah, however, his parents, Wanda and Donald Olden of Hagerstown, did not hear from their son for more than three weeks. They found the silence unnerving as they carefully followed media coverage of the war. Olden was able to resume the calls once the intense fighting had subsided.

Physical training is an important part of Marine Corps routine wherever they may be. The desert is no exception. This photo (below) shows members of Olden's unit on an evening run across dunes in Iraq in 2004.

Keeping their small craft in working order was an important part of the unit's responsibility. Here, Olden performs routine maintenance on the small craft's engine.

(Photographs contributed by Wanda Olden, Shane Olden's mother)

Olden's home away from home was this sand-bagged, mud-bricked compound known as "the Villa," south of the Haditha Dam, where the small craft company was housed. The housing was made of stone and mud, which Olden said made the rooms surprisingly cool, and was fortified with protective sandbags. Some enterprising Marines were able to install a satellite TV so they could tune in to the 2004 Super Bowl. As for the food, Olden reported that "the food was great depending upon where you were," but the field rations, which Olden likened to "opening up a can of dog food and putting it on your plate," got old, real fast.

Olden stands in front of the Haditha Dam, which provides hydro-electric power for a significant portion of Iraq. The dam is deemed to be an attractive target for insurgents and others, so security on the river side of the dam and the resulting lake behind it are a priority. Olden spent much of his seven months in Iraq patrolling the river banks and lake shores 300 meters north and south of the dam, in what was known as "the Safe Zone."

John D. Sales — Army Reserve — Operation Iraqi Freedom

John D. Sales joined the Army Reserve in February 2000 and was deployed to Iraq three years later. He served there from February 2003 to March 2004 as an 89B Ammo Specialist with the 811th Ordnance Company. He expected to return to Iraq in June 2006, but instead was sent to Kuwait with the 811th, in charge of a camp that loads ammunition for convoys and destroys captured ammunition. While participating in Operation Iraqi Freedom, he met Gen. David H. Petraeus and received an award from him for excellence in combat. Petraeus became the commanding general of the Multi-National Force in Iraq in February 2007.

John D. Sales is deployed to Iraq in February 2003.

Sales received a welcome from USO volunteers while home for a break.

Sales and his girlfriend, Sgt. Rebecca K. Hamrick, in Iraq in February 2003. Both 89B Ammo Specialists with the 811th Ordnance Company, they met in Iraq when Sales "yelled at her for drinking his soda." The two are now serving in Kuwait, but they split up after being assigned to different camps.

Rebecca Hamrick with Kurdish children in the city of Dahook in northern Iraq in October 2003.

Sales' buddy and best friend, Sgt. Hedy Ridore of Silver Spring, is also an 89B Ammo Specialist with the 811th Ordnance Company. He and Sales served together in Iraq and are in the same company in Kuwait.

(Photos courtesy of Douglas L. Sales, father of John D. Sales)

Michael Kamas — Navy — Global War on Terrorism

Lt. Michael Kamas (center) on board a P-3 Orion military patrol aircraft, returns from a deployment in Europe on Feb. 5, 2003. A graduate of Saint Maria Goretti High School, Kamas is flanked by Lt. Mark Domenico (left), a Martinsburg High School graduate, and Lt. Bryan Hager (right) of Texas.

The men were returning from a six-month deployment with Patrol Squadron Sixteen, based out of Naval Air Station Jacksonville, Florida. The VP-16 "War Eagles" were deployed from August 2002 to February 2003 in support of the Global War on Terrorism in the European Command. All three aviators held flying billets on combat aircrews. Hager and Kamas would serve another deployment in 2004, supporting Operation Enduring Freedom and Operation Iraqi Freedom. The P-3 Orion is a Maritime Patrol Aircraft for the Navy which is equipped to support land and naval forces in the areas of intelligence, surveillance and reconnaissance.

Domenico and Kamas later served as instructor naval flight officers. Hager became an instructor pilot at the P-3 Orion Fleet Replacement Squadron aboard NAS Jacksonville.

Kamas, who joined the Navy on May 12, 2000, when he was 22, served in Sicily, Crete and South America as part of Operation Enduring Freedom, Operation Active Endeavor and the Global War on Terrorism. He said his most memorable experience is "the pride I took in performing a challenging mission against an unseen enemy. I learned how to interact with a diverse, motivated group of Americans who were among the most selfless and modest people I have ever met."

(Photo courtesy of Michael Kamas)

Warren V. Middlekauff Jr. — Army Reserve — Bosnia / Air National Guard — Kuwait

Warren V. Middlekauff Jr. was photographed in combat gear during active duty in Bosnia in 2001. Middlekauff, of Hagerstown, joined the Army Reserve in 1980 and was assigned to the 357th Transportation Company in Greencastle, Pennsylvania. He completed his basic training at Fort Leonard Wood, Missouri.

In 1986, he served with the 109th Quartermaster Co., Fort Lee, Virginia, and from 1992 to 1998 was assigned to the 515th Engineer Battalion at Fort Lee, to help lay pipeline and unload ships in the Gulf.

(Photographs courtesy of Warren Middlekauff's father, Warren V. Middlekauff Sr.)

In 1998, Middlekauff joined the Air National Guard and served in Kuwait in 2006 with "B" Co., 2-224th AVN Battalion, as a crew chief and gunner on a Black Hawk helicopter. Part of his assignment was performing search and rescue missions with the Marines.

U-60 Black Hawk helicopters are the Army's front-line utility helicopter used for air assault, air cavalry and aerial evacuations. They were first deployed in 1978.

Michael Lee Mardres — Army — Operation Iraqi Freedom

Michael Lee Mardres of Smithsburg catches up on sleep after pulling a 12-hour nighttime guard shift at the airport at Balad Air Base, 50 miles north of Bagdhad, Iraq, in June 2003. A 2002 graduate of Smithsburg High School, Mardres joined the Army in June of that year and after basic training was based at Fort Sill, Oklahoma.

But three days after President George W. Bush declared Operation Iraqi Freedom on March 20, 2003, Mardres was on his way to Iraq. Deployed with the 226th Maintenance Company under 3rd Corps, his job was fixing computers that ran artillery. He was discharged on April 20, 2004, as a private 1st class. Of his experience in the war, he said, "it was all a huge reality check."

Iraqi children wave at American soldiers as a convoy passes. Mardres said his most memorable experience in Iraq was "seeing a little Iraqi boy about 5 or 6 years old holding a tiny American flag as we went over the border from Kuwait into Iraq."

Soldiers guard a pass between Kuwait and Iraq. "Any photo showing green grass or vegetation was in Iraq. There's no green in Kuwait," Mardres said.

(Photos courtesy of Michael Lee Mardres)

Hurlbrink Siblings — Army — Operation Iraqi Freedom
Kevin Hurlbrink & Kelly Hurlbrink-Zamora

Kevin Hurlbrink and Kelly Hurlbrink-Zamora graduated from Boonsboro High School — Kevin in 1999 and Kelly in 2001. Both joined the Army and became members of the 82nd Airborne Division, based at Fort Bragg, North Carolina.

This photograph was taken in Kuwait in September 2003 before the final push into Iraq as part of Operation Iraqi Freedom. The siblings were not necessarily supposed to be assigned to the same base at the same time — the Army tries not to place family members in the same setting, in the event of a calamity — but for eight-and-a-half months, the brother and sister served together at Ar Ramadi, in the Al Anbar province, 100 miles west of Baghdad. Ar Ramadi is the central headquarters for the 82nd Airborne, the commanding general and his supporting staff, and one of the most dangerous cities in Iraq.

Among the items Kelly took with her when she was deployed to Kuwait and then Iraq were snapshots of her family members and pets, a ring given to her by her mother "that I never took off," rosary beads, a Miraculous Medal, a St. Michael's Medal and prayer cards. She came back with Iraqi money, a small handmade bag purchased from a roadside stand, and a souvenir mug that said "All I see is Iraq in my rearview mirror."

Upon her return to the United States, she later helped provide humanitarian support for Hurricane Katrina victims. As a result of her experiences, Kelly said, "I appreciate life a lot more. And it has definitely made me grow up. It's amazing all the things we take for granted. I thank the Army for all the life experience it has given me, and I am particularly appreciative of all the men and women who risk their lives every day for our freedom."

(Photograph taken by Sgt. Michael Carden, courtesy of Kelly Hurlbrink-Zamora)

Among the most vulnerable places for American troops to be are in the convoys that routinely transport soldiers and materiel from one location to another and patrol roads in Iraq. IEDs [improvised explosive devices] and insurgent ambushes are daily hazards for men and women serving in uniform in Iraq. Kevin looks over his shoulder into the interior of a Humvee in this 2004 photo.

"Being able to share my deployment with my sister" was the most memorable aspect of his service overseas, according to Kevin. "Having her there for me, made things bearable." He, too, believes that his experience in the military, and particularly in that part of the world, "made me appreciate what I have."

The emblem of the famed 82nd Airborne Division is worn by members of the largest parachute force in the Free World. Every soldier in the "All American Division" — from cook to computer operator — is jump-qualified and trained to deploy anywhere, anytime. In addition to its fighting force, virtually every piece of equipment needed by the division can be dropped by parachute into battle.

No one was more surprised than Lynn Jones when her son, Kevin, was awarded his airborne wings. She recalls that on a Boonsboro Elementary School field trip to Antietam Battlefield years ago, young Kevin refused to go up into the observation tower on the battlefield because he was afraid of heights. Both Kevin and Kelly, courtesy of the 82nd Airborne training, are now experienced jumpers.

Kelly Hurlbrink-Zamora in an observation tower at Ar Ramadi, Iraq.

Kelly, armed to the teeth with an M4A1 Carbine, the newest version of the M16, stands watch in an observation tower at Ar Ramadi in 2004. A month later, the tower, which had been turned over to the Marines, was overrun and 12 Marines were killed. Kelly knew several of the Marines who died in the same post where she had served as an observer only weeks before.

Kelly is no longer on active duty, but she will soon return to Iraq in her role as a civilian contractor. Kelly is married to fellow 82nd Airborne paratrooper Sgt. David Zamora, of Victorville, California. Although they were deployed in Iraq at the same time, they didn't start dating until they met again at a mutual friend's welcome home party. They were married on June 17, 2006. Sgt. Zamora, a psychological operations specialist with the 4th PsyOp Group, is currently serving in Kenya.

View from observation tower.

In 82nd Airborne tradition, only another former or present member of the 82nd Airborne is allowed to present paratrooper wings to a newly jump-certified soldier. Here Kevin Hurlbrink does the honors for his sister, Kelly, during a ceremony at Fort Benning, Georgia, in March 2003.

(Photographs courtesy of Lynn Jones, mother of Kevin Hurlbrink and Kelly Hurlbrink-Zamora)

Lynn Jones knows what it is like to have a child in the military serving in Iraq. In fact, she knows what it is like to have two children serving in uniform in Iraq at the same time.

The Keedysville mother of Kevin Hurlbrink and Kelly Hurlbrink-Zamora learned to live "with the fear of a car in your driveway," a reference to the Army's policy of sending officers to give personal notification in the event of a combat soldier's serious injury or death. "But every day, you live with that," said Jones. Her only comfort when her son and daughter were in harm's way in Iraq during Operation Iraqi Freedom was knowing "they were with each other." She is also grateful for the support of family and members of the South Washington County Military Support Group — a group she helped found.

The group is made up of 12 families — all of whom have, or have had children serving in uniform. It supports American servicemembers by organizing holiday card drives and distributing care packages. They recruit volunteers to mail cards, personal care items, batteries and phone cards to servicemembers overseas. In 2006, the group sent 58,905 holiday cards and two packages each to 115 servicemen and servicewomen serving in Iraq and Afghanistan. This is something she does to help support the sons and daughters of other mothers who are serving their country far from home.

Jones is relieved to have both children stateside again, although Kevin continues to serve as a member of the Air Guard, based in Martinsburg, West Virginia, and Kelly will soon be on her way back to Iraq. "I can't tell you how proud I am having raised such patriotic kids. They know the risks involved. Some say young people just join the service because of the money and college benefits, but that's not the only reason. These kids are the warriors of the 21st century defending our freedoms. I am extra proud of my children and everyone else's children who are serving our country," Jones said.

Ricky A. Pike — Army National Guard — Operation Iraqi Freedom

When Williamsport native Sgt. Ricky A. Pike decided to join the National Guard in 1998, he might not have imagined that he would spend most of his overseas service in Kuwait and Iraq, participating in the U.S. invasion of Iraq in 2003, and serving again in a training and liaison capacity with the newly configured Iraqi army, as a U.S. advisor to an Iraqi Special Forces Support Battalion.

In March 2006, Pike found himself on patrol in an M1114 Up-Armored Humvee, manning a M240 B machine gun, in the "Green Zone" in Baghdad. "Humvee" is an abbreviation for High Mobility Multipurpose Vehicle.

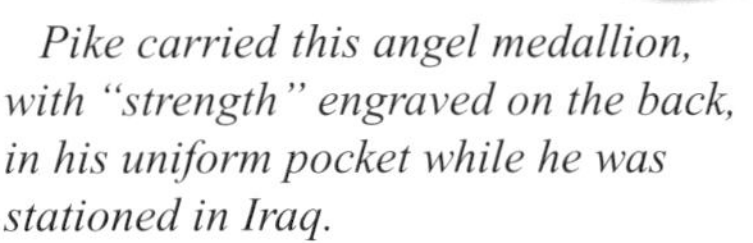

Pike carried this angel medallion, with "strength" engraved on the back, in his uniform pocket while he was stationed in Iraq.

Looking over the barrel of a machine gun at an Iraqi highway is one of the most common views American and British forces have of Iraq. Armored vehicles and weapons are the forces' main protection from ambush.

One of Pike's most memorable experiences was a Jan. 2, 2006, ambush. Pike and his convoy of U.S. and Iraqi soldiers were entering the town of Taji, approximately 20 miles north of Baghdad, on a logistical support mission. On their way back, the road was blocked. Three IEDs [improvised explosive devices] were discovered under a bridge overpass.

Suddenly a black car rolled up to within 500 meters of the convoy and opened fire on American soldiers in an attempt to try to draw U.S. forces away, so they could ambush the Iraqi soldiers. The attempt failed when Iraqi forces "cleared the vehicle" — "clearing," a term used to describe elimination of enemy combatants.

A second attack erupted from a nearby house. American soldiers stormed the house and cleared it as well. A third attack came when the allied forces were fired upon by a tree line to the left of the house, apparently from two insurgents, who headed toward the nearby mosque. The men were shot and killed.

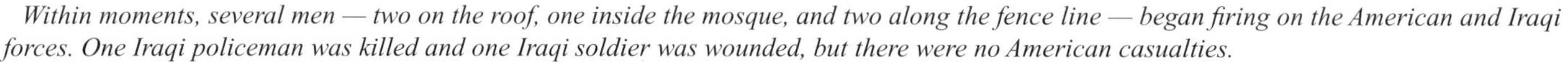

Within moments, several men — two on the roof, one inside the mosque, and two along the fence line — began firing on the American and Iraqi forces. One Iraqi policeman was killed and one Iraqi soldier was wounded, but there were no American casualties.

In many ways this was a test of Pike's work with the newly trained Iraqi Special Forces. "I was impressed and happy that the Iraqi Special Forces reacted the way they had been trained," said Pike, who is "hopeful about the competency of the new Iraqi military."

Pike was awarded the Army Commendation Medal as a result of this action.

The entrance to Baghdad International Airport features a large winged statue, commonly known as the "Flying Man." The statue commemorates Abbas Ibn Firnas, a medieval Arab astronomer, who in 852 saw a man dive off a tower in Córdoba, Spain, using a huge wing like cloak to break his fall. The daredevil survived with minor injuries, and the young Ibn Firnas witnessed what is considered to be use of the first parachute.

But American soldiers thought the statue more closely resembled Icarus, the mythological figure who fashioned wax and feathers into artificial wings in an attempt to fly to the sun. When the wax melted, Icarus fell to the ground. Pike said the soldiers thought it was funny that Saddam Hussein would choose a figure for his prized airport "who died trying to fly."

Pike took this photograph of a palace built for Saddam Hussein's oldest son, Uday, southwest of Baghdad. The elaborate structure was nicknamed the "Perfume Palace" because of the number of prostitutes who were always there, according to Pike. Among the souvenirs Pike brought home with him was a chunk of Saddam Hussein's Radwaniya Palace, in central Baghdad. Uday and Qusay, another of Saddam's sons, were killed in a raid on July 22, 2003.

The image of the Iraqi Tomb of the Unknown Soldier appears on Saddam Hussein-era Iraqi currency that Pike brought back to the States.

Although Pike is dressed in full battle gear with Kevlar vest, helmet, and automatic rifle, a significant part of his mission was to help Iraqi soldiers establish credibility with Iraqi civilians. In the photo above, he stands beside an Iraqi military counterpart who has hoisted a small child on his shoulders. Later, in northern Iraq, while on a public relations mission, Pike and the Iraqi soldiers he was training handed out small Iraqi flags to young boys in an effort to build trust in the country's new troops.

Shoulder patches in Arabic representing Iraqi paratroopers, Pike's Special Forces Support Battalion and a Combat Action Badge, a new award for uniformed personnel who encounter hostile fire. The badge is awarded to members of all U.S. branches of service, no matter the individual's specialty, who have come under fire since Sept. 18, 2001. The 2-inch silver pin, akin to the Combat Infantryman Badge, bears an oak wreath featuring an M9 bayonet and M67 grenade.

(Photographs and memorabilia courtesy of Ricky A. Pike)

Pike loved the sunsets in the Middle East — the most beautiful ones he has ever seen.

Pike (right) and his cousin Darren Jessop (left), a civilian contractor working in Iraq, had a family reunion of sorts at Al-Faw Palace in Iraq. The building, known as the "Water Palace," was one of Saddam Hussein's 99 palace complexes. It was built with an artificial lake surrounding it to commemorate the retaking of the Al-Faw Peninsula by Iraqi forces during the Iran-Iraq conflict, which lasted for eight years beginning in 1980. Located just outside Baghdad, Hussein's onetime duck-hunting lodge was used as a secondary location for Baath Party meetings before the U.S. invasion in 2003, Pike said.

One of Pike's more gratifying memories of his time in Iraq was distributing school supplies to a girls school. The supplies were donated by U.S. forces. Pike said his experience in Iraq had a "very positive impact on my life," with one downside: "I love being on active duty, but I miss my family when I am on extended deployments."

Iraqi flag that Pike was given by the Iraqi support battalion he advised when they learned he was leaving. He also came home with a Special Forces Handbook, printed in Arabic, that was used in training, and a piece of marble from Saddam Hussein's Radwaniya Palace.

Christina "Tina" Carpenter Lawler — Army — Global War on Terrorism

U.S. Army notebook Christina "Tina" Carpenter Lawler used to chronicle her experiences during Advanced Individual Training (AIT) at Aberdeen Proving Ground, Maryland, from December 2005 to March 2006. Her Dec. 9, 2005 entry testifies to the physical demands placed on the new enlistees: "The day after we arrived here at APG we took our first PT test. 47 push-ups, 66 sit-ups, and 17:30 on my 2-mile run — the best I've done since I enlisted!"

She was trained as a power generation equipment repairer and assigned to Fort Riley, Kansas, with the 3rd Brigade, 1st Armored Division.

Christina holds a copy of ***The Daily Mail*** *in front of a bronze "Every Soldier is a Warrior" plaque at Aberdeen Proving Ground, in Harford County, Maryland. Army values expressed include: loyalty, duty, personal courage, integrity, honor, selfless service and respect.*

A beaming Christina accepts her graduation certificate for successful completion of advanced training at Aberdeen Proving Ground from Sgt. 1st Class Conroy in 2006.

Christina, a 2005 graduate of North Hagerstown High School and Washington County Technical High School, completed basic training at Fort Jackson, South Carolina. She had her photograph taken with drill Sgt. Owens at Aberdeen Proving Ground, the Army's oldest proving ground, established in 1917, where she completed Advanced Individual Training (AIT) in 2006.

09 FEB 06
WEEK #11, APG, MD

PASTOR AIKENS,

I RECEIVED YOUR LETTER A FEW WEEKS AGO - SORRY FOR THE DELAYED RESPONSE. THANK YOU FOR ALL OF YOUR SUPPORT AND PRAYERS. THESE OBSTACLES HAVE BEEN QUITE UNFAMILIAR TO ME, BUT GOD IS TAKING CARE OF ME. EVERYDAY I WITNESS HOW GOD WORKS IN MYSTERIOUS WAYS AND ITS A GREAT COMFORT KNOWING THAT ALL OF YOU ARE BEHIND ME SUPPORTING MY SERVICE FOR THIS WONDERFUL COUNTRY. AT TIMES I QUESTION WHY I ENLISTED BUT THEN GOD REMINDS ME OF ALL THE REASONS WHY I SHOULD. WHEN I REALIZE THAT MY SERVICE IS PROTECTING EVERYONE'S WAY OF LIFE I FEEL A SENSE OF HONOR KNOWING THAT I'M NOT ONLY REPRESENTING THE US. BUT I'M REPRESENTING CHRIST'S ARMY, TOO. PLEASE PRAY FOR ALL OF US IN THE MILITARY; MOST OF MY BATTLE BUDDIES - INCLUDING MYSELF - ARE BEING DEPLOYED BY 2007 AND I CAN ASSURE YOU THAT NONE OF US ARE READY FOR THE URBAN WARZONES. I HONESTLY DON'T KNOW HOW I'M GOING TO HANDLE LOSING ONE OF MY BUDDIES IN IRAQ - I CAN'T EVEN HANDLE SEEING THEM ALL GRADUATE AND LEAVING FOR THEIR DUTY STATIONS. MENTAL STABILITY IS DEFINITELY A MUST FOR PRAYER. IF THINGS WORK OUT, I'LL BE HOME FOR PRESIDENT'S DAY SO PRAY THAT WORKS OUT. I HOPE TO SEE ALL OF YOU SOON BEFORE I DEPART FOR KANSAS. THANKS FOR ALL YOU'VE DONE AND WILL CONTINUE DOING! GOD BLESS!

II TIM 1:7
PSALMS 56:3

PVT CARPENTER
Christina Carpenter

PRAYER REQUESTS

AND FOR MYSELF - MENTAL PEACE + STABILITY, PATIENCE, AND THE ABILITY TO SURVIVE MY FINAL FTX 21 FEB - 24 FEB.

Copy of letter Christina sent to her pastor, the Rev. Larry Aikens of Hagerstown's Emmanuel Baptist Temple, expressing appreciation for prayers and support of the congregation. The letter also forwards prayer requests on behalf of fellow soldiers. "Everyday I witness how God works in mysterious ways and it's a great comfort knowing that all of you are behind me supporting my service for this wonderful country," Christina wrote in February 2006.

Inset photo of Christina in fatigues during basic training at Fort Jackson, South Carolina.

Christina met her future husband, Pfc. Shawn Patrick Lawler, from Maine, while she was serving at Fort Riley, Kansas. They were married June 24, 2006, and their daughter, Loralei Lawler, was born April 11, 2007. Christina completed her regular Army service on March 9, 2007, but was placed on Individual Ready Reserve. Christina's husband, who is stationed at Fort Riley, is standing by for possible deployment to Iraq.

(Photographs and memorabilia courtesy of Ramon Joy, Christina Carpenter Lawler's grandfather, and Joyce and David Carpenter, Christina Carpenter Lawler's mother and father)

Michael S. Ingram — Army
Operation Iraqi Freedom

One of the aspects of a military career that appealed to Staff Sgt. Michael S. Ingram was the ability to travel "and go places that I could not have gone on my own." Kuwait and Iraq might not have been the places that immediately leapt to the top of Ingram's list, but the "tons of pictures" he took during his 24-year military career are testimony to his travels.

The Sharpsburg native entered the service in 1982 and retired in October 2006. Among the mechanic's assignments was duty at Fort Hood, Texas, as well as Kuwait and Iraq during Operation Iraqi Freedom. Here he is shown standing next to a bomb crater near Balad, Iraq.

(Photographs courtesy of Michael S. Ingram)

Ingram in full battle gear in Kuwait just prior to leaving for Iraq.

Weapon in hand, Ingram stands next to a glorified painting of an Iraqi war plane at an Iraqi air base in Balad.

Mark Wiley — Air Force — Cold War, Global War on Terrorism

Since he joined the Air Force in 1989, Wiley, a native of Hagerstown, has traveled to Greenland, Spain, Germany, Luxembourg, Belgium, Slovakia, Turkey, Korea, Japan, Thailand, Vietnam, Italy, the Netherlands, Ireland and Qatar.

"The Air Force is my life," Mark Wiley said. It is also where he met his future wife. Wiley is shown with his wife, Catrin, who is now an Air Force master sergeant, both in Air Force mess dress. She recently completed duty as a paralegal in Kuwait. Both Wileys are currently assigned at MacDill Air Force Base, Florida.

(Photographs courtesy of Dorothy A. Cooper, mother of Mark Wiley)

As superintendent of aircrew life support, Wiley is keenly aware of the vulnerability of fighter pilots in the air. Wiley has worked in support of numerous campaigns including Allied Force (Kosovo, March 24 - June 10, 1999), Operation Northern Watch (Kurdish no-fly zone, Jan. 1, 1997 - March 17, 2003), Operation Enduring Freedom and Operation Iraqi Freedom.

While on a three-week assignment to Japan on Dec. 11, 2000, Wiley boarded an F-16 for his second flight in the fighter jet.

Wiley stands next to an F-16 fighter jet at Aviano Air Force Base in Italy in 2000, where he suited up to take his very first ride in the high-speed jet. The air base in northeastern Italy is the home of two F-16 squadrons.

Wiley had his photo taken with village children in Vietnam. He was there as part of a JPAC mission — the military acronym for the Joint-Pacific POW-MIA Accounting Command. Wiley traveled extensively in Vietnam during the 60 days he was part of a team identifying and preparing sites for excavation in the search for the remains of American soldiers and airmen killed in the Vietnam War.

Daniel L. Watson — Navy Reserve — Operation Iraqi Freedom

Builder Petty Officer 2nd Class Daniel L. Watson Jr. on duty in Iraq. Watson and his fellow Seabees were required to wear their Navy dog tags in Iraq.

When Navy Seabee Daniel L. Watson Jr. left for Iraq in 2004, he took with him a banner made by his family, Hallmark cards from friends, and a video camera. When he returned home in 2005, he brought with him a Thanksgiving place mat signed by Secretary of the Navy Gordon England, some "Wanted" posters, and a marker from his gun truck.

He also came home with some memorable experiences that are not all the "feel good" kind.

The Hagerstown resident served a four-year tour of duty with the Navy beginning in August 1990, and entered the Navy Reserve in July 2000. He continues to serve in the reserves. He has served all over the world, most recently in Iraq, and has participated in several major campaigns including Operation Iraqi Freedom, Operation Noble Eagle, Operation Enduring Freedom, and Operation Southern Watch.

Watson said, "The military changed me when I was a teenager, making me a little more focused. My Iraq experience changed me by making me a little more jumpy."

Talking about his experiences in Iraq, Watson said his outfit was hit several times by small arms fire, IEDs [improvised explosive devices], rockets and mortars. "Out of my entire service in the Navy my most memorable time was probably one of the worst times," he recalled. His tactical movements team was providing security for a convoy that was to go from Ar Ramadi, Iraq, to Fallujah, on to Al Asad, and back to Ar Ramadi, where he was based. "This was to be one of the longest missions during my time in Iraq, and we never made it back to our final destination," he said.

"On our way to Fallujah, we came under small arms fire around a very well known overpass in Fallujah. An IED exploded about 50 meters from my gun truck, but we were able to continue on the mission. On our way to Al Asad our convoy located an IED, so we stood watch over it until EOD [explosive ordnance disposal] arrived to disarm it. That took about three hours just sitting there in the open. We then pushed on to Al Asad on a road called Uranium. As we approached the intersection of Uranium and Maverick, a very dangerous area, one of our trucks ran off the road, running over a triple stacked mine. The truck driver and a passenger were injured. While we were setting security around the burning vehicle, the first two gun trucks in the convoy began a security watch at the intersection. This intersection became a very busy place with small arms fire from approaching vehicles. Our gun trucks opened up on them, and additional air support assisted until the enemy forces fled the area."

Continuing his narrative, Watson said, "We finally made it to Al Asad, and I think the most memorable time was when I went to the hospital and saw that both (truck) driver and passenger were doing fine. When I saw them, it was all I could do to keep from breaking down."

Watson was not one to overlook sacrifices made on the home front while he was far from family.

When he deployed to Iraq, he left behind a wife and two children. "Many oceans and countries separated us," he said. "This was a tremendous hardship on our family, but one that I felt was necessary." He remembered how his wife Coleen "kept everything together," and during telephone conversations lifted his spirits so that "I was reassured in my heart that I was where I needed to be ... "

Currently assigned to Naval Mobile Construction Battalion 23 as a reservist, Watson pointed out Iraq was not his first military assignment. He served from 1990 until 1994 as a radioman in the Navy. Most of that time was spent aboard the USS *Theodore Roosevelt*. He served in Operations Desert Storm, Provide Comfort, Provide Promise, Deny Flight and Southern Watch during those four years of service. He has been in the Navy Reserve since 2000. His unit was called to active duty in the summer of 2004 and trained in California. In September it went to Iraq, where it provided convoy security and the occasional patrol.

"The overall mission of our battalion was to make life better for soldiers on other bases and also to help rebuild the infrastructure of Iraq," he said. Besides convoy duty, his team was assigned to patrol the streets of Akashat, Iraq, during the January 2005 Iraqi elections.

A deputy with the Washington County Sheriff's Department, Watson said he believes his military duty has made him a better person. "Although there have been many adverse effects on my life, including the long periods away from my wife and children, I feel proud that I serve my country."

As guest speaker at the downtown Hagerstown observance of Veterans Day on Nov. 11, 2005, Watson recalled that several generations of his and his wife's families had served their country.

"All veterans know that there is always a set mission to accomplish," he said, "and that we will work together as a team to accomplish that mission, or we will die together."

Navy Seabee Combat Warfare Specialist pin belonging to Daniel L. Watson Jr.

Watson's ribbon rack, which contains ribbons representing, top row (left to right): the Navy & Marine Corps Achievement Medal, Joint Meritorious Unit Award, Navy Commendation Medal; (second row from the top) Navy Meritorious Unit Commendation, Navy "E" Ribbon, Navy Good Conduct Medal; (third row from the top) Naval Reserve Meritorious Service Medal, National Defense Service Medal with one bronze star, Southwest Asia Service Ribbon with two bronze stars; (fourth row from the top) Global War on Terrorism Service Medal, Global War on Terrorism Expeditionary Medal, Navy Sea Service Deployment Ribbon with two bronze stars; (bottom row) Armed Forces Navy Reserve Medal with "M" device, Saudi Arabia Medal for the Liberation of Kuwait, and the Kuwait Medal for the Liberation of Kuwait.

When Watson could take a break, he liked to stretch out on the cold rocks in Fallujah, Iraq, but he soon found the sand fleas were more than he could take. So he bought a three dollar chair to carry with him for those rare moments of rest and relaxation.

This angel pendant which Daniel Watson wore on his vest was sent to him by a Washington County resident.

Marines gave these "smart cards" to all tactical movement teams involved with Iraqi citizens.

Watson's Seabee gear while serving in Iraq included a jacket, load-bearing vest and boots.

Watson returned from Iraq this "Wanted" poster and informant card.

Watson in action in a glass factory outside Ar Ramadi, where insurgents were firing mortars.

This MTRV [Medium Tactical Replacement Vehicle], a six-wheel drive, all-terrain vehicle, sometimes called a "7-Ton" because of the amount of weight it can carry, was just ahead of Watson's truck when it ran over a triple stacked-mine. Two men were injured in the explosion.

Watson's Navy Reserve unit displays the flag which flew over its headquarters in Ar Ramadi the day his unit provided security for admirals who were checking bases where Seabees were stationed.

Watson on the gun truck that he nicknamed "Deputy Dan."

Watson's team poses in front of the Camp Fallujah welcome sign in Iraq.

Watson and the medic in his outfit rounded up "goodies sent from home" for an impromptu Christmas party in the barracks in 2004.

Watson in a photograph with his wife Coleen, son Quentin and daughter Carissa at Hagerstown's 2005 Veterans Day observance.

(Photographs and memorabilia courtesy of Daniel L. Watson Jr.)

Watson's Cub Scout troop, along with his wife and children (front row right, spelling "Dad"), sent this Christmas photo greeting to him in Iraq in 2004.

Among the items Daniel Watson brought back with him from Iraq are a flag that flew over Ar Ramadi and a map that he bought at the international airport in Baghdad before coming home, to mark where he had been in the country. The plaque shown resting at the corner of the map was presented to Watson in 2005 by the Washington County Sheriff's Department in recognition of his service to country and community.

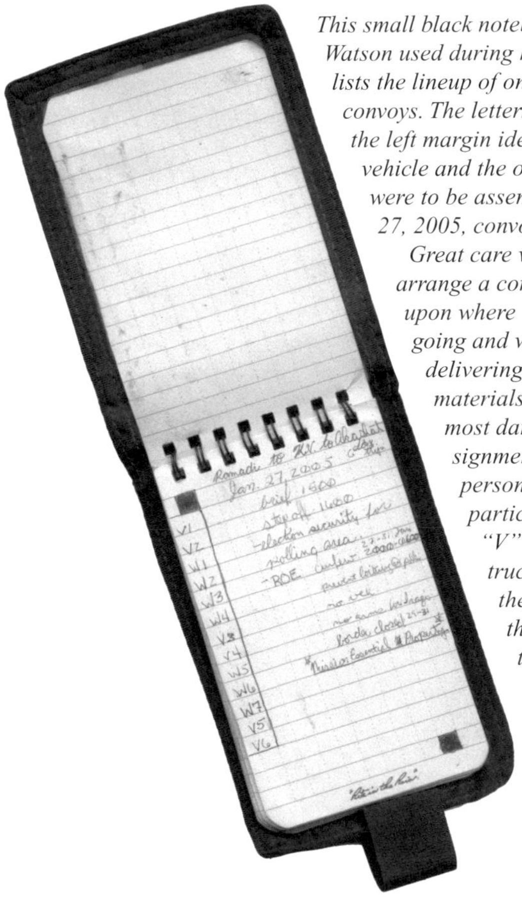

This small black notebook, one of many Watson used during his time in Iraq, lists the lineup of one of Watson's convoys. The letters and initials in the left margin identify the type of vehicle and the order in which they were to be assembled for this Jan. 27, 2005, convoy.

Great care was taken to arrange a convoy depending upon where the convoy was going and what it would be delivering. Transporting materials is among the most dangerous assignments for military personnel in Iraq. In this particular convoy the "V" stands for gun trucks — placed at the front and rear of the convoy — with the "W" signifying supply vehicles in between. Watson drove the gun truck identified as "V5."

Post cards from Iraq included in Daniel Watson's collection.

Editor's Note:

In compiling the information for the following listing of veterans and their service information, we have relied exclusively on information supplied by the veterans and their families.

Errors and omissions are an inevitable part of this process. We also highlighted overseas assignments and elected not to enumerate the many stateside military postings. This informal snapshot of each of the military careers is an attempt to convey some sense of the breadth of each individual's service to their country.

Key to abbreviations:

We spelled out the names of medals and awards where possible.
When space was limited, we used the following abbreviations:

AFCM - Armed Forces Commendation Medal
AFACH - Air Force Achievement Medal
AFEM - Air Force Expeditionary Medal
AIT - Advanced Individual Training Ribbon
ARCOM - Army Commendation Medal
ARACH - Army Achievement Medal
ATO - American Theater of Operations Medal
DMSM - Defense Meritorious Service Medal
GCM - Good Conduct Medal
GWOT - Global War on Terrorism Medal
GWOT-EM - Global War on Terrorism Medal Expeditionary Medal
MSM - Meritorious Service Medal
NDSM - National Defense Service Medal
PUC - Presidential Unit Citation
OLC - Oak Leaf Cluster

Killed In Action

Prisoner of War

Homer Abbott
Branch of Service: Army; Army Reserve
Occupation: Artilleryman
Rank: Specialist 5th Class
Dates of Service: Feb. 1957 - Feb. 1959 (Army); 1959 - 1961 (Army Reserve)
Place of Service: Germany
Decorations/Ribbons: Good Conduct Medal; Expert Rifleman Badge

Percy Albert Jr.
Branch of Service: Army
Occupation: Rifleman
Rank: Private 1st Class
Dates of Service: March 12, 1943 - Feb. 14, 1946
Place of Service: Europe
Decorations: Good Conduct Medal; Bronze Star; Purple Heart w/oak leaf cluster; European-African-Middle Eastern Campaign Medal w/3 bronze stars; American Campaign Medal; WWII Victory Medal; Liberation of France Medal; Combat Infantryman Badge

Marvin Lee Alexander
Branch of Service: Army
Occupation: Military Policeman
Rank: Specialist 4th Class
Dates of Service: Jan. 8, 1962 - Jan. 7, 1968
Place of Service: Europe
Decorations: Good Conduct Medal; Sharpshooter Badge w/rifle bar; Driver Badge w/W-bar (wheeled vehicles)

George R. "Dick" Ambrose
Branch of Service: Army
Occupation: Tank Destroyer
Rank: Private 1st Class
Dates of Service: June 26, 1943 - Dec. 3, 1945
Place of Service: England; France; Luxembourg
Decorations: Good Conduct Medal; Purple Heart-2; Bronze Star; American Campaign Medal; European-African-Middle Eastern Campaign Medal w/2 bronze stars; WWII Victory Medal; Expert Marksman Badge w/rifle bar

Glenn W. Andrews
Branch of Service: Army Air Forces; Air Force Reserve
Occupation: Construction Foreman
Rank: Staff Sergeant
Dates of Service: May 12, 1942 - Dec. 27, 1945 (AAF); Aug. 14, 1950 - Aug. 13, 1953 (AF Reserve)
Place of Service: South Pacific (Guadalcanal; New Caledonia; New Guinea; Biak)
Decorations: Good Conduct Medal; Marksman Badge (Carbine); Asiatic-Pacific Campaign Medal w/1 battle star; Philippine Liberation Medal; WWII Victory Medal

Paul R. Andrews
Branch of Service: Army
Occupation: Infantryman
Rank: Sergeant
Dates of Service: April 1945 - Dec. 1946
Place of Service: Europe
Decorations: European-African-Middle Eastern Campaign Medal; WWII Victory Medal; Army of Occupation Medal (Germany)

Peter Badrich
Branch of Service: Army Air Forces
Occupation: Entertainment Director
Rank: Staff Sergeant
Dates of Service: Jan. 13, 1942 - Jan. 6, 1946
Place of Service: India; Burma; China
Decorations: Good Conduct Medal; American Campaign Medal; Asiatic-Pacific Campaign Medal; WWII Victory Medal

Paul D. Bailey
Branch of Service: Army
Occupation: Infantryman
Rank: Technician 5th Grade
Dates of Service: May 29, 1944 - June 6, 1946
Place of Service: Europe
Decorations: Good Conduct Medal; Combat Infantryman Badge; Bronze Star; European-African-Middle Eastern Campaign Medal w/2 battle stars; WWII Victory Medal; Army of Occupation Medal (Germany)

Samuel Baker

Branch of Service: Army Air Forces
Occupation: Training
Rank: Private
Dates of Service: Dec. 1942 - 1943
Place of Service: Stateside

Paul H. Barr

Branch of Service: Navy
Occupation: Seabee
Rank: Apprentice Seaman
Dates of Service: July 1, 1943 - Jan. 31, 1945
Place of Service: New Guinea; South Pacific

John L. Beair

Branch of Service: Army; Army Reserve
Occupation: Infantryman; Communications Sergeant
Rank: Staff Sergeant
Dates of Service: Jan. 1, 1945 - Nov. 1946 (Army); Aug. 21, 1951 - March 24, 1953 (Army Reserve)
Place of Service: Japan; Korea
Decorations: Good Conduct Medal; Asiatic-Pacific Theater Medal; WWII Victory Medal; Army of Occupation Medal (Japan); Korean Service Medal w/bronze star

Houston L. Bell

Branch of Service: Army
Occupation: Physician
Rank: Captain
Dates of Service: 1943 - 1947
Place of Service: Stateside

Charles R. Berry

Branch of Service: Navy
Occupation: Electrician
Rank: Electrician's Mate 3rd Class
Dates of Service: 1944 - 1945
Place of Service: Stateside

Lee Foster Blickenstaff

Branch of Service: Army Air Forces
Occupation: Food Handler
Dates of Service: July 1943 - Dec. 1944
Place of Service: Stateside

Paul W. Blickenstaff

Branch of Service: Navy
Rank: Seaman 1st Class
Dates of Service: Nov. 1943 - April 29, 1945
Place of Service: Died at sea of tuberculosis at age of 19

Frederick W. Bolland Jr.

Branch of Service: Army
Occupation: Mechanic
Rank: Specialist 4th Class
Dates of Service: Dec. 1963 - Dec. 1966
Place of Service: Stateside; Dominican Republic
Decorations: Parachutist Badge; Combat Infantryman Badge

Glenn S. Bolland

Branch of Service: Army
Occupation: Medical Corps
Rank: Sergeant
Dates of Service: Feb. 19, 2001 - Present
Place of Service: Iraq; Afghanistan; Kosovo; Hungary; Tunisia; Germany; Poland; Italy
Decorations: Good Conduct Medal; National Defense Service Medal; Army Service Ribbon; Global War on Terrorism Medal; Global War on Terrorism Expeditionary Medal w/arrowhead; Afghanistan Campaign; Army Achievement Medal; Army Commendation Medal w/gold leaf cluster; Combat Medical Badge; Overseas Service Medal

Eleanor G. "Ellie" Briggs Bowles

Branch of Service: Army
Occupation: Registered Nurse
Rank: Captain
Dates of Service: May 19, 1967 - April 1, 1970
Place of Service: Stateside; Vietnam
Decorations: Bronze Star; National Defense Service Medal; Vietnam Service Medal; Republic of Vietnam Campaign Medal w/1960 device; Meritorious Unit Citation

Robert L. Bragunier

Branch of Service: Army
Occupation: Infantry Rifleman
Rank: Corporal
Dates of Service: Nov. 7, 1942 - Feb. 9, 1946
Place of Service: Stateside; Pacific
Decorations/Ribbons: Good Conduct Medal; American Campaign Medal; Asiatic-Pacific Campaign Medal; Philippine Liberation Medal; WWII Victory Medal; Sharpshooter Badge w/carbine and rifle bars

Kenneth L. "Buzz" Brandenburg

Branch of Service: Army
Occupation: Motor Pool
Rank: Private 1st Class
Dates of Service: 1945 - 1947
Place of Service: Stateside

Kenneth L. "Lee" Brandenburg II

Branch of Service: Army
Occupation: Supply
Rank: Specialist 4th Class
Dates of Service: July 7, 1965 - July 7, 1967
Place of Service: Stateside; Vietnam

Max A. Brandenburg

Branch of Service: Army
Occupation: Motor Pool
Rank: Master Sergeant
Dates of Service: 1944 - 1952
Place of Service: Stateside; Germany

Harvey L. "Teter" Brown

Branch of Service: Navy
Occupation: Carpenter
Rank: Carpenter's Mate 2nd Class
Dates of Service: Aug. 27, 1943 - March 17, 1946
Place of Service: New Guinea; Admiralty Islands; Philippines
Decorations: Pacific-Asiatic Campaign Medal; WWII Victory Medal; Philippine Liberation Medal

Stanley R. Brown Sr.

Branch of Service: Navy
Occupation: Gunner; Coxswain's Mate
Rank: Gunner's Mate 3rd Class
Dates of Service: July 21, 1943 - October 10, 1949
Place of Service: South Pacific; Europe
Decorations: Asiatic-Pacific Campaign Medal w/4 battle stars

Robert E. Bruchey Sr.
Branch of Service: Army
Occupation: Military Policeman
Rank: Specialist 3rd Class
Dates of Service: 1950-1956
Place of Service: Stateside; Italy; Austria
Decorations: Good Conduct Medal; National Defense Service Medal

Marian L. Freed Cain
Branch of Sevice: Nurse Cadet Corps
Occupation: Nurse
Dates of Service: July 1, 1943 - June 1946
Place of Service: Washington County Hospital

Pete Callas
Branch of Service: Navy
Occupation: Fire Controlman; Radar Range-Finder Operator
Rank: Fire Controlman 3rd Class
Dates of Service: Feb. 1944 - May, 1946; 1951-1952
Place of Service: Pacific; Indian Ocean; Korea
Decorations: Asiatic-Pacific Campaign Medal; American Campaign Medal; Navy Combat Medal; WWII Victory Medal; Occupation Service Medal; Korean Service Medal; Republic of Korea War Service Medal

Paul L. "Pete" Carbaugh
Branch of Service: Army
Rank: Private 1st Class
Dates of Service: Jan. 13, 1943 - Oct. 2, 1945
Decorations: WWII Victory Medal

William F. Carpenter
Branch of Service: Army
Occupation: Clerk-Typist
Rank: Private 1st Class
Dates of Service: April 12, 1966 - May 18, 1967
Place of Service: Vietnam
Decorations: National Defense Service Medal; Vietnam Campaign Medal; Vietnam Service Medal; Marksman w/rifle & M14 bars; Army Commendation Medal

Ellis T. Cline
Branch of Service: Army
Occupation: Supply Clerk
Rank: Technician 4th Grade
Entered Service: March 7, 1941
Place of Service: Africa; Europe

E. Ross Cline
Branch of Service: Army
Occupation: Infantryman; Heavy Machine Gunner
Rank: Private 1st Class
Dates of Service: Oct. 17, 1944 - July 17, 1946
Place of Service: France; Germany
Decorations: Good Conduct Medal; Bronze Star; European-African-Middle Eastern Campaign Medal w/bronze star; WWII Victory Medal; WWII Army of Occupation Medal (Germany); Combat Infantryman Badge

Thurman P. Cline
Branch of Service: Army
Occupation: Utility Repairman
Rank: Private
Dates of Service: March 3, 1943 - Oct. 13, 1943
Place of Service: Stateside

Walter L. Cline

Branch of Service: Air Force
Occupation: Aircraft Mechanic
Rank: Airman
Dates of Service: Feb. 21, 1952 - Dec. 30, 1955
Place of Service: Germany; France; Africa
Decorations: Good Conduct Medal; National Defense Service Medal; WWII Army of Occupation Medal (Germany)

Warren Conner

Branch of Service: Navy
Occupation: Electrician
Rank: Electrician's Mate 3rd Class
Dates of Service: 1944 - 1945
Place of Service: Stateside

Roscoe D. Corderman

Branch of Service: Army
Occupation: Cook
Rank: Tech Sergeant 4th Class
Dates of Service: Jan. 1, 1945 - June 30, 1946
Place of Service: Philippines
Decorations: Good Conduct Medal; Asiatic-Pacific Campaign Medal; WWII Victory Medal

Barry M. "Rick" Cunningham

Branch of Service: Army
Occupation: Infantryman
Rank: Private 1st Class
Dates of Service: Jan 20, 1967 - Feb. 27, 1968
Place of Service: Vietnam
Decorations: National Defense Service Medal; Purple Heart-2; Combat Infantryman Badge; Army Commendation Medal; Vietnam Service Medal; Republic of Vietnam Campaign Medal w/1960 device; Sharpshooter Badge w/rifle & M14 bars

William E. Daley

Branch of Service: Navy; Naval Reserve; Army National Guard
Occupation: Cook
Rank: Seaman 1st Class (Navy); Sergeant 1st Class (Army National Guard)
Dates of Service: Jan. 1945 - Jan. 1946 (Navy); 1946 - 1948 (Navy Reserve); 1948 - 1992 (Army National Guard)
Place of Service: South Pacific (Navy); Stateside (Army National Guard)
Decorations: Good Conduct Medal; National Defense Service Medal; Army Reserve Components Medal-4; Army Service Ribbon; Maryland Commendation Medal; Maryland Service Medal-6; Maryland Distinguished Service Cross

Carl E. Davis

Branch of Service: Marine Corps
Rank: Corporal
Dates of Service: Feb. 1944 - July 1946
Place of Service: Pacific

Dan Davis

Branch of Service: Marine Corps
Occupation: Engineer
Rank: Corporal
Dates of Service: 1953 - 1961
Place of Service: Stateside

Leonard J. Davis

Branch of Service: Army
Rank: Corporal
Dates of Service: 1951 - 1954
Place of Service: Korea

Roger E. Davis
Branch of Service: Army
Occupation: Communications
Rank: Technician 5th Class
Dates of Service: 1947 - 1950
Place of Service: Hawaii

Roy E. Davis
Branch of Service: Navy
Occupation: Radioman
Rank: Seaman
Dates of Service: April 20, 1955 - July 1, 1958

Wilbur W. Davis
Branch of Service: Army
Occupation: Rifleman
Rank: Private
Dates of Service: Nov. 1948 - Aug. 1950
Place of Service: Stateside

William M. DeLauder
Branch of Service: Navy
Occupation: Unknown
Rank: Petty Officer 2nd Class
Dates of Service: 1943 - April 1946
Place of Service: South Pacific; Philippines
Decorations: Good Conduct Medal; American Campaign Medal w/3 stars; Asiatic-Pacific Campaign; WWII Victory Medal

Thurman W. "Sonny" Divelbliss Jr.
Branch of Service: Army
Occupation: Infantryman; Machine Gunner
Rank: Specialist 4th Class
Dates of Service: Oct. 13, 1967 - Oct. 1969
Place of Service: Vietnam
Decorations: Air Medal; Vietnam Campaign Medal; Vietnam Service Medal; National Defense Service Medal; Sharpshooter Badge

Julia Hogan Donovan
Branch of Service: Women's Auxiliary Army Corps
Occupation: Administrative Specialist
Rank: Sergeant
Dates of Service: Oct. 1942 - Nov. 1945
Place of Service: Stateside; Egypt
Decorations: Good Conduct Medal; Women's Army Corps Service Medal; American Campaign Medal; European-African-Middle Eastern Campaign Medal; WWII Victory Medal

Charles L. Downey
Branch of Service: Army
Occupation: Quartermaster
Rank: Major
Dates of Service: July 1941 - Dec. 1945
Place of Service: Europe
Decorations: Bronze Star; American Defense Service Medal; European-African-Middle Eastern Campaign Medal/w 2 bronze stars

Lawrence E. Downey
Branch of Service: Army Air Forces
Occupation: Supply Officer
Rank: Major
Dates of Service: July 1942 - Oct. 1945
Place of Service: Europe
Decorations: Bronze Star

Mary Shinham Downing
Branch of Service: Army
Occupation: Nurse
Dates of Service: 1943 - 1945
Place of Service: Europe

Carol Easterday
Branch of Service: Army
Occupation: Clerk-Typist
Rank: Private 1st Class
Dates of Service: 1975 - 1977
Place of Service: Stateside

Edmund Ray Easterday
Branch of Service: Army Air Corps
Occupation: Military Policeman; Gunner
Rank: Corporal
Dates of Service: 1942 - Jan. 12, 1946
Place of Service: Europe; Africa; Pacific
Decorations: Good Conduct Medal; American Campaign Medal; Air Medal; WWII Victory Medal

Dwayne R. Ebersole
Branch of Service: Army
Occupation: Accounting Specialist/Supply
Rank: Specialist 5th Class
Dates of Service: June 29, 1966 - June 28, 1969
Place of Service: Vietnam; Stateside
Decorations: Good Conduct Medal; National Defense Service Medal; Army Commendation Medal; Vietnam Campaign Medal; Vietnam Service Medal; Bronze Star; Republic of Vietnam Campaign Medal w/device; Survival Escape and Evasion Certificate

Leon G. Ecton
Branch of Service: Army
Occupation: Tank Commander; Trainer
Rank: Staff Sergeant
Dates of Service: June 9, 1942 - March 1, 1963
Place of Service: Europe; Stateside
Decorations: Good Conduct Medal; American Campaign Medal; European-African-Middle Eastern Campaign Medal; WWII Victory Medal; Army of Occupation Medal (Germany)

Harry L. Ecton
Branch of Service: Army
Occupation: Reconnaissance
Rank: Private 1st Class
Dates of Service: June 1, 1967 - Jan. 31, 1968 KIA
Place of Service: Vietnam
Decorations: Bronze Star; Purple Heart; Combat Infantryman Badge; Sharpshooter Badge w/machine gun & rifle bars; National Defense Service Medal; Vietnam Service Medal; Republic of Vietnam Campaign Medal; Republic of Vietnam Gallantry Cross

C. V. Eldridge
Branch of Service: Army
Occupation: Camouflage
Rank: Private 1st Class
Dates of Service: Dec. 29, 1942 - Nov. 7, 1945
Place of Service: Europe
Decorations: Good Conduct Medal; Expert Marksman Badge w/rifle bar; Sharpshooter Badge; European-African-Middle Eastern Campaign Medal; American Campaign Medal; WWII Victory Medal

John "Jack" Elgin
Branch of Service: Air Force
Occupation: Mechanic
Rank: Sergeant Major
Dates of Service: 1940 - 1965
Place of Service: Pacific
Decorations: Good Conduct Medal w/5 clasps; Air Force Longevity Service Award w/3 OLCs; National Defense Service Medal; WWII Victory Medal; Asiatic-Pacific Service Medal; American Defense Service Medal; numerous marksmanship awards

Leroy "Roy" Elgin

Branch of Service: Army
Occupation: Artilleryman
Rank: Chief Warrant Officer
Dates of Service: 1937 - 1952
Place of Service: Europe; Stateside
Decorations: Good Conduct Medal w/clasp; American Defense Service Medal; American Campaign Medal; European-African-Middle Eastern Campaign Medal; WWII Victory Medal

William L. Embly

Branch of Service: Army
Occupation: Power Lineman
Rank: Technician 4th Class
Dates of Service: Feb. 13, 1941 - Oct. 12, 1945
Place of Service: France; Germany; Central Europe
Decorations: Good Conduct Medal; Purple Heart; American Defense Service Medal; European-African-Middle Eastern Campaign Medal; American Campaign Medal; WWII Victory Medal

Helen Powell Eslick

Branch of Service: Army Nurse Corps
Occupation: Operating Room Nurse
Rank: 1st Lieutenant
Dates of Service: March 1943 - January 1946
Place of Service: Europe

Joseph Charles Finfrock

Branch of Service: Marine Corps
Occupation: Infantryman
Rank: Corporal
Dates of Service: Jan. 1942 - Jan. 1946
Place of Service: South Pacific
Decorations: Good Conduct Medal; Purple Heart-2; American Defense Service Medal; Asiatic-Pacific Campaign Medal; Presidential Unit Citation

Walter H. Fitzgerald

Branch of Service: Army
Occupation: Security
Rank: Private
Dates of Service: Sept. 1945 - March 1946
Place of Service: Panama Canal
Decorations: Good Conduct Medal; WWII Victory Medal; Overseas Service Ribbon (Panama)

Bart Fraker

Branch of Service: Navy
Occupation: Hospital Corpsman
Rank: Master Chief
Dates of Service: Sept. 23, 1958 - Dec. 27, 1988
Place of Service: Stateside; Japan; Vietnam; Philippines; Taiwan; Hong Kong
Decorations: Good Conduct Medal w/5 stars; Combat Action Medal; Vietnam Service Medal; Vietnam Campaign Medal; Navy Command Medal w/1 star; Navy Achievement Medal w/2 stars; National Defense Service Medal; Meritorious Unit Commendation

Fred S. French

Branch of Service: Navy
Occupation: Gun Maintenance
Rank: Gunner's Mate 3rd Class
Dates of Service: Sept. 1943 - Jan. 1946
Place of Service: South Pacific; Japan
Decorations: Good Conduct Medal; American Campaign Medal; Asiatic-Pacific Campaign Medal; Army of Occupation Medal (Japan)

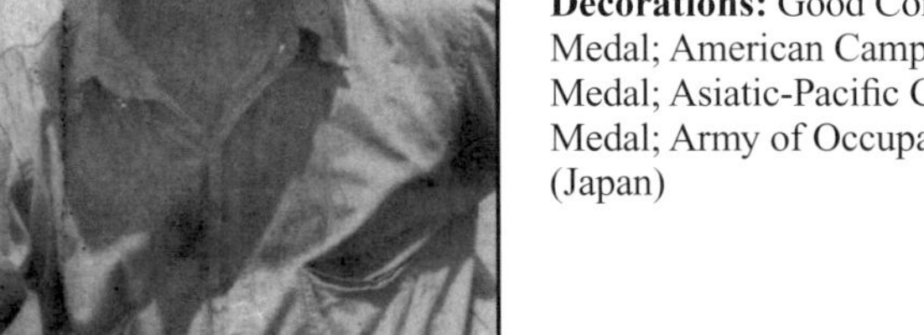

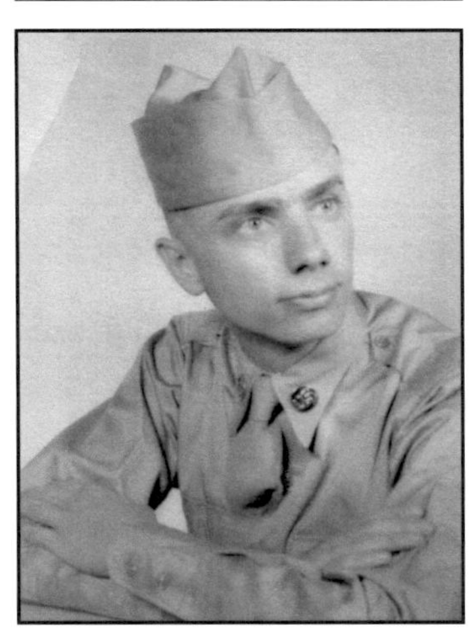

John Frye

Branch of Service: Army
Occupation: Combat Correspondent
Rank: Specialist 4th Class
Dates of Service: July 1953 - June 1961
Place of Service: Stateside

Clyde M. "Pete" Gaylor

Branch of Service: Army
Occupation: Infantry; Military Policeman
Rank: Corporal
Dates of Service: Sept. 14, 1943 - Feb. 1945
Place of Service: Sicily; Italy; France; Stateside
Decorations: Combat Infantryman Badge; European-African-Middle Eastern Campaign Medal; Purple Heart

Charles R. Gehr Jr.

Branch of Service: Navy
Occupation: Machinist's Mate
Rank: Petty Officer 1st Class
Dates of Service: Sept. 1943 - Dec. 1945; Nov. 1950 - Oct. 1953
Place of Service: Pacific; Korea
Decorations: GCM; European-African-Middle Eastern Campaign Medal; American Campaign Medal; WWII Victory Medal; Philippine Liberation Medal w/1 battle star; Asiatic-Pacific Campaign Medal w/1 battle star; U.N. Service Medal; Korean Service Medal w/1 battle star; Chinese Service Extended Ribbon; Republic of Korea Presidential Unit Citation

Francis W. Geiser

Branch of Service: Army Air Forces
Occupation: Engineer/Gunner
Rank: Technical Sergeant
Dates of Service: 1942 - 1946
Place of Service: Italy
Decorations: Air Medal/w 3 OLC

Samuel J. Geiser Jr.

Branch of Service: Army
Occupation: Infantryman
Rank: Technician 4th Grade
Dates of Service: March 23, 1942 - Nov. 11, 1944 KIA
Place of Service: France
Decorations: Purple Heart

Harry M. Gelwicks

Branch of Service: National Guard; Army
Occupation: Armored Crewman
Rank: Specialist 4th Class
Dates of Service: 1962 - 1963 (National Guard); Dec. 1963 - Dec. 1, 1966 (Army)
Place of Service: Stateside; Germany
Decorations: National Defense Service Medal

John R. Gelwicks

Branch of Service: Army
Occupation: Structural Specialist
Rank: Specialist 4th Class
Dates of Service: Feb. 26, 1959 - Feb. 25, 1965
Place of Service: Europe

Joseph R. Gelwicks

Branch of Service: Army
Occupation: Combat Engineer
Rank: Specialist 5th Class
Dates of Service: Jan. 12, 1955 - Jan. 11, 1963
Place of Service: Stateside; Europe
Decorations: Good Conduct Medal; Parachutist Badge

Ronald L. Gelwicks Sr.

Branch of Service: Army
Occupation: Wheeled Vehicle Maintenance
Rank: Specialist 4th Class
Dates of Service: July 11, 1957 - April 16, 1962
Place of Service: Stateside; Europe
Decorations: Good Conduct Medal

Ralph I. Gibney Jr.

Branch of Service: Army
Occupation: Infantryman
Rank: Private 1st Class
Dates of Service: June 1, 1944 - Jan. 13, 1946
Place of Service: England; France; Belgium; Germany
Decorations: Good Conduct Medal; Combat Infantryman Badge; European-African-Middle Eastern Campaign Medal; WWII Victory Medal

Milton M. Gillan

Branch of Service: Army Air Forces
Occupation: Ground Manager
Rank: Corporal
Dates of Service: 1941 - 1945
Place of Service: Aleutian Islands

William S. Gossard

Branch of Service: Army
Occupation: Military Policeman
Rank: Private 1st Class
Dates of Service: 1954 - 1956
Place of Service: Stateside; Germany
Decorations: Good Conduct Medal; Sharpshooter Badge w/rifle & pistol bars; Marksman Badge w/carbine & machine gun bars; Army of Occupation Medal (Germany); National Defense Service Medal

Albert C. Gray

Branch of Service: Army
Occupation: Supply
Rank: Private
Dates of Service: Discharged 1944
Decorations: Good Conduct Medal

Arvine A. Green

Branch of Service: Army Air Corps; Air Force
Occupation: Gunner
Rank: Master Sergeant
Dates of Service: July 3, 1938 - 1960
Place of Service: Pacific

Paul C. Green

Branch of Service: Army; Army Reserve
Occupation: Infantryman
Rank: Staff Sergeant
Dates of Service: Oct. 17, 1944 - 1946 (Army); 1946 - 1949 (Army Reserve)
Place of Service: Europe
Decorations: Good Conduct Medal; Combat Infantryman Badge; Bronze Star; Presidential Unit Citation

Russell L. Green

Branch of Service: Army; Army Reserve
Occupation: Medical Corps
Rank: Staff Sergeant
Dates of Service: Jan. 16, 1937 - 1946 (Army); 1946 - 1951 (Army Reserve)
Place of Service: Europe; Statcsidc

Richard H. Grimes

Branch of Service: Army
Occupation: Food Services
Rank: Sergeant First Class
Dates of Service: Oct. 1, 1941 - Dec. 30, 1945; Sept. 4, 1950 - Sept. 2, 1952
Place of Service: Stateside; New Guinea; Philippines
Decorations: Good Conduct Medal; American Defense Service Medal; American Campaign Medal; Asiatic-Pacific Campaign Medal; Philippine Liberation Medal; WWII Victory Medal

John Grosh

Branch of Service: Navy
Occupation: Fireman
Rank: Fireman 1st Class
Dates of Service: 1944 - 1946
Place of Service: Stateside; South Pacific
Decorations: American Campaign Medal; Asiatic-Pacific Campaign Medal; WWII Victory Medal

Marjorie Grumbacher

Branch of Service: WAVES
Occupation: Communications; Legal Officer
Rank: Lieutenant
Dates of Service: Oct. 1942 - Dec. 1945
Place of Service: Stateside

Dr. Harry C. Grove, Jr.

Branch of Service: Army Air Forces
Occupation: Dentist
Rank: Captain
Dates of Service: Oct. 20, 1942 - June 6, 1946
Place of Service: Okinawa, Japan
Decorations: Asiatic-Pacific Campaign Medal/w bronze star; Philippine Liberation Medal; American Campaign Medal; WWII Victory Medal

Aubrey Grumbine

Branch of Service: Army
Occupation: Medical Technician-
Rank: Staff Sergeant
Dates of Service: July 14, 1941 - Oct. 19, 1945
Place of Service: England
Decorations: Good Conduct Medal; American Campaign Medal; European-African-Middle Eastern Campaign Medal

Ray E. Gruber

Branch of Service: Army
Occupation: Truck Driver
Rank: Technician 5th Grade
Dates of Service: Sept. 14, 1943 - Jan. 1, 1946
Place of Service: New Guinea; Philippines
Decorations: Good Conduct Medal; Expert Sharpshooter Badge w/carbine bar; Asiatic-Pacific Campaign Medal; Philippine Liberation Medal; WWII Victory Medal

Ray L. "Jimmy" Haines Jr.

Branch of Service: Army
Occupation: Radio Operator
Rank: Private 1st Class
Dates of Service: 1966 - 1969
Place of Service: Stateside; Vietnam
Decorations: National Defense Service Medal; Vietnam Campaign Medal w/4 stars

Richard Grumbacher

Branch of Service: Air Force
Occupation: Squadron Commander
Rank: Captain
Dates of Service: Summer 1941-Sept. 1945
Place of Service: Europe; North Africa

Stephen C. Haines

Branch of Service: Army
Occupation: Company Commander
Rank: Lieutenant
Dates of Service: Oct. 1966 - Aug. 1971
Place of Service: Vietnam
Decorations: Good Conduct Medal; Combat Infantryman Badge; Army Commendation Medal; Vietnam Service Medal; Vietnam Campaign Medal w/2 bronze stars; Bronze Star w/ "V" for valor and one for merit; Purple Heart; National Defense Service Medal

Albert H. Hamby

Branch of Service: Army
Occupation: Infantryman; Headquarters Company
Rank: Corporal
Dates of Service: June 1, 1953 - May 11, 1955
Place of Service: Stateside; Germany
Decorations: Good Conduct Medal; Army of Occupation Medal (Germany)

James M. Hamby

Branch of Service: Navy
Occupation: Gunner
Rank: Seaman 1st Class
Dates of Service: WWII
Place of Service: Pacific

Allen A. Harbaugh

Branch of Service: Army
Occupation: Field Observer
Rank: Sergeant
Entered Service: Nov. 27, 1942
Place of Service: Germany; Belgium
Decorations: Good Conduct Medal; Silver Star; Purple Heart; WWII Victory Medal; WWII Army of Occupation Medal (Germany)

Martin I. "Jack" Harbaugh

Branch of Service: Army
Occupation: Engineer
Rank: Private
Dates of Service: June 1943 - Oct. 1945
Place of Service: Europe
Decorations: Good Conduct Medal; Purple Heart; WWII Victory Medal; WWII Army of Occupation Medal (Germany)

William L. Harbaugh

Branch of Service: Army
Occupation: Ammunition Bearer; Machine Gunner
Rank: Private 1st Class
Dates of Service: March 3, 1943 - Oct. 17, 1945
Place of Service: England; France; Belgium; Holland; Germany
Decorations: European-African-Middle Eastern Campaign Medal w/4 campaign stars; Bronze Arrowhead; Purple Heart

Edward A. Harp Jr.

Branch of Service: Army
Occupation: Communications
Rank: Sergeant 1st Class
Dates of Service: Jan. 18, 1953 - May 31, 1973
Place of Service: Stateside; Europe
Decorations: Good Conduct Medal; National Defense Service Medal; Vietnam Service Medal; Army Commendation Medal; Air Force Commendation Medal

Jayne C. Harple

Branch of Service: Air Force
Occupation: Communications Specialist; Military Training Instructor
Rank: Master Sergeant
Dates of Service: Nov. 11, 1965 - Jan. 31, 1986
Place of Service: Stateside; Philippines
Decorations: Good Conduct Medal w/silver oak leaf cluster; Meritorious Service Medal; Air Force Commendation Medal w/2 bronze OLC; Philippine Presidential Citation

Gary Hayes

Branch of Service: Air Force
Occupation: Aircraft Maintenance
Rank: Master Sergeant
Dates of Service: July 11, 1978 - Aug. 1, 2000
Place of Service: Stateside; Germany; Korea; Turkey
Decorations: GCM-6; MSM-3; AFCOM-2; AFACH-5; AF Training Ribbon; Overseas Short-Tour Ribbon; Overseas Long-Tour ribbon w/3 devices; NDSM; AF Longevity Service Awd. w/4 devices; NCO Military Education Ribbon w/1 device; Expert Marksmanship Badge w/small arms bar; Out. Unit Award w/5 devices; Joint Meritorious Unit Award

Robert Lee Heiberger

Branch of Service: Navy
Occupation: Shipfitter Striker
Rank: Seaman 1st Class
Dates of Service: Dec. 30, 1941-Nov. 2, 1945
Place of Service: Pacific

John Aubrey Hill

Branch of Service: Army
Occupation: Clerk; Gunner
Rank: Corporal
Dates of Service: Dec. 22, 1942 - Jan. 11, 1946
Place of Service: Australia; New Guinea; Philippines; Japan
Decorations: Good Conduct Medal; Expert Rifleman Badge; Philippine Liberation Medal; Asiatic-Pacific Campaign Medal; WWII Victory Medal

Wilbur R. Hershberger

Branch of Service: Army
Occupation: Infantry; Squad Leader; First Scout
Rank: Sergeant
Dates of Service: Feb. 20, 1943 - Oct. 12, 1945
Place of Service: Europe
Decorations: Good Conduct Medal; Purple Heart; Combat Infantryman Badge; European-African-Middle Eastern Campaign Medal

John "Jack" Aubrey Hill II

Branch of Service: Army
Occupation: Radar Operator
Rank: Corporal
Dates of Service: Feb. 11, 1962 - Feb. 11, 1965
Place of Service: Stateside
Decorations: Sharpshooter Badge

Jeremy S. Hiett

Branch of Service: Marine Corps
Occupation: Infantryman
Rank: Corporal
Dates of Service: June 1995 - Aug. 1999
Place of Service: Stateside; Bosnia; Albania; Congo; Zaire

Terence Lynn "Terry" Hill

Branch of Service: Navy
Occupation: Seaman
Rank: Seaman 1st Class
Dates of Service: 1967
Place of Service: Stateside

Frederick G. Hill

Branch of Service: Army Air Forces
Occupation: Pilot
Rank: Tech Sergeant
Dates of Service: July 11, 1941 - Aug. 1943
Place of Service: Stateside

Robert Carl Hixson

Branch of Service: Army Air Forces
Occupation: Draftsman
Rank: Sergeant
Dates of Service: Sept. 30, 1942 - Nov. 9, 1945
Place of Service: Alaska; Aleutian Islands
Decorations: Good Conduct Medal; Distinguished Unit Badge; Asiatic-Pacific Campaign Medal w/bronze star; American Campaign Medal; WWII Victory Medal Award w/5 devices; Joint Meritorious Unit Award

Ralph C. "Dutch" Hoover

Branch of Service: Army
Occupation: Infantry; Operations; Training; Headquarters Commandant; Troop Commander
Rank: Major
Dates of Service: 1943 - 1945; 1948 - 1968
Place of Service: Pacific; Korea; Stateside; Europe
Decorations: Purple Heart; Combat Infantryman Badge; Distinguished Unit Citation; Korean Service Medal w/7 campaign stars; UN Service Medal; Army Occupation Medal (Japan, Germany & Korea); NDSM w/1OCL; Philippine Independence Medal; Armed Forces Reserve Medal w/1 OCL; ARCOM w/2 OLC; Joint Service Commendation Medal

Stanley T. Hoover

Branch of Service: Air Force
Occupation: Mechanic
Rank: Sergeant
Dates of Service: March 9, 1951 - March 8, 1955
Place of Service: Stateside
Decorations: Good Conduct Medal; National Defense Service Medal

Carroll S. Hose

Branch of Service: Army
Occupation: Supply Clerk
Rank: Private 1st Class
Dates of Service: March 2, 1942 - Nov. 12, 1945
Place of Service: South Pacific
Decorations: Good Conduct Medal; Combat Infantryman Badge; American Campaign Medal; Asiatic-Pacific Campaign Medal w/1 battle star; WWII Victory Medal

Richard W. Huntzberry

Branch of Service: Army
Occupation: Infantryman
Rank: Sergeant
Dates of Service: January 1943 - Sept. 22, 1944 KIA
Place of Service: North Africa; Italy
Decorations: Good Conduct Medal; Bronze Star w/2 OLC; Purple Heart w/1 OLC; European-African-Middle Eastern Campaign Medal; WWII Victory Medal; Medaille Commemorative de la Campagne d'Italie; and the Croix du Combattant Voluntaire

Wilbur E. Huntzberry

Branch of Service: Army
Occupation: Infantryman; Mess Sergeant
Rank: Sergeant
Dates of Service: Aug. 15, 1944 - March 21, 1946
Place of Service: Europe
Decorations: Good Conduct Medal; American Campaign Medal; Combat Infantryman Badge; Marksman Badge/w M1 and rifle bars; European-African-Middle Eastern Campaign Ribbon; WWII Victory Medal

Kelly Hurlbrink-Zamora

Branch of Service: Army
Occupation: Topographic Analyst
Rank: Specialist
Dates of Service: Aug. 2002 - May 2006
Place of Service: Stateside; Kuwait; Iraq
Decorations: GCM; Airborne Wings; Joint Service Achievement Medal; Army Commendation Medal; NDSM; Global War on Terrorism Service Medal; Iraq Campaign Medal & others

Kevin Hurlbrink

Branch of Service: Army
Occupation: Network Switching Systems Operator
Rank: Specialist
Dates of Service: June 28, 2001 - June 27, 2005
Place of Service: Stateside; Kuwait; Iraq
Decorations: GCM; Airborne Wings; Army Commendation Medal; Army Achievement Medal; NDSM; Global War on Terrorism Expeditionary Medal; Global War on Terrorism Service Medal; Iraq Campaign Medal; Army Service Ribbon

J. Robert Hyssong Jr.

Branch of Service: Army
Occupation: Supply Sergeant
Rank: Master Sergeant
Dates of Service: Dec. 4, 1942 - Jan. 21, 1946; Sept. 1950 - Sept. 1951
Place of Service: Africa; Europe; Stateside
Decorations: European-African-Middle Eastern Campaign Medal

Vernon Jenkins

Branch of Service: Army
Occupation: Ranger
Rank: Private
Dates of Service: 1942-1945
Place of Service: Italy
Decorations: European-African-Middle Eastern Campaign Medal; WWII Victory Medal; Prisoner of War Medal

Weston Jenkins

Branch of Service: Army
Rank: Private
Dates of Service: 1942
Place of Service: Stateside

Robert W. "Bob" Johnson

Branch of Service: Army Air Forces
Occupation: Aviation Cadet
Rank: Cadet Flight Sergeant
Dates of Service: Sept. 21, 1944 - Oct. 31, 1945
Place of Service: Stateside
Decorations: Good Conduct Medal

Harold Elwood Jones

Branch of Service: Air Force
Occupation: Supply Sergeant
Rank: Staff Sergeant
Dates of Service: Jan 3, 1951 - Dec. 10, 1954
Place of Service: Alaska
Decorations: Good Conduct Medal; National Defense Service Medal

Leon Jones

Branch of Service: Army
Occupation: Clerk; Mechanic
Rank: Staff Sergeant
Dates of Service: June 1945 - Dec. 1946; June 1950 - June 1953
Place of Service: Pacific; Atlantic; Germany
Decorations: Asiatic-Pacific Campaign Medal; Army of Occupation Medal (Germany); WWII Victory Medal

Lewis E. Jones Jr.

Branch of Service: Army
Occupation: Medic
Rank: Corporal
Dates of Service: May 7, 1951 - April 30, 1953 (Army); April 31, 1953 - Jan. 17, 1957 (Army Reserve)
Place of Service: Stateside; Korea

Lester F. Joy

Branch of Service: Army
Occupation: Machine Gunner
Rank: Private 1st Class
Dates of Service: May 16, 1950 - Feb. 14, 1951
Place of Service: Korea
Decorations: Combat Infantryman Badge; Purple Heart; Meritorious Unit Commendation; National Defense Service Medal; United Nations Service Medal

Michael Kamas

Branch of Service: Navy
Occupation: Naval Flight Officer
Rank: Lieutenant
Dates of Service: May 12, 2000 - present
Place of Service: Sicily; Crete; South America
Decorations: Navy & Marine Corps Achievement Medal; Global War on Terrorism Expeditionary Medal; Meritorious Unit Commendation; Navy Battle "E" Ribbon

Larry E. Keller

Branch of Service: Navy
Occupation: Communication Technician
Rank: Petty Officer 2nd Class
Dates of Service: 1957 - 1961
Place of Service: Stateside; Turkey

Charles L. Kendall

Branch of Service: Army
Occupation: Company Commander
Rank: Major
Dates of Service: 1932 - April 27, 1946
Place of Service: Hawaii; Panama; North Africa; Italy
Decorations: Purple Heart w/OLC; European-African-Middle Eastern Campaign Medal w/4 bronze stars; American Campaign Medal; WWII Victory Medal

Oscar K. "Bud" Keller

Branch of Service: Navy
Occupation: Gunner
Rank: Seaman 1st Class
Dates of Service: July 9, 1943 - March 21, 1946
Place of Service: Atlantic; Europe
Decorations: American Campaign Medal; WWII Victory Medal

Edward Kendall

Branch of Service: Navy
Occupation: Communications Tech
Rank: Petty Officer 3rd Class
Dates of Service: June 1951 - June 1955
Place of Service: Japan; Stateside
Decorations: Good Conduct Medal; United Nations Service Medal; K orean Service Medal; American Service Medal

Greyson Julius Kelsh

Branch of Service: Army
Occupation: Driver
Rank: Private
Dates of Service: Jan. 19, 1942 - Dec. 29, 1945
Place of Service: Stateside
Decorations: Good Conduct Medal; American Campaign Medal; WWII Victory Medal

William K. Kendall

Branch of Service: Army Air Corps
Occupation: Turret Gunner
Rank: Staff Sergeant
Dates of Service: April 9, 1943 - May 29, 1945
Place of Service: Europe
Decorations: Good Conduct Medal; Air Medal w/12 OLC; European-African-Middle Eastern Campaign Medal w/3 bronze stars

Robert Henry Kelsh

Branch of Service: Army
Occupation: Cook
Rank: Sergeant
Dates of Service: Sept. 26, 1939 - Sept. 3, 1945
Place of Service: Africa; Tunisia; Middle East; Europe
Decorations: Good Conduct Medal; American Defense Service Medal; European-African-Middle Eastern Campaign Medal

Edwin M. Kershner

Branch of Service: Navy
Occupation: Ship Repair
Rank: Shipfitter 2nd Class
Dates of Service: Oct. 1, 1943 - Dec. 11, 1945
Place of Service: Pacific

Fred J. Kershner

Branch of Service: Army
Occupation: Rifleman
Rank: Private 1st Class
Dates of Service: Aug. 15, 1944 - Oct. 5, 1945
Place of Service: Europe
Decorations: Combat Infantryman Badge; European-African-Middle Eastern Campaign Medal w/1 bronze star; Purple Heart

John R. Kershner

Branch of Service: Army
Occupation: Messenger
Rank: Private 1st Class
Dates of Service: July 25, 1944 - Nov. 20, 1945
Place of Service: Europe
Decorations: Good Conduct Medal; WWII Victory Medal w/2 bronze stars; Silver Star

Albert L. Keyser III

Branch of Service: Air Force
Occupation: Fire Control Systems Operator
Rank: Staff Sergeant
Dates of Service: 1970 - 1973
Place of Service: Stateside; Thailand; Laos; Cambodia
Decorations: Good Conduct Medal; National Defense Service Medal; Vietnam Service Medal; Air Force Combat Action Medal; Presidential Unit Citation; Outstanding Unit Award

Gisele Luipersbeck Klincewicz

Branch of Service: WAVES
Occupation: Medical Corpsman
Rank: Pharmacist's Mate 3rd Class
Dates of Service: April 16, 1947 - June 14, 1949
Place of Service: Stateside
Decorations: WWII Victory Medal

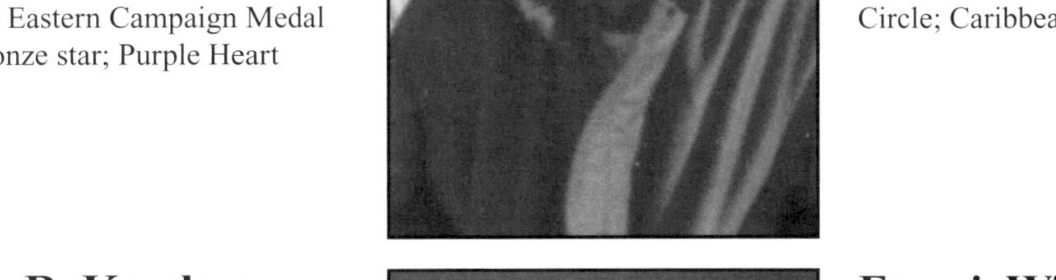

Thomas F. Kline

Branch of Service: Navy
Occupation: Fire Control Technician
Rank: Fire Technician 3rd Class
Dates of Service: Jan. 1949 - Jan. 1950 (released to inactive reserve duty); reactivated April 1952 - Dec. 23, 1953
Place of Service: Atlantic; Arctic Circle; Caribbean

Francis Wilbur Knight

Branch of Service: Navy
Occupation: Fire fighter
Rank: Seaman 1st Class
Dates of Service: Jan. 11, 1944 - Dec. 17, 1945
Place of Service: Philippine Islands
Decorations: Philippine Liberation Medal

Orville Lee Knight

Branch of Service: Army
Occupation: Radioman
Rank: Corporal
Dates of Service: Nov. 5, 1968 - April 8, 1969 KIA
Place of Service: Vietnam
Decorations: National Defense Service Medal; Vietnam Service Medal; Combat Infantryman Badge 1st Award; Expert Marksman Badge w/rifle bar; Sharpshooter Badge w/machine gun bar; Marksman Badge w/rifle bar; Purple Heart

David H. Knode

Branch of Service: Navy
Occupation: Seaman
Rank: Seaman
Dates of Service: Oct. 15, 1963 - Oct. 14, 1966
Place of Service: South China Sea
Decorations: Good Conduct Medal

Gary L. Knode

Branch of Service: Marine Corps
Occupation: Infantryman; Administration
Rank: Corporal
Dates of Service: Feb. 9, 1961 - Feb. 8, 1965
Place of Service: Cuba; Stateside
Decorations: Good Conduct Medal; Marine Corps Expeditionary Medal; Marksmanship Badge (Rifle)

Harry E. Knode

Branch of Service: Army
Occupation: Draftsman
Rank: Sergeant
Dates of Service: Aug. 2, 1961 - July 31, 1967
Place of Service: Germany
Decorations: Good Conduct Medal

Michael David Knode

Branch of Service: Air Force
Occupation: Electronic Systems Security Assessment Analyst
Rank: Technical Sergeant
Dates of Service: March 1, 1990 - Present
Place of Service: Stateside; Germany; Korea
Decorations: Joint Service Commendation Medal; AF Commendation Medal-2; Joint Service Achievement Medal-2; AF Achievement Medal-3; GCM-5; NDSM-2; GWOT; Korean Defense Service Medal

Thomas M. Knode

Branch of Service: Air Force
Occupation: Administration
Rank: Airman 1st Class
Dates of Service: April 1960 - May 1964
Place of Service: Stateside
Decorations: Good Conduct Medal; Marksmanship Badge

John C. Koontz Sr.

Branch of Service: Army
Occupation: Infantry
Rank: Technical Sergeant
Dates of Service: Dec. 2, 1952 - Nov. 4, 1954
Place of Service: Korea
Decorations: Good Conduct Medal; National Defense Service Medal; Korean Service Medal w/bronze star; Republic of Korea Presidential Unit Citation; United Nations Service Medal

Paul D. Koontz

Branch of Service: Army
Occupation: Military Policeman
Rank: Corporal
Dates of Service: Nov. 11, 1942 - Nov. 30, 1945
Place of Service: Africa; Italy
Decorations: Good Conduct Medal; European-African-Middle Eastern Campaign Medal; WWII Victory Medal

Andrew Albert Lewis Krumpe

Branch of Service: Marine Corps
Occupation: Infantryman
Rank: Corporal
Dates of Service: Oct. 2002 - Present
Place of Service: Stateside; Iraq

Max Krumpe

Branch of Service: Merchant Marine
Occupation: Deck Hand; Cook; Baker
Rank: Seaman
Dates of Service: 1943 - 1947
Place of Service: Europe; Middle East; India; China; Africa
Decorations: Atlantic War Zone Bar

Wilbert F. Latney

Branch of Service: Air Force
Occupation: Paratrooper
Rank: Sergeant
Dates of Service: 1954 - 1958
Place of Service: Okinawa; Stateside

Robert Logan

Branch of Service: Navy
Occupation: Interior Communications Electrician
Rank: Electrician's Mate 3rd class
Dates of Service: Nov. 7, 1968 - Nov. 7, 1972
Place of Service: Atlantic; Caribbean

Christina "Tina" Carpenter Lawler

Branch of Service: Army
Occupation: Power Generation Equipment Repairer
Rank: Private 1st Class
Dates of Service: Sept. 21, 2005 - March 9, 2007 (Army); March 10, 2007 - Present (Individual Ready Reserve)
Place of Service: Stateside
Decorations: Sharpshooter Badge

Terry Lee Logan

Branch of Service: Army Reserve
Occupation: Data Processing Operator; Aircraft Maintenance
Rank: Specialist 4th Class
Dates of Service: March 4, 1966 - Oct. 6, 1969
Place of Service: Vietnam; Stateside
Decorations: Good Conduct Medal; National Defense Service Medal; Vietnam Service Medal; Vietnam Campaign Medal; 2 overseas bars; Sharpshooter Badge (M14; Expert M16)

Harry J. "Blackie" Layman

Branch of Service: Marine Corps
Occupation: Combat Engineer
Rank: Lance Corporal
Dates of Service: 1968 - 1970
Place of Service: Vietnam
Decorations: Good Conduct Medal; Combat Action Ribbon; Vietnam Service Medal; Vietnam Campaign Medal; National Defense Service Medal

William Russell Long

Branch of Service: Army
Occupation: Infantryman
Rank: Technician 5th Grade
Dates of Service: Dec. 3, 1942 - Dec. 22, 1945
Place of Service: Europe
Decorations: Good Conduct Medal; Purple Heart-2; Meritorious Unit Award; American Campaign Medal; European-African-Middle Eastern Campaign Medal; WWII Victory Medal

Elmer O. "Whitey" Lewis

Branch of Service: Army
Occupation: Medic
Rank: Private 1st Class
Dates of Service: May 11, 1943 - April 28, 1946
Place of Service: France; Germany
Decorations: Good Conduct Medal; American Campaign Medal; European-African-Middle Eastern Campaign Medal; WWII Victory Medal; Army of Occupation Medal (Germany); Army Commendation Medal

George W. Lushbaugh Jr.

Branch of Service: Army
Occupation: Combat Engineer
Rank: Private
Dates of Service: Oct. 15, 1943 - Jan. 1946
Place of Service: Europe
Decorations: Good Conduct Medal

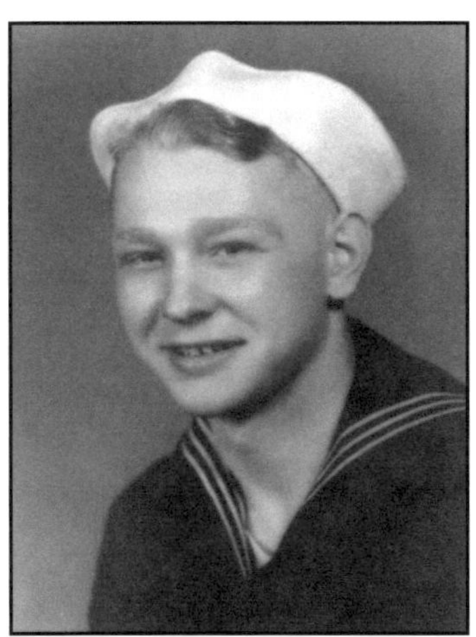

Richard Pierce Lynch
Branch of Service: Navy
Occupation: Machinist
Rank: Motor Machinist's Mate 2nd Class
Dates of Service: Jan. 27, 1944 - May 4, 1946
Place of Service: Pacific; Philippines
Decorations: Asiatic-Pacific Campaign Medal w/1 star; American Campaign Medal; WWII Victory Medal; Philippine Liberation Medal; Combat Action Ribbon

Michael Lee Mardres
Branch of Service: Army
Occupation: Computer Maintenance, Artillery
Rank: Private 1st Class
Dates of Service: June 25, 2002 - Apr. 20, 2004
Place of Service: Stateside; Iraq
Decorations: Army Commendation Medal

Carl V. Martin
Branch of Service: Army
Occupation: Medic
Rank: Staff Sergeant
Dates of Service: June 2, 1944 - April 19, 1946
Place of Service: Stateside; Philippines; Japan
Decorations: Good Conduct Medal; American Campaign Medal; Asiatic-Pacific Theater Medal; WWII Victory Medal; Army Occupation Medal (Japan)

Ernest W. Martin
Branch of Service: Army
Occupation: Tank Driver
Rank: Private
Dates of Service: May 9, 1945 - Nov. 9, 1945
Place of Service: Stateside
Decorations: WWII Victory Medal

Ernest W. Martin Jr.
Branch of Service: Marine Corps
Occupation: Rifleman; Automotive Mechanic
Rank: Sergeant
Dates of Service: Jan. 14, 1954 - Jan. 13, 1957
Place of Service: Stateside
Decorations: Good Conduct Medal; Sharpshooter Badge w/ rifle bar; National Defense Service Medal

Lawrence R. Martin
Branch of Service: Army
Occupation: Mechanic
Rank: Technician Four
Dates of Service: August 1943 - January 1946
Place of Service: Stateside; England; France; Germany
Decorations: Good Conduct Medal; European-African-Middle Eastern Campaign Medal w/5 campaign stars (Normandy, Northern France, Ardennes, Rhineland, Central Europe); WWII Victory Medal

Robert L. Martin
Branch of Service: Army Air Forces
Occupation: Air Traffic Controller
Rank: Technical Sergeant
Dates of Service: Dec. 22, 1942 - 1945
Place of Service: Stateside; England; Italy; France
Decorations: European-African-Middle Eastern Campaign Medal w/7 battle stars; Presidential Unit Citation

Theodore M. Martin
Branch of Service: Army
Occupation: Military Policeman
Rank: Specialist 4th Class
Dates of Service: Jan. 29, 1962 - Nov. 4, 1964
Place of Service: Stateside; Philippines
Decorations: Good Conduct Medal; Sharpshooter Badge w/rifle & carbine bars; National Defense Service Medal

Victor W. Martin

Branch of Service: Army
Occupation: Counterintelligence
Rank: Chief Warrant Officer-4
Dates of Service: May 1968 - Aug. 1993
Place of Service: Germany; Stateside
Decorations: GCM; ARCOM; ARACH; MSM w/OLC; Reserve Components Achievement Medal w/OLC; NDSM w/1 bronze star; Armed Forces Reserve Medal; Army Service Ribbon; Overseas Service Ribbon

Elvin E. Mason

Branch of Service: Air Force
Occupation: Radio Controller
Rank: Airman 1st Class
Dates of Service: June 1953 - June 15, 1957
Place of Service: Germany

Walter J. Mason

Branch of Service: Army
Rank: Private 1st Class
Dates of Service: July 11, 1950 KIA
Place of Service: Korea
Decorations: Purple Heart; Combat Infantryman Badge; Korean Service Medal; United Nations Service Medal; National Defense Service Medal; Korean War Service Medal

Earl E. May

Branch of Service: Army
Occupation: Tank Corps
Rank: Private
Dates of Service: Sept. 14, 1943 - Aug. 4, 1945
Place of Service: Europe
Decorations: Purple Heart; Marksman Badge w/rife bar

Paul F. May

Branch of Service: Army Air Forces
Occupation: Airplane Electrical Mechanic
Rank: Sergeant
Dates of Service: Sept. 30, 1942 - Oct. 22, 1945
Place of Service: Stateside; New Guinea; Philippines
Decorations: Good Conduct Medal; Asiatic-Pacific Campaign Medal; Philippine Liberation Medal w/bronze star

George F. McAllister Jr.

Branch of Service: Army Reserve
Occupation: Ammunition Specialist
Rank: Staff Sergeant
Dates of Service: 1980 - 1992; 2001 - 2004
Place of Service: Saudi Arabia; Kuwait; Iraq
Decorations: Army Commendation Medal w/2 bronze stars; Global War on Terrorism Service Medal

Gary Lynn McDonald

Branch of Service: Air Force; Navy
Occupation: Morse System Operator (Air Force); Operation Specialist (Navy)
Rank: Sergeant (Air Force); Operation Specialist 2nd Class (Navy)
Dates of Service: Jan. 1970 - Feb. 1976 (Air Force); Jan. 1980 - Nov. 1980, Mar. 1985 - June 1998 (Navy)
Place of Service: Alaska; Turkey; Vietnam (Air Force); Atlantic; Mediterranean; Persian Gulf; Caribbean (Navy)
Decorations: Good Conduct Medal w/2 OLC; Armed Forces Service Medal; Vietnam Service Medal

Ronald McNeer

Branch of Service: Army
Occupation: Artillery
Rank: Specialist 4th Class
Dates of Service: Dec. 9, 1965 - Sept. 1967
Place of Service: Vietnam
Decorations: National Defense Service Medal; Vietnam Service Medal; Vietnam Campaign Medal w/2 Oak Leaf Clusters

Richard E. Messersmith

Branch of Service: Marine Corps; Navy
Rank: Corporal (Marine Corps); Yeoman 1st Class (Navy)
Dates of Service: Sept. 21, 1936 - Sept. 13, 1940 (Marine Corps); Feb. 1942 - Sept. 1945 (Navy)
Place of Service: China; Pacific
Decorations: American Defense Service Medal; American Campaign Medal; Asiatic-Pacific Campaign Medal; WWII Victory Medal

Benjamin A. Michael

Branch of Service: Army
Occupation: Ranger; Medical Corps
Rank: Second Lieutenant
Dates of Service: May 2003 - Present
Place of Service: Stateside; Afghanistan

George Michael

Branch of Service: Army
Occupation: Intelligence Officer
Rank: First Lieutenant
Dates of Service: March 1969 - April 1972
Place of Service: Stateside
Decorations: Army Commendation Medal

Joseph Elwood Michael

Branch of Service: Army
Occupation: Quartermaster Corps
Rank: Sergeant
Dates of Service: 1936 - 1939; 1940 - 1945
Place of Service: Stateside; New Guinea

Larry F. Michael

Branch of Service: Army
Occupation: Infantryman
Rank: Staff Sergeant
Dates of Service: Oct. 1967 - July 1969
Place of Service: Vietnam
Decorations: Good Conduct Medal; Purple Heart; Combat Infantryman Badge; Vietnam Service Medal; Vietnam Campaign Medal; National Defense Service Medal

Robert Harding Miles

Branch of Service: Army
Occupation: Military Policeman
Rank: Chief Warrant Officer - 4
Dates of Service: March 1939 - Aug. 31, 1969
Place of Service: Europe; Korea; Vietnam
Decorations: Bronze Star; Army Commendation Medal w/2 OLC; Korean Service Medal; National Defense Service Medal w/1 OLC; United Nations Service Medal; Overseas Service Bar-4; Vietnam Service Medal; Vietnam Campaign Medal w/1960 device; Basic Missileman Badge

Robert Benson Miller

Branch of Service: Navy
Occupation: Engine Room Crewmember
Rank: Water Tender 3rd Class
Dates of Service: June 1, 1944 - June 8, 1946
Place of Service: Pacific; Philippines
Decorations: Asiatic-Pacific Campaign Medal; American Campaign Medal; Philippine Liberation Medal; WWII Victory Medal

Daniel J. Minnich

Branch of Service: Navy
Occupation: Gunner; Merchant Marine Armed Guard
Rank: Seaman 1st Class
Dates of Service: 1943 - 1946
Place of Service: Atlantic

James W. Minnich

Branch of Service: Army
Occupation: Military Police; Cook
Rank: Staff Sergeant
Dates of Service: Nov. 1947 - June 1955
Place of Service: Korea; Japan; Stateside; Germany
Decorations: Army of Occupation Medal (Japan)

Wallace T. Minnich

Branch of Service: Army
Occupation: Scout Crew Chief; Military Police; Infantry
Rank: Sergeant 1st Class
Dates of Service: March 9, 1943 - Sept. 5, 1950 KIA
Place of Service: Europe; Korea
Decorations: Good Conduct Medal; Combat Infantryman Badge; European-African-Middle Eastern Campaign Medal w/bronze star; Purple Heart (Italy); Purple Heart (Korea)

Dennis Lynn Mongold

Branch of Service: Navy
Occupation: Radioman
Rank: Petty Officer 3rd Class
Dates of Service: June 17, 1970 - June 12, 1974
Place of Service: Pacific
Decorations: National Defense Service Medal; Meritorious Unit Commendation

James "Dale" Mongold

Branch of Service: Marine Corps
Occupation: Aviation Group
Rank: Corporal
Dates of Service: Aug. 12, 1965 - May 1, 1970
Place of Service: Vietnam
Decorations: GCM; NDSM; Presidential Unit Commendation Ribbon; Vietnam Service Medal w/2 stars; Combat Action Ribbon; Republic of Vietnam Campaign Medal w/1960 device; Republic of Vietnam Meritorious Unit Citation; Vietnam Cross of Gallantry Medal w/palm; Vietnam Civil Actions Medal 1st Class Color w/palm

James Charles Mongold

Branch of Service: Marine Corps
Occupation: Mechanic
Rank: Sergeant
Dates of Service: April 8, 1943 - Dec. 6, 1945
Place of Service: Pacific
Decorations: Good Conduct Medal; American Defense Service Medal; Asiatic-Pacific Campaign Medal; Army of Occupation Medal (Japan)

Alvey C. Moser

Branch of Service: Air Force
Occupation: Food Service
Rank: Staff Sergeant
Dates of Service: Sept. 18, 1950 - Dec. 21, 1953
Place of Service: Stateside; Japan; Korea
Decorations: Good Conduct Medal; National Defense Service Medal; United Nations Medal; Korean Service Medal w/3 bronze stars

David L. Murray

Branch of Service: Air Force
Occupation: Radio Communications
Rank: Airman 2nd Class
Dates of Service: July 5, 1951 - July 4, 1955
Place of Service: Japan; Stateside
Decorations: Good Conduct Medal; United Nations Service Medal (Korea); Korean Service Medal; National Defense Service Medal

Donald C. Murray

Branch of Service: Army
Occupation: Unknown
Rank: Sergeant
Dates of Service: WWII
Place of Service: France; Germany
Decorations: Purple Heart

Allen W. Myers

Branch of Service: Army
Occupation: Messenger
Rank: Private 1st Class
Dates of Service: April 3, 1943 - Aug. 23, 1945
Place of Service: Europe
Decorations: Good Conduct Medal; European-African-Middle Eastern Campaign Medal; Purple Heart

Charlie "Gordy" Myers

Branch of Service: Navy
Rank: Petty Officer 2nd Class
Dates of Service: May 1943 - 1945
Place of Service: Cuba; Atlantic

Earl Sam Myers

Branch of Service: Army
Occupation: Paratrooper
Rank: Sergeant
Dates of Service: May 1942 - Jan. 1946
Place of Service: Scotland; Africa; Holland; Belgium; Germany
Decorations: Combat Infantryman Badge; Purple Heart-2; European-African-Middle Eastern Campaign Medal; WWII Victory Medal

Eugene Y. Nakada

Branch of Service: Army
Occupation: Supply Officer
Rank: Major
Dates of Service: 1953 - 1977
Place of Service: Stateside; Germany; France; Vietnam; Korea; Japan
Decorations: Bronze Star-2 w/4 campaign stars

Ray Lewis Nalley

Branch of Service: Army
Occupation: Reconnaissance
Rank: Staff Sergeant
Dates of Service: Sept. 17, 1948 - May 1952
Place of Service: Stateside; Germany
Decorations: Good Conduct Medal; Army of Occupation Medal (Germany)

Freda D. Nunamaker

Branch of Service: Women's Army Corps
Occupation: Clerk
Rank: Private
Dates of Service: Jan. 17, 1945 - Dec. 9, 1945
Place of Service: Stateside
Decorations: American Campaign Medal; Women's Army Corps Service Medal; WWII Victory Medal

Harold B. Nunamaker

Branch of Service: Army Air Forces
Occupation: Airplane Sheet Metal Worker
Rank: Sergeant
Dates of Service: March 6, 1943 - March 21, 1946
Place of Service: China; India; Burma
Decorations: Good Conduct Medal; American Campaign Medal; Asiatic-Pacific Campaign Medal; WWII Victory Medal

Shane M. Olden

Branch of Service: Marine Corps
Occupation: Infantryman
Rank: Corporal
Dates of Service: Oct. 6, 2003 - Present
Place of Service: Stateside; Lebanon; Africa; Jordan; Kuwait; Iraq
Decorations: National Defense Service Medal; Sea Service Deployment Ribbon w/bronze star; Combat Action Ribbon; Humanitarian Service Medal w/bronze star; GWOT; GWOT-EM; GCM; Iraqi Campaign Medal; Navy & Marine Corps Achievement Medal; Navy Unit Citation Medal

Linwood E. Orange

Branch of Service: Army Air Corps
Occupation: Pilot
Rank: 2nd Lieutenant
Dates of Service: June 26, 1942 - Oct. 1945
Place of Service: Stateside
Decorations: Good Conduct Medal; American Campaign Medal; WWII Victory Medal

Elwood C. "Woodie" Pearman

Branch of Service: Army
Occupation: Military Policeman; Postal Clerk
Rank: Sergeant
Dates of Service: Oct. 1, 1941 - Oct. 7, 1945
Place of Service: Stateside; Central and South America
Decorations: Good Conduct Medal; American Defense Service Medal; American Campaign Medal

Ed Peters

Branch of Service: Army
Occupation: Military Police
Rank: Corporal
Dates of Service: Oct. 12, 1952 - Aug. 26, 1954
Place of Service: Korea
Decorations: Good Conduct Medal; National Defense Service Medal; United Nations Service Medal; Korean Service Medal w/2 bronze stars; Republic of Korea Presidential Unit Citation

Ricky A. Pike

Branch of Service: Army
Occupation: Petroleum Supply Specialist; General Supply Specialist
Rank: Sergeant
Dates of Service: Dec. 19, 1998 - Present
Place of Service: Stateside; Iraq; Kuwait
Decorations: ARCOM; Iraq Campaign Medal; Army Service Ribbon; NDSM w/bronze star; Combat Action Badge; Iraq Campaign Medal; MD Recruiting, Commendation, Service & Active Duty medals; Nat. Guard Unit of Excellence Awd.; Overseas Service & Army Service ribbons; Armed Forces Reserve Medal w/M device; Army Reserve Ach. Medal w/OCL; Army Meritorious Unit Cit.; Presidential Unit Cit.; Drivers Badge

Allan Powell

Branch of Service: Navy
Occupation: Aviation Ordnanceman
Rank: Aviation Ordnanceman 2nd Class
Dates of Service: 1942 - 1945
Place of Service: Caribbean; Pacific
Decorations: Good Conduct Medal; Caribbean and Pacific service medals; ribbons of merit; Gunner's Wings

Bob "Moe" Powell

Branch of Service: Navy
Occupation: Quartermaster
Rank: Quartermaster 2nd Class
Dates of Service: 1946 - 1951
Place of Service: Pacific; Caribbean

C.K. Powell

Branch of Service: Navy
Occupation: Radio and Radar Operator
Rank: Aviation Radioman 1st Class
Dates of Service: 1941 - 1952
Place of Service: Pacific

David F. Powell

Branch of Service: Navy
Occupation: Diver
Rank: Boatswain's Mate 2nd Class
Dates of Service: 1946 - 1957
Place of Service: Atlantic; Caribbean; Mediterranean; Persian Gulf
Decorations: Good Conduct Medal; American Campaign Medal

Francis Bernard Rang

Branch of Service: Army Air Forces
Occupation: Navigator/Bombardier
Rank: Major
Dates of Service: 1941 - July 14, 1943 KIA
Place of Service: Stateside; North Atlantic; Mediterranean
Decorations: Distinguished Flying Cross; Silver Star

Murray Baechtel Reed

Branch of Service: Air Force
Occupation: Classified Support w/Flight Status
Rank: Airman 2nd Class
Dates of Service: 1961 - 1962
Place of Service: Stateside
Decorations: Good Conduct Medal

Carl J. Reed

Branch of Service: Army
Occupation: Armorer; Infantry
Rank: Corporal
Dates of Service: Nov. 7, 1942 - Jan. 31, 1946
Place of Service: England; Europe
Decorations: Good Conduct Medal; American Campaign Medal; European-African-Middle Eastern Campaign Medal; WWII Victory Medal

Roderick C. Reed

Branch of Service: Army Air Forces
Occupation: B-17 Maintenance Crew Chief
Rank: Captain
Dates of Service: January 1940 - 1949
Place of Service: Newfoundland; England; North Africa; Italy; Germany
Decorations: Good Conduct Medal; Aerial Gunner's Wings; Air Medal w/1 OLC; Presidential Unit Citation w/1 OLC; European-North African-Mediterranean Campaign Medal w/6 battle stars; American Campaign Medal; American Defense Service Medal w/1 battle star

Douglass C. Reed

Branch of Service: Marine Corps
Occupation: Rifleman; Interpreter-Translator
Rank: Sergeant
Dates of Service: Sept. 6, 1966 - Dec. 5, 1969
Place of Service: Caribbean; Panama; Vietnam
Decorations: Good Conduct Medal; National Defense Service Medal; Vietnam Service Medal; Vietnam Campaign Medal; Combat Action Ribbon; Sharpshooter Badge w/rifle bar

Dennis E. Reeder

Branch of Service: Marine Corps
Occupation: Infantryman
Rank: Corporal
Dates of Service: November 1966 - 1970
Place of Service: Vietnam
Decorations: Good Conduct Medal; Purple Heart; Combat Action Ribbon

Jeffrey C. Reed

Branch of Service: Army
Occupation: Artillery (Nike Hercules Missiles)
Rank: Specialist 4th Class
Dates of Service: May 1968 - March 1971
Place of Service: Alaska

Samuel Ray Rhodes

Branch of Service: Army
Occupation: Military Policeman
Rank: Sergeant
Dates of Service: March 1943 - Feb. 1946
Place of Service: Central Europe
Decorations: Good Conduct Medal; Glider Badge; Sharpshooter Badge w/rifle & carbine bars; American Campaign Medal; European-African-Middle Eastern Campaign Medal; WWII Victory Medal

Jimmy Ridenour

Branch of Service: Army
Occupation: Rifleman
Rank: Private 1st Class
Dates of Service: July 12, 1944 - Sept. 28, 1945
Place of Service: Europe
Decorations: Good Conduct Medal; Combat Infantryman Badge; European-African-Middle Eastern Campaign Medal; Bronze Star; Purple Heart; WWII Victory Medal; Presidential Unit Citation

Paul W. Rodeffer

Branch of Service: Navy
Occupation: Deck Hand; Motor Launch Driver
Rank: Seaman 1st Class
Dates of Service: Nov. 1944 - July 1946
Place of Service: Pacific
Decorations: China Service Medal; Asiatic-Pacific Campaign Medal; WWII Victory Medal

Ernest R. "Dick" Rider

Branch of Service: Marine Corps
Occupation: Motor Sergeant
Rank: Sergeant
Dates of Service: Sept. 10, 1951 - 1953
Place of Service: Stateside; Korea
Decorations: Korean Service Medal w/3 stars; National Defense Service Medal; United Nations Service Medal; Korean Presidential Unit Citation; Republic of Korea War Service Medal

William H. Ruck Jr.

Branch of Service: Army
Occupation: Cook
Rank: Technician 5th Class
Dates of Service: Feb. 1, 1943 - Dec. 2, 1945
Place of Service: Europe
Decorations: Good Conduct Medal; European-African-Middle Eastern Campaign Medal; American Campaign Medal; WWII Victory Medal

Charles W. Riggs

Branch of Service: Army Air Forces
Occupation: Administrative NCO
Rank: Technical Sergeant
Dates of Service: Sept. 30, 1942 - March 10, 1946
Place of Service: Stateside; Brazil
Decorations: Good Conduct Medal; American Campaign Medal; WWII Victory Medal

Lewis Stanley "Pat" Rudesill Jr.

Branch of Service: Navy
Occupation: Firefighter
Rank: Seaman 1st Class
Dates of Service: April 19, 1945 - July 4, 1946
Place of Service: Hawaii
Decorations: Asiatic-Pacific Campaign Medal; American Campaign Medal; WWII Victory Medal

Ray Ritchie

Branch of Service: Army
Occupation: Anti-aircraft
Rank: Sergeant
Dates of Service: 1943 - 1945
Place of Service: Europe
Decorations: Good Conduct Medal; Army of Occupation Medal (Germany); American Campaign Medal; European-African-Middle Eastern Campaign Medal; Sharpshooter Badge

Charles R. Russell

Branch of Service: Army
Occupation: Truck Driver; Rifleman
Rank: Private 1st Class
Dates of Service: Feb. 11, 1943 - March 14, 1946
Place of Service: Stateside; Pacific (Okinawa)
Decorations: Good Conduct Medal; American Campaign Medal; Asiatic-Pacific Campaign Medal; WWII Victory Medal

Brian D. Ruth

Branch of Service: Army
Occupation: Helicopter mechanic; Tool room clerk; Quartermaster Corps cook
Rank: Specialist 4th Class
Dates of Service: Jan. 30, 1987 - April 3, 1997
Place of Service: Stateside; Germany; Korea; Egypt
Decorations: Good Conduct Medal; Overseas Service Ribbon; Army Service Ribbon; NCO Professional Development Ribbon; National Defense Service Medal; Reserve Components Achievement Medal; Army Achievement Medal w/2OCL; Expert Marksman Badge w/rifle bar.

Donald M. Ruth

Branch of Service: Air Force
Occupation: Musician
Rank: Sergeant
Dates of Service: Jan. 1950 -
Place of Service: Stateside

Lewis Ruth

Branch of Service: Army
Occupation: Artillery Mechanic
Rank: Technician 5th Grade
Dates of Service: August 1943 - January 1946
Place of Service: Stateside; England; France; Germany
Decorations: Good Conduct Medal; European-African-Middle Eastern Campaign Medal w/5 campaign stars (Normandy, Northern France, Ardennes, Rhineland, Central Europe); WWII Victory Medal

Doris Stevenson Sager

Branch of Service: WAVES
Occupation: Communications Officer
Rank: Lieutenant Senior Grade
Dates of Service: August 1943 - Fall 1946
Place of Service: Stateside
Decorations: American Campaign Medal; WWII Victory Medal; Navy Unit Commendation

John D. Sales

Branch of Service: Army Reserve
Occupation: Ammo Specialist
Rank: Staff Sergeant
Dates of Service: Feb. 18, 2000 - present
Place of Service: Iraq; Kuwait
Decorations: National Defense Service Medal w/M device; Iraq Campaign Medal; Global War on Terrorism Service Medal; Army Commendation Medal

Jack Schaffer

Branch of Service: Army
Occupation: Infantryman; Anti-tank Gun Crewman
Rank: Private 1st Class; Sergeant
Dates of Service: July 15, 1943 - Dec. 8, 1945; Feb. 12, 1947 - Sept. 7, 1949
Place of Service: Wales; France; Germany; Belgium; Luxembourg; Czechoslovakia
Decorations: Good Conduct Medal; Purple Heart; Bronze Star; European-Africa-Mediterranean Campaign Medal; WWII Victory Medal; Army of Occupation Medal (Germany); French Croix De Guerre

David Schwartz

Branch of Service: Naval Reserve
Occupation: Communications Officer; Navigator; Operations Officer
Rank: Lieutenant
Dates of Service: July 12, 1953 - Nov. 11, 1956
Place of Service: Stateside; Japan; Korea; Indochina; Philippines; Taiwan; Cuba; Greece; Italy; France; Spain; Algeria; Canada; various Atlantic ports
Decorations: National Defense Service Medal; Korean Service Medal; China Service Medal; Republic of Korea Presidential Unit Citation

Lewis W. Shanholtz

Branch of Service: Army
Occupation: Infantry Squad Leader
Rank: Sergeant
Dates of Service: May 18, 1943 - Dec. 3, 1945
Place of Service: Europe
Decorations: Good Conduct Medal; Marksman Badge w/rifle bar; Combat Infantryman Badge; Presidential Unit Citation; Purple Heart; Bronze Star; European-African-Middle Eastern Campaign Medal; American Campaign Medal; WWII Victory Medal; Army of Occupation Medal (Germany)

Donald Mendenhall Shank

Branch of Service: Army Air Forces; Air Force
Rank: Captain
Dates of Service: 1936 - 1961
Place of Service: North Africa; Egypt; Europe; Pacific
Decorations: Good Conduct Medal w/5 bronze stars; European-African-Middle Eastern Campaign Medal w/9 bronze stars; Bronze Star; Asiatic-Pacific Campaign Medal; WWII Victory Medal; Air Force Commendation Medal

Ernest M. Shank

Branch of Service: Navy
Occupation: Seaman
Rank: Seaman
Dates of Service: Feb. 21, 1945 - July 13, 1946
Place of Service: Pacific
Decorations: Asiatic-Pacific Campaign Medal; American Campaign Medal; WWII Victory Medal

Hunter Orville Shank

Branch of Service: Army
Occupation: Ordnance
Rank: Sergeant
Dates of Service: June 1935 - 1945
Place of Service: Italy; France; Belgium; Germany; South Pacific
Decorations: Army Commendation Medal; Asiatic-Pacific Campaign Medal; WWII Victory Medal

James Merle Shank

Branch of Service: Army
Occupation: Signal Corps
Rank: Technician 3rd Grade
Dates of Service: WWII
Place of Service: Europe
Decorations: Good Conduct Medal; European-African-Middle Eastern Campaign Medal

Kenneth Benjamin Shank

Branch of Service: Army
Occupation: Engineer
Rank: Technician 5th Grade
Dates of Service: 1944 - 1945
Place of Service: Europe; Japan
Decorations: Good Conduct Medal; America Campaign Medal

Thomas H. Shank

Branch of Service: Army
Occupation: Anti-aircraft Gunner
Rank: Corporal
Dates of Service: Oct. 15, 1951 - Oct. 11, 1953
Place of Service: Stateside
Decorations: Korean Service Medal

Calvin Sheeler

Branch of Service: Navy
Occupation: Yeoman
Rank: Seaman 1st Class
Dates of Service: April 26, 1944 - May 25, 1946
Place of Service: Atlantic; Pacific
Decorations: American Campaign Medal; Asiatic-Pacific Campaign Medal; WWII Victory Medal; Occupation Service Medal (Japan)

Ralph Sheeler

Branch of Service: Army
Occupation: Infantryman
Rank: Private 1st Class
Dates of Service: Oct. 2, 1943 - Oct. 6, 1945
Place of Service: Europe
Decorations: Good Conduct Medal; Combat Infantryman Badge; European-African-Middle Eastern Campaign Medal w/4 battle stars; Bronze Star

George F. Shinham

Branch of Service: Army Air Forces
Occupation: Flight Engineer; Gunner
Rank: Technical Sergeant
Dates of Service: Mar. 8, 1943 - Oct. 31, 1945
Place of Service: Europe
Decorations: Good Conduct Medal; European-African-Middle Eastern Campaign Medal w/4 battle stars; American Campaign Medal; Air Medal; Purple Heart; Prisoner of War Medal

Irvin H. Shipley

Branch of Service: Army
Occupation: Infantryman
Rank: Private 1st Class
Dates of Service: Feb. 1944 - April 10, 1945 KIA
Place of Service: France; Belgium; Holland; Germany
Decorations: Purple Heart

Curtis E. Shives

Branch of Service: Navy
Occupation: Radioman
Rank: Radioman Petty Officer 1st Class
Dates of Service: July 26, 1979 - July 1999
Place of Service: Stateside; Europe; Guam; Diego Garcia
Decorations: Meritorious Unit Commendation-2; Navy and Marine Corps Overseas Service Ribbons-3; Coast Guard Special Operations Service Ribbon; National Defense Service Medal; Navy "E" Ribbon-2; Sea Service Deployment Ribbon; Armed Forces Service Medal; NATO Medal; Military Outstanding Volunteer Service Medal; Joint Meritorious Unit Award; Enlisted Surface Warfare Special Breast Insignia; Joint Service Commendation Medal

Joseph W. Shobe

Branch of Service: Army
Occupation: Engineer
Rank: Specialist 5th Class
Dates of Service: 1963 - 1966
Place of Service: Stateside; Korea

Michael David Shobe

Branch of Service: Army
Occupation: Apache Helicopter Maintainer
Rank: Sergeant
Dates of Service: Sept. 2002 - Present
Place of Service: Stateside; Germany; Afghanistan; Kosovo, Czech Republic
Decorations: Aviation Badge; Sharpshooter Badge w/M9 pistol & M16 bars; Expert Marksman w/M203 bar; Army Achievement Medal/w 3 oak leaf clusters; Good Conduct Medal; National Defense Service Medal; Kosovo Campaign Medal; Afghanistan Campaign Medal; Global War on Terrorism Service Medal; NCO Professional Development Ribbon; Army Service Ribbon; Overseas Service Ribbon; NATO Medal (Non-Article 5 Operations in the Balkans)

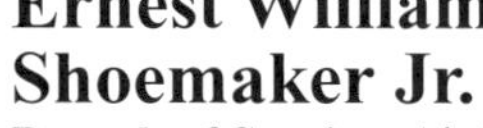

Ernest William Shoemaker Jr.

Branch of Service: Air Force
Occupation: Firefighter
Rank: Senior Airman
Dates of Service: Sept. 4, 1990 - Nov. 3, 1994
Place of Service: Iraq
Decorations: Good Conduct Medal; National Defense Service Medal; Armed Forces Expeditionary Medal (Egypt)

Howard H. Small

Branch of Service: Army
Occupation: Infantryman
Rank: 1st Lieutenant
Dates of Service: June 4, 1941 - Feb. 7, 1946
Place of Service: South Pacific
Decorations: Combat Infantryman Badge; Bronze Star; Purple Heart; American Defense Service Medal; WWII Victory Medal

Darryl Smith

Branch of Service: Army
Occupation: Electrical Technician; Clerk
Rank: Sergeant
Dates of Service: 1986 - 1990
Place of Service: Stateside

Ernest R. Smith
Branch of Service: Army Air Forces
Occupation: Airplane Sheet Metal Worker
Rank: Sergeant
Dates of Service: Feb. 1, 1943 - Oct. 18, 1945
Place of Service: Europe
Decorations: Good Conduct Medal; European-African-Middle Eastern Campaign Medal; Distinguished Unit Citation

Richard William Smith
Branch of Service: Army
Occupation: Military Police
Rank: Sergeant
Dates of Service: Oct. 3, 1939 - July 21, 1945
Place of Service: Stateside; Pacific
Decorations: Good Conduct Medal; American Defense Service Medal w/1 bronze star; American-Pacific Campaign Medal

Jim Smith
Branch of Service: Air Force; Air Force Inactive Reserve; Maryland Army National Guard
Occupation: Clerk
Rank: Airman 1st Class (Air Force); Staff Sergeant (MD National Guard)
Dates of Service: 1951 - 1954 (AF); 1954 - 1960 (AF Reserve); 1960 - 1964 (Army National Guard)
Place of Service: Stateside; Korea
Decorations: Good Conduct Medal; Korean Service Medal

Eugene Porter Snyder
Branch of Service: Army Air Corps
Occupation: Pilot
Rank: 1st Lieutenant
Dates of Service: 1942 - 1945
Place of Service: England; Germany
Decorations: Good Conduct Medal; American Defense Service Medal; Distinguished Flying Cross

John Alvey Smith
Branch of Service: Army Air Forces
Occupation: Tail Gunner
Rank: Staff Sergeant
Dates of Service: Jan. 28, 1943 - Nov. 2, 1945
Place of Service: England; France; Germany; Holland
Decorations: Good Conduct Medal; Air Medal w/5 bronze OLC; Distinguished Flying Cross; European-African-Middle Eastern Campaign Medal w/5 battle stars; American Campaign Medal; WWII Victory Medal; Presidential Unit Citation

Donald Austin Spence
Branch of Service: Army
Occupation: Engineer
Rank: Corporal
Dates of Service: April 19, 1949 - March 26, 1953
Place of Service: Japan; Korea
Decorations: Bronze Star; Army of Occupation Medal (Japan); Korean Service Medal

Kevin Smith
Branch of Service: Navy
Occupation: Dentist
Rank: Lieutenant
Dates of Service: 1988
Place of Service: Stateside

Elwood B. Sterling
Branch of Service: Army Air Corps; Air Force
Occupation: Pilot
Rank: Lieutenant Colonel
Dates of Service: Sept. 2, 1941 - July 31, 1971
Place of Service: Stateside; U.K.
Decorations: Marksmanship Badge w/rifle, bayonet, hand grenade, machine gun & automatic rifle bars; American Defense Service Medal; American Campaign Medal; European-African-Middle Eastern Campaign Medal; WWII Victory Medal; Armed Forces Reserve Medal; Air Force Longevity Service Award

Albert G. Stotelmyer

Branch of Service: Army; Army National Guard
Occupation: Infantryman
Rank: Private
Dates of Service: 1942 (Army); 1943 (National Guard)
Place of Service: Stateside

Denzil E. Viands

Branch of Service: Army
Occupation: Wrecker Operator; Driver; Mechanic
Rank: Technician 4th Grade
Dates of Service: March 22, 1943 - Nov. 6, 1945
Place of Service: Italy
Decorations: Good Conduct Medal; Distinguished Unit Badge; American Campaign Medal; European-African-Middle Eastern Campaign Medal; WWII Victory Medal

Roger E. Stottlemyer

Branch of Service: Army
Occupation: Intelligence officer
Rank: Sergeant
Dates of Service: Dec. 4, 1942 - Dec. 7, 1945
Place of Service: Europe
Decorations: Good Conduct Medal; European-African-Middle Eastern Campaign Medal w/3 battle stars; Bronze Star; Sharpshooter Badge

Galen R. Warden

Branch of Service: Merchant Marine; Army
Occupation: Seaman; Infantryman
Rank: Corporal
Dates of Service: 1945 - 1946 (Merchant Marine); 1946 - 1947 (Army)
Place of Service: At sea; Stateside

Roy U. Talhelm

Branch of Service: Army
Occupation: Paratrooper
Rank: Private
Dates of Service: Sept. 1, 1942 - June 12, 1944 KIA
Place of Service: Europe
Decorations: Good Conduct Medal; Combat Infantryman Badge; European-Middle Eastern-North African Campaign Medal; Purple Heart; Bronze Star; WWII Victory Medal; Presidential Unit Citation

William J. Warden

Branch of Service: Navy
Dates of Service: 1946 - 1948
Place of Service: Stateside; Atlantic

Russell "Clarke" Urich Jr.

Branch of Service: Army; Army Air Forces
Occupation: Artillery; Bombardier
Rank: 2nd Lieutenant
Dates of Service: April 11, 1941 - Dec. 1943; Dec. 24, 1943 - July 1945
Place of Service: Pacific; Europe
Decorations: Air Medal w/5 OLC; European-African-Middle Eastern Campaign Medal w/3 stars; Asiatic-Pacific Campaign Medal w/1 star; American Defense Service Medal

Gilbert Ware

Branch of Service: Army
Occupation: Infantry; Military Police
Rank: 1st Lieutenant
Dates of Service: June 1955 - Sept. 1959
Place of Service: Stateside; Germany

Daniel L. Watson Jr.

Branch of Service: Navy; Navy Reserve
Occupation: Seabee; Builder
Rank: Radioman (Navy); Builder 2nd Class Petty Officer (Navy Reserve)
Dates of Service: Aug. 1990 - Aug. 1994 (Navy); July 2000 - Present (Navy Reserve)
Place of Service: Assignments around the globe, including Iraq
Decorations: Seabee Combat Warfare Pin; Navy & Marine Corps Ach. Medal; Joint Meritorious Unit Award Ribbon; Meritorious Unit Comm. Ribbon w/1bronze star; GCM; Naval Reserve Meritorious Service Medal; Navy "E" Ribbon; NDSM w/bronze star; SW Asia Service Medal w/2 bronze stars; GWOT-EM; GWOT; Sea Service Ribbon w/2 bronze stars; Armed Forces Navy Reserve Medal w/M device; Saudi Arabia & Kuwait Liberation of Kuwait Medals

Lewis R. Watson Sr.

Branch of Service: Marine Corps
Occupation: Motor Pool
Rank: Sergeant
Dates of Service: May 1954 - June 1960
Place of Service: Stateside; Lebanon

Thomas E. Watts

Branch of Service: Marine Corps
Occupation: Aviation Ordnance
Rank: Private
Dates of Service: Nov. 1982 - Nov. 1986
Place of Service: Stateside

Douglas P. Weaver Jr.

Branch of Service: Navy
Occupation: Gunner on Merchant Ship
Rank: Gunners Mate 3rd Class
Dates of Service: July 1943 - Feb. 1946
Place of Service: Stateside; South Pacific (Tulagi)
Decorations: Good Conduct Medal; Asiatic-Pacific Campaign Medal; American Campaign Medal; WWII Victory Medal

D. Tolly West Jr.

Branch of Service: Navy
Occupation: Supply Officer
Rank: Chief Petty Officer
Dates of Service: Feb. 6, 1942 - Nov. 13, 1945
Place of Service: Stateside; South Pacific (Tulagi)

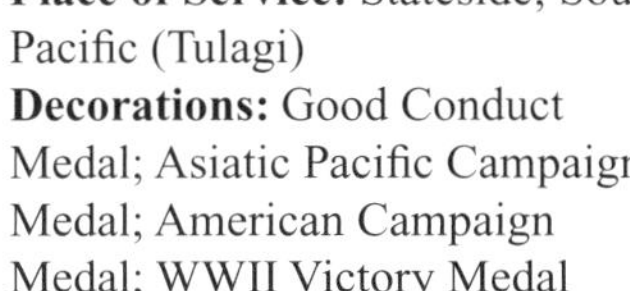

Decorations: Good Conduct Medal; Asiatic Pacific Campaign Medal; American Campaign Medal; WWII Victory Medal

Charles N. White Jr.

Branch of Service: Army
Occupation: Infantryman
Rank: Tech Sergeant
Dates of Service: Dec. 1943 - Nov. 1945
Place of Service: Germany
Decorations: Combat Infantryman Badge; Bronze Star; GCM; American Campaign Medal; European-African-Middle Eastern Campaign Medal; WWII Victory Medal; Army of Occupation Medal (Germany)

Mark Wiley

Branch of Service: Air Force
Occupation: Superintendent, Aircrew Life Support
Rank: Master Sergeant
Dates of Service: Sept. 5, 1989 - Present
Place of Service: Stateside; South Korea; Italy; Turkey
Decorations/Ribbons: Meritorious Service Medal; Air Force Commendation Medal; Air Force Achievement Medal; Kosovo Campaign Medal

Russell B. Wingerd

Branch of Service: Air Force; Air Force Reserve
Occupation: Munitions and Weapons Maintenance
Rank: Sergeant
Dates of Service: Dec. 26, 1961 - Dec. 23, 1965 (Air Force); 1965-1967 (Air Force Reserves)
Place of Service: Libya; Japan; Stateside
Decorations: Good Conduct Medal

Guy Wingert

Branch of Service: Army
Occupation: Infantry
Rank: Corporal
Dates of Service: 1942 - 1945
Place of Service: Europe

William P. Young Jr.

Branch of Service: Army
Occupation: JAG
Rank: Captain
Dates of Service: Jan. 26, 1966 - Dec. 4, 1971
Place of Service: Stateside; Vietnam; Germany
Decorations: Army Commendation Medal; Bronze Star; Meritorious Service Medal; National Defense Service Medal; Vietnam Service Medal; Vietnam Campaign Medal w/2 bronze stars

Walton Roscoe Wolf

Branch of Service: Army
Occupation: Rifleman
Rank: Private 1st Class
Dates of Service: May 21, 1943 - Nov. 4, 1945
Place of Service: North Africa; Italy
Decorations: Good Conduct Medal; Combat Infantryman Badge; European-African-Middle Eastern Campaign Medal w/3 bronze stars

Glenn E. Younker

Branch of Service: Army
Occupation: Driver
Rank: Corporal
Dates of Service: Nov. 12, 1952 - Dec. 5, 1960
Place of Service: Korea; Stateside
Decorations: Combat Infantryman Badge; Expert Rifleman Badge

William C. Wolfinger

Branch of Service: Air Force
Occupation: Combat Cameraman
Rank: Master Sergeant
Dates of Service: Air Force, 1966 - 1972; Air National Guard, 1978 - 2005
Place of Service: Europe; Bosnia-Herzegovina; Greece; Crete; Central & South America; Saudi Arabia; Turkey
Decorations: Aerial Ach. Medal; AFACII w/5 devices; AFCOM w/4 OLCs; NDSM w/2 devices; Longevity Service & Overseas Ribbons; Armed Forces Service & Expeditionary Medals; Armed Forces Reserve Medal w/M; Combat Readiness Medal; SW Asia Service Medal w/1 device; Joint Meritorious Unit Awd.; Outst. Unit Awd. w/2 OLCs; GCM; MSM w/8 devices; GWOT & others

Jonas William "Buck" Zeigler

Branch of Service: Navy
Occupation: Seabee
Rank: Machinist Mate 3rd Class
Dates of Service: Aug. 28, 1944 - Feb. 18, 1946
Place of Service: Guam
Decorations: Pacific-Asiatic Campaign Medal; American Campaign Medal; WWII Victory Medal

Kent Wyndham

Branch of Service: Army
Occupation: Infantryman; Company Commander
Rank: Captain
Dates of Service: April 8, 1966 - April 30, 1972
Place of Service: Vietnam
Decorations: National Defense Service Medal; Vietnam Service Medal; Vietnam Campaign Medal; Combat Infantryman Badge; Expert Rifleman Badge [M-14]; Bronze Star Medal w/2 OLCs

Jack A. Zirkle

Branch of Service: Army
Occupation: Infantry
Rank: Private 1st Class
Dates of Service: September 1949 - July 27, 1950 KIA
Place of Service: Korea

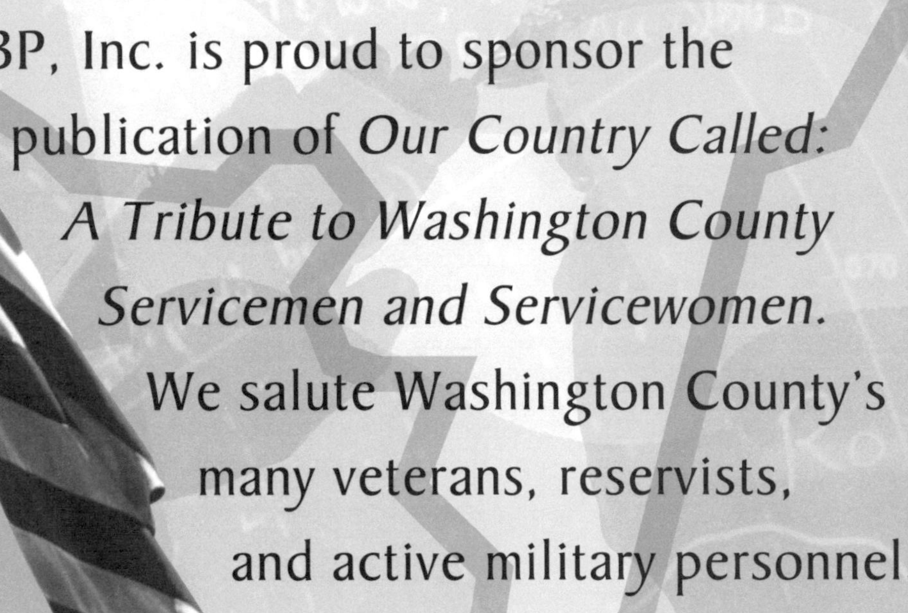

History does not long entrust the care of freedom to the weak or timid.

—Dwight D. Eisenhower

The Herald-Mail Company
is pleased to present Vol. II of this tribute to
Washington County servicemen and servicewomen.

Lest we forget . . .